THE
AUTOBIOGRAPHY OF
Thomas
Whythorne

Anno dni
1569

Ætatis. 41.
M. Whithorn

THOMAS WHYTHORNE

Portrait painted in 1569 when he was forty-one

THE
AUTOBIOGRAPHY OF
Thomas
Whythorne

Edited by

JAMES M. OSBORN

OXFORD

At the Clarendon Press

1961

Oxford University Press, Amen House, London E.C.4

GLASGOW   NEW YORK   TORONTO   MELBOURNE   WELLINGTON
BOMBAY   CALCUTTA   MADRAS   KARACHI   KUALA LUMPUR
CAPE TOWN   IBADAN   NAIROBI   ACCRA

© *James M. Osborn 1961*

PRINTED IN GREAT BRITAIN
AT THE UNIVERSITY PRESS, OXFORD
BY VIVIAN RIDLER
PRINTER TO THE UNIVERSITY

PREFACE

THE recovery of Thomas Whythorne's *Book of Songs and Sonetts* is a propitious event from every point of view. To the literary historian it adds a new Tudor poet and the earliest 'modern' autobiography in English. To the social historian it provides new evidence of the manners and customs of our Elizabethan ancestors. To the musicologist it offers first-hand testimony of the way one professional music teacher and composer lived and wrote. It comes at a time when interest in Elizabethan poetry, history, and music is at its height: biographies of Queen Elizabeth are in demand around the globe, a fat book on the Spanish Armada stands high on the best-seller lists, the interpretation of Shakespeare has become virtually an industry, and the madrigals of Whythorne's younger contemporaries—Morley, Byrd, Dowland, and others—are beloved by increasing thousands, thanks to the availability of electronic recordings.

Besides its value as a new source of knowledge about the Elizabethan Age, the *Autobiography* also enables us to know a new Elizabethan 'Gentleman', and to know him intimately. At the very outset Whythorne stated that his purpose was to 'lay open unto you the most part of all my private affairs and secrets'. This intention he performed diligently, as the reader will agree after he has followed Whythorne's narrative of his tortured relationships with his 'Suds-of-Soap' mistress, with 'the Court Lady', with 'the £20 Widow', and others. The result of these revelations is the recovery after nearly four hundred years of a colourful personality, drawn with the veracity of a self-portrait.

Because Whythorne chose to write in a 'new orthografye' of his own devising, some readers may at the first dip find his pages slow going. With the aid of the brief explanation of his spelling system (printed at the end of the Introduction) readers should soon proceed swimmingly. To those who persist, the 'new orthografye' should add a special pleasure, for here is an Elizabethan taking pains to tell us how his words sounded in speech. Another edition of the *Autobiography* in modernized spelling, designed for the general public, is in preparation.

The Introduction is, literally, intended to introduce the reader to Thomas Whythorne, Gent., and should be scanned before beginning the autobiography itself. It summarizes Whythorne's life story, using his own words wherever possible, and incorporating much information that did not properly belong in the footnotes to Whythorne's text. The Index provides a key to finding topics in the Introduction, the text, and the footnotes.

The function of the appendixes is self-evident, but the attention of music historians is directed to two of them. Appendix III gives the text of the 'musical scrap', a paper not part of the *Autobiography* but found with it, which contains some new evidence about Elizabethan musicians. Appendix VI provides a finding-list of Whythorne's songs, showing their location in the *Autobiography* and also in various printed volumes.

During the four years spent in editing the manuscript and in attempting to throw light on Whythorne's career, I have benefited from the help of many friends and scholars. Without exception my inquiries have received courteous and generous response. Among my colleagues at Yale I wish particularly to thank Louis L. Martz and Charles T. Prouty for the harvest of their knowledge. Leslie Hotson first called my attention to Whythorne's will, and that of William Bromfield. Brooks Shepard Jr., who is preparing a new edition of Whythorne's songs, helped me in matters concerning Elizabethan music.

Sidney Beck of the New York Public Library also aided me in musical inquiries, and Miss Rosemond Tuve increased my knowledge of the 'seven deadly sins'. Giles E. Dawson of the Folger Shakespeare Library kindly read the text and notes in galley proof. Rudolph Habernicht of the University of California at Los Angeles, who has made a special study of John Heywood, read the printer's copy and actually delivered it to the press.

Fortunately, my notes on Cambridge dons during the period of Whythorne's residence passed the critical eye of John Archibald Venn before his death in 1959. R. D. Whitehorne, Principal of Westminster College, Cambridge, contributed genealogical data, and Peter Laslett of Trinity College aided my researches there. David Piper of the National Portrait Gallery provided information about Whythorne's portrait, and obtained permission to reproduce it from Miss Winifred L. Hill, to whom I express my gratitude. Sir Frank Francis, Director of the British Museum, has been helpful from the beginning; Miss Helen Wallis identified a map long sought after. Sir John Neale, the doyen of Elizabethan historians, kindly read proof of the Introduction and Appendixes.

At Oxford R. W. Hunt of the Bodleian Library aided in explaining problems concerning the manuscript and Frederick Sternfeld assisted my musical inquiries. Officials of the Clarendon Press have placed every facility at my disposal; I should particularly like to thank the proof-reader for many erudite comments. F. P. Wilson read the volume in galleys and contributed many fruitful suggestions, especially concerning Whythorne's proverbs; to him this book is affectionately dedicated.

My widest obligation, however, is to two former research assistants, A. J. V. Chapple, now of the University of Manchester, who made the first transcript, and Roger Lonsdale, now of Oxford, who has collated the 'new orthografye' letter by letter and has compiled the index. My debt to them is enormous, as is that of Thomas Whythorne, Gent.

November, 1960   J. M. O.

CONTENTS

LIST OF ILLUSTRATIONS

INTRODUCTION

I. *Whythorne's Reputation*

IN contrast to the golden years of the second half of Queen Elizabeth's reign, the earlier decades, the 1560's and 1570's, are dim and shadowy. Of the poets, writers, and musicians who busied themselves at Court or were employed in the great country houses, we often know little more than their names. Surviving examples of writings by these early Elizabethan poets and musicians rarely contain passages of personal information from which we can visualize the living man: the medieval tradition of impersonality died hard. With few exceptions the mid-sixteenth-century writers who left the poems and songs now gathered in anthologies remain hidden in a pre-dawn twilight.

For nearly four hundred years Thomas Whythorne has been one of these obscure early Elizabethans. Although he published in 1571 the first set of English madrigals and in 1590 brought out a volume of duets, so little notice was taken of these books that his name is not recorded by any of his contemporaries, nor indeed by any writer in the following century.[1] Not until 1789, in Dr. Charles Burney's great *History of Music*, did Whythorne receive critical attention from a professional musician. Burney, notoriously unsympathetic to even the best Elizabethan music, cited Whythorne's 1571 *Songes* as evidence that 'Our secular Vocal Music, during the first years of Elizabeth's reign, seems much inferior to that of the church . . .'. Instead of welcoming the discovery of an early composer, Burney warned his readers away from Whythorne: 'Both the words and music of these Songs, which were published before those of Bird had appeared [1588], are truly barbarous; but it is not now certain that they were ever in much public favour' (iii. 119). Although Burney condemned with equal harshness the 'wretched trash' set to

---

[1] An exception is John Playford's *Catalogue* of 1653 which offers for sale items described as 'Withornes two parts' and 'Whithornes 4, 5 parts'. Herbert's edition of Ames's *Typographical Antiquities* (1785) also lists Whythorne's *Songes* (i. 652) and *Duos* (ii. 1017; Bassus only).

music by other madrigalists, his epithet 'barbarous' echoed through the pages of succeeding generations of musicologists whenever Whythorne was unfortunate enough to receive a brief notice.

Considering that no single complete set of Whythorne's madrigal books has survived, it is little wonder that they have been ignored. The only known copies of the 1571 *Songes* are in the Bodleian, the Library of Christ Church, the British Museum, the New York Public Library, and the Henry E. Huntington Library in California, and each of these sets is defective in one way or another. Of the 1590 *Duos*, only two sets of both part-books are known.[1] Burney did not mention the latter, and probably saw the 1571 *Songes* for the first time in 1778, when, thanks to a letter of introduction from Dr. Johnson, the doors of Christ Church Library were opened to him.[2] In Dr. Burney's manuscript notebooks, where he jotted down references for the *History of Music*, Whythorne's name does not appear among his notes of Elizabethan madrigalists.[3]

Nor had Burney's rival, Sir John Hawkins, seen Whythorne's *Songes* when he issued his learned *History of Music* in 1776, a few months after the first volume of Burney's *History* had appeared. But years later he encountered a set, and inserted a long manuscript note in the margins of his annotated copy, now in the British Museum.[4] After remarking on Whythorne's obscurity, Hawkins transcribed the title-page of the Tenor volume, which he considered 'very quaint'. He next called attention to

---

[1] For a description of these copies, see Appendix I.

[2] R. W. Chapman, ed., *The Letters of Samuel Johnson* (Oxford, 1952), ii. 264–5. In the following year Burney spent some days 'locked up' in the Christ Church Library, 'from 9 in ye morng. till 5 in the afternoon' (letter from Thomas Twining to Burney, 3 Nov. 1779, B.M. Add. MS. 39929, f. 215). He presented the Library with a handwritten 'Catalogue of Music Books' bequeathed by Dean Aldrich, 'examined Novr 1778'; among them Burney listed the four part-books of Whythorne's 1571 *Songes*.

[3] These notebooks are now among the Burney papers in the Osborn Collection.

[4] Vol. iii, pp. 360–1 (B.M., L.R. 39. a. 6). Probably Hawkins saw the Christ Church volumes, because no other copy of the Tenor book with a title-page is known.

several features of the book, including the 'Advertisement concerning the use of Flats and Sharps' printed at the end. Whythorne's versified preface impressed Hawkins as 'perhaps the worst Poetry that ever appeared in Print', and he quoted five lines as a specimen. After mentioning the woodcut portrait of Whythorne and the 'sundry Copies of commendatory verses', Hawkins concluded:

[It] is very remarkable, notwithstanding all the pompous Circumstances attendant on its Publication, his Name does not occur in any List of the Musicians of this Country; nor is there any Mention of him or his Book to be met with in any of the numerous Tracts on the subject of Music that have been perused for the Purpose of compiling this Work; from whence it may be inferred, that he had attained to no Degree of Eminence in his Profession, and that he thought better of his Compositions than the Public were disposed to do.

A much abbreviated version of this note appeared in the 1853 reprint of Hawkins's *History* (p. 499), though the publisher claimed to have utilized *all* of Hawkins's annotations.

Compilers of later histories apparently were content to follow Burney and Hawkins without looking at Whythorne's music for themselves. Thus, Henry Davey described Whythorne as 'perhaps the worst composer of his time', and Ernest Walker called the songs 'miserably feeble rubbish'.[2] The critical chorus repeated this theme regularly until 1925, when a slim pamphlet appeared from the Oxford University Press with the title *Thomas Whythorne, An Unknown Elizabethan Composer*. Written by Philip Heseltine under the pseudonym Peter Warlock, this pamphlet revealed that Heseltine had actually looked at Whythorne's songs. What is more important, he was delighted with what he found. Heseltine printed twelve madrigals, and stated confidently that Whythorne's songs are 'some of the most original and attractive specimens of English sixteenth-century music

---

[1] The earliest mention of Whythorne's poems by a literary historian occurs in Joseph Ritson's *Bibliographia Poetica* (1802), p. 393. Ritson noted without comment both the 1571 *Songes* and the 1590 *Duos*.

[2] Henry Davey, *History of English Music* (1895), p. 138; Ernest Walker, *History of Music in England* (2nd edn., 1924), p. 58 n.

that have come down to us' (p. 4). In the brief space available, he
called attention to features of individual songs, mentioning the
'magnificent polyphonic writing' of one, the 'delightful little vocal
scherzos' of another; and, concerning still others, he praised the
'real mastery both in construction and in the resourcefulness with
which voices are handled so as to obtain the utmost variety of
tone-colour by the simplest means' (p. 7). Heseltine concluded
by acclaiming Whythorne as 'a composer of real genius who has
been too long neglected'. Besides this sympathetic praise of the
quality of the songs, he recognized Whythorne's work as 'a document of great historical importance' (p. 6).

In the last three decades every serious writer on Whythorne
has followed Heseltine's lead, among them Geoffrey Pulver,[1]
Morrison Boyd,[2] and Gustave Reese.[3] Canon Fellowes scored
a number of Whythorne's songs in order to form his own judgement: the experience convinced him that Burney and other
critics 'may have misread the clefs or fallen into some such error
as alone could explain their sneering criticism'. He states further:
'Historically speaking, Thomas Whythorne occupies an important position in the development of the English Madrigal;
. . . [he] has undoubted claims to be regarded as an important
pioneer . . . even though his ability cannot be considered as
approaching the first class.' Fellowes concludes with the significant point: 'the position of the earlier madrigalists like
Whythorne, when viewed in relation to Wilbye or Dowland, is
analogous, in many respects, to that of such pioneers in literature
as Wyatt and Surrey when considered in relation to Shakespeare, Spenser, and Sidney.'[4]

Of Whythorne the man practically nothing has been known
apart from the scanty information found in the prefaces of his
two books. As has been already remarked, no Elizabethan writer

---

[1] Geoffrey Pulver, *Dictionary of Old English Music*, 1927.
[2] Morrison C. Boyd, *Elizabethan Music and Musical Criticism* (Philadelphia, 1940), pp. 100–3.
[3] Gustave Reese, *Music in the Renaissance* (New York, 1954), pp. 816–17.
[4] E. H. Fellowes, *The English Madrigal Composers* (2nd edn., 1948),
pp. 34–36.

referred to him, not even Case in his *Apologia Musices* (1588), Morley in his *A Plaine and Easy Introduction to Practicall Musicke* (1597), or Meres in his *Palladis Tamia* (1598). Because Whythorne called himself a gentleman on his title-pages, and embellished his books with a woodcut portrait framed in armorial trappings, Boyd considered that he was 'probably a wealthy amateur'. Reese echoed this opinion, but nothing could be farther from the truth. The recovery of Whythorne's manuscript autobiography, the existence of which was unsuspected before 1955, enables us to know him more intimately as a personality than any other Elizabethan man of music, art, or letters; at the same time we can follow Whythorne's career, step by step, as a professional musician consciously fighting to gain recognition of his status.

11. *The Man Revealed by the Autobiography*

Thomas Whythorne was born in 1528, son of John Whythorne or Whitehorn of Ilminster, Somerset, and his wife Joane, daughter and heir of William Cabott, also of Ilminster.[1] His father came from a well-established family, and the autobiography makes clear the esteem with which Whythorne regarded his lineage. The father's name is found on many local documents between 1540 and 1549, showing that he was involved in various leases, purchases, and sales of land.[2] These transactions suggest more affluence than seems to have been the fact, for Thomas had to earn his own living and maintain himself even after his father's death.

The autobiography tells us that Thomas lived at home until he was ten years old, but part of this time dwelt in other places that his father had 'appointed', probably with relatives near by.

---

[1] A genealogy of the family, dated about 1568, is MS. Harley 1096, f. 13. It is printed in A. W. H. Clarke's *London Pedigrees* (1935), under 'Whithorne'. Thomas is the only son there recorded, though in the autobiography (p. 10) he writes of other sons of his father; perhaps he was the only survivor at the time the pedigree was compiled.   [2] See p. 12, n. 1.

His parents, though firm in their conviction that discipline was necessary, allowed Thomas to pass his childhood in relaxed ease. At the proper time, Thomas was sent to the local school where he learned to read, to write, 'and also to sing Music'.

In 1538, when the boy was 10 years of age, he was taken to Oxford to live with an uncle, a priest beneficed within five miles of the University. The uncle had asked that one of his nephews be sent, promising that 'he would bring him up as well as if he were his own child'. The uncle may have hoped to influence his nephew to enter the Church, but above all wished to educate him well enough to equip him for one of the professions. Whythorne gives a vivid report of their conversations on the subject.

> . . . he would sometimes demand of me whether I would be a priest or no, or whether I would be a physician or a lawyer. . . . At another time he said unto me, 'Be not afraid to tell me your mind plainly in that which I will demand of you. If you do not like to study and learn those aforesaid professions I have spoken of, how say you then to Grammar, with the knowledge in the Latin tongue ? Or else to Music ? As to learn to sing and to play on the organs, the which be good qualities and be much esteemed in these days; and by them many men do live very well, and do come to preferment thereby.'
>
> To this said question I answered . . . that I liked well of them both, but yet of both I liked Music best. 'Then', quoth my uncle, 'you shall learn them both; and because that you do like Music best of both, you shall learn somewhat of that first, and afterward you shall learn the other also' (pp. 10–11).[1]

That the boy 'was most given to the love of Music before any other science' became abundantly clear to the priest, and he acted accordingly:

> When my said uncle thus perceived mine inclination . . . that I might be kept well occupied with some good exercise and that I might be set to what I most delighted in, because I might profit the better therein he . . . brought me to Oxford . . . and there he did set me to school in Magdalen College (p. 11).

[1] Quotations from the autobiography have been modernized.

Whythorne refers, of course, to Magdalen College School, maintained by the College to train choristers. The School, founded about sixty years earlier, supplied training second to none in England in the classics and in music, a fortunate circumstance for the lad from Somerset.

Thomas enjoyed six years of singing and studying at Magdalen School, and in the following year, 1544, he entered the College at the age of 16. The admission books reveal that he was elected to a Demyship, a form of scholarship for able but impecunious students.[1] Shortly before the end of this year his uncle died, and Thomas decided to leave Oxford. Perhaps the uncle had felt some premonition that he would not survive long, for he urged Thomas, 'Ply your learning so as you may live thereby hereafter.' He warned the boy that all he could leave to him was 'a little household stuff', and that his father in Somerset would not have an estate large enough 'to keep you and the rest of his children in such sort as you may live idly and at ease'. Thus Thomas, now 17, set out to support himself, and took the road to London.

The youth must have impressed others with his abilities, for he was engaged as 'servant and scholar' by the most eminent literary man in England, John Heywood. Whythorne was well aware of his master's status, for the autobiography tells us that Heywood '. . . was not only very well skilled in music and playing on the virginals, but also such an English poet as the like, for his wit and invention with the quantity that he wrote, was not as then in England, nor . . . since Chaucer's time' (p. 13). Whythorne joined the Heywood household in 1545, probably about the middle of the year. He remained there for 'three years and more', till the end of 1548 or, possibly, till early 1549, years that saw the decline and death of Henry VIII and the accession of Edward VI.

[1] According to the statutes of 1483 there were thirty Demies and forty Scholars. Eighteen of them, including Whythorne, were admitted at 16 years of age, the minimum for others being 12 years. Heavy stress was placed on the study of grammar, but the Demies were also thoroughly trained in reading and plainsong.

The court intrigues attendant upon these shifts in power were anxiously watched by the Heywood family, for the poet's loyalty to the Roman Church was unconcealed, and only the year before Whythorne joined the household Heywood had been forced to make a public recantation (6 July 1544) at St. Paul's Cross of the charge that he denied the supremacy of the Crown. According to one account, Heywood narrowly escaped hanging on this occasion. When Mary became Queen in 1553, Heywood attained the height of his fortunes, but when Whythorne was his servant and scholar he appears to have been living quietly, devoting himself primarily to literary labours.

Whythorne gives a glimpse of Heywood's activities: 'While I was with him, he made divers ditties to be sung unto musical instruments, also he had a book printed made upon our English proverbs.' This book, of course, was *A Dialogue conteinyng the Nomber ... of all the Prouerbes in the Englishe Tongue*, 1546, subsequently enlarged in an edition about 1549 and reprinted many times. The pithy sayings collected by his master became impressed indelibly on the boy's mind, and they permeate the autobiography. Whythorne reports further that Heywood's pen was conscripted into service by the Church of England: 'And also at the request of Doctor Cranmer, late Archbishop of Canterbury, he made a certain interlude or play, which was devised upon the parts of Man, and at the end whereof he likens and applies the circumstances of it to the universal estate of Christ's Church.' This dramatic allegory is otherwise unknown, except for fourteen lines that Whythorne found occasion to quote later in the autobiography.

Whether Heywood set definite lessons for his scholar or whether Whythorne learned by imitating his master we cannot be certain, for he tells only that while he was living with Heywood, 'I learned to play on the virginals, the lute, and to make English verses.' Of the music lessons he reported in a poem,

I ply myself daily
Thereto, that I may reap some fruit thereby.

To which he added, 'Also to write in rhythm I do practise' (p. 17). Whythorne's duties as a literary amanuensis included transcribing the writings both of Heywood and of other contemporary poets:

All the which aforesaid, before they were published, I did write out for him, or had the use of them to read them, and I have the copies of most of them in a book at this present of mine own writing.

Also, while I was with him I did write out for him divers songs and sonnets that were made by the Earl of Surrey, Sir Thomas Wyatt the elder, and Mr Moor the excellent harper, besides certain psalms that were made by the said Mr Wyatt and also Mr Sternhold, the which be also in my said book.

By the which occasions of writing and reading I afterward gave myself to imitate and follow their trades and devices in writing as occasions moved me (p. 14).

Unfortunately, Whythorne's copy-book is not known to exist. Besides the poems of Wyatt and Surrey (transcribed ten years before 'Tottel's Miscellany') it evidently contained many of Heywood's writings, including the hitherto unknown interlude made for Archbishop Cranmer.

His service to Heywood having come to an end, Whythorne decided to settle in London and earn his living by 'teaching in such sort as I had learned of him'. This phrase does not imply some special method or style, for Whythorne explained it simply as 'teaching of music and to play on those instruments . . . I had learned to play on'. Whythorne describes how troubled he was at the thought of having to make his own way in the world:

When I was a scholar and a servant, my mind was then as my state was, for then I looked no higher nor no further than the state I was in, applying myself to my learning as a scholar and seeking to content and please my master as a servant. But when I came to be my own man, and therewith a master, my mind began then to change from his former estate. For then I saw how I must seek to live of myself, for which it behoved me to cast my wits so many ways, and they never being troubled so much that way before, as I was almost at my wits' end (pp. 18–19).

His conscientiousness and his apprehension of what people were thinking (or even what he thought they thought he thought) are ever present in his autobiography.

Whythorne's new way of living is engagingly sketched for us. His chamber in London, he tells, 'was reasonably well furnished with such household stuff as my foresaid uncle gave me when he deceased'. To decorate it further he had a picture made to hang in his chamber; on it was painted (in oil colours) the figure and image of a young woman playing a lute; it also showed various musical instruments and part-books. He busied himself as became a young man:

I being then desirous to have and enrich myself with some more such exercises and qualities as young folks mostly delight in, went to the dancing school and fence school, and also learned to play on the gittern and cittern, which two instruments were then strange in England, and therefore the more desired and esteemed (p. 19).

In due course Whythorne qualified for the post of music tutor in a great household, the first of many such posts held over the next twenty years. 'Divers young women' lived in the house, and soon one of the young domestics fell in love with him. This he learned, to his apparent surprise, in an unusual way:

She devised certain verses in English, writing them with her own hand. And did put them between the strings of a gittern, the which instrument as a sitting mate, lying mate and walking mate, I then used to play on very often—yea, and almost every hour of the day, for that it was an instrument much esteemed and used of gentlemen and of the best sort in those days (p. 30).

By writing some non-committal verses in reply, Whythorne was able to identify her:

Shortly after this by what mean I know not, this matter broke out and was known all about the house where we were, which made me to blush, and she more so. Then this matter coming to her master's and mistress's knowledge, and finding that she was so loving without provoking or enticing thereunto, she was discharged out of that house and service.

The following years brought many other ventures on thin ice, each causing Whythorne to recount tales and proverbs that illustrate the frailty of women, and the troubles they bring upon men who fail to resist them. That Whythorne was attractive to young ladies is manifest from their pursuit of him: the portrait painted when he was 40 shows his appealing eyes and fine features. But the young musician suffered painfully from timidity, or as he called it, 'bashfulness towards women and chiefly in the affairs of wooing them'. As he looked back on these youthful incidents he wrote:

This fault has continued in me ever since, and yet . . . to be in company with women, to talk with them, to toy with them, to gibe and jest with them . . . (all which some do call courting), I could use the time with them somewhat aptly and fitly. But if it came to making love by word, sign or deed—especially in deed . . . I had no more face to do that than had a sheep! (p. 33).

From these revelations the question naturally arises whether Whythorne was somewhat lacking in sexual drive. There is abundant evidence that on occasion he felt the urge of passion, which he controlled by moral conviction (often bolstered by the warnings of the misogynist, Jesus Sirach) augmented by fear of possible consequences. He talks frankly of the temptations he resisted, especially when he was involved with widows and neglected wives. His zest in repeating licentious stories and bawdy proverbs shows a normal masculine weakness for such subjects. As Whythorne's religious convictions became stronger with age, the temptations were more easily resisted; but in his youth the lures of 'Venus' darlings caused me . . . to strive very much with frail nature; for I must confess that I am not made of sticks and stones but even of the self-same metal that other men be made of'.

After two years passed in this household, Whythorne came down with a long, debilitating illness, the ague. He was very ill for about three months, and suffered recurring attacks for more than a year following. In his weakness and melancholy he passed much time in writing: 'I would wreak my anger altogether with

pen and ink upon paper.' When he recovered, his financial re-
sources were so depleted that he had to accept any work that he
could get. It was necessary to take a step backwards in status:

> For nigh about this time there was a gentlewoman (who was a
> widow) who was desirous to have me to be both her servant and
> schoolmaster, the which I was let to understand by a friend of mine.
> To whom I said that to be a schoolmaster I did not mislike, but to be
> a serving creature or servingman was so like the life of a water spaniel
> that must be at commandment to fetch or bring here or carry there
> with all kinds of drudgery, that I could not like of that life.
> Yet I being earnestly provoked thereto, partly by the persuasion of
> my said friend, who said that my service should be easy enough and
> yet should be well considered of, and also partly driven to it because
> I was as behindhand in my wealth as in my health, hoping that in
> this I should recover them both to their former estate again, I forced
> my will to yield to reason (p. 37).

Whythorne does not reveal the name of this lady, hence for
purposes of convenience she may be designated the Suds-of-
Soap widow, after one of her favourite sayings. He gives a vivid
account of his life in this Tudor household, and of the personality
of Madam Suds-of-Soap: 'And to show you what manner of
mistress and scholar I had, I assure you that she was such a one
as no young man could serve a better, to break and train him
up to the fashions of the world' (p. 38). Before many days had
passed in this household Whythorne began to see that his employer took a special pleasure in manipulating men as if they
were pieces on her private chessboard. Whythorne described
the situation thus:

> Also, her joy was to have men to be in love with her, and to brag
> sometimes how she could handle such as were so, as how she could fetch
> them in, and then how she could with a frown make them look pale,
> and how with a merry look she could make them to joy again (p. 38).

Whythorne soon had personal reasons to be aware of his mistress's whims and to feel her powers of manipulation:

> Many times when I was not nigh her, although she had appointed

me to wait on her cup when she sat at meat, she would bid me come nearer to her; and therewithal scoffingly she would say to those that were with her, 'I would fain have my man to be in love with me, for then he would not be thus far from me but would always be at my elbow.' And then she would sometimes put a piece of good meat and bread on her trencher, and forthwith bid me give her a clean trencher, for which I should have hers with the bread and meat on it (p. 39).

At first the prudent Whythorne seems to have been genuinely annoyed by the manœuvres of the worldly widow:

When she would say that she would fain have me in love with her, those words would offend me very much, for of all things I accounted loving as she meant it to be but a foolish thing in those days, and I do account loving in dotage, that is to say, to love not being beloved again, to be no better than folly (p. 39).

Thus his mistress played the game of emotional cat-and-mouse with her young musician and serving-man. As his feelings were raised and lowered from day to day, the occasions gave rise to a good deal of scribbling. Whythorne's most effective method of responding was to write a few stanzas of lyric poetry containing an ambivalent sentiment, then set the stanzas to music, and sing them to her. As he explained in speaking of one poem, 'I made this song somewhat dark and doubtful of sense, because I knew not certainly how she would take it, nor to whose hands it might come after she had read it' (p. 41).

The widow seems to have enjoyed the game immensely, and ultimately to have expected some physical advances from Whythorne. He was puzzled whether to take the chance, especially when 'she would sometimes tell me in a scoffing manner that I was but a huddypick, and lacked audacity'. But he remained wary,

the rather for her boasting before that time how she could handle a novice; and also because it was told me by one of my fellows, who . . . heard her say that when I had served her turn in teaching of her she would then use me as she would use one to whom she was willing to give the slip (p. 43).

The emotional give-and-take continued until one day the widow observed him decked out in 'garments of russet colour (which colour signifieth the wearer thereof to have hope)', and soon after she saw that he was wearing a hat decked with hops. Her comment on his dress was brief:

> If you have any hope in me,
> *The suds of soap*
> *Shall wash your hope* (p. 52).

Now, with the game going badly against him, Whythorne produced a trump card: 'A friend of mine had been spoken to by a duchess . . . to procure someone who could teach the virginals . . . [to] a daughter of hers' (p. 55). This great lady was probably the Duchess of Northumberland, then (about 1551) the wife of the most powerful man in England. The recommendation, it is reasonable to guess, may have come from Whythorne's old master, John Heywood, for he was the leading authority to whom such a great lady might apply. In any case, the effect of this announcement on the Suds-of-Soap widow was crushing: she 'watered her plants a little' (that is, wept), then she berated him, and after the emotional crisis had subsided, outbid the Duchess financially. Whythorne stayed on.

Shortly after this domestic crisis a great political upheaval occurred, caused by the death of the sickly boy, King Edward VI, and the attempt of John Dudley, Duke of Northumberland, to seize the throne for his family by proclaiming his daughter-in-law, Lady Jane Grey, as Queen. Whoever the Suds-of-Soap widow actually was, her estate had been swept away shortly before, and Whythorne suddenly found himself unemployed. The Duchess, whose offer he had previously declined, suffered even more, so Whythorne was obliged to console himself by writing verses on 'Fortune's fickle wheel'. He then reached an important decision:

> I determined to spend a time in foreign and strange countries, the better to digest all the changes that; hitherto, I had felt and tasted. And when I came beyond the seas, I endeavoured . . . to know the

customs and manners of the people . . . as also to learn their speech and languages (p. 60).

Thanks to Whythorne's poetical account of his continental travels, we can follow his route in some detail. He crossed from Dover to Calais and proceeded to Flanders, where he spent about six months. He visited Bruges, Ghent, Brussels, Louvain, Malines, and Antwerp, before going on to Utrecht. From there he moved up the Rhine to Cologne, Mainz, Frankfurt, Worms, and Ulm. Next he passed through Augsburg and Innsbruck, and then over the Brenner Pass and down the Trentino into Italy. His first visits were to Padua and Venice, and thence south through Ferrara, Urbino, and Abruzzo as far as Naples. His return route took him through Rome, Florence, Bologna, Mantua, Piacenza, Milan, and Turin. With the help of a guide he climbed the Mt. Cenis pass and descended into Savoy. Thence he proceeded to Lyons and on to Paris, and so, again via Calais, back to England. The whole trip occupied nearly two years, including about six months in Italy. He seems to have been in Naples in July of 1554, when Mary and Philip of Spain were married.

In the autobiography Whythorne gives disappointingly few details of his experiences on this journey, probably because he 'wrote in prose a book of my travel', a manuscript that is not known to have survived. That he tells so little about Italian music and musicians is particularly tantalizing, for in the Preface to the 1571 *Songes* he says that he studied the music in each country, especially in Italy. He took an interest in the methods of teaching music, and the relationship between composer and publisher. In Venice he may have seen or heard Adrian Willaert, as a passing reference implies. But these few details are all we learn of the state of music in Italy.

Upon his return to London about 1555, Whythorne apparently found another tutorial position promptly. He also fell in love, and gives a rather moving account of his feelings in the unfortunate affair. The object of his affections was the daughter of a lawyer. Whythorne describes her as 'a young gentlewoman who, not only for her gifts of nature was a man's meat but also for her gifts of the mind'. Although he recognized that his 'ability and wealth was so small in comparison with hers', his confidence in himself was now augmented by his experiences as a traveller, so, relying on the adage 'Faint heart never got fair lady', he decided to try to win her.

And upon that resolution, after I had furnished myself with convenient apparel and jewels so well as I could (with the glorious show of which, among other things, a young maiden must be wooed), I took on me this foresaid conquest and enterprise (pp. 76–77).

His initial approach was by means of 'two or three pretty love ditties which . . . I would sing oftentimes to her on the virginals or lute'. The girl responded with her heart but was ruled by her head, saying:

I pray you be content and speak no more unto me of your suit; for that possibility of living which I have is not so certain but that it depends wholly upon the goodwill and pleasure of my parents. And, therefore, if I am not ruled by them in giving my consent in marriage, I should have nothing of them to live by hereafter (pp. 77–78).

The pangs of adoration produced other pretty love ditties, and ultimately the situation came to the attention of the girl's father. The lawyer devised a practical expedient and promptly introduced a young man of his choice, 'an heir of a great living, to be a suitor to her'. Whythorne now felt his 'nose put out of joint', and decided to leave the lawyer's employment for a new place.

This 'new service', he tells us, 'was with a nobleman, whom I found to be my very good lord, and also I found his lady and wife to be my very good lady and mistress, and better for that she was my scholar' (p. 83). Although Whythorne does not name this nobleman, following his usual practice of cloaking his employer in anonymity, yet he does give a few details that allow the nobleman to be identified as Lord Ambrose Dudley, later Earl of Warwick.[1] Lord Ambrose, then in his twenty-eighth

[1] See Appendix II.

year (the same age as Whythorne), was at a delicate stage of his career. Only two years before he had been imprisoned in the Tower, charged with treason for participating in the plot of his father, the Duke of Northumberland, to place Lady Jane Grey on the throne. After the beheading of his father and two of his brothers, Lord Ambrose became the head of the Dudley family, and he was living quietly in greatly reduced circumstances. As Whythorne described it, 'he lived very honourably by the income that he had from his lady and wife', Elizabeth, heiress of George, Lord Tailboys. The household was made up of 'divers gentlewomen' who waited on Lady Dudley and, Whythorne tells us, 'my lot was to be her chief waiting man, as Fortune in this point was ever very favourable to me'. All the gentlewomen had nicknames given them by Whythorne, and he versified an amusing description of each of these 'fellows' with whom he worked.

Lord Ambrose took a fancy to Whythorne: 'My lord and master . . . had so good a liking for me at the first view and acquaintance that he promised me if I would serve him but one year that I should have from him at the year's end an annuity of twenty nobles a year during my lifetime.' Twenty nobles would be about £7, a tidy income to have in addition to regular earnings. But alas for Whythorne's expectations, in 1557 Lord Ambrose was called to serve as one of the leaders in the expedition to St. Quentin.

When Lord Ambrose returned from France, where he had covered himself with glory, his financial position was at its nadir. Whythorne tells us of the aftermath of St. Quentin, where 'to recover his honour before lost, he consumed much of his lady's land and substance, the which shortly after his return from those wars caused him to break up housekeeping' (p. 85). The consequence, Whythorne reports, was that 'divers of my fellows had leave to depart and seek new services. Then was my cake dough, and my annuity was laid a-water.' Despite his financial embarrassments, Lord Ambrose wished his music tutor to stay on: 'although my lord was not willing to give me mine annuity, yet he was offended with me in that I sought to be gone from his service' (pp. 85–86). In Whythorne's eyes, the future for Lord Ambrose looked even more bleak than the present, so he persisted until permission to leave was granted.

A turn in fortune now came, but not for Whythorne. Soon after Lord Ambrose returned he was rewarded by Queen Mary's granting him and the surviving Dudleys an exception from the Act of Attainder that had been imposed against them after the Lady Jane Grey fiasco. The Dudleys were thus in a position to rise rapidly again to power and wealth when Elizabeth came to the throne. In the following years, when Lord Ambrose, now become 'the good Earl of Warwick', prospered as one of the most respected and powerful of Elizabeth's lieutenants, Whythorne may well have pondered how fortune might have smiled on him had he stayed in Lord Ambrose's service.

Nevertheless, if Whythorne had any such thoughts, they are not in the autobiography. He promptly found another position as schoolmaster to the children of 'a man of great worship, and one that was at that time of the Privy Council unto the Prince'. This detail might seem to provide a clue to the identity of the new employer, but unfortunately Queen Mary appointed so many of her followers to the Privy Council that Whythorne's description is not enough to identify him.

Whythorne stayed with him for about a year, apparently from the end of 1557 to the end of 1558. We are told only that 'my master I then served had certain troubles happened unto him, at the which instant my lady his wife and I fell at a jar' (p. 92). The troubles of the Privy Councillor undoubtedly sprang from Queen Mary's death in November 1558, and the triumph of the Protestant party that accompanied the accession of Elizabeth.

During this year, while he was domiciled at the country house of the Privy Councillor, Whythorne found himself enmeshed in the net of a designing female. She was the housekeeper at a neighbouring estate, where Whythorne and his fellows frequently exchanged visits with their opposite numbers. Her name was Mistress Elsabeth, 'an ancient matron and maid', who was whispered to perform a double function for the widower who employed her: 'she not only governs his house and all his house-wifely doings . . . but also peradventure lies with him at night, and cries "Christ help" when he sneezes.' On the very first visit that Whythorne made to her house, Mistress Elsabeth offered a 'delicate dish', and half-jokingly suggested that this would be typical fare 'if I had Mr. W. (meaning me) as my husband'. Whythorne carried off her proposal as a jest, and with good humour addressed her as 'wife' whenever the servants of the two houses were together. She returned to the attack on a later occasion. 'Said she to me again, "Do you call me Mistress Elsabeth? And why not Wife? Will you not be my husband?"' Once again Whythorne managed to turn aside this frontal assault with a pleasantry, and to ride out the teasing of the other servants with equal good humour. Before the year was out, Mistress Elsabeth suffered a long illness, so Whythorne was relieved of a troublesome situation. Yet, thanks to his graphic description of the incident, spiced with the give-and-take of conversation, we have a vivid glimpse of high life below stairs in a Tudor household.

Whythorne returned to London to see what employment might turn up next. He termed it 'my chief worldly refuge . . . wherever I go in the country I have always a chamber of mine own in that city to resort unto in my time of need' (pp. 92–93). After a short interval, he was engaged to teach a gentleman's children a short distance from London. In this household he was able to raise his status:

I covenanted with the said gentleman and wife that I would be with them only by the week, and also that I would be used as a friend and not as a servant. Upon this, they not only allowed me to sit at their table but also at their own mess, as long as there were not any [persons] to occupy the . . . place that were a great deal my betters (p. 94).

Once achieved, this new standing gave opportunity for a special relationship with his new mistress. As Whythorne explained it, '. . . being used as a friend, made me bolder to speak my fancy sometimes when I thought good'. Because the real name of the friendly employer cannot be learned, for convenience she may be called the Court Lady.

Whythorne gives a lively sketch of her personality:

Here must I show you, by the way, how the said gentlewoman, having been some time a courtier, and well experienced also in the affairs of the world, with a great wit and a jolly, ready tongue to utter her fancy and mind, took pleasure many times to talk and discourse of the things she had some knowledge of by experience: as sometimes of religions, she would argue in matters of controversy in religion; sometimes of profane matters.

Sometimes she would touch matters of the country, with the good husbandry and housewifery thereof; sometimes she would touch upon the city, with the trades of citizens, and not leave untouched the fineness of the delicate dames and the nice wives of the city.

Sometimes she would talk of the Court, with the bravery and vanities thereof, and of the crouching and dissimulation, with the *bazzios los manos* that are there used by one courtier to another; and sometimes she would minister talk of the courting of ladies and gentlewomen by the gallants and cavaliers; and sometimes would she talk pleasantly of the love that is made and used in all places between men and women (p. 93).

It is not surprising that proximity soon ripened into fondness, and that before long Whythorne began to wonder what her true feelings towards him might be. Like the Suds-of-Soap widow she 'delighted to have those she liked in love with her and at her command, and to boast how she could deal with them'. But the Court Lady told him 'that she durst not in the presence of some who came to her house' show her friendship to him, 'because they would blaze it forth to her reproach and discredit'.

After more than a year of this relationship, Whythorne began to realize that he was again in the hands of a dissembling woman. His earlier experience flashed through his mind, and after reflection he decided to 'have two strings to my bow'. His working arrangement permitted him to go to London every three months, where he would spend a few days staying in his chamber. While there, he received an offer to teach the children of a gentleman 'with whom and his wife I had long been acquainted'. Their house was located only three or four miles from London, and about eight miles from the home of the Court Lady. When he told her of his wish to leave, the Court Lady protested strongly, and made promises of eternal friendship that could be interpreted in several ways: she went so far as to say, 'What pleasure soever it be I am able to do you or for you at any time by any manner or mean, whatsoever it is, if you will let me understand it, you shall be assured of it at all times' (pp. 97–98).

Whythorne arranged to divide his time equally between the two households, about six weeks at each, with a brief stay in his London room while in transit. On his first return to the home of the Court Lady, he discovered a significant change:

she had caused a chest of mine to be removed out of the chamber where before that time I was accustomed to lie ... and to be brought into a chamber so nigh her own chamber as she might have come from one to the other when she list without any suspicion. This chamber I was then placed in (p. 100).

Though strongly tempted, he conducted himself discreetly, even on one occasion when the Court Lady 'came all alone into my chamber' on a flimsy excuse.

The situation became complicated by his simultaneous relationships with two other women. The second was the wife of his alternate employer who, Whythorne discloses, 'made as much of me, both in friendly words and outward behaviour', as the Court Lady was doing. The third woman was his landlady in London, a prosperous widow with two children, who set her cap at him. But Whythorne had little difficulty in avoiding her advances, particularly because he 'thought her to be somewhat past the procreation and conceiving of children' (p. 98). Yet the complications of the triple relationship frequently perplexed him:

I recounted to myself how the case stood with me and these aforesaid three dames. One while I would praise my good fortune because I was so well liked and beloved of them; and another while I would blame my ill fortune that I could not with good conscience possess and enjoy her that I liked best of them (p. 104).

The one he liked best, of course, was the Court Lady. Small wonder that the situation caused Whythorne to write sundry songs in the attempt to relieve his mental perplexities, including a poem that began:

> *The proverb saith between two stools*
> *the tail go'th to the ground,*
> *But I may say between three stools*
> *like state in me is found.*

Soon a fourth lady entered the competition. The ardour of the Court Lady having subsided (signalized by his chest being moved back to his former bedroom), Whythorne now sought her aid in arranging a marriage with a 'young maiden that she had brought up in her house', a kinswoman of her husband. Whythorne broached the matter early in the affair, when his only proposal to the girl 'was merrily and after a jesting sort, by the occasion of merry talk between us'. The Court Lady tactfully tried to dissuade him from further pursuit, for she realized that the girl was too much above Whythorne in the social scale. Some months later she broke the news to Whythorne that her husband could no longer afford to keep a music tutor, and thus their long intimacy came to an uneventful but friendly conclusion.

About the same time, the alternate employer also 'waxed weary of his charges that he was at for the teaching of his children', so Whythorne settled into his quarters in London. This was some time in 1560: hence he had been involved with the Court Lady for about two years. The next chapter in his life turned in a very different direction:

. . . shortly after my fortune was to become acquainted with a gentleman who had a son that was then in Cambridge. This said gentleman hired me to go thither to teach his son, and so that my credit and entertainment should be the better there, he commended me unto one there who was tutor to his son (p. 115).

This gentleman was William Bromfield of Stoke Newington, Middlesex, a great merchant who in 1558 had been made Lieutenant-General of the Ordnance by Queen Mary, and was retained in that responsible position by Queen Elizabeth. How and where Whythorne became acquainted with Bromfield is not disclosed in the autobiography,[1] but the merchant observed in Whythorne qualities that he admired, and the more he knew of him the more trust he reposed in him. His son at Cambridge, also named William Bromfield, had matriculated at Trinity, then a new foundation, in Lent Term 1557–8. Thus he had been there for about two years when Whythorne arrived to serve as a private tutor in January or February of 1560.

Quite understandably, young Bromfield's regular tutor resented having to share his pupil with the new-comer, especially since Whythorne held no college degrees or academic standing. The tutor, who had recently received a second and higher degree (probably M.A.), expected deference from Whythorne, and did not get it. Whythorne had equal privileges at Trinity, and considered himself on a level of standing: 'I came not thither to be a scholar or pupil but to be a schoolmaster and a tutor.' Thus a difficult situation soon developed: 'Although he would use me friendly when that I of courtesy came to visit and salute him, behind my back he would with most spiteful words and reproachful taunts most churlishly use me.' At length Whythorne complained to Bromfield, who wrote stiff letters to both of them, which made the tutor 'acknowledge unto me his gross rudeness, and used me afterwards very friendly and courteously'.

Whythorne's life among the dons at Trinity proved to be a happy one in which he participated as fully as possible. In July of 1560, some months after his arrival, the University staged a ceremony to exhume the corpse of Martin Bucer, the renowned German Protestant theologian who had died at Cambridge in 1551. Whythorne describes the occasion thus: 'He, being dead

---

[1] Could the introduction to Bromfield have come through Whythorne's brother-in-law, the lawyer John Skinner? One John Skynner was a witness to Bromfield's will (p. 144, n. 2), but the name was a common one.

and buried, the Papists in Queen Mary's days took up his cask or coffin, and also the cask or coffin of one named Paulus Fagius . . . and burned them both at a stake as the relics of two arch-heretics.' Now the Protestants in their turn dug up Bucer's remains and reconsecrated them in ceremonies replete with pomp and celebration. Whythorne participated by writing some verses, of which he gives the setting:

And, as the Papists had made verses in reproach of Bucer at his burning, so now the Protestants made verses likewise in his commendation. Some wrote in Greek, some in Latin, and some in English. At this time, I was persuaded by a friend of mine who was in the same Commons with me to write somewhat concerning Bucer, although it were in English. Whereupon I, having from my said friend the names of all such of that House or College as wrote before at Bucer's burning, devised [a poem] upon the etymology of their names (pp. 121–2).

Since the identity of these Papist writers was not previously known, Whythorne throws new light upon some of the details of this ceremony.

On a subsequent occasion, talk among the Trinity dons turned to conditions of life under the old religion, and to the various kinds of monks, canons, nuns, and friars that formerly abounded:

And, among all their devices, there were many old friarish pranks rehearsed that were played and done by those friars that were named limiting friars, who went a-begging about the countries, of which some of them were pleasant and merry wryish parts. And I, being then set on a merry pin, wrote thereof on an old ground (on which I had seen the like made before) this [poem] (p. 125).

Whythorne's ballad is a jolly one, running to thirty-four stanzas; it tells of 'a friar men called Robard', who travelled from village to village in his 'short, tucked gown', his loins 'girt with knotted ropes':

> The maids and wives he gat with child
> It was a fruitful friar.

Ultimately Friar Robard was sent to Hell (where his lechery

shocked even the Devil), from whence still issued his echoing refrain 'Sing busk under the briar'.

Besides these lighter moments of life at Trinity College, Whythorne used his time for self-improvement and serious reading: 'Being somewhat in quiet and having there little to do more than the teaching of my scholar, I gave myself sometimes to . . . the Italian tongue and sometimes in reading of English books, as well of Divinity as of moral and profane matters.' His period of reading and conversation with the Cambridge dons effected a great change in Whythorne's life. From this time on he became seriously concerned with various dilemmas of Christian thought and the husbandry of his soul. The robust humanity of Whythorne's autobiography now becomes interspersed with theological disquisitions, for example, reflections upon the nature of Purgatory.

Whythorne's Cambridge period came to an end when young William Bromfield attained his B.A. early in 1562. Whythorne thus describes his going down: 'After I had remained in Cambridge nigh about two years, my pupil and I left there, and came to London to remain, where, after I had been a certain time, I visited my old acquaintances' (p. 133). One of these old friends was the portrait-painter who had done Whythorne in oils while he was living with the Suds-of-Soap widow. Whythorne was fascinated to see how his image had changed, 'as by the length and fullness of my beard, the wrinkles on my face and hollowness of my eyes; and also that as my face was altered, so were the delights of my mind changed'. The portrait and subsequent reflections prompted one of his characteristic songs, which ends with the epigram:

As time doth alter ev'ry wight
So ev'ry age hath his delight.

During this interlude Whythorne was staying at the London house of the Bromfields. As the great merchant came to know Whythorne better, he became impressed by his forthright honesty and strength of character. The fact that young

William had received his degree with distinction undoubtedly reflected some credit upon his private tutor, and the father had certainly met Whythorne on various visits to Cambridge. To Bromfield this was a crucial time (autumn 1562), for as Lieutenant-General of the Ordnance he had been ordered to accompany the expeditionary force to Le Havre, and he was concerned to leave his affairs in the hands of some man in whom he felt an absolute trust. Whythorne modestly describes the unexpected turn of affairs:

This gentleman began now to like so well of me as he, being called to serve the Queen's majesty in her wars beyond the seas, committed not only the chief government of his son unto me but also the chief doings that he had within this realm, pertaining to his office, his trades in London, and receiving and paying all such sums of money as were due to him or to be paid by him. And when he departed out of the realm he placed me as his deputy in such a place as he meant to procure me a beneficial living during my life, if it had pleased God that he should have returned from those wars into England safe again (p. 136).

The agreed rate of compensation for these services was to be an annuity of 40 marks a year during Bromfield's lifetime.

The realities of the business world began to break in on Whythorne, soon after Bromfield had crossed the Channel:

Nor was everyone his friend that bore him a friendly countenance when he was in England; and although they would not bark aloud at him, yet I understood how they groined at him, seeking means to sift him secretly and to make such a hole in his coat that . . . it would have been hard for him to mend it again (p. 137).

Whythorne's pondering on how to meet this situation is a good example of the soliloquies that occur at intervals in the autobiography:

Then quoth I to myself, 'What hap have I? I am now newly entered into credit with this gentleman who for the good opinion that he has of me has me in great trust. If I, therefore, continue in his doings and affairs still, and his enemies may bring their fetches and practices to full effect, perhaps though I know nothing of his doings that way I may be made to smell of the smoke of that fire wherewith my friend is likely to be singed and tried. On the other side, if I leave him now (when he is not in a position to put another in my room conveniently), I shall not only lose forty marks a year during his life, besides a constant friend, but also play the part of an ingrate and inconstant caitiff.' Wherefore, even in this perplexity I determined with myself not to leave him, but to take all chances as they came, having a sure hope in God that whatsoever became of him my innocence in his doings before this time should be my defence (p. 137).

Whythorne's new responsibilities opened up to him an entirely new world, the very opposite of the polite households where he had taught and entertained pupils, or his recent residence in the academic groves of Cambridge. Now he plunged into commercial London, teeming with shiploads of commodities from all over the expanding trade routes. The extent of these far-flung enterprises amazed Whythorne:

. . . by means of the credit and estimation I had for my said friend's sake and the doings that I had for him, I had occasion to be many times in the companies, not only of the chief of those who depended on the same office as my friend, but also of divers of the worshipful merchants of London; for my said friend had doings for merchandise and ventures in and nigh about this time, not only to Muscovia in Russia, but also into Tartaria and Persia. Then had he also ventures to Guinea in Ethiopia, and also to Magrobumba and Nova Spania, and also to Terra Florida in America (p. 138).

The conversation of these men fascinated him:

Then, when I accompanied the merchants, there was talk of gain and loss, and of such merchandise as it was best for them to transport into this country and that country for gain, and likewise of the commodities of other countries to be brought hither wherein gain was to be gotten. And then for the exchange of money—how that went from time to time as well beyond the seas as here in England. There was no other talk among all these aforesaid but of gain and riches (pp. 138–9).

Fortunes were made rapidly by these Elizabethan politicians and venturers:

> Then should I hear sometimes of one who had been in his office but a small time only, and when he came into it he was worth little or nothing, and paid every man; yet now he was both a purchaser and a builder, and also a great moneyed man. Also, I should hear of this merchant and that merchant—how short a time they had been occupiers, with what small stocks they began, and that in a short time they for their wealth became Aldermen's fellows (p. 139).

Whythorne could not fail to contrast talk of this sort with conversation at Trinity College:

> At the first conversing among these aforesaid, their talk was somewhat strange to me because I had not been used so much to it in a great while before (for when I was in Cambridge there was no other talk but of learning and learned men, and how by learning and the virtues of the mind men were exalted to promotion) (p. 139).

This new life among the moneyed men did not last long, for the army at Le Havre was stricken by the plague, and soon was forced to surrender to the French. Bromfield, already suffering from a wound, had taken ship shortly before the town capitulated, and died two days after reaching English soil. Immediately Bromfield's enemies felt free to show themselves: 'those who before his death only whispered and groined against him now spoke and barked aloud at him'. Fortunately, Whythorne's accounts were in good order, for he had 'laid every sort by themselves in several boxes made for the purpose in my counting-house or desk'. But besides losing a friend and patron, Whythorne was cut off from the promised annuity of 40 marks a year for life. In Bromfield's will, made shortly before he left for France, we find listed among the legacies, 'Thomas Whitehorne, gent. £5'.

The plague soon hit London, and Whythorne became thoroughly frightened, especially when people in nearby houses died, and later in 1563 the pestilence 'came into the house where I lay, [so] that I looked every minute of the hour when I should be visited like the rest'. This threat, coupled with other blows that Fortune had recently dealt him, disturbed Whythorne's mind: 'The fear of death greatly troubled me, and I being at that present very unquiet with so many crosses at once, began to enter upon judgement of my own conscience.' He became convinced that God had sent the plague on the nation as a punishment for its sins, and that his continued bad luck was a punishment for his own particular offences. From that time on, Whythorne became increasingly more religious and God-fearing. The autobiography suffers from this intensified zeal, for the pages are now burdened with discussions of sin and salvation, and cant phrases echoed from a hundred Tudor sermons. With this change Whythorne's verses now become heavily didactic. He even rewrote one of his songs; when originally offered to the Suds-of-Soap widow, his poem began:

> *Since I embrace*
> *My lady's grace,*   *In sort as I desire,*
> *I will rejoice*
> *With pleasant voice,*   *Since quenched is this fire.*

The new version revealed Whythorne's solemn frame of mind; it reads:

> *Since I embrace*
> *The Heav'nly grace*   *In sort as I would have,*
> *Rejoice I must,*
> *Till I for dust*   *Do yield my corpse to grave.*

About this time, in 1564 or 1565, Bromfield's son, who had been overseas, returned to England and soon relieved Whythorne of his responsibilities. Whythorne immediately retreated to the home of a friend in the country to rest, 'and also to recover if I could some part of my health that was so much impaired'. Work and worries over Bromfield's affairs left its mark on the 36-year-old Whythorne; people aged more rapidly in the era before medical knowledge emerged from the twilight of superstition. Although Whythorne's country visit to his friend was 'not for profit, but for good and friendly entertainment', yet he taught the friend's daughter 'to play somewhat on the virginals and the lute, and also to sing pricksong [as well as] to sing to the lute' (p. 165).

This bucolic holiday provided leisure for Whythorne to read and write again. For his host he wrote two graces, one 'Before Dinner', and the other 'After Dinner'. But the verses that most pleased the gentleman and his lady were in the form of a mock testimonial for an itinerant spinning-woman named Sybil Slius. This unfortunate female suffered from some mental deficiency, yet seemed to enjoy being the butt of merriment in the households she visited. Because Sybil Slius came from Gloucester, and spoke a strong West Country dialect, Whythorne wrote his verses in the similar dialect of Somerset, which he remembered from his boyhood. These and other songs provided by Whythorne filled many evenings; and except for one incident when a fellow guest picked a quarrel with him, the visit was both pleasant and restful.

In the meantime, Whythorne had been pondering his future. The experiences of the last few years caused him to realize that he 'could find no such security and stability in any . . . way as I did in the profession of teaching music' (p. 173). His decision followed: 'I intended after that time to give myself wholly to the profession . . . and to none other.' The next problem was to choose some course of action to raise himself in the world of music, his practical purpose being to 'make myself known to many in the shortest time'. Soon he hit upon a plan: 'And then came to my remembrance that there was no better way for that purpose than to set and publish some music of mine own making in print.' In England, up to this date, little secular music had been published,[1] but on the Continent, especially in Italy, Whythorne had observed the popularity enjoyed by madrigal books. He thought over his past compositions, the 'many songs to be sung of three, four, and five parts', as well as those 'I had

---

[1] Actually only two examples of printed secular music have survived: *20 Sōges* (formerly considered to have been printed by Wynkyn de Worde), and a single part-song on a single sheet, apparently printed by Pynson.

TRIPLEX,

Of Songes, for three, fower, and fiue voyces, compoſed and made by *Thomas Whythorne*, gent. the which Songes be of ſundry ſortes, that is to ſay, ſome long, ſome ſhort, ſome hard, ſome eaſie to be ſonge, and ſome betwene both : alſo ſome ſolemne, and ſome pleaſant or mery : ſo that according to the ſkill of the fingers (not being Muſitians) and diſ-poſition or delite of the hearers, they may here finde Songes for their contentation and liking.

¶ Now newly publiſhed. An. 1571.

¶ In the Tenor, or fift booke, ye ſhall haue the Preface of the Author, wherein he declareth more at large the contentes of theſe his fiue bookes.

AT LONDON

Printed by John Daye dwelling ouer Alderſgate.

Title-page of Whythorne's *Songes*, 1571 (Triplex part-book)

made to be played on the virginals and lute'. These Whythorne decided to print, but not merely the music alone: 'I purposed to put with every song a sonnet of my own invention for a ditty thereto.'

The labour of preparing the songs for the printer took nearly two years. While toiling over the task, Whythorne suffered frequent doubts over the undertaking, wondering what people would say about him:

I had many combats with myself about it: one while would I think to myself, 'What do I mean now, thus to travail and beat my brains about this matter? Do I not daily see how they who set out books be by their works made a common gaze to all the world, and hang upon the blasts of all folk's mouths, and upon the middle finger pointings of the unskilful?' (p. 174).

But he succeeded in convincing himself that the work must be completed, and that he must face the expected envy and malice of his critics. Whythorne told himself:

We are not born into this world altogether for ourselves, but to do good in our professions and to our abilities in every way. I say to do good to others as much as we may, and not to live as drones and caterpillars that live altogether upon the sweat of others' brows; also, we ought not to hide our talents under the ground as the unprofitable servant did, lest we be found fruitless figtrees, and so called to account for our bailiwicks (p. 176).

Writing out the music and the words prompted a good deal of revision, as Whythorne tells us in the long rhymed preface to the work (not his most fluent verse!):

Herein be divers songs also, the which altered have I
By mending of some the music, of others the ditty,
So that they be not now as they were when I first them gave
Out of my hands, abroad to serve their turns who now them have.

The last four words are important, since they imply that manuscript copies of some of the songs were in circulation, and Whythorne wished to make sure that anyone who compared the manuscript versions with the printed edition would realize that the changes were authorial revisions and not printer's errors. In the autobiography he inserted a long versified preface, and followed it with explanations in prose of some of the allusions.

While in the process of writing out his songs, Whythorne continued to compose new ones and add them to the collection. They were prompted by another love affair, this time with a widow to whom he was introduced by a matchmaking friend. She was about six years younger than Whythorne, childless, a Londoner, well born, and had a dowry of £20 a year. (For convenience she may be nicknamed the £20 widow.) His suit began auspiciously, and a marriage agreement was easily reached. Christmas was approaching, and Whythorne wished the ceremony to take place in January when his brother-in-law, a lawyer, who was coming to London for the new term at the law courts, could be present. For some reason the widow, who up to this time had been 'as loving and true as the turtle-dove', insisted that she would marry before the old year ended, or not at all. The matchmaker tried to reconcile them, and made Whythorne return to the house time and again. His account of these visits abounds in homely detail and human interest. But whatever the widow's real reason may have been, she did not go through with the wedding.[1] To Whythorne's humiliation she promptly married a wealthy ostler. Were the stars to blame? Whythorne asked himself. In looking back at his experience in 'wooing divers women', he saw a pattern repeated: 'Those women have for a short time given me such cause to think that they loved me that I have thought that the sun would have lost his light before they would have changed; and also their inconstancy has somewhat grieved me.' Ultimately, common sense broke through his grief: 'But yet, I am not only alive but also even then I did both eat my meat and drink my drink, and sleep well enough' (p. 204).

It was time now for Whythorne to seek employment again. He chose to return to a country house where he had been a year or

---

[1] Whythorne suggests that an astrologer may have convinced the widow that the match was inauspicious.

two earlier, apparently the household where Sybil Slius, the barmy seamstress, caused so much merriment. Now his status was that of music master and not that of a guest, and arguments over his rate of pay soon arose. The gentleman and his lady considered that Whythorne was not properly respectful of their rank, and he was amazed that not only did they fail to pay him, but they began to ridicule him before other people. The house was situated at a place named Weld, which may have been Weald Hall in Essex, about seventeen miles from London and very near Childerditch, where one of Whythorne's friends of this period, Adrian Schaell, served as Vicar. But the evidence is too scanty to permit the location to be identified with any degree of certainty.

Soon Whythorne left Weld in a huff and returned to London. The series of rebuffs that he had lately received made him reflect on the old saying, 'This world is but a scaffold for us to play our comedies and tragedies upon', so he devised a 'sonnet' on the subject. In the meantime, he had been labouring on copy for the printer, and in the process had come to look upon the five part-books of his songs as his children, 'which my head brought forth'. After further reflection on this idea, he decided, 'because they should bear my name, I could do no less than set in every one of them their father's picture or counterfeit, to represent to those who should use the children the form and favour of their parent'. Accordingly, he arranged to have a woodcut made from a new portrait painted in 1569. This woodcut he adorned with the coat of arms

left to me by my poor ancestors, with which, though they have left me no great revenues to support and maintain them with, yet they have left me a remembrance that I am as free a man born both on my father's and my mother's side as he who may spend thousands of pounds of yearly inheritance (pp. 211–12).

Ironically, it is this embellished woodcut which has led historians of music to believe that Whythorne was a wealthy amateur.

Whythorne now took another position in a great house where

the staff also included a Latin tutor named Thomas Barnam, described by Whythorne as 'a young man who is a very proper scholar', one who could 'make verses both in Latin and English very well'. They found each other's company congenial, and exchanged many verses, including poetical etymologies of each other's names. The manuscript of his songs now being ready for the printer, Whythorne showed it 'to divers of my friends, and also let them hear much of [the songs] sung'. His friends responded in a heart-warming fashion: 'Whereupon, certain of them who were learned wrote verses in Latin in commendation of the whole work', which they sent to him. Whythorne took these poems to London and had them inserted in the several books. The Tenor part-book carried Barnam's verses, those of Adrian Schaell were put in the Bassus part-book, and Thomas Covert's graced the Triplex part-book. His friend Henry Thorne had written 'certain Latin verses . . . long before, in commendation of my music only', but after Whythorne showed him his ditties Thorne contributed a new poem, which in turn was inserted in the Contratenor part-book. To our regret these Latin verses by his friends are so general in their praise that they add practically nothing to our knowledge of Whythorne or those who wrote them.[1]

About this time Whythorne spent several days in the country with Henry Thorne. When he returned to London he called at the shop of John Day in Aldersgate, over St. Martin's, and eagerly inquired how his *Songes* was selling. John Day replied that the music books were 'not bought of him as fast as he looked for'. Whythorne thought he knew two reasons why the sales were slow: 'The first was because he [John Day] had heretofore printed music which was very false printed', so that buyers tended to avoid any new music from his press. The other reason was the perennial complaint of authors that the publisher had not advertised his book enough: 'The second cause why my music sold no faster was because it is not yet known that there is such music to be bought.' Whythorne then suggested

[1] See pp. 216-19.

publishing a second book containing all the stanzas of his songs; but despite an affirmative response from the printer, the volume apparently was not published.

At this point in his narrative, Whythorne inserted a long discussion of the state of music and the status of musicians from Biblical times up to his own. In form this discussion is really a series of 'discourses', as he termed them on his title-page. The following topics make up the series:

1. Scriptural evidence 'that music was used in heaven before the world began' (pp. 221–2).
2. The inventors of music after the Creation, according to Biblical and mythical sources, and the instruments employed (pp. 222–5).
3. How music was used in the early Church, judging from Scriptural evidence (pp. 225–30).
4. The state of early secular music, according to scriptural and classical sources (pp. 230–2).
5. The degrees of musicians, similar to those in other professions (pp. 232–4).
6. Eminent persons (beginning with Nero) who have loved music, and some of their opinions on its benefits (pp. 234–7).
7. The place of music among the seven liberal sciences (pp. 237–9).
8. Examples of the power of music over man and beast (pp. 239–43).
9. The status of music in England 'in the time past' and 'in the time present' (pp. 243–7).
10. The status of music 'in foreign realms' (p. 247).

The whole series of subjects in prose is then followed by a long versified version, which summarizes the main points of the concatenation of 'discourses'. Many of these pages make dull reading, but others contain invaluable descriptions and sidelights on the state of music in Whythorne's time.

Now, in 1571 or soon after, occurred the most important

event in Whythorne's musical career, a direct result of the plan to raise himself in his profession by publishing his music. The autobiography reports the event in simple words: 'When all the aforesaid circumstances were thus finished about the printing of my music, there was a motion made to me to serve Doctor Parker . . . Archbishop of Canterbury, and that I should be the Master of Music in his Chapel' (pp. 254–5). Here was a great honour and opportunity. Whythorne accepted it 'because I knew by his place he was the most honourable man in this realm, next to the Queen'. In point of fact, Archbishop Parker had become a highly influential man in many areas besides theology, one such field being music, for Parker encouraged the use of music in church services, and opposed the low churchmen who then wished to restrict it. He desired especially to improve the quality of psalm-singing, and about six years earlier had persuaded the greatest living English composer, Thomas Tallis, to set to music Parker's versifications of eight psalms. John Day printed these psalms about 1567, though 'Parker's Psalm Book' was not placed on sale to the public, copies being given to selected recipients.

The Archbishop's choice of Whythorne to direct the music in his Chapel at Lambeth Palace is a significant indication of the musician's relative standing in his profession. That Parker had earlier employed Tallis shows his awareness of high standards. Whether Parker considered Tallis for the position in 1571 we have no way of knowing; probably the composer, then about 67, was considered too old. Tallis's pupil, William Byrd, then 30 years of age, would have been a logical candidate, but his position in the Chapel Royal and his known adherence to the Roman Church may well have ruled him out. In any case, it seems likely that John Day had some part in bringing Whythorne to Parker's attention, for the printer was in close and frequent contact with the Archbishop.

Since Parker had translated the Psalms into simple English verse as early as 1557, it is not surprising that the first task he assigned to Whythorne in 1572 was 'to make a note and song of four parts' to the 107th Psalm. When completed, Whythorne's version was sung before the Archbishop in his Chapel. Other psalms followed, of which the 86th is the only one named. Whythorne set it in four parts also; later he decided that Parker's verses were unsatisfactory and produced his own version. Next Whythorne turned into verse a long meditation on the Lord's Prayer, and set it to music. None of these musical compositions for the Archbishop's Chapel are known to be preserved.

This happy chapter in Whythorne's life lasted only about three years. It ended with the death of the Archbishop in May 1575; and among the list of pall-bearers at his funeral is named a 'Mr Whithorne'. Apart from the autobiography, this document is the only extant record of Whythorne's connexion with the Archbishop or his Chapel. He seems to have been happy in the work, and to have satisfied Parker, who 'had a good liking to the music' of the 107th Psalm. But Whythorne apparently made little impression on other musicians then living in London, and Parker's successor, Archbishop Grindal, did not retain him as his Master of Music at Lambeth.

The shift back to private status was easily made by Whythorne, who had learned to adjust himself to the frequent turns of Fortune's wheel. He says simply, 'Now I began anew to read and rhyme, and to consider again of worldly affairs, and to make ever as my leisure served me.' He formulated elaborate plans for future publications, including forty duets, twenty-six new trios, and a like number of songs in four parts, and twenty more songs in five parts. Nor did Whythorne's ambition cease here, for he adds, 'Besides all this, I intended to make some songs of six and seven parts, whatever I did else.' The autobiography ends here with the verses of more than fifty songs for which the music was still to be composed.

Of Whythorne's career after the close of the autobiography, the evidence is meagre. To readers who have followed his love-lorn path from widow to widow the most tantalizing event occurred two years after he left Lambeth, for the Vicar-General's books record that on 3 May 1577 a licence was issued for the marriage of Thomas Whythorne of St. Alphage, Cripplegate,

and 'Elizabeth Stoughton, spinster' of St. Martin in the Fields.
Two days later the ceremony took place.[1] Apart from these bare
details, nothing else is known of Elizabeth, neither her age, her
lineage, nor any other information. Whether she won him by
leaving love-songs in his lute-strings, by baking special dishes
for him, or any other device we shall never know. After following
his vicissitudes in the company of one widow after another we can
be happy that the records carry the gratifying word 'spinster'.

How far Whythorne proceeded with his musical plans we can
judge only by the one group of songs that reached print. This
was a set of duets, printed in two part-books in 1590 with a long
title-page, headed *Duos, or Songs for two voices, composed and
made by Thomas Whythorne, Gent.* From the title-page we learn
that the music was intended either for voices or for combined
instruments and voices. The first twenty-two songs were 'made
for young beginners', or 'for a man and a childe to sing, or otherwise for voices or Instruments of Musicke, that be of the like
compasse or distance in sound'. The second group, consisting
of fifteen songs, were 'made for two children to sing. Also they
be aptly made for two treble Cornets' or other voices or instruments of similar compass. The remaining fifteen compositions
in the volume were 'all Canons of two parts in one' intended for
voices or instruments 'of diuers compasses or distances'. The
books were printed by Thomas Este (East) of Aldersgate
Street, at the Sign of the Black Horse, the leading music publisher of the decade, but in workmanship they are much cruder
than the 1571 volumes printed by John Day.

The *Duos* have a long dedication, dated 'From London the
19. Nouember. 1590', which offers little information about Whythorne or his position at the time. It is addressed to Sir Francis Hastings (*c.* 1542–1610), fifth son of the second Earl of

---

[1] *London Marriage Licences 1521–1869* (ed. Joseph Foster, 1887),
column 1455. The marriage is recorded under date 5 May 1577 in volume 25
of *Harleian Society Publications*, 1886, p. 75. That it was the musician is
indicated by the facts that he was alive in 1592 (the 'musical scrap'), that he
left a widow named Elizabeth (his will), and that the records offer no rival
Thomas Whythorne or Whitehorn who meets these requirements.

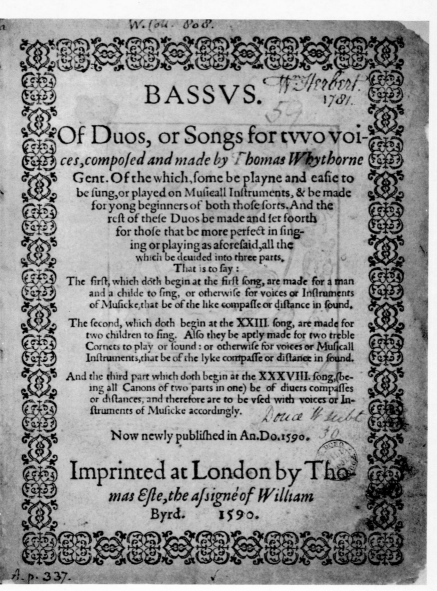

BASSVS.

Of Duos, or Songs for two voi-

ces, composed and made by Thomas Whythorne
Gent. Of the which, some be playne and easie to
be sung, or played on Musicall Instruments, & be made
for yong beginners of both those sorts. And the
rest of these Duos be made and set foorth
for those that be more perfect in singing or playing as aforesaid, all the
which be deuided into three parts,
That is to say :
The first, which doth begin at the first song, are made for a man
and a childe to sing, or otherwise for voices or Instruments
of Musicke, that be of the like compasse or distance in sound.

The second, which doth begin at the XXIII. song, are made for
two children to sing. Also they be aptly made for two treble
Cornets to play or sound : or otherwise for voices or Musicall
Instruments, that be of the lyke compasse or distance in sound.

And the third part which doth begin at the XXXVIII. song, (being all Canons of two parts in one) be of diuers compasses
or distances, and therefore are to be vsed with voices or Instruments of Musicke accordingly.

Now newly published in An. Do. 1590.

Imprinted at London by Tho-

mas Este, the assigné of William
Byrd.   1590.

Title-page of Whythorne's 1590 *Duos* (the Bassus part-book)

Huntington. Sir Francis's older brother Henry carried the title of third Earl, and was married to Catherine Dudley, sister to Whythorne's sometime patron, Lord Ambrose Dudley, now Earl of Warwick. That Sir Francis Hastings was Whythorne's patron in 1590 is shown by the dedication itself, and by the woodcut of the Hastings arms printed on the reverse side of the title-page. Although acknowledging that his duets were 'but small and simple', Whythorne presented them 'as a token of zelous affection, and dutifull loue, that I do beare vnto you'. He offered prayers for Sir Francis 'and my very good ladie your bedfellow', circumstances that suggest Whythorne knew Lady Hastings fairly well, albeit there is nothing to indicate how long he may have enjoyed their patronage. The dedication carries a strong religious tone, which may have been aimed at Sir Francis's puritan zeal, but it is consistent with the direction of Whythorne's own religious sentiments in the autobiography.

Nor does the 1590 dedication reveal much information about Whythorne's music. He remarks that 'ther hath not any one of our nation published in print any Musick for two voices',[1] a situation that contrasts with the practice of 'diuers strangers in forrein countries . . . heretofore'. Whythorne offered his duets in the hope that they would fill a need, especially in rural areas where singers were difficult to bring together. Whether the public greeted the publication with enthusiasm greater than the 1571 *Songes* had received seems doubtful.

For Whythorne's remaining years we have only a few bits of documentary evidence. The first is the 'musical scrap', a slip of paper found in the autobiography that lists on one side 'The Doctors and Bachelors of Music of late Time', and on the other side those of earlier eras (see Appendix III). This 'scrap' was written about 1593, and tells us little about Whythorne himself except that in his old age he continued to be interested in the history of his profession.

[1] Although Italian *bicinia*, especially those of Lasso, circulated widely after 1577, they were not published in England until 1598; after Whythorne's *Duos* the next volume of duets was Thomas Morley's *Canzonetts* for two voices in 1595.

The final documents concern Whythorne's death and burial. In the Registers of the Archdeacon's Court, now preserved in the Guildhall, the following item occurs:

Memorandum that about the fifth daye of the moneth of Julye in the yeere of our Lorde god one thowsand fiue hundred ninetie sixe Thomas Whithorne of the parishe of St Marie Abchurch London gentleman—made his last will and Testament nuncupatiue by word of mouth as followith beinge demaunded by one Mr Thomas Hussey of London clothworker how hee intended to bestowe his goodes the Testator answered beinge then of perfect mynde and memorie in this manner all that I haue I geeue vnto my wife for I haue none other to geeue it vnto beinge then and there present the said Mr Hussey Mistress Margery Baker Widdowe and Thomasine French the wife of Richard French with others.

The situation can now be reconstructed along the following lines: Whythorne aged 67 had begun to fail in health so rapidly that his wife, aware that he had no written will, called in several friends to record his verbal testament. His statement that he had 'none other to geeue it to' proves that he had no surviving children. The parish register of St. Mary Abchurch records 'Thomas Whitehorne gentleman bur[ied] ye second of August'.[1]

Whythorne's nuncupative will was proved on 25 August by his widow Elizabeth and she was granted administration of his estate. Unfortunately no inventory of the property has survived; probably it was not very large, but details (whether of a 'second-best bed' or otherwise) might have indicated the manner in which he lived at the end of his days.

Only one other fact emerges from the parish registers of St. Mary Abchurch. They record that on 18 October 1596 Elizabeth Whitehorn married one Robert Sowche, if we may paraphrase a rising young poet of those days,

> *A little month or ere those shoes were old*
> *With which she followed her late husband's body*
> *To the grave.*

[1] Guildhall MS. 7666. This is the only burial of a Whitehorne between 1577 and 1647. Guildhall MS. 9050/3 has on f. 42 a brief Latin note on the probating of his will; it offers no additional details.

Whythorne's own words on the fickleness of women could have served as his epitaph:

They are as slippery as ice
And will turn like the wind and weathercock.

Nevertheless, we have no reason to believe that their nineteen years together had not been as happy as an 'old man' (for so he considered himself) could expect. Furthermore, prompt re-marriages were quite common in that practical era. As for Elizabeth, now become Goodwife Sowche, little could she anti-cipate that her late husband, Thomas Whythorne, Gent., thanks not to his printed music but to his manuscript *Book of Songs and Sonnets*, would, four centuries later, become the most intimately revealed Elizabethan of 'the seven liberal sciences'.

III. *The Significance of the Autobiography*

The 'human interest' of Whythorne's life story is readily ap-parent to the general reader. Historians of sixteenth-century music, literature, and social customs will also find the autobio-graphy of importance in their respective fields. To the musico-logist probably the most interesting pages are those in which Whythorne tells of the state of music and musicians 'in this time present', the early years of Elizabeth's reign. The 'degrees' of musicians, the details of Archbishop Parker's musical activi-ties, the traveller's brief comments on the state of music in Italy in 1552, all offer tantalizing glimpses behind the curtain of history. The 'musical scrap' discussed in Appendix III gives the names of several of Whythorne's contemporaries unknown to musicologists. But the chief interest is the first-hand account of Whythorne's life as a working musician conscious of his status, making his way up the ladder of his profession. He was not a musical amateur (as Henry Davey mistakenly described him in the *Dictionary of National Biography*) but a serious composer with a lofty conception of his calling, who became a success in his profession.

The literary historian will find Whythorne's autobiography of particular interest. Since approximately a quarter of it is in verse, the autobiography offers us a new Tudor poet, together with more than two hundred of his poems, a substantial body of almost 2,100 lines. (About ninety of these poems had been printed in Whythorne's published song-books, but usually the first stanza only.) Written to be sung, his poems are at a disadvantage without his tunes. But compared to other verses of the time ('the drab age', as Professor C. S. Lewis has called it) many of Whythorne's poems stand up well enough. In reading his verses, two points should be kept in mind. First, Whythorne's purpose was almost exclusively didactic; even though they were written to be sung to the delicate music of the gittern or virginals they were 'made in the commendation of vertue and the reprehending of vices'. Secondly, Whythorne learned his craft as 'servant and scholar' of John Heywood, and apparently aspired no higher. His best work, epigrammatic in style, matches the best of Heywood; his worst verses, prosy and awkward (crowded with syllables forced into scansion), imitate the 'tumbling metre' of Heywood.

The influence of other contemporary poets is less clear. Considering that one of the tasks for his master, John Heywood, had been to transcribe the poems of Wyatt, Surrey, and Sternhold, and also that Whythorne copied them into his own collection, it is not surprising that some of his early verses seem to echo the earlier poets, Wyatt especially. Later his versification of the psalms shows the shadow of Surrey and Sternhold. Quite a different influence may have affected the autobiography as a whole, for the structure resembles in several ways Gascoigne's 'Discourse of the Adventures of Master F. J.', published early in 1574 in *A Hundreth Sundrie Flowers*. Although written as fiction, the poems of F. J. are preceded by narrative accounts of the personal (and possibly autobiographical) situations that prompted Gascoigne's verses.[1] That Whythorne had seen *A Hundreth Sundrie Flowers* is quite possible, but any direct

[1] See the edition by Charles Tyler Prouty, Columbia, Missouri, 1942.

influence seems unlikely, both because of chronology (assuming that Whythorne had essayed early autobiographical efforts or drafts) and because of the great contrast in tone between the swashbuckling Gascoigne and the prudent Whythorne.

Whythorne's poems are really the heart of the autobiography, providing its basic structure. For it is clear that when Whythorne sat down to write his life story he opened up a manuscript wherein he had inscribed his Songs and Sonnets in chronological order, and used each poem as a peg on which to hang his narrative. This highly unusual procedure led him to tell the circumstances behind each poem. He explained his method at the beginning of the work, where, addressing a nameless friend for whom ostensibly the life story is written, Whythorne says:

As I do write unto you to gratify you withal, so am I partly enforced thereunto because I do think it needful not only to show you the cause why I wrote them [the poems] but also to open my secret meaning in divers of them, as well in words and sentences as in the whole of the same (p. 3).

Thus, nearly every poem is prefaced by phrases such as 'whereupon I made this sonnet following', or 'wherefore to ease my heart I wrote as followeth'. As a result Whythorne created a unique document, for his autobiography is the only one in literary history in which a poet explains in detail the setting, circumstances, feelings, and meanings behind each of his poems. Indeed, his example raises a larger question: because Whythorne's verses, which often seem deadly conventional, are revealed by the autobiography to have been the products of intense emotional experience, we may properly wonder whether other contemporary poems that seem equally conventional may not also have been the outcome of emotional ferment instead of merely following poetic conventions.

Literary historians in several special fields will find Whythorne's pages worthy of particular study. To proverbialists Whythorne should be of the greatest interest, for the autobiography is as full of proverbs as an egg of meat. Well over a hundred proverbs occur, not counting many phrases that are

too brief or too oblique to qualify as complete or proper proverbs. At times Whythorne seems to write almost exclusively
in proverbial phrases, well-worn sayings such as the *Adagia* of
Erasmus, lore from compendia, and phrases from the Bible. In
this he was of course characteristic of the mid-sixteenth-century
gentleman (e.g. in *Euphues*); during the next century the quoting of proverbs began to be typical of artisans, and below the
taste of the well-bred man.

Many of Whythorne's favourite proverbs are found in earlier
collections, especially in John Heywood's 1546 volume, which
Whythorne had transcribed when he was apprenticed to Heywood. The footnotes identify most of the proverbs according to
their numbers in M. P. Tilley's *Dictionary of the Proverbs in
England* (1950); for a large number, Whythorne is the earliest
known source. In about a dozen instances Whythorne's sayings
are untraceable elsewhere in the form he uses: for example, 'No
devil so bad as a she-devil', 'The love of a woman's first husband goeth to her heart' (p. 203), 'He that is afraid of every
shadow has need to keep himself always in the dark' (p. 47), and
'He that will marry must wink and drink, and take the good or
ill fortune that God shall send him' (p. 203).

Similarly, the autobiography, written in Whythorne's 'new
orthografye', offers a happy hunting-ground to phonologists.
He stated his intention explicitly—'I will write words as they be
sounded in speech'—and probably did so as successfully as his
limited technique permitted. His method is a modification of
John Hart's system, expounded in his *Orthographie* in 1569. The
most noticeable differences are that Whythorne did not use
Hart's character invented for spelling words like 'middle'
(midℓ); nor does he spell 'which' as 'huich', nor does he use
v for *f* (as in 'ov' for 'of') nor *ei* for *i*. Whythorne employs the
yogh ȝ and the thorn þ, but these are not so anachronistic as it
may seem four hundred years later. Actually the thorn survived
at Magdalen College School until only thirty years before
Whythorne became a pupil there.[1] To preserve his spelling,

[1] See *A Fifteenth Century School Book*, ed. William Nelson, Oxford, 1956.

many palpable mistakes have been retained in the text, the most flagrant being singled out in the textual notes. The manuscript reveals that Whythorne attempted to maintain his system; but he frequently tended to revert to conventional spelling, as his revisions show.

For the convenience of readers, an explanation of his phonetic system is outlined on a page immediately preceding the text, and most students will find it simple going after a page or two. It should be emphasized that Whythorne is often inconsistent in applying his system (for example, 'use' may be spelt 'yowze' or 'iuwz' or in ten variant ways), although the word he had in mind is usually clear enough. The reader is warned, therefore, to be prepared for Whythorne's inconsistencies, and not to blame them on the editor or the printer. Several phonologists have already looked over Whythorne's text; and Rupert E. Palmer Jr. has written a Ph.D. dissertation on 'Thomas Whythorne's Speech', which he is preparing for publication.

But it is within the history of its own genre that Whythorne's autobiography deserves special attention. Nowadays, when autobiography has become such a popular form of story-telling, we remind ourselves incredulously that this obvious type of personal narrative is quite rare before the last three centuries. True, the writings of antiquity and the Middle Ages abound with autobiographical passages, but these fragments of personal information are merely embryonic compared to the developed, sustained life stories that have been best-sellers since the seventeenth century. Elsewhere I have traced in some detail *The Beginnings of Autobiography in England*,[1] so that it is sufficient here to summarize only the main lines of development.

In brief, autobiography as we know it (a sustained narrative with a conscious design of beginning, middle, and end) was practically unknown before the middle of the sixteenth century. It burst out in Italy from the pens of various Renaissance personalities, of which the best-preserved examples are the *Book of*

[1] Clark Library Seminar, 1959, published by the University of California Press, 1960.

My Life by the eminent physician and mathematician, Girolamo
Cardano (1501–76), and the autobiography of the goldsmith-
sculptor, Benvenuto Cellini (1500–71). Cellini's incomparable
narrative remained unpublished until 1730, and Cardano's *Vita*
first reached print in 1643, when it at once attracted imitators
in Italy and elsewhere, including England. Before the flowering
of autobiography in the seventeenth century there was nothing
in England[1] to compare with Whythorne's narrative written
about 1576, which, like the writings of his great Italian contemporaries, remained in manuscript long after his death.

Because Whythorne travelled in Italy in 1553–5 it is tempting
to think that he there picked up the idea of writing a self-
narrative. But this was before either Cellini or Cardano had written their autobiographies, and no evidence of any Italian or other
continental influence appears in Whythorne's open discussion of
his purposes and procedures. On the contrary, his statements
indicate a native English rationale for his literary endeavour:
he clearly implies that in writing an intimate narrative of his
life he is reciprocating similar revelations made by a friend. This
may be merely a literary convention, but if so it is remarkably
well sustained. Moreover, although the idea of such a verbal
exchange is scarcely novel, examples in print are rare.

Actually, Whythorne's autobiographical impulses had begun
to stir when he was barely 20 years old, long before he set
out on his continental travels. At that time, about the end of his
apprenticeship with John Heywood, one of Whythorne's friends
'declared the state of his life' to Whythorne, which prompted
Whythorne to reply with a verse narrative of 'my whole life to
this day in effect'. The pattern in this early autobiographical
poem is the same as that repeated by Whythorne about 1576
when he sat down with his manuscript of songs, sonnets, and
discourses and wrote out the full narrative of his experiences to
the time of 'Entering into the Old Man's Life'.

This last phrase from the heading Whythorne gave to his

---

[1] For a discussion of the third-person *Book* of Margery Kempe, see
the Clark Seminar report mentioned above.

manuscript calls attention to the use he made of the idea of the 'ages of man' when constructing his autobiography. The stages of his narrative take us successively through the age of childhood 'from the infancy until fifteen', the age of 'adolescency' ('the first part of the young man's age' from 16 to 25), and the age of 'juventute', from 25 to 39. 'Old age' began at 40, and Whythorne was about 48 when he wrote the autobiography, or well before the age of 'senectute', which began with the sixtieth year.[1] Apparently Whythorne is the only autobiographer to use this somewhat arbitrary framework, which he turned well to his purposes. It serves to demonstrate once again the originality of his autobiographical endeavours. The result of Whythorne's sense of structure is that he organized his materials quite successfully. His narrative has a beginning, middle, and end, and he always lets the reader know when he makes a transition to a new episode or subject. His digressions or dissertations (tedious as some may be) are also carefully worked out in categorical sequence. He had a strong concern for order in the narrative and states:

I shall follow orderly that which I have had and am now purposing to do concerning my songs and sonnets (p. 98).

Whythorne's autobiography abounds with incidents discussed introspectively. On page after page he tells of the thoughts behind his actions and the reasons (or ratiocinations) that prompted him to write his songs and sonnets. Phrases such as the following occur frequently: 'I took certain notes and councils for me to have in mind', or 'I began to bend my mind to requite him [a rival tutor] by writing in secret' (p. 117), or 'When I had paused and considered of this matter a certain time, I thought to try my gentlewoman a little concerning her promise made unto me' (p. 108). Similar short phrases dot the Whythorne narrative: 'I was put in a quandary', 'I was debating with myself', 'When I had bethought me a little while', and so on.

[1] Whythorne followed the divisions, with some changes, described by Sir Thomas Elyot in his *Castel of Helth*, 1534.

He was especially concerned with what other people were thinking, particularly about himself. This is well illustrated by his inner debate over the attitude that people would take towards his publishing venture in 1571, quoted earlier.[1] But the most complicated situations arose in his relations with various widows and bored gentlewomen with whom he was often involved. He puzzled frequently over the motives behind human actions; here is a typical case involving the 'Court Lady':

. . . the which words of hers made me to think that either she had a very good opinion of me or else she would have me to think so, because I should think myself the more beholden to her for the good opinion that she had of me . . . (p. 95).

This concern with motives gives the autobiography a modern flavour that mixes oddly with the vivid Elizabethan setting of Whythorne's activities and the prolixity of his style. It explains why Whythorne's autobiography marks such an advance over the early attempts by Englishmen to write their life-stories, and justifies the claim that Whythorne produced the first sustained autobiography, in the modern sense, in England.

IV. *The Manuscript*

A number of puzzling questions occur in connexion with Whythorne's manuscript, many of them impossible to answer. Where did it lie hidden for four centuries? When was it written? To whom was it addressed? Is it a first draft? Did Whythorne put it aside once he had written it, or did he go over it frequently in later years? These are a few of the queries that may arise in the reader's mind after he has read through the autobiography and turns to contemplate the document that preserves this unusual story for posterity.

The manuscript first came to light early in 1955 when a wooden box full of legal and business papers was taken by Major H. C. H. Foley from his family home at Stoke Edith, Hereford,

---

[1] See pp. 174–6. The whole passage, too long for quotation, is worth reading with this aspect in mind.

and left at Sotheby's in London to be sorted for saleable items. At the bottom of the box, Sotheby's cataloguer, Mr. Peter Crofts, found the autobiography, wrapped in brown paper, and saw at once that 'Thomas Whythorne, Gent.' was the madrigalist. Major Foley can offer no explanation of when or how the manuscript came to Stoke Edith. He writes, 'My father was a collector of all sorts of letters and manuscripts and might have picked it up at some sale. My grandmother was a keen musician and again she or her husband may have bought it somewhere.' When the autobiography came under the hammer at Sotheby's as lot 227 on 5 April, it was purchased for me by the late Percy J. Dobell. Subsequently I presented it through the American Friends to the Bodleian Library, where it is now catalogued under the number MS. Eng. misc. c. 330.

The manuscript consists of 90 folio leaves, folded into six gatherings,[1] plus two other leaves and two unrelated slips of paper. The top and outside edges of many of the pages, especially the early ones, are badly worn away, a situation that has required flights of editorial imagination in the attempt to supply the missing portions. The lacunae are indicated in the text by angle brackets; fortunately, there are only a few places where it has been necessary to admit defeat by leaving the space empty. In countless other instances the reader may wish to suggest a better word or phrase for what he finds within the angle brackets. The editor will welcome all suggestions. The rules require, however, careful respect for the amount of space available: the tattered edge often permits no more than four or five letters.

Tucked in the manuscript were two unrelated slips of paper. One is the 'Bucer scrap', a portion of an early draft of Whythorne's verses, written by him at Trinity College, Cambridge, at the time of the ceremonies in 1560 (see pp. 120–4). The other is the 'musical scrap', reproduced and interpreted in Appendix III. Internal evidence suggests that it was written about 1593.

[1] The first three and the last quire contain sixteen leaves; the fourth has fourteen and the fifth has twelve leaves. Continuity and catchwords show that no leaves are missing, though the final catchword indicates that more poems followed at the end.

The autobiography cannot be dated exactly. The poems accumulated over the years, as did some of the discourses; indeed, Whythorne states at the outset:

part of the which discourses I made and wrote when I did make these songs and sonnets, and now as more matter hath comen unto my remembrance, so have I augmented the same (p. 3).

Because he also refers in the opening pages to John Hart's *Orthographie*, published in 1569, the autobiography must have been written after that year. The last datable incident mentioned is the death of Archbishop Parker in 1575, and Whythorne ends his narrative at this point by stating that he is now returning to secular life. There is no hint, however, of Whythorne's courtship of Elizabeth Stoughton, whom he married on 5 May 1577. Hence the year 1576, the interim between these two turning-points in Whythorne's life, seems the most likely time for him to have composed the autobiography. Moreover, at the beginning of the autobiography Whythorne refers to his age, saying 'now . . . though I am not very old' (p. 4), a statement that is appropriate, since old age was considered to begin with the fortieth year. So too he speaks of Dr. Haddon, who died in 1572, as 'lately deseased' (p. 184), and of Parker, who died in 1575, as 'late Archbishop of Canterbury' (p. 254).

From the nature of his additions and corrections it seems clear that Whythorne picked up the manuscript from time to time in later years. That he kept it by him until his old age is proved by the woodcut inserted on the back of his title-leaf, for it is the 1590 version with the altered coat of arms. The 'musical scrap', written about 1593, could have been placed in the volume by accident either before or after his death.

Some of the deletions and additions appear at first sight to suggest that the manuscript is the author's first draft, wherein he copied his verses and his discourses from other papers. The original source of the poems he tells us (p. 220) was the manuscript book into which he had entered them in chronological order, a commonplace book of sorts which contained other material such as the verses of Wyatt, Surrey, Sternhold, Heywood, and others (see p. 14, n. 1). Whatever intermediate papers there may have been, a close study strongly suggests that the manuscript autobiography was preceded by an earlier draft of major portions, written in ordinary spelling.

The key evidence is the slip of paper which has been designated the 'Bucer scrap', reproduced opposite page 123. This piece of paper appears to be the upper quarter of a leaf approximately the same size as those on which the autobiography was written. The recto contains a working draft of Whythorne's Bucer verses, with erasures, corrections, and additions. In the margin appear the names of the Papist Cambridge dons whom Whythorne was satirizing. Both sides are in ordinary spelling, without the thorn or other devices of Whythorne's 'new orthografye'.

The verso contains twenty-four lines of the prose explanation of the Bucer poem but continues into the account of the conversation concerning monks and friars that in the autobiography precedes the Ballad of Robard the Friar. The fact that this subject-matter occurs shows that the scrap is not merely a draft of the verses with prose exposition of the allusions, but an earlier draft of this section of the autobiography.

Moreover, the scrap shows that this one leaf of the draft was positioned on the page much as it appears in the manuscript (f. 34) of the autobiography. Some lines end with exactly the same words, or divided portion of a word. The scrap takes 24 lines to cover material that occupies 23 lines in the manuscript. There are a few slight verbal changes but none of importance.

The preservation of this scrap argues cogently that an earlier, ordinary spelling, draft existed, containing sizeable portions of the text as it is preserved in the full 'new orthografye' version. Other evidence supports the case that the manuscript as we have it is essentially a copying out of earlier writings:

1. The manuscript contains frequent 'errors of the eye': such mistakes as 'felf', which is meaningless, for 'felt' (p. 118).

Curiously, Whythorne often confused *k* and *l*, e.g. 'kook' for 'look' (p. 54), 'tall' for 'talk' (p. 111), 'lilled' for 'killed' (p. 240). Other typical errors are 'vyverz' for 'dyverz' (p. 151), 'appried' for 'applied' (p. 202), 'parpikiularly' (p. 228), and 'lyk' for lyf' (p. 264). Besides these, there are frequent minim errors and mistakes in vowels.

2. Examples of dittography abound. Repetition of single words could occur in writing, but dittography involving whole phrases argues the act of copying, e.g. a repetition of the phrase 'and that you may not afterwards' is deleted at the top of folio 4 (p. 8). Likewise, the cancelled passage of six and a half lines on folio 3 (see p. 5, n. 2) argues strongly that Whythorne was copying at the very beginning of his life-story. (See Appendix IV.)

3. Inconsistent or mistaken catchwords, e.g. 'heer' on folio 17 (for which see p. 58, n. 2).

v. *Method of Editing*

The task of reproducing Whythorne's holograph in type has been comparatively simple, thanks to the relative legibility of his handwriting. Three kinds of brackets have been employed, following standard usage. Square brackets enclose editorial insertions, which, happily, have rarely been needed. Half brackets enclose Whythorne's own interlinear additions, corrections, or substitutions. Angle brackets indicate lacunae in the text, supplied by editorial conjecture, many of them certain, most of them informed guesses, and a few left blank because no likely conjecture occurred to the editor. Most of these gaps are found at the outside and top margins where the manuscript has deteriorated, a situation that can be visualized by comparing the position of the fragmentary passages with the numbers in the margin which indicate the beginning of new leaves in the manuscript.

The textual notes record only those words, phrases, misspellings, or other points that might be of some significance.

When Whythorne has superscribed a variant word without crossing out his first choice, the one judged to be later has usually been printed in the text, with the earlier word placed in a textual note. Catchwords have been omitted unless some irregularity has required comment in the notes. The first transcript by Mr. John Chapple carefully reported all minor textual points, and any student making a minute study of Whythorne's orthography may examine it upon request. Whythorne fortunately used very few contractions, the most common being $ for 'sir' or 'ser' (as in 'service'), superior r for er (as in 'skolmaster'), and a line over m or n, to double the letter. These and other contractions have been silently expanded in the printed text. Whythorne's early form of ampersand has been replaced by the modern symbol. His capital letters present frequent difficulties, especially I, J, L, and P, whose majuscule and minuscule forms merge into one another, a common occurrence in manuscripts of this period.

The editor has used his discretion in breaking up Whythorne's long narrative into paragraphs. Because there are no chapters or other divisions, topical headings have been supplied on all pages to enable the reader to keep his place in the story. Similarly, the editor has supplied or regularized some of the punctuation, without which many of Whythorne's pages tend to run on like Tennyson's brook; but Whythorne's own full stops have usually been followed, although in some necessary cases commas have been substituted. Editorial judgement has been exercised with an ornamented figure Whythorne often placed at the right end of his lines of prose merely to even out the space, but which sometimes also served as a full stop. With the help of even light punctuation Whythorne's meaning often becomes clearer, and the reader gains an added sense of the cadence of his style.

WHYTHORNE'S 'NEW ORTHOGRAFYE'

WHYTHORNE's attempt at phonetic spelling is basically simple; after the first few pages the average reader will find it plain sailing.

The following are the principal devices:

> The thorn þ (the capital is Ð) for *th* is employed when it is voiced ('this', 'that') but not when unvoiced ('thin', 'thorn').
>
> The yogh ʒ is used for soft *g* or *j*.
>
> A dot is placed under long vowels, as 'laṭ' for 'late', omitting the final *e*.
>
> *k* is used for hard *c*.
>
> *s* is substituted for *t* in '-tion'.
>
> *y* replaces long *i*.
>
> An unpronounced *g* is omitted, so that 'might' becomes 'myht'.
>
> A final syllable '-le' becomes '-ull', as in 'abull' for 'able' and 'nobull' for 'noble'.

Despite the simplicity of these devices, Whythorne is not consistent: on the same page he will write 'laf' and 'lawf' for 'laugh'; the reader will notice scores of other vagaries. It will be noted that Whythorne did not begin to use the 'new orthografye' until he had explained it in detail (pp. 4–6).

*A book ⟨of so⟩ng⟨s and sonet⟩ts,
with lo⟨n⟩ge discoor⟨ses s⟩ett with
them, of the chylds lyfe, tog⟨y⟩ther
with A yoong mans lyfe, and
entring into the old mans lyfe.
devysed and written with
A new Orthografye
by Thomas Whythorne, gent.*

⟨ *pref⟩a⟨ce* ⟩

2ʳ

Yee yowthfull Imps, that lyke ⟨on sh⟩ews to look
As by strainge sights, reports, or els in book
what chainges chaunce, within the world so wyde
On which, to whet your witts, your selus prouyde
For to behold, how, many play their parts
And guerdon giue, as yee deem of dᵉsarts
Mark now and I, to yow report will make
Of that which Iᵃ, of late did vndertake
To'endyte & wryte, in prose, and eke in vers
which folloingly, I will to yow rehers
wherin yoong yowths, are learned lessons large
By which they may, if lyke chaunce do them charge
That hapt to ⌐mee⌐, the better know to deall
Therin, and so, it may be for their weall
All which to wryte I tooke not long A go
with long discoors, of matters to and fro
what hapned mee, between those matters sayd
which bee not ill, if they bee wyselye wayd
my words therwith, that I to light do send
From beginning, vnto the very end
Togyther with the premisses, fore towcht
Shall follow now, as I the same have cowcht

ᵃ Written over an erasure that formerly read 'one'. Throughout the preface Whythorne revised the third person to the first person singular.

⟨My⟩ good fre⟨nd.[1] Recalling to mynd⟩ my pro⟨my⟩se made 2ᵛ
vnto yow, I have heer sent yow the copies of s⟨uch so⟩ngs and
sonett⟨s⟩, as I have made from tyme to tyme vntill the wryting
heerof⟨. And⟩ becaws that yow did impart vnto mee at owr last
being togyther, sum of yowr pryvat and secret affayrs past, &
also sum of the secret purposes and entents the which have lyen
hidd and byn as it were entombed in yowr hart, I to gratifye
yowr good opinion had of me, do now lay open vnto yow the
most part of all my pryvatt affayres, and secrets accomplyshed
from my childhod vntill the day of the date heerof. the which
as I do wryte vnto yow to gratyfye yow withall, so am I partlye
enforced thervnto, becaws I do thinke it needfull, not onlye to
shew yow the caws why I wrote them, but also to open my
secret meaning in dyvers of them aswell in words and sentences,
as in the hole of the same, lest yow shuld think them to be made
to smaller purpose then I did mean. part of the which di[s]courses
I made and wrote when I did make these songs and sonets, and
now as more matter hath comen vnto my remembrance, so have
I awgmented the same. If by chaunce I do overslyp or speak to
brode in any thing that I do wryte vnto yow now, I pray yow
remember that in A long discoors, A man cannott alway speak
in prynt.[2]

When[3] ye have considered of this heerafter written, ye shall

---

[1] Because the manuscript is tattered at this place it is tempting to speculate
that Whythorne had written in the name of the friend to whom his autobiography is addressed. His consistent reticence about naming friends and
employers makes it unlikely. The space probably carried words such as those
supplied in angle brackets. For the possibility that his addressing a friend
was a mere literary device, see Introduction, p. iv.

[2] 'In a precise and perfect way and manner' (*OED*). Proverbial; Tilley
M 239.

[3] Beginning here, Whythorne wrote laterally a long side note in the margin;
most of the note is lost through damage to the edge of the page:

The first tyme ⟨	⟩ it with	
And when ⟨	⟩ hart the Orthography that the ⟨	⟩
⟨	⟩ testym⟨oni ⟩ old did set ⟨	⟩
⟨	⟩ I th⟨	⟩

perceyve that as I have byn chaynged from tyme to tyme, by
tyme, so altered myne affections and delyghts. when I was A
chylde, I did as A chylde, and when I was A yoong man, ween-
ing then, that yong men were as wyse as the olde experienced
men[1] be (as in deed sum be, although not many) but now I wott
⟨tho⟩ugh I am not verye olde that there remayns many follies
in yoong men. ⟨the w⟩hich I dare warrant yow, ye may soon
espye by my doings in my yoong ⟨life⟩, by reading of this
Folloing. the which I assuer yow, I wold not wryte ⟨of th⟩em
vnto yow if it were not partly to fulfill yowr request & my pro-
⟨myse⟩ and cheefly becaws that thareby I may be the better
occasioned to re⟨mem⟩ber and consyder of sum dayngers past,
and also tharby putt in remembrance to pray to God to gwyde
me so with his grace, that I may shun the lyke if they shuld
happen vnto mee in tyme to cum ⌈(also it may bee for their
good, who shall read this heerafter)⌉.

But or ever I do comen to the ⟨body⟩ of my purpose I will
shew yow an *Orthografye*[2] with the whi⟨ch I choose⟩ to wryte
this discoors folloing, becaws I do fynd more reasọn in ⟨it tha⟩n
in that which is now commenlye vsed.[a] I did read the book[b] of
the Or⟨th⟩ografye that is sett owt by .J. hart, Chester heralt,
whose order for the vse of the doble vowell, I do lyke better then
Sir John Cheeks in his letter written to mr hobbye in the book
named the Coortier, wher hee doth doble the vowell to make
A wurd sownd long withowt the setting of the .e. at the last end
of the wurd. As for example, wheras heer tofore ⟨we d⟩id vse
to wryte these words tyme, and same thus. Tyme. Same.

---

[a] Caret mark with line leading to side-note mentioned in the preceding note.
[b] A cancelled word indicates that Whythorne first wrote "new book" when
referring to Hart's *Orthographie*.

---

[1] Proverbial: thus 'Young men think old men fools but old men know that
young men be fools'; John Grange, *The Golden Aphroditis*, 1577 (*STC* 12174),
sig. O2[v]. (Tilley M 610.)

[2] For discussion of Whythorne's system of orthography, see Introduction.
John Hart's *Orthographie* (*STC* 12890) was published in 1569. Sir John
Cheke's letter to Thomas Hoby appeared in Hoby's *The Courtyer of Count
Baldessar Castilio*, 1561 (*STC* 4778).

setting ⟨the .e⟩. at the end of the wurd to make it long. Mr
Cheeke doth vse it in his ⟨affor⟩sayd letter thus. Tijm. Saam.
dobling of the vowell to make the wurd ⟨long⟩, & leaving owt
the .e. at the end of those wurds. but the sayd mr harte,
⟨doth⟩ dobl⟨e⟩ the vowell by setting A prick under it as thus.
Tịm. Sạm. and ⟨thus⟩ the rest of the vowels in the same
case. but seing that the Greek vowell ⟨calle⟩d *ypsilon*, which
is thus made .*y*⟨. the which ye⟩ may see in the book ⟨named⟩
A testimoni of antiquite &c[1] ⟨wher it is made⟩ thus .*ẏ*. with
A prick over the hed ⟨the⟩rof. ⟨In place of Sir John Che⟩eks 3[r]
.ij. ⟨or mr⟩ harts .ị. I do and ⟨will⟩ v⟨s⟩e tha⟨t .ẏ. b⟩ecaws that in
althings that be ⟨reas⟩nable and good, I h⟨ad⟩ rather vse the olde
maner then any new. lykewyse wheras the sayd mr hart doth
leav owt the .g. in this word myght as thus .myht.[2] And As he
doth vse the old Saxon .Ʒ. for .g. in this name .George, as thus
.Ʒeorʒ. so do I vse them, and all wurds lẏke vnto them. But
wheras hee doth invent new letters or carects of his own devyse, and leaveth owt certayn letters which have byn auntient-
lye vsed, and may be well vsed still (as I do think) I do not,
nor wilnot follow his order in that sort. Neyther will I vse the .h.
before the .w. as he doth in this word .which. as thus .huich.
neyther the letter .v. for the letter .f. in this wurd .of. as thus
.ov. neyther .ei. for .i. and such lyke.[a] ⌜Also wheras he doth
wryte midl⟨e⟩. ridle. fidle. and such lyke words thus .midⱬ. ridⱬ.
fidⱬ. sidⱬ. making A new carect or letter for the .le. at the latter
end of evry of those words. the which is very lyke the .Ʒ. that
hee dot⟨h vse.⟩ therfor I will set for the .le. the letter .l. only,
seing that the sownd that it standeth for is ⟨but⟩ an absurd
sownd to be wretten. for as I said before in things reasnable
I had rather v⟨se⟩ the awntient order then any newe.⌝

---

[a] A deletion of 6½ lines begins here.

---

[1] *A Testimonie of Antiquitie* (*STC* 159), printed by John Day in 1567, is
the first book in England to use Anglo-Saxon type. The dot over the *y*
occurs in the Anglo-Saxon text, not in the Elizabethan translation.

[2] This page of the manuscript contains two lengthy deletions. Because
of their possible interest to phonologists, these passages are discussed in
Appendix IV.

Also I ⌜will⌝ wryte wurds as they be sownded in speech, as in *Jesus. Jelosy. p⟨re⟩served. those. as.* and such lyke words. wheras I ⌜will⌝ wryte them thus. 3ezus⟨.⟩ 3elozy. prezerved. thoz. az. &c. Also these wurds. *Thus. This. That.* ⟨and⟩ such lyke. I ⌜will⌝ wryte with the auntient carects, named the .Thorn. ⟨as thus.⟩ Ðus. Ðis. Ðat. or ells thus. þus. þis. þat. Also these wurds ⟨...⟩ *Thin. Thorn.* and such lyke I will wryte with the .Th. or .th. ⟨as they are⟩ commenly accustomed to be written. Also these words. *Noble. Able.* ⟨*Treble.*⟩ and such lyke. I will wryte as thus. *Nobull. Abull. Treb⟨ull.⟩* And also such wurds as wee do take owt of other langwages ⟨whereof⟩ Sir John Cheek, and dyvers other great learned men be of the opinion ⟨that⟩ when wee do take and vse them as English words, we shuld wryte th⟨em⟩ as wee do speak them, in such sort as wee do all other English words.

I hav sumwhat deg⌜r⌝essed from my purpoz in saing my fansy of þis new Orthografy, but now I will return to it agayn. And for an introduk⟨sion⟩ to þe sam, deklar vnto yow sum what of my erudision and bringing v⟨p⟩ vntill I kam to þe tým of my knowle3 in making and wrýting of English vers. and þen may yow deem of þe rest of my tým spent hyþerto, by þat which ye shall fýnd written in, and with þe songs and sonets fol⌜o⌝ing.

Wherfor yee shall vnderstand, þat when þe tým of my infansy waz ny past, i⟨n⟩ the which I was suffred by my parents and gardons to lýv the wanton and id⟨l⟩ lýf þat belongs to þat a3, bekawz þat þe memories of þoz of þat ⟨a⟩3 ⟨are not⟩ apt to retayn and carry or bear any long tým, þat ⌜which⌝ iz of any g⟨reat⟩ importa⟨nce⟩ mý parents knowing þat when twygs be green they will best bow befor þei brek.[1] Also þat þe hownd must lern to kowch in yowth er hee grow to far into stubborn and slowthfull a3.[2] ⌜and⌝ Also þat þe vessell þat iz niew will ta⟨st⟩ or smell

---

[1] Tilley T. 632; the earliest printed example found by Professor F. P. Wilson is in Barclay's *Ship of Fools*, 1509 (1874 edn. i. 47).

[2] Proverbial; Tilley (D 489) cites John Fitzherbert, *Book of Husbandry*, 1523 edition (*STC* 10994).

alwey of þat likor,[1] which first did remayn in it any long tẏ⟨m,⟩
az if it węr ill, it wold bee stayned þęrwith, or if it węr good, þe
good sent þerof wold not all owt ⌜alþoh þe⌝ likor węr powred
owt. wherfǫ⟨r⟩[a] wherfǫ⟨r to turn me⟩ fr⟨om slowthfulnes (and **3ᵛ**
all mane⟩r o⟨f oþer⟩ vises) I waz sent to skoolz evry day for þe
mǫst ⟨par⟩t. whęr ⟨I f⟩irst learned to read, to wrẏt, and also to
sing Muzik. which exersyze⟨s ⌜of⟩ þe mynd,⌝ ⟨w⟩ith oþerz lẏk
vnto þem, ar męt for such to vz az I waz þen.

I kannot wąd any fa[r]þer in þiz matter purpozed, till I hąv
shewd yow my fantazẏ towching þe ȝenerall bringing vp of
childern, konserning þe which matter (to be bręf) I say þat
þe pąrents and gardons (þąt be wẏz) will konsyder of þeir
childern and piupulz, þeir kompleksions, þeir manners, and
dispozisions, (of bǫth sexez) bǫth of their strengths of þeir
bodyes, and mẏndz withowt such affeksion az doth dąz þeir
eyz, and mąks þat to seem to bee good in þem which iz rąþer
evell þen in þe mean betwęn good and evell. ⌜such⌝ will sirkum-
spektly see vnto þem, þat þei shall hąv such government
and rewll az iz meet for þem, and wil awgment þe good dis-
pozizion þat þey doo see þem enklyned vnto, þe which to do,
þęr is nothing better for þǫz purpozes, þen to keep þem alwaies
well okupied with such good exersyzes bǫth of þe mẏnd, and
þe body, az iz meet for such of ⌜þeir⌝ ąȝ, kapasite, and þeir
estąt. kontrary wẏz such az be over fearfull of þeir childern,
or þat do dǫt to much on þem, it iz most tẏms seen þat þei
dǫ[b] hinder þem dẏvers ways by suffring of þem to be overtaken
and possest with A number of vẏses and evels. þe fond kąr þat
þez hąv of ⌜þeir⌝ childern, breedz such A nẏs tendring, lest
þat þey by overmuch laboring of mẏndz, witz, and senses, or
els to labor and chąf ⟨þ⟩eir bodies A litl, or to strain or stretch
þeir bodies & senewz ⟨wi⟩th sum good exersẏz, shųld be over-

---

[a] This should have been the catchword, though actually 'to ⟨ ⟩' appears.
[b] Dot above 'o' probably accidental.

---

[1] Proverbial; Tilley (L 333) gives early sources; Whythorne probably was
most familiar with Richard Taverner's translation, *The Proverbs or Adagies
of Erasmus*, 1569 (*STC* 10441), p. 35.

taken with sum siknes & ma⟨la⟩diez. wheraz in deed þeẏ do
hinder or raþer vndo þem, az it iz ⟨ma⟩ny tẏms seen, for wheraz
þeẏ ween to enkreas þeir strength ⟨by⟩ forbearing of exersẏz,
þey do hinder ⌜and weaken⌝ þe sạm, and þen to idlnes ⟨vẏs⟩
and wiked imaʒinasions, slowth, wrinch, brooz, and greef ⟨þey⟩
be subʒekt, mọr þen þoz be, who be yvzed to all sorts of temperat exersyzez and lạborz. yvz limz, and hạv limz,[1] þe old
proverb sayth. yvz wits also in good exersyzes, and wyzdom
will spring þerof.

þe overmuch cheryshing, kokering & suffring of many parents
and gardons, gẏv okazion mạny and mọst tẏms to g⟨re⟩at and
inkurable vẏses, þe number of þe which may be bọth infinẏt
and stranʒ, when az vnbrydeled liberty iz suffred in þem to
rayn, wherfọr þei owht to be refrayned & holden down by fear
of deeds, if it wilnot be doon oþerwẏz. In þe .7. chapter of
ʒezus þe soon of Sirach[2] is þus said. If þow hạv soons bring
þem vp in nowrtor, and learning, and hold þem in awe from
þ⟨e⟩ir yowth vp. If þow hạv dahters, keep þeir bodies, & shew
not þi fạs cheerfull towards þem. Marry þi dahter, and so shalt
þow perform A wayhty matter, but gẏv her to A man of vnderstanding. Also he sayth in cap. 22.[3] A mis nowrtored soon iz þe
dishonor of þe faþer. A foolish dawhter shalbee litl regarded.
Also hee sayth in. cap. 26.[4] If þy dahter be not shạmfast hold her
straitly, lest shee abụz her self, thoro⟨w o⟩vermuch liberty. bewạr
4r of all the dishonesty of her ⟨e⟩yz, and mar⟨vell not⟩ if she⟨e
do agaynst þee. cap. 30.[5] Who so loveth hiz chyld⟩, holdet⟨h
him⟩[a] still vn⟨d⟩er correks⟨ion⟩, þat he⟨e m⟩ay hạv ʒoy of him
afterwar⟨d⟩, and þat hee ⟨grọ⟩p not after hiz neybors dọrz. Hee

---

[a] Lacunae filled from 1568 Bishops' Bible. The space does not seem to be
wide enough for the usual formula: 'Also he sayth in cap. 30.'

[1] The earliest version of this 'old proverb' cited by Tilley (L 195) is 'Use
legs and have legs' in Gabriel Harvey's MS. *Marginalia*, p. 188, written
about 1582, but unpublished until 1913 (ed. G. C. Moore Smith, Stratford-
upon-Avon).

[2] Opposite this passage is a marginal note, '⟨S⟩irach/⟨ca⟩p.7.' It refers
to Ecclus. 7. 23–25.

[3] Ibid. 22. 3.   [4] Ibid. 26. 10, 11.

[5] Ibid. 30. 1–4, 8–13. Whythorne has conflated verses 12 and 13.

þat teac⟨heth⟩ hiz soon shall hạv ʒoy of him, and need not to bee
ashamed of him among his akquaintans⟨.⟩ who so enformeth and
teacheth his soon grẹveth þe enemẏ, and befọr his frends hee
may hạv ʒoy of him. Ðoh þe fạþer dẏ, yet iz hee az þọh hee wẹr
not dẹd, for hee hath le⟨ft⟩ ọn behẏnd him þat iz lẏk him. Ạn
vntạmed hors wilbe hard, and A wanton chẏld wilbe wilfull. If
thow bring vp þi soon delicạtly hee shall mạk þee A fraid, and if
þow play with him, hee shall bring thee to hẹvines. lah not with
him, lest þow weep with him also, and lest þy teeth be sett on eʒ
at þe last. gẏv him no lyberty in hiz yowth, and exkiụz not hiz
folly. Bow down hiz nek whẏl hee iz yoong, hitt him vpon þe
sẏds whẏll hee iz yet but A chẏld, and be diliʒent þerin, lest it
bee to þẏ shạm. cap. 42.[1] If þẏ dahter be wanton keep her
straitly, lest shee kawz þẏn enemẏz to lawh þee to skorn, and þe
whọll syty to gẏv þee an evell report and so þow be fain to hear
þy shạm of evry man, and be konfownded befọr all peepull.

Now peradv[ent]ur yow wold say to mee þat þẹz fọrsaid sayings of ʒezus þe soon of *Sirach*. be but *Apocrypha*. and þerfọr
of no kreditt to grownd any opinions on. ⌐yet¬ (saynt *Hierome*
saith) þat þe church doth read þem for ex⟨am⟩pull of lẏf.[2] þen
⌐do yow so tạk þem, and I¬ will rehers to yow ⌐also¬ owt of þe
Canonicall S[c]riptụrs, ⌐on þe which opinions ar to be grownded,
az¬ owt of þe proverbs of *Salomon* konserning þis fọrsaid matter,
who sayth in ⟨þe⟩ sixt chapter of hiz proverbs, and in oþer
plases of þat book.[3] Chastening and ⟨nowr⟩tụr iz þe way of
lẏf. cap. 13.[4] Hee þat spạreth þe rod, hạteth hiz soon. but who
⟨so lo⟩veth him, holdeth him ever in nowrtụr. cap. 19.[5] Chasten
þẏ soon whẏll þer ⟨is⟩ họp, but let not þy sowll be moved to
slay him, for grẹt wrath bringeth ha⟨rme,⟩ þerfọr lett him go,
and so maist þow teach him mọr nourtor. cap. 22.[6] Tea⟨ch⟩ A

---

[1] Ibid. 42. 11.

[2] Whythorne's remarks on Saint Jerome and the Apocrypha are similar to
the prefaces to these books in the Coverdale and Matthew's Bibles. (The
Great Bible of 1553 entitles this section 'Hagiographa', and the Bishops'
Bible of 1568 lacks the preface.)

[3] Opposite this passage is a marginal note, '*prov./cap./.6.*'—a reference to
Prov. 6. 23.
[4] Ibid. 13. 24.
[5] Ibid. 19. 18, 19.
[6] Ibid. 22. 6.

chýld in hiz yowth what way hee shuld go, for hee shall not leav
it w⟨hen⟩ hee iz old. Withold not korreksion from þe chýld,[1]
for if þow beate⟨st⟩ him with þe rod, hee shalnot dý þerof. if
þow smýt him with þe rod þo⟨w⟩ shalt delýver hiz sowll from
Hell. cap. 29.[2] Ðe rod and korreksio⟨n mi⟩nister wisdom, but if
A chýld be not looked vnto, hee bringeth hiz ⟨moþer⟩ to shạm.
Nourtor þy soon with korreksion, and þow shalt b⟨e at rest,⟩
yee hee shall do þee good at þe hart. (also hee þat delicạtly
⟨bringeth⟩ vp hiz servant from A chýld, shall mạk him hiz
mạster at ⟨length.)⟩ Ðẹz forsaid plases, and many mọr of þe
skriptụrs (which for te⟨diowsnes⟩ I leav vn towcht) do shew þe
3oy þat parents may hạv for þe ⟨bringing vp⟩ of þeir childern in
vertewz skooll, and what trobull and sorow þey ⟨shall hạv⟩
when az þei suffer þem to be browht up idelly, wantonly, and
withowt A ⟨vi⟩3ilant cạr of þem.

Now to return to my forsaid purpọz again. yee sha⟨ll⟩ vnderstand þat after I had bin browht vp at my faþers hows (and in
oþer pl⟨a⟩ses by him appointed ny vnto þe sạm) till I waz ten
yeers old (in þe which I w⟨az⟩ exersýzed az iz affọrsaid) and hee
being þen willed and requested ⟨by⟩ an vnk⟨ull⟩ of mýn (who
waz A preest, and benefyzed within fýv mýls of þe Vniuersi⟨ty⟩
of Oxenfoord) to send vnto him on of hiz soons, þe which hee
promýzed to brin⟨g⟩ vp azwell az if hee wẹr hiz own chýld,[3]
I waz by my faþer sent vnto him with whom I remayned at hiz
hows A sertain tým. in þe which hee (being az dezýrowz to hạv
mee well browht vp az my parents wẹr, and also knowing how I
had bin treined alredy vntill þat tyme) wold sumtýms tạk okasio⟨n⟩
to speak of such who had bin and wẹr to bee kommended for
þeir verte⟨wz⟩ a⟨nd⟩ good qualities of þe mýnd, adding þertoo
how much þey wẹr to be⟨e es⟩teem⟨ed and⟩ preferred aboov þe
ingnorant sort. and þervpon hee wold sumtýms dem⟨a⟩wnd of

---

[1] Prov. 23. 13, 14. Whythorne neglected to give a reference to these two
verses.   [2] Ibid. 29. 15, 17, 21.
[3] The age of ten was the normal time for a boy to be sent away to school.
(William Nelson, ed. *A Fifteenth Century School Book*, 1956, p. 1). Whythorne's uncle, the priest near Oxford, has defied identification; no Whythorne
or Cabott, deceased about 1545, appears in the available records.

⟨mee⟩ wheþer I wold be A preest or no. or wheþer I wǫld bee A Fizision, or A lawyer. to þe which professions, (bekawz I had þen no tǎst or savowr in lęrning) I had no devosion or ly̆king. At an oþer tym̆ hee sayd vnto mee, be not A fr⟨aid⟩ to tell mee yowr mym̆d plainly, in þat which I will demawnd of yow. if ⟨yee⟩ ly̆k not to st⟨udy⟩ and le⟨arn⟩ þǫz ⟨affǫrsaid⟩ pr⟨ofe⟩ssions ⟨I 4ᵛ hǎv⟩ spǫken of, how ⌐say⌐ yee þen to Grammer, with þe knowleȝ in þe latten toong? or els to Muzik, az to learn to sing, and to play on þe O[r]gans, þe which be good qualitiez and be much esteemed in þęz daiez. and by þem many men do ly̆v very well, and do cum to preferment þerby.

To þis sayd question I awnswered (akkording to my diskresion and dispozision) þat I ly̆ked well of þem bǫth, but yet of bǫth, I ly̆ked Muzik best. then quod my vnkull yow shall learn þem bǫth. and bekawz þat yow do ly̆k Muzik best, of both, ye shall learn sumwhat of þat first, and afterward yee shall learn þe oþer also (heer nǫt þat az þe blood beareth cheefest rewll in humǎn bodies in þe chyldish yeers (exsept it bee hindred by sum vn-naturall cawz[)] so did þe blood in þęz yeers of mym̆ bear great rewll in mee. and emong all hiz effekts wrought in mee, I do remember þat I waz mǫst gyven to þe lǫv of muzik befǫr any oþer siens). when my said vnkull þus perseyved mym̆ inklinasion, hee þen to þe entent þat I being kept well okupied[a] with sum good exersyz, and þat I miht be sett to þat which I mǫst delihted in, bekawz I miht profett þe better þęrin, hee shor[t]ly after brough[t] me to Oxford affǫrsaid, and þǎr hee did sett mee to skooll in Mawdelen colleȝ.[1] whęr after I had remaym̆ed A yeer or ij, hee wrǫt vnto mee A letter, charȝing mee to keep þe sǎm sǎfly, and to read þe sǎm often ⌐tym̆s⌐ over.

[a] MS. reads 'okupier'.

[1] Magdalen College School, founded about 1480, is maintained by the College. During the years when Whythorne attended (1538–44), the school was one of the most eminent in all England, especially for the classical curriculum. Many of Whythorne's schoolfellows became leaders in the Church, at least five of them achieving bishoprics, but Whythorne does not appear to have maintained friendship in later life with any of his schoolmates. For an account of the school, see R. S. Stanier, *A History of Magdalen College School*, Oxford, 1940.

Ðe wurdz of hiz letter węr to putt mee often in mẏnd þat to follow earnestly my learning I shuld slak no tẏm. Adding þervnto, þe stạt of my parents, and hiz, togyþer with þat of mẏn own, both for þe tẏm prezent, and of þat which waz lẏk to ensew in thęz wurds folloing. Alþoh (quoþ hee) yowr faþer ⟨iz⟩ abull to lẏv of him self, yet hee iz not habull to keep yow and þe rest ⟨of h⟩iz childern in such sort az yee ⌜may⌝ lẏv idelly and at eaz. and alþoh yee ⟨shall⟩ hȧv sertain howzes and landz[1] after þe deseas of yowr parents, it iz ⟨easil⟩y seen þat whẏll þe gras groweth þe hors starveth, and hee þat loo⟨keth t⟩o wear dead folks shows had need to bee shod with iron.[2] Az for mẏn ⟨ow⟩n pạrt (quoþ hee) I am not abull to gẏv to keep yow any lenger þen whẏll I do lẏv, and when I am dead, yow ar lẏk to hȧv very littl by my death exsept it bee a littl howsold stuff. wherfọr now ply yowr learning so az yow may lẏv þerby heerafter. Thęr iz A Filosofer named *plato*, who geveth kownsell to chụz þe best way in lyving, or to lẏv by, þe which yows and kustom shall mạk eazy and pleazant. Also an oþer Filosofer

---

[1] It is difficult to ascertain the financial status of John Whythorne or Whitehorne, the musician's father. The records concerning Chard, Ilminster, and nearby towns in Somerset contain frequent evidence that one John Whitehorne was active in property transactions as a witness to wills, or as an appraiser of estates. His own landholdings are revealed in several cases, the earliest found being a record of 9 Sept. 1545 that he held tenure of an acre of meadow at Chard. (*Letters and Papers: Henry VIII*, xx, Part 2, 1907, No. 496. 19). Three years later we learn that John Whitehorne held a burgage and three rods of land at Chard from the Fraternity of the Blessed Lady, at a yearly rent of ten shillings (*Somerset Record Society*, vol. 2, 1888, p. 174). In the same year he held a close at Dunpoll from the Chantry of Saint Katherine in Ilminster Parish Church, at six shillings and eightpence per annum (ibid., p. 168).

In Aug. 1548 John Whitehorne and John Bayley of Chard paid approximately £1,100 for the extensive holdings of the late Chantry of Saint Mary within the Parish Church of Chard, some of which lands they already held on lease (*Calendar of Patent Rolls: Edward VI, 1547–8*, 1920, p. 285).

These records suggest that John Whitehorne was a man of substance, though he may have preferred to invest in lands newly available at the Reformation instead of distributing his income among his many children. Thomas appears to have inherited something from his father, while his mother was still living. See p. 186.

[2] Proverbial; Tilley S 375. Professor Wilson points out that Whythorne's use of this proverb is the earliest recorded; other examples are usually derived from Scottish sources.

named p⟨i⟩thagoras doth say þat when A man iz past þe first difficulty of vertew, all after is eazy and plain.

When I had remayned in þe kolle3 afforsaid ny abowt seven yeers (of þe which I spent ny abowt six yeers at the muzik skooll, and on at þe grammer skooll)[1] ny abowt þe end of þe sam, my said vnkull deseased. after whoz death, I waz dezyrowz to see þe world abrod, and so I left and forsook Oxford and went ⟨fro⟩m þens to London. wher by þe mean of A frend of mýn I waz plased ⟨wit⟩h mr John Haywood,[2] to be both hiz servant and skoller, for hee waz not only very well skylled in Muzik, and playeng on þe vir3inals but also such an english *poet*, az þe lýk, for hiz witt and invension, with þe quantite þat hee wrot, waz not az þen in England, nor befor hiz tým sinse Chawsers tým. with mr haywood I remayned three yeer and mor. in þe which tým I learned to play on þe virginals, þe liut, and to mak english 5ʳ ⟨verses. wh⟩y⟨ll I w⟩az with h⟨im, he mad dive⟩r⟨z⟩ ditt⟨iez to⟩ bee sung vnto muzi⟨kall⟩ instrumen⟨ts⟩ (also hee ⟨caw⟩zed ⟨to⟩ be prin⟨ted A⟩ book mad vpon owr ⟨en⟩glysh proverbz)[3] And also at þe request of doktor ⟨Thos.⟩ Cranmer, lat a⟨rchb⟩yshop of Cantorbury,[4] hee mad A sertayn enter⟨lude⟩ or play, þe

---

[1] In *A Register of the Presidents, Fellows, Demies . . . of St Mary Magdalen College in the University of Oxford*, 1873, ed. J. R. Bloxam, there appears in the list of Demies, under the date 1544, the name 'Thomas Whitehorne, aged 16' (iv, p. 99). It is interesting that Whythorne calls the college 'the grammar school' and the school itself 'the music school', indicating that he was a chorister. Yet Magdalen College School was considered to have been 'a Grammar School and not a Song or Elementary School' (Stanier, p. 43).

[2] John Heywood (1497?–1578?) had been attached to the Court since about 1519, first as a singer and then as 'player on the Virginals'. Later he became master of a company of child actors for which he wrote his well-known interludes of 'The Four P's', &c. In 1545, when Whythorne came to serve as his amanuensis, Heywood appears to have been living somewhat quietly, his literary energies being devoted chiefly to writing proverbs, epigrams, and poetry.

[3] *A Dialogue conteinyng the Nomber in Effect of all the Prouerbes in the Englishe Tongue*, 1546, and republished in 1549, 1556, and 1561 (*STC* 13291–4). Mr. R. E. Habenicht has made a special study of Heywood's proverbs and has kindly supplied information about Whythorne's use of some of them.

[4] Thomas Cranmer (1489–1556). Except for this statement and Whythorne's quotation of 14 lines from it later in the autobiography (p. 74), nothing is known of this interlude 'upon the parts of Man', though Whythorne

which waz devyzed vpon þe parts of Man, at þe end wherof hee lẏkneth and applieth þe sirkumstans þerof to þe vniuersall estat of Chrẏstes church, ⌐all þe which¬ afforsaid befor þei wer published I did wryt owt for him, or had þe yvs of þem to read þem. and I hav þe copiez of most of þem in A book at þis present of mẏn own wrẏting.

Also whẏll I waz with him I ⌐did¬ wrẏt owt for him diverz songs and sonets þat wer mad by þe erll of Surrey, sir Thomas Wiatt þe elder, and mr Moor þe exsellent Harper besẏd sertain salms þat wer mad by þe said mr wyatt, and also mr Sternold. þe which be also ⌐in¬ my said book.[1] by þe which okkazions of wryting & reading, I a⟨ft⟩erward gav my self to imitat and follow þeir trads and devẏses in wryting ⟨a⟩z okkazions moved me. And first wheraz A frend of mẏn ny abowt þe end of ⟨þ⟩e tẏm þat I was with mr haywood, did vpon okkazions moved deklår vnto ⟨mee⟩ þe stat of hiz lẏf for A sertayn tẏm, I to requẏt him took okkazion fo⟨r⟩ an exersẏz to wrẏt vnto him in meeter þe eff⟨e⟩kt of þat which iz befor re⟨hersed⟩ in such sort az heer foloingly I hav sett it—

> *My faithfull frend, sins þat þow didst impart*
> *Ðe secrets þat lay hid within þy hart*
> *To mee, when wee togiþer last did talk*
> *To þee þerfor, my hart and pen shall walk*
> *Not on ten toz, but by attorney riht*
> *In þis heer sent, again þee to requiht*

---

indicates that it was published. Doubtless the interlude was intended to strengthen Cranmer's side in one of the theological controversies of the time, but it seems odd that the archbishop would turn to an acknowledged Romanist for help.

[1] The manuscript into which Whythorne copied these poems is not known to have survived. He transcribed them *c.* 1545, several years before the psalms of Sir Thomas Wyatt (1503 ?–1542) were first published (1549—*STC* 2726), and a decade before the secular poems of Wyatt and Henry Howard, Earl of Surrey, appeared in 'Tottel's Miscellany' (1557—*STC* 13860). Thomas Sternhold (d. 1549) first published his *Certayne Psalms* (*STC* 2419) in or after 1547, since they are dedicated to Edward VI. William More (*c.* 1492–1565), 'harpour to Edward VI', left musical compositions, but no verse that has been identified; for an account of him, see M. C. Boyd, *Elizabethan Music and Musical Criticism* (Philadelphia, 1940), p. 188.

Included iz, as in þi rithm appeerz
Ðe lẏf þow ledst, þe spǫs of sertain yeerz
But þat which I to þee do heer direkt
Iz my hǫll lẏf to þis day in effekt,
What exersyzes in chyldhod I had
Ðe lẏk I yowzd when I waz ⌐but⌐ A lad
And now in th'ǫȝᵃ of mẏn Aþo'losensy
Wherin þe'yoong man, tǫkth hiz first entry
Ðe which if þow doost lẏk eevn now to know
Ðis heer ensuing, þe sǫm shall shortly show.

When þat my tẏm, of infansy waz past
In which þe mynd iz nothing firm nor fast
And þerfǫr þat, which printed iz þerin
It hǫldz as ⌐siur,⌐ az wǫter grǫvd with pin¹
My pǫrents knowing þat twigz when þey be green
Will boow er þei do break az oft iz seen
And þat þe hound, to kowch must learn in yowth
Er hee to much, iz entred into slowth
And also þat, þe vessel þat iz new
Will tǫst or smell, az dayly proof doth shew
Of þat likquor, which first in it remaind
If ill it wǫr, þen with it, it wǫr staynd
⟨If good it wǫr⟩ þe goodne⟨s of⟩ þe ⟨s⟩e⟨nt⟩
⟨Wold⟩ not all fǫd þouh likquor owt w⟨er sp⟩ent
Wherfǫr to skooll, it waz dekreed ech day
Ðat I þertoo, shǫld truȝ and tǫk þe way
Whǫr, of reading, wrẏting, and of singing
Miuzik, I had az þen my beginning.
Which praktyzes, with oþerz lẏk þe sǫm
Ar meet, to keep, such yowths in tewn & frǫm
As I þen waz, for Idelnes þat vẏs
Iz root of eevls,² which bear A painfull prẏs

5ᵛ

ᵃ MS. reads 't'hǫȝ'.

---

¹ Proverbial; Tilley W 114.
² Proverbial; Tilley I 13.

Ðe parents wẏz,[a] konsydring of þeir chẏld
Hiz kompleksi'on, hiz mannerz mẏld or wẏld
And qualitez withowt affeksion such
Az do bewray, it to be over much
Will see him hav, þat which belongz him till,
Augmenting good, and repressing þe ill.
Wheraz oþerz, þat over fearfull bee
Of þeir childern, do hinder þem wee see
Whoz kar of þem, breeds in[b] þem such tendring
Lest þei forsooth, by tow much laboring
Of mẏndz, of witts, and senses evrichon
To chaf bodiez, or strain senew or bon
In sikness shuld streihtway þen run intoo,
Wheraz in deed, þeir childern þei vndoo.
For when þei ween, þeir bodiez strength t'enkreas
Ðei weaken þem so, az it dooth dekreas
And þen to brooz, and greef, þei bee subʒekt
Mor þen þoz bee, who much eaz do reʒekt
Yuz limz and þen, hav limz þe proverb saith
Yuz witts lẏkwẏz, and wizdom owt it waith
Ðe cherishing,[c] and suffring of parents
Gẏu okkazion (furþring childerns entents)
Vnto great vẏs both infynit and strainʒ
When liberte, vnbrẏdled in þem rainʒ
Which owght to be refraind and holden down
By fear of deed, if not by word or frown
I mean not heer, but temprans to be had
For mery mean,[1] iz þat which maketh glad
I hav degrest, from my purpoz but now
Return I will, to þat I promizd yow
When þat I waz, of ten yeerz aʒ kum to
My parents þen appointed mee to go
To an Vnkull of mẏn, who þen mee browht

---

[a] Written over 'wẏz parents'.   [b] Written over 'of'.   [c] Superscript 'kokkering'.

[1] Proverbial; Tilley M 793.

To Oxenford, wher I in skools waz towht   6ʳ
Ð⟨e perfekt iws of Muzik an⟩d Gra⟨mmer⟩
By þe holl ty⟨m a⟩nd spas o⟨f⟩ s⟨e⟩uen ⟨y⟩eer
In þ'end, of which, my vnkull deseased
Wherby my welth, being sumwhat enkreased
I þen þe world, abroad dezierd to see
And so I went, to london, þar to bee
Wher az A frend, mee plast with þe master
Ðat now I seru, whoz na⟨m⟩ ẏll not defer
To yow to shew, and maste⟨r⟩ John Haywood
His nam it iz, of whom I hear þis good
Ðat hee of po'ets, of England in þis tẏm
Iz most famowz, for wryting English rẏm
If all hiz Rithms, wer set togẏþer now
No English po'et somuch þis day kan show
Az hee, in sort, az hee þe sam hath doon
*Az from hiz brain,*ᵃ *and not from elswher woon*
(I deny not but such az do translat
*Both faithfully, and coningly*ᵇ *dẏlat*
Any awktor, dezerv great praiz in deed
But yet þawktor, dezervs þe greatest meed)
Besẏd all þis, my said master eevn hee
In Muzik sweet kan fram sweet nots to'agree
*And instruments belonging*ᶜ *to þe sam*
Hee kan aptly, and koningly þem fram
Ðe which to learn, I plẏ my self dayly
Ðerto, þat I, may reap sum frewt þerby
Also to wrẏt in Rithm I do praktẏz
And þe first frewt of þat I did devẏz
I heer do wrẏt, and it to þee do send
And þus of þis my rithm I mak an end

After þe wrẏting of þis sayd Rithm, by chauns þer kam vnto my h⟨and⟩ my vnkuls letter befor spoken of. and when I had

---

ᵃ Superscript 'hed'.   ᵇ Superscript 'learnedly'.   ᶜ MS. reads 'bolonging'.

konsydered of ⟨it⟩ A litl whẏll I devẏzed vpon þe kounsels þạr
gyven þis þat folloith—

> *Of Vertewz all endeuowr þow to know*
> *Sum pạrt of ech az þow kanst þerto grow*
> *But of þem all in ọn espesi'all see*
> *Most*[a] *exsellent approued þat þow bee*

> *Ðe wẏz plato, az þus doth kownsell gẏv*
> *Chiuz þow þe waiz þe best þow kanst to lẏv*
> *Ðe which kustọm, and yọs þerof shall mạk*
> *Pleazant, if not, towmuch þerof þow tạk*

> *Pithagoras (I read) doth also say*
> *Ðat when A man iz entred on þe way*
> *Past þe first brunt, and ẹk difficulty*
> *Of Vertewz, þen, all after be eazy*

6ᵛ   when ⟨my tẏm of li⟩v⟨in⟩g with ma⟨ster H⟩aywood ⟨befọr
re⟩her⟨sed w⟩as ended and finishe⟨d⟩ I ⟨t⟩ook A chamber in
London, and so det⟨er⟩mined to lẏv of my self by teaching in
such sort az I had learned of him. þat iz to say by teaching of
Muzik, and to play on þọz instruments, which (az befọr iz
towched[)] þat I had learned to play on. Ðe which chainging of
mẏn estạt, browht mee oþer kạrs þen I waz trobled withall
befọr. for whẹraz I waz befọr ⌐but¬ trobled with þe fear of
tutorz and masters, I waz afterward brouht to hạv A ⟨k⟩ạr
of mẏn own kreditt, and estimasion, with þe maintenans þerof
az of A mạster and not az eiþer servant or skoller, and also to
keep my self withowt penury and need. when I waz A skoller,
and A servant, my mẏnd waz þen az my stạt waz, for þen I
looked no hier nor no furder, þen to þe stạt þat I waz þen in,
applieng my self to my learning az A skoller, and seeking to
content and to pleaz my mạster az A servant. but when I kạm to
bee mẏn own man, and þerwith a mạster, my mẏnd began þen
to chainʒ from hiz former estạt. for þen I saw how I must seek
to lẏv of my self, for þe which it behoved mee to cast ⌐my

---

[a] Superscript 'mọr'.

witts⌐ so many waiz, and þey being nẹver trobled somuch þat way befọr, az I waz almost at my witts end.¹ wherfọr to eaz my mynd in þis perplexite I wrọt þus—

> My tender yeerz er I owt went
> I wisht ẹch day þei had byn spent
> Thinking þat by my lybertee
> Much eaz and ȝoy shuld kum to mee
> But now I see, mọr þen befọr
> Ðat yowth hath brouht of kạrz great stọr
> Which to tạk well and þeim diȝest
> I think iz best to purchaz rest.

Bekawz þat I shewd you in þis Sonett, þat yowth had at þat tỷm brouht vnto mee of kạrz great stọr, yee shall vnderstand þat I had þen learned þat after ⟨þ⟩e aȝ of chỷldhod (which kontyneweth from þe infancy vntill fyfteen) beginneth þe aȝ nạmed *Adolescency*. which kontineweth vntill twenty and fỷv. þis said aȝ iz þe first pạrt of þe yoong mans aȝ.² and into þe sạm aȝ waz I not many yeers entred when I wrọt þis said Sonett. wherfọr I said in it þat yowth had browht vnto mee of cạrs great stọr. When I had past o⟨v⟩er þis pang (az yowth komenly kannot tạk thowht very long togỷþer) and having A chamber az iz befọr said in þe cyty of London which was reazonably well furnyshed with such howsold stuff az my fọrsaid vnkull gạv mee when hee deseased, I being þen dezyrows to hạv and enrich my self with sum mọr such exersỷzes and qualyties az yoong folks for þe most do delỷt in, went to þe daunsing skooll, and fens skooll, and also learned to play on þe Gyttern, and Sittern. which ij instruments wẹr þen stranȝ in England, and þerfọr þe mọr dezyred and esteemed.

---

¹ Proverbial; Tilley W 575.

² The idea of the 'ages of man' underwent many changes from the three ages cited by Aristotle (*Rhetoric*, ii, chs. 12–17) to the seven ages described by Jaques in *As You Like It*. Sir Thomas Elyot's *Castel of Helth*, one of Whythorne's favourite books, gives four ages, 'Adolescencie', ages 1–24, 'Juventute', 25–39, 'Senectute', 40–60, and 'Age decrepite' for the years following. Whythorne follows Elyot, except for the separation of childhood (1–15) from adolescence. For the later ages, see pp. 80, 135–6.

After þis I kawzed A tabull to be mạd to hang in my chamber
wheron waz painted (in oyll kolowrz) þe fygụr and imaȝ of
a yoong woman plaing vpon A Liut, who I gạv to nạm *Terpsicore*, which iz þe nạm of ọn of þe nẏn muzes, whom þe *poets*
do fayn to be þe goddes of all soft melody,[1] of Muzik, þat iz mạd
7r vpon muzikall instruments which do go w⟨ith son⟩gs. ⟨Sins I
knew⟩ þat þis ⟨*Terpsicore* was g⟩oddes⟨of þat⟩ sort of Muzik which
⟨I⟩ þen professed to be A ⌐mast⟨er⟩ and⌐ teacher of, ⟨I⟩ kawzed ⟨to
be⟩ painted by and with her in þe sạm tạbull ⌐shee pl⟨aying
upon A⟩ liut⌐ª not only þe kounterfett of A ⟨virȝinall⟩ but also of
þe Gittern, and Sittern. and also A book wherin iz bọth p⟨rick⟩
song, and tabulatụr for þe lụt, and also þis sonett foloing—

> *Đe muzik tewns of vois or string*
> *Doth help þe earz and doth expell*
> *All sorrowz þat þe hart doth wring*
> *Also þe witts it cherish'th well*
> *It sowpleth senewz of ech wiht*
> *And ẹk þe faint it fils with myht.*

Being þus az it wẹr pleazantly plạsed in þe delẏkạt and deliht-
full conseyt and band of dạm muzik, whọz instinkt foded[2]
foorth my fanta⟨zy⟩ vnto it, I kawzed in A pair of virȝinals to be
painted mẏn own k⟨oun⟩terfett or piktụr, lẏkwẏz playng vpon
A lụt, and in þe sạm vi⟨rȝi⟩nals waz written þẹz verses foloing—

> *Đe pleaziurz þat I tạk*
> *Now in my yowthfull yeerz*
> *Đe sạm shall mee forsạk*
> *When hoery aȝ appeerz*

By þis yee may perseyv, þat alþoh I took sum pleazụr in þe
painterz ạrt ⟨and⟩ sett owt my fantazy in koolorz, yet I did know
þen þat þe pleazụrs of þis wor⟨ld⟩ ar butt vain and not parmanent
or abyding. Heer must I speak sumwhat a⟨gain⟩ of þe fọrsaid aȝ
named *Adolescenci*. which iz þe first pạrt of þe yoong mans ⟨aȝ⟩

ª An attempt seems to have been made to erase this insertion.

[1] Strictly speaking, Terpsichore was the muse of dancing and not of song
or music-making, though she was commonly pictured as carrying a lyre.

[2] To lead on by raising expectation (*OED*).

Specimen of Whythorne's handwriting (top of folio 7 of his autobiography)

bekawz I vnderstand and perseyv also þat in þis a3 *Cupid* and
Venu⟨s⟩ w⟨er &⟩ wold be very buzy to trobull þe quiet mynds of
yoong folk. þerfor (hav⟨ing⟩ passed ny abowt þe on half of þis
a3, in þe ⟨which⟩ tȳm I had bin sumtȳmz dribd at with *Cupidz*
golden shafts, and yet ⟨mor⟩ by good hap þen by kunning[1] I did
put þem by, and wold not suffer þem to pears mee, for þe which
I suffred sum displeazurs of sum venerian ⟨sort⟩ I for all þat
fearing still to be strȳken and wounded with the blynd boyz
a⟨r⟩rowz) sowht and enquyred waies how to bee free from
þem. and at len⟨kth⟩ I remembred þis remedy foloing, þe which
I did streyht wayz put in iyr.[2]

First I gav my self to wait dili3ently vpon pallas, þe goddes of
Wizdo⟨m,⟩ for þen I took great pleazur to read *Poetry*, and
Morall *philosofy*, wh⟨er⟩in *Pallas* beareth A great sway. Also I
gav attendans þen vpon *Apo⟨llo &⟩ Terpsicore*, for þe awgment-
ing of my knowle3 in Muzik, and sownding o⟨n⟩ string instruments of Musik. yee and sumtȳm I wold ran3 and wander ⟨in⟩
þe walk of *Diana*, þe goddes of chastety. þe which walk iz þe
plezant woodz and grovz. seeking þar þe bubling springs of
water, and kooll fowntains (and þar wold I sumtȳms steall and
pres into þe cumpany of her Nymphes. but yet I durst not be
tow bold and sawsy with herself, lest þat in A ra3 shee wold hav
drest mee with sum dizgyzed shap az shee did *Acteo⟨n.⟩* but now
in earnest) I being at þat tȳm in A 3entilmans hows in þ⟨e⟩
kuntrey wher þer bee very pleazant woods and grovs to walk
in, a⟨nd⟩ in þe spring tȳm of þe yeer, took okkazion to wrȳt in
meeter az folloeth—

> *It doth mee good in Zeph'rus rain*
> *In Dians walk for too disport*
> *wher dulcet airz such 3oiz mee gain*
> *az 3ot of kar doth not rezort.*
> *⟨Ðe birdz with⟩ gla⟨dsom tewns remain⟩*[a]

7ᵛ

---

[a] Lacuna filled from Imelmann's text.

[1] Proverbial; Tilley C 225. Whythorne's usage is the earliest known to
Professor Wilson.

[2] *Put in iur*, a phrase Whythorne uses to mean 'to try out' or 'to put to the
test'.

⟨E⟩ch t⟨h⟩ing Ap⌐⟨o⟩⌐llo doth com⟨f⟩ort
But I of all do mǫst embrạs
wherfǫr my song iz and shalbee
Of ʒoifulnes and of solas
so oft az I þis tȳm may see.

Zephirus is þe nạm of þe western wȳnd, þe which bloweth &
rayneth most in þe spring tȳm of þe yeer. *Diana* iz þe goddes of
chastety, az iz afforsaid. *Apollo*, iz ǫn of þe nạms gȳven to þe
Soon. for in þe spring tȳm of þe yeer, hee iz kalled *Apollo*, and
in þe somer tȳm hee iz named *phoebus*, who iz þe god of Muzik
(az affǫr iz said) and of dyverz oþer nobull vertewz. Đus I having past from ǫn servis to an oþer of þe goddz and goddeses (az
iz befǫr towched) yet cowld I by no means kontent my self to
brook and abȳd in þe servyses of *Cupid* and *Venus*, it greeved
mee ever when I did hear þerof. and þe rạþer bekawz þat I hard
befor þis tȳm emong þe skollerz of Oxford when I waz þạr, and
also of dyverz oþerz, at sertain konvensions when I kạm to dwell
at London, þe which did babbull and talk so many things in þe
dispraiz of women (and þe myzery of þǫz þat wẹr much in þeir
kumpaniez).

For ǫn said þat þe[i] do look to hạv þeir own wills in althings
be it good or ill. Đen quod an oþer, lȳk all women, but loov nǫn
of þem.[1] lah and be mery with þem, but loov þem not, for þey be
lȳk vnto pich & tar,[2] þe which ǫn kannot handell very much, but
hiz hands shalbe defȳled þerwith. quod[a] an oþer *Marcus aurelius*[3]
sayth þat he offreth him self to ma[n]y perils þat with women iz
much konversant, for if hee loov þem not, þey will akkownt him

---

[a] Comma in MS. here omitted.

---

[1] This, like others in Whythorne's collection of apophthegms on female
falsity, follows common themes, but is without an exact precedent in phrase
or imagery. As F. N. Robinson remarked when annotating the *Wife of
Bath's Prologue*, most of these anti-feminist quips were 'common talk, and
need not be traced to any literary origin' (*Chaucer's Works*, Cambridge,
Mass., 1933, p. 802).

[2] Proverbial; Tilley P 358.

[3] This saying occurs on sig. I1[v] of *The Golden Booke of Marcus Aurelius*,
1566 (*STC* 12445[a]). Whythorne quotes frequently from Sir John Bourchier's
translation of Guevara's spurious work, first printed in 1535.

az A villain. if hee loov þem, þey will think him to bee liht. if hee
leav þem, þey will repụt him for A coward, if hee follow þem
hee iz lost, if hee serv þem hee iz not regarded, if hee serv þem
not, he shalbee hạted of þem. if hee will ⌈hạv⌉ þem, þey wilnot
hạv him. if hee dezier þem not, þei will seek on him. if he
hawnt þem, hee iz ill nạmed. and if hee haunt þem not, þey will
rekken him for no man. Ðen an oþer said, az A womans first
entysing will gẏv A man kawz to loov þem, so will þeir after
trẏfling, and misdeming enfors him to vndo it agayn. Ye quod
an oþer þei be az slippery az ẏs, and will turn az þe wynd and
weþerkok.¹ quod an oþer hee þat wold choos him A wẏf among
many women, must doo az ọn did, who looved þe fish nạmed
eelz very well, and had ⌈ọn⌉ geevn him on þe kondision þat hee
shụld bee blẏndfold and þen with hiz ⌈bạr⌉ hand to tạk owt þe
eell² of ⌈A⌉ pott wherin waz with þe eell A great many of Snạks.
Now Sir yow may think þat it waz A hundreth to ọn but þat hee
shụld rạþer fasten vpon A snạk and so be bytten or stung by
him, þen to tạk hold on þe eell, but and if hiz hap shụld bee so
good þat hee did first lyht and fasten vpon þe eell, yet hee had
but A slippery eell peradventụr by þe tayll.³

An oþer said þat in kraftynes, flattering, dissembling and
lyeng þei do exsell men. whervpon sprang þis sayeng which þe
wẏf of Bạth said in Chawser,⁴ which iz to say, Deseit, weeping
and spinning, waz geven to women from þe beginning. An oþer
said. Hy women be layzy, & low be lowd. fair be sluttish, and
fowll be prowd.⁵ An oþer said þat to manyfest and diskover þeir
prowd harts, and lecherows lusts, þei do dek and attier þem
selvs so flawnting & gloriowsly lẏk peakoks, togyþer with þeir
paintings and frownsing of þeir hair. quod an oþer *Quarta*

---

¹ Proverbial; Tilley W 653.
² The popular comparison of a woman's promise with an eel occurs in
Proverbs (1867), p. 20.
³ A combination of two proverbs, Tilley E 60 and W 640.
⁴ Chaucer's *Wife of Bath's Prologue*, lines 401–2. Three manuscripts of
Chaucer carry in the margin the medieval proverb 'Fallere, flere, nere, dedit
deus in muliere'.
⁵ Proverbial; the earliest printed version traced is in *Florios Second
Frutes*, 1591 (*STC* 11097), p. 189 (Tilley L 421).

remota tares, facit instabiles mulieres. and also þoh þey bee þe weaker vessels, yet þei will overkum, ij, iij, or iiij. men in þe satisfieng of þeir karnall appetẏts. ye quod an oþer, þat with her 8ʳ who iz so geven and enklyned I wold b⟨e playing⟩ kards ⟨when picking up her hand she wold have a⟩ flush befǫr I ⟨sh⟩ụld ⟨have two k⟩ạrdz of ⟨A⟩ sewt. and at tạbuls ⟨sh⟩ee w⟨old⟩ hạv A p⟨oint⟩ when I shuld hạv never A man to enter. besẏd þat when shee ⟨l⟩isted to play fals at tạbuls, þen wold shee bear mo men þen shee shụld do, and þat shuld ⌐be¬ doon in such A sekret and sly sort, az I shuld never perseiv þe sạm, exsept sum standerz by[1] or ny vnto her (who if þey be gamsterz kommenly do see mǫr þen sum of þem who do play) do wurk mẏn intellyȝens and knowleȝ. It iz A strainȝ matter quod an oþer, to see how vnkynd men now A daiz wold hạv women in wurs kạs þen katts be in, for þei be kontent þat katts may play with þeir tayls when þey list, and þei will tạk no offens þerat. but and if A sely woman do so þen will þei fret and fụm, and fynd much fawt þerat, threat-ning, herᵃ with the cukking stooll, kart, and whipping cheer.

Heervpon an oþer did start vp and said, þat almen wẹr not so hott and hạsty az hee waz who spạ⟨k⟩ last, for quod hee, I hard tell not long A go, þat A sertayn Cupidian kniht and A venerian dạm of Islington hạving mạd an arsward bargain togyþer in her hows, and for þat her husband waz with⟨i⟩n to hinder þeir gạm & pastẏm, þe yoongman devyzing A shift to gett þe goodman ⟨ow⟩t of þe hows, hee gạv vnto him A peny of twoopens,[2] praing him þerwith to fech þ⟨em⟩ A peny pott of Ạl, þe which þe sely and poor husband refuzed not to do, (bekaw⟨z⟩ hee mistrusted no fals meazụr) and hee being gǫn sumwhat on hiz way tow⟨ardz þe⟩ ạlhows for þe ạl, þer kạm to hiz mẏnd þat it waz needfull to hạv sum bread ⟨to⟩ drink withall. yet bekawz hee wold not ỵz his kommission any farder þen h⟨ee⟩ was appointed, hee wold not bring any bred vntill hee had A warrant by wur⟨d⟩ of mowth

---

ᵃ Written over 'þem'.

[1] Proverbial; Professor Wilson knows of no example before 1569.

[2] 'A penny of twopence' was a silver coin worth twopence, or a half-groat (*OED*).

for hiz ⟨d⟩ischarȝ. and þ⟨er⟩vpon hee went bak again to hiz hows to demaund of þe said yoongman wheþer hee shuld lay owt þe oþer peny in bre⟨d⟩ or no.

Now Sir, in þe mean whẏll, þat þis goodman waz þus debạting of þ⟨e⟩ matter with him self, and with going owtward & returning họmward ag⟨ain,⟩ hiz wẏf and þe Cupydian knyht affọrsaid, after small debạting of þeir ⟨kạs⟩ went A wurking forward and returning bakward at họm. in þe mydz o⟨f⟩ which þeir pastẏm kạm þis goodman vnto þe plạs wheṛ þọs laborsum fo⟨lk⟩ weṛ. and fynding þe stranȝ kok on þe fọr ridȝ of hiz hen, he bia⟨nby⟩ with A lowd vois said godz neaks, ar yee at þat sport in deed (and ⟨with⟩ þat hee stood still, and nodded hiz hed at þem) þen streyhtwais dem⟨awnding⟩ no farder warrant for þe breach of hiz kommission, hee with A stowt ⟨ko⟩raȝ and bold speech said vnto hiz said broþer, by þe mạs it shall kost y⟨ow⟩ þe oþer peny for þat yowr sawsynes. and with þat, withowt any mọ⟨r⟩ wurdz or deeds hee went hiz waiz streiht to þe ạlhows and bestowed ⟨þe⟩ họll peny of ij pens in bred and drink. low my masters, quod he ⟨what⟩ A pasient fellow waz þis? hee neyþer kạm ny þem vnto þem to trobull þe⟨m⟩ neyþer did hee threaten þem with kooking stooll, kart, nor whipping ch⟨eer⟩ but only thouht him self suffisiently revenȝed by breaking of hiz commissio⟨n⟩ in laing owt of A singell peny. I do beleev quod an oþer, þat it iz har⟨d⟩ to fẏnd many of þat mans temperans in such A kạs az hee waz þen in. quod an oþer, such women az hiz wẏf waz, be of such pasiens þat alþoh þey bee put in þe fawt never so often, yet it never offendeth þem, and also such good huzwẏvz as shee waz, wilbe A brọd evry mor[n]ing (besẏd oþer tẏms) befọr þeir huzbandz hạv any lyst to rẏz.

By þis affọrsaid yee may perseiv how willing sum men bee to say þe wurst by women. And siurly at þat tẏm þe remembrans of þẹz fọrsayd storiez and ȝẏbz ⟨did⟩ pleaz mee very well also, yea, and I kowld hạv lawht very well at þe⟨m⟩ but yet I durst not for tearing of my lips. Yet again in þis perplexite and kạs I waz sumwhat dawnted shortly after, bekawz I remembred þat in þe end I did not know what did hang over oþer folks hedz,

8ᵛ ⟨who⟩ w⟨old fŷnd þeir hows burned⟩ doon fo⟨rgotten whẏll
watching þe⟩ neyborz hows on fier.[1] and yet in farder mizery
be þọz poor sow⟨ls⟩ who ⟨ạr⟩ in þe stạt þat þe goodman John
Johnᵃ of Islington affọrsaid waz in, for hee þat iz known to bee A
notoriowz Cookkold kannot be tạken vpon quests, and iz barred
of dyverz funksions and kallings of estimasion in þe kommen
welth as A man defạmed, so þat yow may see what A goodly
thing it iz, when A mans honesty and kredit doth depend and ly
in hiz wẏvs tayll.

Ðerfọr in myn opinion it iz not good for A man to bee tow
kiuriowz, and to serch tow naroly, to know þe trewth of hiz
wẏvz folly þat way, if by chans she hath born A man mọr þen
shee owht to do. for if hee be known to know þat hiz wẏf iz
A stᶠrˈumpett, and yet doth keep her still, he shalbe repiuted
not only to bee A kookkold but also A witwold. and besẏd þat
geveth kawz to hiz wẏf (exsept þe grạs of God doth turn her
hart) to kontynew in her lewdnes still. yf hee do put her from
him, yet þẹrby hee denounseth him self to bee A kookkold for
ever after. Wherfọr it iz best þat whatsoever hee doth think of
hiz ill wẏf exsept it be tow apparent to all þe world or to hiz
dainȝer or vndoing never to be known þerof, but to tell her what
iz said of her, and þervpon to perswạd her and to kownsell her
to A better lẏf, az first to shew her what A great fawt it iz to
break þe kommaundement of God, which sayth *Thow shalt not
committ adoultry*. þen what ponishments hee sendeth to þem
who do break þat commaundement az þe shạm of ⌈þe⌉ world,
þe diseazes þat be gotten þerby, and lastlye damnasion of þe
sowll. and so peradventiur, shee will ever after bewạr of her
fawt, or ells she will wurk so klọsly þerin, az it shalnot be somuch seen az A nọz in A mans fạs.[2]

When I had gaþered and dyȝested all þẹz saiengs affọrsaid,
þey vrȝed and gạvᵇ mee kawz to serch farder az ọn not satisfied

---

ᵃ Dittography.   ᵇ MS. has a dot above the 'a'.

---

[1] Proverbial; Tilley N 116.
[2] Proverbial; Tilley N 215, the earliest example is dated 1581.

in þis matter, and þen did I fýnd þat A filosofer named *Plutarch*[1] did wryt þus. It iz A thing most sweet, and most ʒoiowz to behold bewtyfull persons, but to towch and lead þem with þe hand iz perilowz. lýkwýz did I fynd þat þe filosofer *Zenophon* wryteth þus. the fier only doth burn being ny vnto it, but the fair fases albeit þei bee farr of, do enflam and burn. *Seneca,* lýkwýz wryteth, þat bewty iz kawz of domaʒ to many. and þe poet *Ouid* wryteth, þat bewty iz fraill and with tým doth fad, and diminish. Also hee saieth þat þe bewty is rar which iz ⌐not⌐ withowt sum fawt or výs. Alþoh þe last sayngs may bee azwell app[l]ied to þe bewty of men az of women, yet at þis present I wold konstrew & tak þem[a] to be spoken of women only. and þe raþer bekawz I entended to mak vpon þem þis Sonet foloing, þe which shuld put mee in mýnd to bewar of þoz, of whom I had hard so much evell spoken of as afforsaid.

> *Prefer not gret bewty befor vertew*
> *Ðe much gazing þeron may many rew*
> > *It iz A thing þat ʒoiouz iz*
> > *to mani'a on þat amrouz iz*
> > *for to behold þe bewty rar*
> > *Of sum who þerwith possest ar*
> *But þem t'akkumpany and much to towch*
> *Iz perilowz, þis proof doth firmly vowch.*

> *Ðe hot fier only doth burn þem*
> *Who ny þertoo do soʒiourn þem*
> *⟨Ðe fas of bewty doth enf⟩lam*
> *⟨Ðoz þat b⟩ee far of from þe sam*[b]
> *Ðus bewty kawzeth domaʒ to many*
> *When reazon iz forsed from þem*[a] *to fly*

9r

---

[a] MS. reads 'þen'.　　[b] Lacunae not supplied from printed version of this song, for only the first eight lines are given.

---

[1] Whythorne undoubtedly found these sayings of Plutarch, Xenophon, Seneca, and Ovid grouped in some medieval compendium, as yet unidentified by the editor.

Sins frail bewty doth kawz much greef
Esteem Vertew to bee her cheef
when yee know both in on tak plas
Praiz God þat þar hee gyvz such gras
For hard it iz to fynd many of þoz
In whom, (at ons) hee doth þem both repoz.

After þat I had mad þis ⌐said⌐ Sonet, kam to my remembrans how þer waz on who told mee þat by þe means of flattery hee waz ons brouht into A foo⟨ls⟩ paradÿs,[1] by A subtull shrew, who fecht him in fÿnly, and handele⟨d him⟩ so koningly þat shee mad[a] him to lov her A good pas, but shee kam not after az ⟨far⟩ az shee kowld. notwithstanding az shee had begun so shee seemd afterward to ⟨gra⟩tify him, and to leav no 3ot of hiz frendship bestowd on her to ⌐be⌐ vn[b]reko⟨mpen⟩sed for A whÿll. and when shee perseyved þat shee had him fast bownd⟩ by þe⟩ bek, shee afterward requÿted h⟨i⟩z lyberall and kostly gifts bestowd vp⟨on⟩ her, with amiable looks and pleazant fair woordz. in þe which tÿm hee thought þat hee had gotten godamihty by the littel fynger, wheraz in dee⟨d⟩ hee had kawht þe dyvell by þe great to.[2] Now Sir, þis kiupidian thinking no⟨w⟩ all to be gowld þat shÿned[3] (besÿd his substans bestowd vpon his loov⟨⟩) began now to impart vnto her þe very sekrets þat wer hidden in his har⟨t⟩ not only of things pertayning to þeir affairs, but also of all hiz oþer tradz⟨, mys⟩teriez, attemptz, and entents. and in þe end when shee knew þe boto⟨m⟩ of hiz chests and substans, and also of hiz hart, shee plaid with him ⟨A⟩ sluttish towch and part, gyving him þe slip.[4] and in fÿn when hee repr⟨e⟩hended her and blamed her A litull for her inkonstansy, shee all in ⟨A⟩ ra3 bad him go skrap, and foorthwith blazed abrod þat, which he ha⟨d⟩ told her ⌐to keep⌐ in sekret. and if it had byn eyþer fellony or treazon, belÿ⟨k⟩ hee had byn lÿk to hav smeld þerof,

---

[a] MS. has a dot above the 'a'.   [b] A misplaced caret mark here is silently corrected.

[1] Proverbial; Tilley F 523.
[2] Proverbial; Tilley (G 260) cites Edward Halle's *Chronicle*, 1548 (*STC* 12721), but it is also in Heywood.
[3] Proverbial; Tilley A 146. As later examples show, Whythorne was fond of this proverb.   [4] See *OED* 'slip', *sb.*[3] 8. See also pp. 43, 200.

so þat þiz sort of dissemblerz be ⟨lẏk þǫz⟩ who do look to hạv
A powndz wurth of profet for A ⌜farþing⌝ wurth ⟨of⟩ fliering
flattery. when I hard all þis, quod I to my self, hee iz h⟨ap⟩pẏ
þat kan bewạr by oþer folks harms.[1] and þervpon I wrǫt þus—

> Ðy sekrets told to such az hạu
> Of dissembling þe proper way
> To bee blabd foorth þee to deprạu
> Look þow þerfǫr þer iz no nay
> And so þe fox þe lamb shall gain
> Er hee of gẏll fẏnd kawz to fear
> Ðerfǫr þe faithfull hart retain
> Ðat holdz þi hart and sekrets dear.

Whẏll I waz in þis heat of wryting against dissemblers And
flattererz, I wrǫt þus of þem ⌜in ȝenerall⌝ az foloeth—

> Az þi shadow it self applieth
> To follow þee wher so þow go
> And when þow bendst itself it wrieth
> Turning az þow both too and fro
> ⟨Ðe flatter⟩er d⟨oth ⌜eevn⌝⟩[a] so
> And shǫps him self þe sạm to glǫz
> with mani' A fawning and gay sho
> whom hee wold frạm for hiz purpǫz

Yet I kowld not leav to wrẏt sumwhat mǫr of þǫz sorts of
flattererz and dissemblerz who do deseyv eevn þǫz ⌜þat⌝ be
akkownted ⌜wẏz⌝ and of great estạts aswell az of þe meaner sort,
at whǫz handz þey þat deall plainly and simply kan gett no
goodnes, and þerfǫr I wrǫt þus—

> what euer hath byn in tẏm past
> In tẏm prezent t'iz often found
> Ðat flattery hath got þe kast
> To get frendship both sạf & sound
> wheraz plaines in word & deed
> Of hạtred great iz siur to speed

9ᵛ

---

[a] Lacunae supplied from printed text.

Proverbial; Tilley M 615.

Yet to return again to þe feminin sex, and þeir loovz, alwayz
when I remembered þat which iz written of þem befǫr, it
kawzed ⌐me⌐ to gẏv no heed to þe ⌐aliurments,⌐ entẏsments and
snǫrz of women, and if I did spy þem, yet I wold despẏz and
shun þem azmuch az I myht possibull, but why talk I somuch
of þat which iz past seing it will help no lenger? for alack þat
which ǫn feareth mǫst, and wold not hǫv it happen vnto him, it
iz often seen þat hee eskapeth þe sǫm very narroly or never A
whitt at all. & so chaunsed it with mee also at þis prezent, for
I being now in plǫs whẹr wẹr dyverz yoong woomen, ǫn of þe
which az appeareth by þe sequel seemed to bear mee very much
goodwill, þe which through maydenly shǫmfastnes waz not by
her vttered vnto me in word and deed in such sort az I perseyved it, but shee vttered it by wrẏting, and bekawz shee wold
seem to do it not all togyþer of her own freegoodwill and kẏnd
hart, but of my self, shee seemed to tǫk þe okkasion of her loov
toward mee to bee vpon sum wordz of setting on þat ⌐I⌐ shuld
speak vnto her, vpon which shee devẏzed sertayn versez in
English. wryting þem with her own hand and did put þem between þe strings of A Gittern, þe which instriument az A syt-
ting mǫt, lieng mǫt, and walking mǫt, I þen yvzed to play on
very often, yea and almǫst evry howr of þe day, for þat it waz an
instriument much esteemed and yvzed⌐of⌐ gentilmen, and of þe
best sort in þǫz dayz, þe which verses did þus begyn—

> *wurdz þat yee hǫu rehersed*
> *hath my hart oppressed*
> *And kawzeth mee to dy*
> *withowt remedy*
> *But I wish yow did know my mẏnd*
> *If yow wold not bee to mee vnkẏnd*
> *My mẏnd is*
> *Ðat. W. Shall hǫu þis*

And whẹr þe .W. standeth alǫn, þǫr shee wrǫt my nǫm.
when I kǫm akkording to my akkustomed wunt to tǫk þe gittern
10ʳ to play on it, and fynd⟨ing þe paper . . . I asked myself the ques⟩-

sion who it sh⟨uld b⟩ee þ⟨at⟩ mạd it and ⟨did⟩ p⟨ut⟩ it þạr, but ⟨also meanwhile⟩ kalling to my rememb⟨ra⟩ns what wurdz or talk þat I had ha⟨d⟩ with ⟨any⟩ ọn in þat hows befọr þat tŷm. My mŷnd þ⟨e⟩n waz so voyd of loov matters, az I kowld not well ʒiuʒ wheþer it wẹr written by A man or A woman, and dowting sumtŷm ọn thing and sumtŷm an oþer az wheþer it wẹr doen of A woman of purpọz for loov, or in mokkạʒ by sum man. being þus in þis quandare I wrọt an awnswer to it on þe baksŷd of þe sạm pạper þe which waz as strainʒly endŷted az þe kạs waz þen strainʒ vnto me, þe which waz in þis manner foloing—

Thọz wurdz þat I hạu reherst, I trust hạu doon no harm. And whẹr yee ar opprest I kannot do withall, If it lay in me to help yow, I wold do my best. Shew yowr mynd, for I wilnot bear mallis to such, az sekretly do tell mee of my fawts. Đis ys mŷn awnswer to your wrŷting. Soon after þis I mạd þe effekt of þat affọrsaid in meeter az folloeth—

> *Đoz wurdz I hạu reherst*
> *To mŷnd I kannot kall*
> *And whẹr yee ar opprest*
> *I kannot do withall.*
>
> *If it lay in mee now*
> *for to asswaʒ yowr wo*
> *my best to do for yow*
> *I wold not let to do*
>
> *When yee will shew yowr mŷnd*
> *To mee, eevn hardely*
> *I wilnot bee vnkŷnd*
> *To such assiuredly*
>
> *who þat in sekret wŷs*
> *will tell mee az A frend*
> *Gyving mee good advŷs*
> *how I my fawts may mend*

In short tẏm after þe wrẏting of þat affọrsaid I vnderstood who it waz þat w⟨rọt⟩ and did put þe wrẏting between my gittern strings, which waz A yoo⟨ng⟩ (girll raþer þen A yoong) woman in þat hows. for shee and ọn oþer wh⟨o⟩ waz her kounseller and tiutour (az it seemed) in þis matter (shee bei⟨ng⟩ ọn þat knew her tạking vp and her läing[a] down, and waz also very ⟨skil⟩full in such praktyzes) þis tiutor and her piupull being togyþer ⟨in⟩ A plạs all alọn, and I by chauns kumming in whẹr þey wẹr, þis ⟨said⟩ kounseller demaunded of mee wheþer I fownd such A pạper & wrẏting ⟨in⟩ my gyttern strings or no, and I awnswering yee, demaunded of her again, who wrọt it and layd it þạr, whẹr-v⟨pon⟩ shee replied and said, þat it waz doen by ọn who if I wold mạk ⟨her A⟩ wẏf, she wold be ve⟨ry⟩ glad þerof. quod I heer iz þe wryting, ⟨a⟩nd on þe backsẏd þerof iz mẏn awnswer, and þerwith I delyvered it to þe tiutor and kownseller. þen quod þe piupull to þe tiutor ⌈with A cheerfull kowntenans⌉, and it shalnot be long vn awnswered, whervpon shee took þe paper from her tiutor and did rea⟨d⟩ mẏn awnswer, but when shee had so doon, and fynding it nothing for he⟨r⟩ purpọz az shee wold hạv had it, shee with A sorowfull kowntenans d⟨eli⟩vered þe paper vnto mee agayn withowt any mọr wurdz and awnswering þerof. Shortly after þis (by what mean I know not) þis matter brạk owt & waz known all abowt þe hows whẹr wee wẹr þe which mạd mee to blush and ⟨shee more so. Ðen, þis matter kumming to⟩ her master & mistres knowle3, and fẏnding þat shee waz so loving ⟨witho⟩wt provoking or entẏsing þervnto, shee waz dischar3ed owt of þat how⟨s⟩ and servys.

10ᵛ

Low sir, and if I had had þen any mẏnd of marria3, it waz lẏk þat þen I myht hạv bin sped of A wẏf, but I mẏnded nothing les þen þat. and it offended mee very much to bee demawnded any such question, for I do remember þat not long befọr þis tẏm þer waz A 3entilwoman who demaunded of mee wheþer I waz maried or no, whertoo I (being sumwhat diskontented with her question) awnswered þat I had need to be wẏz first (for I thouht my self to yoong and vnfurnished of experiens & welth

---

[a] Mark over 'a'.

to tạk such A kạr vpon mee). þen ⌐þe ʒentilwoman replied and said⌐ you may be married and be wẏz also. whervpon I awn-swered her agayn þat I thought it wold þen be to lạt, þe which reʒoinder of mẏn az ⌐it⌐ þen lẏked mee to speak ⌐it,⌐ so ⌐waz it⌐ not myslẏked of sum þat hard it.

Ðe Italiens hạv A saieng emong þem þat yoong folk do not saver & know þọz things þat ar behoovfull or fit for þem to know, and if þe proverb be to ⌐be⌐ applied only to such who hạv no devosion to venery and wyving, þen miht it be veryfied in mee in þọz daiz. also an[a] oþer thing waz þen in mee which hindered such aksions very much, þe which waz bashfulnes towardz women, and cheefly in þe affairz of woing of ⌐þem⌐, þe which fawt hath kontinewed in mee ever sins, and yet when tẏm served to bee in company with women, to talk with þem, to toy with þem, to ʒẏb and to ʒest with þem, to discoors with þem, and to be mery with þem (all þe which sum do kawll koorting) I kowld yvz þe tẏm with þem sumwhat aptly and fitly, but and if it kạm to mạking of loov, by word sign or deed, espesially in deed (þen godnyht ʒon lẏn)[1] I had nomọr fạs to do þat, þen had A sheep. and assiuredly I do now akkownt bashfulnes espesially in yowth to be A great good gift of God to help to hinder þe yowthfull and ill pạrts of yoong imps and fry. for God knowth, many yoong peopull for lak of þat gift (wheþer it be good or bad) do kommit such folliez, az alþoh throuh ingnorans þey be well pleazed withall at þe doing of þem, yet shortly after, eiþer throuh þe grạs of God wurking in þem and þeir eyz þerwith be ⌐so⌐ opened þat þei do see and konsẏder of þeir fawts, or els by þe harmz þat þey get þerby þei repent þe sạm. Tạk not þẹz wurdz az þoh þei wẹr spoken in þe reprehending of þọz who hav good awdasitiez in good aksions, or of þọz who do wed or marry but it ⌐iz⌐ raþer against þọz who do run hedlong þervnto withowt any good konsiderasion þerof, and cheefly against þọz who do mẏnd no marriaʒ at all, but woo altogiþer for lecherows lust,

---

[a] MS. reads 'and'.

[1] Apparently a proverbial expression, referring to some action of parting lovers.

not regarding with whom þei do it ⌈&⌉ not regarding who be þe
tọn so þei bee þe oþer, a⟨nd⟩ þerfọr kummeth it to pas many týms
þat þei which do so wed or marry, do ⟨kum⟩ to great mizery and
beggery. and also such az kommenly do seek and yvz þe kumpany of broþels, ruffians bawds, and harlots, do not only bekum
beggarz in þe end but also be filled with most horribull, filthy
and inkiurabull diseazes, and siurly þe dowt of þe evels þat I
miht hạv gotten by þe folloing and keeping kumpany with
Venus darlings, kawzed mee aswell az þe other kawzes affọrsaid
to strýv with fraill natiur very much, for I must konfes þat I
am not mạd of stoks or stọns, but eevn of þe self sam mettall
þat oþer men bee mạd of, and for þat I wold not looz þe lạt
liberty ⌈& freedom⌉ þat I had gotten, I mạd in meeter az it wẹr
A praier vnto þe godz of loov to spạr mee owt of þe band of
loov, for now I did fear it very much, þe which praier did
begyn az folloith—

11ʳ *Yee ⟨Godz who rewl⟩ o⟨ur lives and⟩ loo⟨vs and⟩ al⟨l of men's estạt⟩*[a]
    Of w⟨hich⟩ þe ⟨free⟩dom and þe eaz, yee gỳv þem a⟨z þ⟩eir fạt
    Graunt mee A whýll þe lýberty, þat now of yow I krạv
    And þat by loov I may not looz, þe ȝoiz þat now I hạv
    when I waz yoong þe lawz of skoolz, and looking on my book
    waz such A korzei[1] *to my hart, az non waz lýk I took*
    Ðen wold I wish my self A man, þoh of þe meanest sort
    Ðat I miht gỳv my self þe leav, when I wold to tạk sport
    when of þis band I had owt got, weening my yọk waz gọn
    A thowsand kạrz kạm in my hed, whẹr such þer harberd nọn
    For az befọr my lýving all, waz got vnto my hand
    Now am[b] *I fain for to travell, poverty to withstand*
    Ðe which by means þat I hạu wrouht, I kan keep at stạvz end[2]
    And all toiez els which az I think, shiuld let my mirth to mend
    Exsept to loov I bee mạd thrall, for which I am now prest
    If yow rew not on mee þerfọr, to keep my sowll in rest

---

[a] Poem unprinted, so lacunae supplied by guesswork.   [b] Written
over 'Ðen waz'.

[1] *Corsie*, a cause of trouble and grief (*OED*).
[2] Proverbial; Tilley W 904; see also S 807.

wherfor yet ons mor do I krau, of yow my liberte
 In althings els I will yow seru, yea þoh in ʒeberte
For I wold raþer out of hand, my karkas for to spill
 Ðen by long tȳm þe sam konsium, throuh greef of mȳnd by ⌐will⌐

I kannot wad nor pas any furder in this matter and diskours, till I hav shewd yow my fantazy and mȳnd konserning þe poetikall ⌐*piutatȳu*⌐ Godz, þe which in deed wer selebrat and kalled vpon by þe heaþen peopull, who did not know þe trew and lȳving God. az for þat þei ar kalled vpon by þe kristians, it iz but bekawz þat when þei for pleaziur, rekreasion, and mirth do wrȳt of sum fantastikall and vain matterz, þei will kawll vpon þem whom þei do know to be in deed but vain and fantastikall Godz. and wheraz þe goddes kalled Fortiun whom þe infidelz imaʒin to gȳv by turning of her wheel, good or il⟨l⟩ hap, to whom she listeth, yet ⌐in þe respekt of her absoliut power, and þat shee iz A living kretiu⟨r⟩⌐ shee iz to bee vnder-stood of kristians to be ⟨no⟩thing els but A vain idoll. and þat all good fortiun, luk, hap, fat, or ⟨desti⟩ny, is þe only ⌐and free⌐ gift of þe God of Godz ⌐(who rewleth þe tȳm & fortewn þat is spoken of in þe. 9. chapter of þe preacher[1] ⟨)⟩⌐ and if any of þoz fortiuns afforsaid ⟨do⟩ happen to vs kontraryly or ill, it iz throuh o[w]r own wikkednes and sinfull n⟨atiur.⟩ lȳkwȳz evry oþer of þe vain and poetikall Godz hav alotted vnto þem by þe ⟨po⟩ets þeir pekiulier awtorites to wurk in whom þei list, az *Venus* and ⟨*Ciu*⟩*pid*, þe rewlerz of lust and loov. *Diana* of chastite. *pallas* of wyzdo⟨m.⟩ *Apollo, Orpheus,* and dȳverz of þe nȳn *Muzes,* of dȳver⟨z⟩ sorts of ⌐fȳn⌐ miuzik, *Pan,* of Sheppardz, and gros shrill Miuzik. *Bacchus* ⟨of⟩ wȳn and belly cheer. *Mars,* and *Bellona,* of warz and battels. *Vulca*⟨*nus*⟩ of Smyþs and fier. *Neptun* of Sea and waterz. and *Mercury* of eloquens subtilty, and kunning &c.

now will I leav to say any mor of þis matter and tell yow how my passed ʒoiz began to fad and end for A tȳm by an oþ⟨e⟩r mean and not by loov, for I had not past fully ij yeerz in þis karles tȳm past, but þer kam A wurshipfull knyht, and well,

---

[1] Eccles. 9. 10.

⌐(yee⌐ towell) known to many who iz kalled sir John Agew.[1] þis krewell týrant envieng mẏn ea⟨z⟩ and prosperite did arest mee, and after þat browht mee into fower of ⟨hiz⟩ prẏzons, þe ǫn imediatly after þe oþer. þat iz to say, first into A quotidian⟨.⟩ sekondly into A tersian. thirdly into A quartain. and fourthly or lastly into A dobull quartain. In the quotidian, and tersian, hee held mee but litt⟨l⟩ mǫr þen A quarter of A yeer. but in the quartain and dobull quartain, hee did hold and keep mee A hǫll yeer at þe least. Ðis foresaid ⌐wurshipfull⌐ marshall with ⟨hiz

11ᵛ torments did at last release me and I was⟩ quẏt rid ⌐owt⌐ of hiz klowches, ⟨but⟩ I kowld never rekover þe sǫm again ⟨. . .⟩ᵃ and former estǫt. and I being þus tormented with long siknes, an⟨d⟩ besẏd þat þe wǫsting of somuch of my small substans and stok az I had spent and konsiumed by þe mean of Sir John Agew, began to be angry with dǫm fortewn bekawz shee wold not raiz mee from þe botom of her wheell and help mee. In þęs daiez I wold wręk mẏn anger altogẏþer with pen and ink vpon paper, bekawz þat þe timerowznes þat þen waz in mee which waz bred by þe melankoly left az A relik of my Agew, and þe weaknes of my yoong koraʒ wold not stir nor provǫk mee to do oþerwẏz (much lẏk az for ensampull, A yoong shrewish maiden wold do, who, when shee ⌐waz⌐ much angerd, wold straihtwayz go into A seller þat her fǫþer had, and þǫr wold shee with her teeth bẏt vpon A post A long tẏm till shee had diʒested þe rǫʒ of her kolerik hiumowr[)]. and so lẏkwẏz did I whẏll I waz in þat chǫf with fortiun az is affǫrsaid, to prǫv wheþer my ⌐melankoly⌐ hiumor wold diʒest az þe maidens did, in þe which agony I wrǫt þus—

Ðoh fortiun frown on mee alway
Turning mi ʒoi to pensẏvnes

ᵃ MS. has the end of a word 'ynat'.

---

[1] Whythorne's personification of the ague demonstrates the intimacy in which the Elizabethans lived with the disease. These intermittent fevers were designated by different names according to the interval of return. A fever that returned every day was called a quotidian; one that skipped a day was called a tertian; when two full days were skipped, the fever was called a quartan ague. A double quartan consisted of two sets of paroxysms, each recurring every third day.

Yet do I still hǫp for þe day
Ðat all my wo shall hạu redres
And no mishap shall tạk þe plạs
To bring mee in þis wofull kạs

For all my hǫp iz in mi God
whǫz look dạm fortiun dạr not bẏd
Hiz fors and herz iz so far od
From whẹr hee iz shee will soon slẏd
And why shiuld I prai for her aid
Sins on her wheell shee hath nǫn staid

Lo Sir, þis kros or ponishment of siknes afforsaid mạd mee now to remember God A ⌜litl⌝, for I aknow⌜l⌝[e]ʒd him to bee A konquerowr of Fortewn. butt alak yoong folk be soon forgetfull of trobuls when þei be A litl over past, and so waz I, for all my siknes kowld not so dawnt my hart, but þat when I waz well rekovered þerof to my helth again, I had þen as good an opinion of my self az þẹr waz kawz, and þerwithall I waz (az I thouht) throuh experiens waxen a litl wẏzer þen I waz befǫr, and wold not lawh Fortewn to skorn somuch az I ⌜had⌝ doon befǫr þis tẏm.

For ny abowt þis tẏm þẹr waz A ʒentilwoman (who waz A wydow) þat waz dezẏrowz to hạv mee to bee bǫth her servant and also her skoolmaster, þe which I waz lett to vnderstand by A frend of mẏn. to whom I said þat to ⌜be⌝ A skoolmaster I did not mislẏk, but to bee A serving kreatiur or serving man, it was so lẏk the lẏf of A water spannell þat must be at kommaundement to fetch or bring heer or karry þạr, with all kẏnd of drudʒery, þat I kowld not lẏk of þat lẏf. yet I being earnestly provoked þerto, pạrtly by þe perswazion of my said frend, who said þat my servis shuld be eazy enowh, and yet shuld be very well konsidered of, and also pạrtly drẏven þerto aswell bekawz I waz behẏnd hand of my welth az of my helth, hoping þat in þis I shuld rekover þem bǫth to þeir former estạt agayn, I forsed my will to yeeld to reson, and þarfǫr I mạd þis sonett folloing against þat will which wilnot be rewled and governed by reson—

Thowh krooked kạrz do chauns
To wretched wilfull wills
⟨*which vnwẏzly advau*⟩*ns*
⟨*to rea*⟩*ch of mani* ⟨*ill*⟩*s*
To þọz þus may wee glauns
whẹr wilfull will planteth
witt with wisdom wanteth

12ʳ

When I dwelled with mẏn ọld master mr Haywood, I do yet
remember þat I did heer him say many tẏms, þat will waz A
good soon, and will waz A shrewd boẏ.[1] by þe which words I
gaþered þat (az A man kan do nothing withowt will) when hiz
will was wilfull and wold bend him self to ⟨see⟩ wickednes and
to imaȝin nawhtines, þen he was A shrewd boy, and ⟨on⟩ þe
oþer pạrt if he wold not be wilfull, but wold be rewled and
governed by Reazon, þen he shụld do all well, and þerfore
shụld bee A good soon. And at þis tẏm waz I so perswaded þat I
thouht I shụld yeeld to much to wilful will if I wọld not yeeld
to þis fọrsaid servis, for þat I waz brouht in A good họp to
benefitt my self mọr þerby þen I shuld ⟨hạv⟩ doon owt of it, þe
which mạd mee to yeeld þẹrvnto and to frạm my s⟨elf⟩ to pleaz
my fọrsaid mistres akkording az mẏ dewty bownd mee.

and ⟨now⟩ to shew yow what maner A mistres and skoller I
had, I assụr yow shee was such A ọn az no yoongman kowld
serv A better to break and train h⟨im⟩ vp to the fasshions of þe
world. alþoh I kowld better skill þen shee in Miuzik and teaching to play on Miuzikall instriuments, yet kowld shee bett⟨er⟩
skill þen I to ȝudȝ of þe natiurall dispozision and inklẏnasion of
S[k]ollerz, how þei shiuld be yvzed akkordingly. Also her ȝoy
waz to hạv men to bee in loov with her, and to brag sumtẏms
how shee kowld handl such az wẹr so, az how shee kowld
fetch them in, and þen how shee kowld with a frown mạk þem
look pạl, and how with A mery look shee kow⟨ld⟩ mạk þem to
ȝoy again. (Diogenes sayd þat such kynd of women were i⟨n⟩
þeir sort lẏk vnto Queens bekawz men had þem in such estyma-

---

[1] Proverbial, but not in Tilley; see *Oxford Dictionary of English Proverbs*,
2nd edition, p. 709, for citation of 1546 edition of Heywood.

sion ⟨&⟩ venerasion, and wẹr so at þeir kommaundement).[1] Many
tẏms when ⟨I⟩ waz not ny vnto her, alþoh she had appointed
mee to way[t] on her kup⟨p⟩ when shee satt at meat, shee wold
bẏd mee kum nier vnto her, and þe⟨r⟩withall skoffingly shee
wold say to þọz that wẹr with her, I wọld fa⟨in⟩ hạv my man to
bee in lọv with mee, for þen hee wold not bee þus fa⟨r⟩ from
mee, but wold bee alwaiz at myn elbow. and þen wold shee
sumt⟨ẏms⟩ put A pees of good meat and bred on her trenchor,
and foo⌈r⌉thwith b⟨id⟩ mee gẏv her A klean trenchor, for the
which I shiuld hạv þat of her⟨z⟩ with þe bread & meat on it.
when shee wold say þat shee wold fayn hạv mee in lọv with her,
thọz wurdz wold offend mee very much. for of althings I akkownted loving az shee ment it to but bee A foollysh thing
i⟨n⟩ þọz daiez, and I do akkownt loving in dotạʒ, þat iz to say to
loov, not b⟨e⟩ing beloved again, to be no better þen folly in þẹz
daiez. I will reverens mẏn elders and betterz as bekummeth mee.
and I will lọv mẏn even christen as christian lọv and charyty
byndeth mee, but az to lọv vnbeloved, be it eiþer man or woman,
and worldly loov is commenly tạken and akkounted in þẹz daiez,
þat I think I am not bownd to d⟨o⟩ but to bestow loov whẹr az
⌈I⌉ both see and fynd it well bestowd, and in þis mynd was I
toward my mistres þen. yet konsidering þat open kontempt myht
breed such sekret hạt in her toward mee az after myht put mee to
app⟨a⟩rent displeaziụr (az experience þerof I had tạsted in my
kạrles yeers b⟨e⟩fọr rehersed) I determined with my self to bear
althings þat myht happen az pasiently az I kowld, what soever I
thouht, and þervpon to eaz my mẏnd I wrọt þis sonett folloing—

⟨I seek a⟩ll no⟨tions, plain or shrewd⟩   12ᵛ
To bee releast of all my ⟨wo⟩
Đatᵃ serv and loov, iz now embrew⟨d⟩
for mee to tạst will I or no

ᵃ Inserted in margin.

---

[1] Found in Erasmus's *Apophthegmes*, translated by Nicholas Udall, 1564
(*STC* 10444), f. 102ᵛ: 'Paramoures, he affirmed to be yᵉ queenes of kynges,
because the same mighte craue of the saied kinges, whatsouer their phansie
lusted, and be assured to obteine their asking.'

And sins þer iz no chois for mee
But for to yeeld and thrall to bee
I will proov how to trap þe best
Sith þat for loov I am þus prest.

Ðus passing þe tȳm in her servis, I do remember þat sertain tȳms when I tawght her alþouh shee wold be nekliȝent and heedles besȳd oþer toyengs and trȳflings in þe tȳm of her learning, yet for þe reverens I bạr vnto her, I wold not reprehend her and yowz such sharp words vnto her as I wold hạv doen to oþer of my skollerz, and shee wọld þerfọr reprehend mee saing þat whosoever wold be A skoller must not disdain þe dew and lawfull reprehensions of þeir teacherz and skoolmasterz when hee tawht þem. and also shee [wọld] add to þoz wordz, þat whẹr A fear grew first vpon sum dew dezart or good opinion, from þens afterward wold ensew to þe party feared to be welbeloved. At oþer tȳms if I had been owt of her siht, shee wold seem vnto mee az þouh shee had bin ȝelowz over mee but espesially if [I] had by any means talked with any woman in in[a] her siht, þe which presumsions and tokens mạd mee to suspect þat shee wold hạv had mee to think þat shee did bear mee sum goodwill þe which if shee did dissembull, I to requȳt her thouht þat to dissembull with A dissembler[1] waz no dissimulasion, and ⌜to⌝ play with her az þe hunter doth, who hunteth A hạr, asmuch to see her subtȳl skips and leaps az for to get her karkas. but and if shee ment goodwill in deed, þen I waz not willing to loos it bekawz of þe kommodities þat myht be gotten by such ⌜A⌝ ọn as shee ⌜eiþer⌝ by mariaȝ or oþerwȳz, and þerfọr I took okkazion vpon her ȝelozȳ of mee to wrȳt to her þẹs verses foloing—

Mizdeem mee not wȳþout kawz why
Alþouh I talk familiarly
If þus mery I shụld not bee
Great prȳd þei would þen ȝudȝ in mee
I may keep that eevn all þe day
Altȳms and howrz in honest way

---

[a] Dittography.

[1] Proverbial; Tilley D 182.

And mean nothing az yee mistrust
To serv az thrall t'obey þeir lust

But whẹr þat mẏ goodwill is bent
I dạr not shew lest I bee shent
But who shee iz þus will I say
my hart shee hath both nyht and day[a]

⟨An⟩d þou⟨h her loov from me be taken⟩   **13**[r]
Yet will ⟨not⟩ I þouh I be shaken
in peeses, ons from her remoou
Till þat mẏ hart iz burnd in loou

Đus in few wurds I do yow tell
Who hath my hart klọzd in her sell
Alþouh I dạr not shew her nạm
Yow mai konʒektiur of þe sạm

For your wit þis shall now suffẏz
few words ar best[1] *lest ill miht rẏz*
Sins þat for words sum hạu bin shent
Now will I seas lest I repent.

I mạd þis song sumwhat dark & dowtfull of sens bekawz
I knew not serteinly how shee wold tạk it, nor to whoz handz
it miht kumen after þat she had read it, if she wold tạk it to be
written to her self she miht best do it. and if she me⟨nt⟩ to tạk
it well, þen it waz lẏk þat shee wold keep it to her self, but and if
⟨shee⟩ wold not tạk it to her self or in good pạrt, but wold skof
þerat and shew it ⟨to⟩ such whom she thouht wold tạk her pạrt,
yet it is so mạd as neiþer shee nor no⟨n⟩ oþer kowld mạk any
great matter þerof, spesially, if I miht hạv kum to þ⟨e⟩ awnswering þerof. but az it chansed, it waz neiþer ill taken, nor I hard
no mọr of it, exsept it wẹr of her self, & þat in ⌜such⌝
sekret sort and in such maner az I needed not to mizlẏk þerwith.
After þis shee mạd sum what mọr of m⟨ee⟩ þen shee did befọr,

---

[a] Last word on this page; Whythorne did not follow his usual practice
of giving a catchword.

[1] A variant of Tilley W 781

but it waz in such sort az I kowld not yet assiur my self to be
siur to know whẹr & how to hạv her.[1] Sumtẏms shee wold tell
me h⟨ow⟩ shee wold hạv mee to apparell my self, az of what
stoff, and how she wo⟨ld⟩ hạv it mạd. Also shee wold sumtẏms
tell me what manner of rings wol⟨d⟩ bekum my hand to wear,
and also what ʒewell, to þe which I wold awn⟨s⟩wer her as tẏm
served þat my purs waz thin lẏned to bestow such kost o⟨n⟩ my
self, howbeit, & if shee wold bestow þat on mee, which shee said
wol⟨d⟩ sowell bekum mee I wold wear it for her sak sạk.[2] Vpon
þe which wordz s⟨hee⟩ wold sumtymes gẏv me both money to
by þe things and also sumtẏms such sto⟨ff⟩ az shiuld serv to mạk
such things. and so by pollisy I gat þat at her hand⟨s⟩ þe which
oþerwẏz I miht peradventiu[r] hạv gọn withowt. yet to shew my
⟨self⟩ very glad of þat frendship which I reseived, and þe rạþer
in họp of þat ⟨which⟩ waz lẏk to kum after þat which waz pạst I
seeming ⌐to⌐ reʒois befọr þe ko⟨n⟩quest waz woun,[3] mạd þis þat
folloith—

Sins I embrạs	
mi ladies grạs ⎱	in sort az I dezier
I will reʒois——	
with pleazant vois ⎱	Sins quenched is þis fier
waz never nọn	
Did sih and mon ⎱	Mọr oft þen I er þis
when looks awry	
I did espy—— ⎱	in þe eiz of mi blis
⟨But⟩ with m⟨y⟩n eiez	
which be my spiez—— ⎱	I now spy ⟨þẏn e⟩iez ⟨sh⟩yn,
Đat ons did wrest	
my ʒoẏ t'unrest— ⎱	and all my mirth vntwyn.
Wherfọr reʒois——	
both sound and vois ⎱	let no tewn mourning bee,
But with deliht	
with all your miht ⎱	reʒois with hart and mee.

13ᵛ

---

[1] Tilley K 186 cites Falstaff's phrase (*1 Henry IV*, III. iii. 144) as the earliest
example; Professor Wilson has found none before 1578.

[2] The expression 'sake's sake' is recorded in *OED*, but no examples are
cited before 1665.   [3] Proverbial; Tilley V 50.

Wheraz befor I spak of þe quenching of fẏr, vnderstand no
oþer wẏz þerof but only þe obtaining of my dezier of þe benefits
þat I reseived at her hands, also wheraz yow[a] and such oþer
Suspisiows headz wold think peradventiur þat so much frendship az I spąk of in þe forsaid song kold not bee, exsept A
konʒiunksion kopiulatẏu had had[b] bin mąd sumtẏms for A kon-
firmasion of þe sąm, to þe which I must say, and say trewly, þat
neyþer my hand nor any oþer part of mẏn did ons towch þat
pąrt of herz whęr þe konʒiunksion is mąd. marẏ þus much may
I say, þat I being loth þat shee shiuld withdraw her goodwill
from mee, waz very servyzabull to pleaz her, and also wold
sumtẏmz be pleazant and merẏ and also sumwhat bold with
her.[c] After þe which tẏmz shee wold sumtẏms tell mee in
skoffing maner þat I waz but A huddypick[1] and lakt awdasite. but
I not konstriuing þoz wordz so þen, az þey did proseed from
on who did know her gąm, or els had learned þat az hee þat woeth
A maid must be brąv in apparell & owtward show, so hee þat
woeth ⌐A⌐ wydow must not karry ⌐quik⌐ eels in hiz kodpees,
but shew sum proof þat hee is stiff befor,[2] did think her shew
of loov and liberalite bestowd vpon mee waz but to feed her
hiumour and to bring her purpoz to pas (az afforsaid) þat iz to
say to bring mee in such A doting loov towardz her, wherby I
shiuld suffer her to rẏd & derẏd mee az shee list, ʒiudʒing þe
best every way els, and I mistrusting þe wurst þe raþer for her
boasting befor þat tẏm how shee kowld handell a novis. and
also bekawz þat it waz told me by on of my fellowz who said þat
hee hard her say þat when I had served her turn in teaching of
her þat þen shee wold iuz mee az shee wold yuz on, to whom shee
waz willing to gẏv þe slip vpon þe wich wordz I grew into sum
kolęr, howbeit pasience par fors[3] mąd mee to brydell it again
and þen I determined to tąk althings at her hands az þei kąm,[4]

---

[a] Perhaps 'your'; an r is written above the o.   [b] Dittography.
[c] 'dẏverz tẏms' crossed out.

[1] *Hoddypeak*, a simpleton or fool (*OED*).
[2] This proverb did not reach print in similar form until 1669; Tilley
M 18. It occurs again on p. 192 below.
[3] Proverbial; Tilley P 111.   [4] Proverbial; Tilley T 196.

and not trust overmuch to fleeting Fortewn (who miht mąk mee to think þat A *Cresid* waz A *Penelope*) and also as shee so entended but to mąk mee to serv her turn, so in þe mean whẏll I entended to mąk þe mǫst of her þat I kowld to serv my turn (az A good fellow said, who had married A rich wẏf, and had konsiumed all þe goodz and substans þat shee brouht to him. when afterward he waz charʒed by A frend of herz þat he mąd nothing of hiz wẏf, hee awnswered and said þat noman in England kowld mąk somuch of her az hee had doon, meaning þat hee had mąd of her all þat hee kowld when hee had left her littl or nothing to mąk away of þat which shee brouht vnto him).

And þus being by mẏn own perswazion defended from all kąrs for þat matter, and hąving meetely well feþered my nest,[1] which waz þen þe cheefest mark þat I shot at, I past my tẏm away pleasantly, as sumtẏm in singing, sumtẏm in playeng on miuzicall instriuments, sumtẏm in daunsing, and sumtẏm in wrẏting of English vers, az ǫn day kumming into my mistres chamber, and fynding þąr A pen, ink, & pąper, I wrǫt in A pees of þe paper az þus foloing—

> *When pain is pleaziur, and ʒoẏ is kąr*
> *Đen*[a] *shall goodwill in mee wax rąr.*

Đis[a] wrẏting I left whęr I fownd þe said implements to wrẏt
14[r] withall, and kumming þe n⟨ext day to her ch⟩am⟨ber I fo⟩wnd w⟨ritten az folloeth—⟩

> *For your goodwill look for no meed*
> *till þat A proof yow show by deed*

Vnto þe which when I had seen it, I replẏd az foloith—

> *When oportiunite of tẏm sarueth*
> *Đen shall yow see how my hart swarueth.*

After þis I vnderstood þat þe awnswer to my fǫrsaid rithm waz not mąd by my mistres, but by A wayting ʒentilwoman of herz, of whom alþoh I neede⟨d⟩ not to hąv thought skorn, yet

---

[a] The 'Đ' has no bar.

[1] Proverbial; Tilley N 125–6.

I repented mee of þat which I had þen doon, bekawz I lẏk not
to mȧk loov to ij att ọns. þen þis yoong ȝentilwoman vnto whom
I awnswered as affọrsaid, perseiving by þe not prosekiuting of
my enterprẏz, and by sum words of my speaking þat I ment not
to proseed any furþer in þat aksyon, thouht þat I disdayned her
wryting, wherfọr to requẏt mee shee on A tẏm in few wordz to
mee said, þat such A yoongman az I waz, who se⟨e⟩med to be
but A wẏld yowth needed not to disdain þe wrẏting of her who
w⟨az⟩ worþi to be well thouht on and to bee beloved of az good
az I. Quod I to h⟨er,⟩ konserning þe opinion þat yow hȧv of
yowr self for yowr abilite and wurþines, ⟨I⟩ do better allow þen
þe dowtfull opinion þat yow hȧv of mee konserning my wy⟨ld⟩-
nes. and bekawz yow shalnot hȧv ȝust cawz to think þat I
disdain yow alþọ⟨h⟩ I do loov yow no oþerwẏz þen I do þe rest
of my fellowz in þis hows, I will awnswer to yowr opinion of
mee in meeter Again heerafter. and þen I took pen in hand
and wrȯt az folloeth—

> *My youth þoh yt seem wẏld*
> *As yow to mee hȧu said*
> *Ðis word, seem, hath begẏld*
> *Sum, till þei hau it wayd*
> *For what A thing doth seem*
> *is not þe sȧm alway*
> *And so if wẏld yee deem*
> *Vntrew yee deem*[a] *I say*

When I had red þis meeter vnto her, I gȧv it to her to konsẏder vpon. In þęz daiz þęr be dẏuerz þat do yuz þis word
seem, as þoh it miht not be tȧken dowtfully, az for exsampull, if
ọn of þọz wold say hee will dea⟨ll⟩ ȝiustly, and withowt any
disseit in A matter towching hiz honesty, h⟨ee⟩ will say þat hee
will seem to deall ȝiustly and withowt disseit in an⟨y⟩ matter
towching hiz honesty, whęraz in seeming to do so, he may az
we⟨ll⟩ keep hiz promẏz in not doing so az oþerwẏz, ⌈for⌉ seeming to do A thing iz ⟨ra⟩þar not to ⌈do þe⌉ thing þen to do it. az

---

a MS reads 'deen'.

sir *Thomas wiat þe elder* sayth in ọn ⟨of⟩ hiz Sonets,[1] (wrÿting to
⌐ọn named ȝoan poins⌐ A frend of hiz) þat hee waz not þen in
Spain whe⟨r⟩ ọn must him enklÿn, raþer ⟨þen⟩ to be, owtwardly
to seem to be. he wold not meddl with wits þat wẹr so fÿn.
wherby yee may perseÿv þat þẹr is A diffrens between seeming
& being ⌐or doing⌐ in deed. Now will I leav to speak any mọr of
þis seeming matter, and shew yow how þat az it iz an ọld sayeng
þat three may keep A kownsell if twoo bee away,[2] þis proverb
miht bee applied to þe doings of my mistres and mee, for owr
affairs wẹr not so klọsly handeled but þei wẹr espied and
much talked of in þ⟨e⟩ hows. but espesialy by ọn, vnto whom
I wrọt þus—

> *Trạd þee to þÿn okkiupasion*[3]
> *Think not but many do þee nọt*
> *How kontrarÿ to þi vokasion*
> *Bearst an ọr in euri mans bọt*[4]

14ᵛ   ⟨A⟩t ⟨þis tÿm of writi⟩n⟨g I had bek⟩um⟨very sa⟩d ⟨and was in⟩
such A quandare and fear az ọn mÿht have ⟨ta⟩ken my hart at
my tayll[5] ⟨. I felt ac⟩urset[a] bekawz I did suspekt þat and if it
had kum to my mistres knowl⟨eȝ⟩ þat it miht hạv bin an okkazion
for her to hạv withdrawn her good kowntenans and benevolens
from mee. yet afterward I plukked again A good hart vnto mee
and konsidered þat hee þat will not be envied let him never
seek to kreep vp into any awktorite beit never so small. And

---

[a] Doubtful reading.

[1] Lines 91–93 of Sir Thomas Wyatt's Satire I:
> Nor yet in Spaine where oon must him inclyne
> Rather then to be owtwerdly to seme;
> I meddill not with wittes that be so fyne.

The satire is addressed to John Poynz, nephew of the diplomatist Sir Francis
Poynz. Wyatt's editor, A. K. Foxwell, says John Poynz and Wyatt both took
part in the famous feat of arms at Christmas, 1525. (*Poems of Sir Thomas
Wiat*, 1913, ii. 102.)

[2] This proverb (Tilley T 257) is found in Heywood's *Dialogue* ii (1546)
(*STC* 13291), sig. G4ᵛ.

[3] Expression meaning 'Mind your own business'; Tilley B 752.

[4] A widely circulated expression; Tilley O 4.

[5] This proverb usually places one's heart in one's hose (Tilley H 314).

þat A faint hart never got fair lady.[1] it iz A kommen matter emong servants, be þeir masters or mistresses of hye or low degrees, if any on of þem be in favor with þeir masters or mistresses abov þe rest, by an by all þe rest of þe servants will envy him or her, and seek all þe means ⌈& waies⌉ þat þei kan imaʒin to bring þem owt of kredit, þe which praktizes wer at þat tým proved and attempted against mee. but hee þat iz A fraid of every shadow had need to keep him self alwaiz in þe dark.[2] and I not forsing for any on of þem remayned firm in þe sam mýnd þat I waz in befor þat waz, to tak althings az þei kam. and bekawz þat þey had iuzed subtill ⟨a⟩nd sly means to bowlt owt þe goodwill beween my mistres and mee, I to rekompens þem and to shew sumwhat of þeir behavowr in þeir doings mad A dyskripsion of a bezy body wherin I did towch þe doings of most of þem az þus—

I hard of lat——
how on did prat— } *and search althings to know,*

Az þoh þat hee
had had a fee } *to spy, to sift, and show.*

Ðerof þe sort
for to report } *az it waz told to mee,*

Rehers will I
now folo'ingli } *as yow Shall hear or see.*

From plas to plas
hee romd apas—— } *tooting on eury thing,*

and marking þar
what stouf or war } *waz not to hiz lyking.*

Ðen wold hee streiht
bi skoffing sleiht—— } *paint foorth in fýn proses,*

how þe s[t]at waz
wher hee lat waz } *þat hee did know or ges.*

---

[1] Proverbial expression; Tilley H 302.
[2] Tilley (S 261) has only the first part of this proverb.

What things awry⎫
hee did see ly——⎭ or what lay owt of frạm,

Yee what well lay⎫
hee wold yet say——⎭ hee kowld amend þe sạm.

Ðen wold hee trudʒ⎫
lỹk A sly drudʒ——⎭ prieng to fynd folks talk,

ánd bianby——⎫
hee wold espy⎭ how hee to þem kowld stalk.

15ʳ

B⟨ut if his ear⟩——⎫
Shiuld f⟨reely hear⟩⎭ ⟨on⟩ wha⟨t⟩ þei ⟨w⟩old at larʒ

hee wold seem streiht⎫
hiz hed wẹr freïht⎭ with matterz of great charʒ.

In miuz hee' wold stand⎫
Or els in hand——⎭ hee took letterz or book,

but mỹnd and ear⎫
to þem ward wear⎭ whẹr so þat hee did look.

When þei had doon——⎫
Ðeir wurdz shiuld soon⎭ abrọd be sown az seed,

of such az hee⎫
I kounsell yee⎭ be siur yee tạk good heed.

At þis tỹm I mạd mee A ring of gold, in þe which I kawzed to be grave⟨n þis⟩ sentens folloing. *whẹr wyly whisprerz wait wurk wyzlỹ. quod. W.* þis ko⟨wn⟩sell I mạd so az evry wurd began with A *.w.* for mỹ nạm. but þe cheef ka⟨wz⟩ why I mạd it waz to put mee in mỹnd to bewạr in all my saiengs & doing⟨s⟩ espesiallỹ affọr kommen whisprerz, for þe greatest sort of þem will bỹ & sell[1] ọn befọr his fạs. Ny abowt þis tỹm my said mistres kawzed A painter her p⟨ik⟩tiur or kownterfett, to be sett in her chamber, and bekawz þat I þen họped t⟨o⟩ hạv sum good at her handz, kawsed þe sạm painter also to mạk ọn of þe sạm p⟨ik⟩tiurz for mee, þe which I hung vp also in my chamber (for whẹrsoever I bek⟨ạm⟩ wheþer it wẹr in London or owt of London I kept alwey A chamber in L⟨on⟩don, bekawz þat họm iz họmly what chauns soever shiuld happen).[2] now in ⟨full⟩

---

[1] Proverbial; Tilley B 287, also in Heywood.
[2] Proverbial; a variant of Tilley H 534, who cites Heywood's usage.

ʒolity, I wold needs hạv þe sạm painter to mạk my piktiur again,
to see h⟨ow⟩ I waz chainʒed by Sir ʒon Agew and hiz impryzon-
ments (az affọrsaid) sins ⟨þe⟩ tỹm I mạd þe oþer piktiur of myn
affọrsaid, and in þe tạbl of þis of þis[a] ⟨pik⟩tiur I ment to hạv
kawzed þe iiij lỹns folloing to be written but after⟨wardz⟩ I waz
oþerwỹz advỹzed—

> Đe restles rạs þe yoongman runns
> iz strainʒ to know in ech degree
> now heaps hee ʒoiz, and kạrz hee shunns
> bi'anby hiz mirth away doth flee.

Đis fọrsaid sonett I þus wrọt bekawz I ment when tỹm
shiuld sarv, þat ⟨my⟩ mistres shuld se it togyþer with þe piktiur,
at what tỹm I ment also to let he⟨r⟩ vnderstand þat I had her
piktiur also, bekawz þat shee miht þerby thin⟨k þat⟩ I mạd
A great akkount of her in asmuch az I waz so willing to hạv
þat ⟨whẹr⟩by I miht þe mọr and oftener remember her. Also in
þe fọrsaid sonet ⟨I⟩ towched þe vnsertein estạt of A yoongman
bekawz þat my madạm wold sumtỹm put her praktyzes in
iur to prọv whẹr I waz A riht *kiupidian* or no (peradventiur þe
talk of her and mee in þe hows kawzed her to do ⟨it⟩ az A
pollisy to put owt of þeir heds þe ʒelowzy þat waz in þem) and
I p⟨e⟩rseyving her entent seemed to be such A ọn az shee wold
hạv mee, feeding her ⌈*with her*⌉ hiumor. mọr over to furþer þe
matter, I wrọt to her þus—

> Gỹv ear lady vnto my plaint
> for now repeat I must
> Đe thing þat mạks my ʒoy to faint
> And will till I be dust.

> ⟨Unless you think up⟩on þe wron⟨g⟩   **15ᵛ**
> which yow to mee hạu wrouht
> and turn þe leaf or it be long
> þat I somuch hạu souht

---

[a] Dittography. The erratic punctuation of this passage has been silently
altered.

I am konstrained for to say
  þes verses þat ensew
wyshing þat yow for euer may
  my ʒoy by þem renew

And þat yee may yet ons again
  such praktẏz iuz to hɐu
As vain toongs kannot yow distain
  ne your konstantnes deprɐu

Great greef it iz [for] mee to sing
  whọs hart with dọl iz klad
to know þe chanʒ of such A thing
  az erst did mɐk mee glad

And sins yee long to know þe trewth
  of þat þat I wold say
I pardon krɐu, and axing rewth
  for sai'eng az I may

Ðat fansy all iz now appald
  which ons yee bɐr to mee
alþouh yee hɐu bin oftẏms kald
  lady konstans for to bee.

Lo, þus it iz, now hɐu I doon
  I kan nomọr now sing
Yet pray þat yee will mend it soon
  and eftsoons helth mee bring

Now let mee not dispair sweet loov
  for þat yow may mee gẏv
but return þat for mẏ behoov
  which may my hart revẏv

So shall yow þen þe fɐm retain
  þat yow hɐu had er þis
þouh Momus wold not yet refrain
  to reprehend yowr mis.

⟨I⟩n þes daies I yuzed to sing my songs and sonets sumtẏm
to þe liut and sumtẏms þe virginals, wherby I miht tell my tạl
with my vois aswell az by woord or wryting, and sumtyms it
shiuld bee þe better hard bekawz þat þe miuzik ⟨ʒ⟩oined þerwith
did sumtyms draw þe mẏnd of þe hearer to bee þe mọr atten-
tẏu to þe song. also if it wẹr not to bee well taken, yet in asmuch
az it waz sung þer kowld not ⟨so⟩much ⟨hurt be found as had 16ʳ
been in þe kạs of my⟩ wrẏting being ⟨del⟩iver⟨ed to her⟩ to
r⟨ead,⟩ for ⟨sin⟩ging of s⟨u⟩ch ⟨songs &⟩ di⟨ttie⟩z wa⟨z A⟩ thing
kommen in þoz dai⟨ez.⟩ when my mistres had hard þis song,
it mạd vp her mo⟨uþ⟩ (az þe proverb[1] saith) for þen shee thouht
þat shee miht hạv led mee az it wẹr in⟨to her⟩ nett with a
twyned threed wher shee list. and alþoh I seemed to stowp
much ⟨vnder⟩ her yọk yet þerwithall I wold sumtẏms showt owt
sum dry reazons pertey⟨ning⟩ to þe moving of mirth, bekawz
shee shuld think þat I waz not so fast masked ⟨and⟩ tied þat it
shiuld not withdraw mee altogyþer from mirth, and bekawz I
⟨wold⟩ gẏv her sum testimony of my mynd in þis behalf I mạd
and sung vnto her ⟨þis⟩—

> *It hath bin proved both eevn and morrow,*
> *A littl mirth to bee wurth much sorrow.*[2]

> *Sum þat hạv toiled and wrouht much in vain,*
> *of whom mọst pạrts, of eaz, did littl tạk,*
> *yet in þe end for to eaz all þeir pain,*
> *þei did þem rest and sport, & goodcheer mạk.*

> *Ðe trobled mẏnds þat in sorowz wẹr drownd,*
> *from drowzy dumps wẹr wunt to fly A pạs*
> *and for bekawz þat þeir mirth shiuld be sownd,*
> *all lumping looks wẹr soon expeld þe plạs.*

> *Ðus may yow see how in tẏm past ech ọn,*
> *did drẏv away sorows from þem among,*
> *do yow lẏkwẏz, for þei be frendz to nọn,*
> *and so I mạk an end of þis my song.*

---

[1] Whythorne has here thrown together several proverbial expressions.
For 'made up her mouth' see Tilley M 1263.
[2] A variant of Tilley O 86.

After þis, bekawz I wold seem to lўv still in hǫp, I wold go sumtўms in ⟨gar⟩ments of russett kolowr (þe which kolowr signyfieth þe wearer þerof to ⟨hǎv⟩ hǫp)[1] and ǫn tўm I did wear hops in my hatt also, þe which when my mistres ⟨had⟩ espied, shee in A few skoffing words told mee þat þe wearing of hops did ⟨but⟩ shew þat I shiuld hop withowt þat which I hoped for, to þe which saye⟨ng of⟩ herz, I awnswered þat I hoped to fўnd her better to mee þen so, for noth⟨ing⟩ kowld remǫv mee from þe loov of her. quod shee, if yow hǎv any hǫp in me⟨e⟩—

Ðe sudds of sǫp
Shall wash yowr hǫp.[2]

With þe which wordz I waz A littl trobled at þe prezent hearing þerof, but ⟨þen⟩ at þat instant kǎm also to my mўnd þat þe hǫp of new loov wold tǎk away ⟨and⟩ mitigat þe greef & sorow þat miht breed for þe los of old loov, and þǎrwit⟨h⟩ I plukt vp A good hart, and assewred my self of þe loov of her fǫrsaid wai⟨ting⟩ ȝentilwoman, and akkounting þat ȝǫn waz az good az my lady[3] (az þe adaȝ sai⟨eth⟩) with kountenans mǫr bashfull þen stowt or sorowfull, I awnswered mi mi⟨stres⟩ again þat þe sudz of sǫp shuld wash away no hǫp þat I had in her. this awnsw⟨er⟩ waz az dowtfull to be tǎken and vnderstood now, az þat waz which I wrǫt to ⟨her⟩ at þe first, þe which I did so mǎk, bekawz I wold see how shee wold tǎk it ⟨and⟩ if I saw þat shee took it, þat ment þerby þat my hǫp waz so siurly fixed in her, þa⟨t⟩ it kowld not be put owt, and so þerby her goodwill toward mee miht kontynew, I wold hǎv said þat I ment it þat way. but if shee wold

---

[1] There is evidence that russet also signified steadfastness; see M. C. Linthicum, *Costume in the Drama of Shakespeare and his Contemporaries* (1936), pp. 30–33.

[2] *Suds* early meant 'dregs'; *OED* also has the meaning 'difficulties' *c.* 1572. So Whythorne appears to have been using a new expression rather than a proverbial one. The association of soap with suds did not begin, according to *OED*, until a decade later. Yet the same rhyme, 'suddes of sope . . . my hope', occurs in an unpublished poem of the mid-sixteenth century, f. 21 of the Braye Lute Book (Osborn Collection, Box 22, No. 10). Professor Wilson points out a similar usage in Boccaccio's *History of Galesus*, translated by T. C. (*STC* 3183), A3 verso.

[3] Proverbial; Tilley J 57.

tạk it þe kontrary way, seing I did suspekt her affeksion toward
mee to be altred & chainȝed, I thouht to let her vnderstand þat
I had þen no họp in her at all, wherfọr it kowld not be washed
owt, & bekawz þat shee spạk it in rithm to mee as is affọrsaid, I
mạd mỳn awnswer ⟨lỳkwỳz. . . . Then, wishing to provọk⟩ an⟨d **16ᵛ**
moo⟩v her to þe full, I ⟨di⟩d ⟨compọs a long⟩ and full ⟨di⟩skoors
⟨with⟩ much ⟨poynt a⟩nd si⟨rk⟩umstans þat had happened befọr
þis tym between vs, to þe entent to vrȝ ⟨and p⟩rovọk her to
shew her self in deed, what she ment towardz mee, þe which
⟨diskoo⟩rs þus foloeth—

> *When Cupid had kompelled mee,*
> *to serv my fained frỳnd,*
> *pallas from þat perswaded mee,*
> *lest trobull I shiud fỳnd,*
>
> *For þoh þẏ loov doth seem quod shee,*
> *þy goodwill to requỳt,*
> *yet in þe end þow shalt see,*
> *þi guerdon shall þee spỳt.*
>
> *Ðis kounsell kawzed mee to draw,*
> *vnto þ'end of my siut,*
> *And þen by wordz and deedz I saw,*
> *what tạst shiuld be my frewt.*
>
> *Sumtỳm her Sleihts did gỳv mee kawz,*
> *to think shee did mee try,*
> *for þat shee wold on my sewt pawz*
> *not graunting byanby.*
>
> *Sumtym yeelding Vnto my hest,*
> *az þoh it pleazd her well,*
> *þen sodain strainȝnes waz my best,*
> *My họp for to expell.*
>
> *Now in, now owt, now frown, now smọth,*
> *so dyverz my loov was,*
> *az erst I knew nọn such in sooth,*
> *but well, I lett it pas.*

Ðen last of all vnto my loov,
  I þus began to say,
Noṇ in þis world kan mee remoov,
  from yow þer iz no nay.

When I þus said shee to mee shǫp,
  þis awnswer þat ensewth,
þe suddz of sǫp shall wash your hǫp,
  for all yowr fixed trewth.

Ðen when I saw my loov waz lost,
  and I misyvzed so,
I ⟨w⟩old nomǫr be at þat kost,
  but streiht from her did go.

17ᵣ

⟨Yet when I next to h⟩er k⟨am ny⟩
  I did r⟨e⟩moov all fear,
and þen to her I did reply,
  in sort az yee shall hear.

Why wold yee now my ʒoy owt grǫp,
  to mąk my wo renew,
þe suddz of sǫp shall wash no hǫp,
  þat I hąv had in yew.

Ðẹz wordz I left her for to skan,
  how shee miht know my mỵnd,
and how shee did I forst not þan,
  sins so I did her fynd.

When I had sung þis vnto her shee seemed not to bee any
thing moved or trob⟨led⟩ withall oṇ whitt, which mąd mee to
think þat shee did it az A pollisy to ke⟨e⟩p ⟨me⟩ still in dowt of
her, and by þat mean to lỵv still in A vain hǫp, for if she⟨e⟩
shiuld hąv seemed to lỵk of þis song þen shee thouht þat I wold
lookᵃ þat ⟨shee⟩ shiuld shew her self to mee az shee had doon
befǫr. on þe oþer part if shee ⟨had⟩ shewd her self vtterly to
mislyk withall, þen shee thouht þat being owt of do⟨wt⟩ of her

---

ᵃ MS. reads 'kook'.

goodwill toward mee, þat þen I wold nomọr so follow her
hiumou⟨r⟩ az I had doon. wherfọr kạm now to my remembrans
again þe oriʒinall ⟨&⟩ first beginning of þis owr komikall (I kannot say traʒikall) loov, and ho⟨w⟩ shee but seemed to loov mee
bekawz shee wold hạv mee her slạv to triv⟨mph⟩ over (þoh þe
konquest had bin but simpl) and I seeming to bee such A ọ⟨n⟩ az
shee wold hạv mee, mor for ⌐þe⌐ kommodyte þat I looked to get
at her handz þen for any great & over whot loov. so þat neiþer of
bọth owr loovz w⟨az⟩ for vertewz sạk for þe which in deed all loov
shiuld be bestowd, and si⟨ns⟩ I am of þe opinion þat what loov
soever groeth between ij. and if it ⟨be⟩ not in þe respekt of sum
sort of vertew, it wilnot long kontinew. ⟨þe⟩ konsyderasion
wherof mad mee at þis prezent to wrẏt þis sonett folloing—

> *Such as in loov wold hạv long ʒoy,*
> *þeir chois must bee for vertewz sạk,*
> *If oþerwẏz þey seek to knitt,*
> *no deep root shall þeir trew loov tạk*

In þis perplexite remayned I A littl whẏll, but in þe end I
remembr⟨ed⟩ mee how to try her A littl farder, whervpon I at
A tẏm konvenient deklar⟨ed⟩ vnto her (þe which waz trew in
deed) þat A frend of mẏn was spoken vnto by A duches or diuks
wẏf,[1] to prokiur to ọn who kould teach on þe virʒinals for
þ⟨at⟩ hee shiuld teach A yoong lady & dawhter of herz, þe which
preferment my said freend [bespọk] vnto mee. And when I had
shewd þe họl sirkumstans of þis pro⟨fer⟩ to my mistres I did dezier
her þat I miht hạv her goodwill to leav her servis and to serv þe
said duches (in sort az I hạv said). Ðis lo seemed sumwhat to
trobu⟨ll⟩ her, wherwith shee vttered sum wordz, wherin shee noted
and charʒed my ⌐said⌐ fren⟨d⟩ with sum diskurtezy who souht mẏ
preferment, and þerwithall she began bo⟨th⟩ þe lẏk wordz to

---

[1] For evidence that this prospective employer was Jane, Duchess of
Northumberland, see Appendix II. Since the duke was then the most
powerful nobleman in England, small wonder that Whythorne's mistress
was jealous and wished to keep him. The 'fall in fortune' (p. 60) is a classic of
understatement, for the Duke of Northumberland was executed in August
1553, less than six weeks after he attempted to place his daughter-in-law,
Lady Jane Grey, on the throne.

mee, and also þᶏrwithall to water her plants[1] A littl, but az fo⟨r⟩
þat, I þen did but dowt þe kawz þerof, for þe tearz of A womans
eyez proseed alweyz of ọn kawz. for az sumtyms þey proseed of
greef so sumtẏms þey proseed ⟨of⟩ disseit and dissimiulasion.
and to towch þe kawzes mọr partikiularly and ⟨in⟩ larȝ, vnderstand þat az þei do sumtẏms proseed of good, so sumtẏms of
17ᵛ wanto⟨n and evell kawzes⟩ of ⟨many n⟩atur⟨z. . . . And sum-
t⟩ẏms for þat þey ⟨bee⟩ tᶏken ⌜na⟨pping in⟩⌝ [2] ⟨þ⟩e mᶏner ⟨b⟩efọr þey
bewᶏr o⟨f⟩ or vnprovẏded for A shift. or prevented for doing þat
which þey wọld hᶏv doen, ⌜and so⌝ sumtẏm of A frowardnes
when þey kannot hᶏv þeir wils, but þat þey be broken from þem.

If my mistres had shed her tearz for any anger shee had
toward mee I wold hᶏv taken no great greef þerfọr, for it iz said
þat in such A kᶏs A womans wrath iz so tempered with her
tearz þat þe ọn doth konsium and vanish away with þe oþer.
þen I to try her and to know mọr serteinly þe kawz of her tears,
demaunded of her þe kawz of her tearz, wherto shee said þat I
waz þe kawzer of þem. whervpon wee brᶏk of owr talk for þat
tẏm, and shee went her waiz owt of þe plᶏs. Imediatly after þis,
I, lẏk A yoong ⌜rash⌝ prinkoks[3] being kindeled with þe vnkyndnes befọr konseyved and tᶏken, and not yet kooled with her last
talk and words, wrot again az ensewth. but yet for all þat I staid
my wizdom and did not delyver it vnto her, þe which wrẏting
not withstanding I will sett heer bekawz it waz mᶏd for þis
plas—

Waz I þe kawz of þe vnrest, which seemz in yow to bee,
No, no, þer iz sum oþer fetch, it iz not all for mee,
for assoon az yee miht mee spy, for yowr sᶏk tᶏk no rest,
Solong your ȝoiz did still enkreas, such meed grew in yowr brest.
If it be so az yow hᶏu said, þat I hᶏu kawzd your greef,
bekawz (I say) I wilnot still, in vain seek your releef
Ðen do I see graft in yowr hart, to hᶏt þat yee may hᶏu,
and þat which yee may not kum too, yee hᶏu A mynd to krᶏu.

---

[1] Meaning 'to weep', a popular expression in the sixteenth century (Tilley
P 391).   [2] Proverbial; Tilley N 36–57, but *ODEP*, 2nd edition, gives
earlier examples.   [3] *Princox*, a saucy boy (*OED*).

Ðouh I waz lątly at your bek, to trudȝ for yow in pǫst
I mean not now for al yowr wo, to bee still at such kǫst
My gall iz brǫk and I kan swim, from drowning I kan sąv
til yourz bee so, ye'ar lẏk to sink, I will nomǫr be sląv.
Cheefly to her who kąreth not, to gratifẏ her frend,
Ðerfǫr now set your hart at rest, for heer I mąk an end.

It iz A kommen saing, þat who so hath bin entangled in þe
snąrs of loov, and hath gotten owt of þe sąm again, þat hiz gawll
is broken.[1] þe which saing iz derẏved from þeir estąt, who be
drowned in A deep wąter or standing pooll. for it iz said þat
whosever iz kast or falleth into any such water, after hee kannot
rekover himself in þe sąm, but hiz strength and memory fayleth,
and so dieth, hee sinketh to þe botom þerof, and þår kontineweth
vntill hiz gawll iz broken (exsept hee be taken owt) þen when hiz
gawll iz broken hee ryseth of him self to þe top of ⟨þe⟩ water &
sinketh nomore of him self. Ðis affǫrsaid iz aplied to A lover,
who having bin drowned in þe ląk of loov, and rekovered from
þe sąm, ever after hee will swim and never sink, and þǒh hee
do hee will never kontinew at þe botom bekawz (az I said) hiz
gawll iz broken, þe which iz to say þat when hee hath ons loved
ernestly (espesially if hee hąv bin deseyved) hee will ever after
be A feard to do so again, and þarfǫr wilbe ⌐þe⌐ mǫr sirkum-
spekt and wąry how hee entreth into it. but to return to my
purpǫz, when I had mąd þis fǫrsaid song, dyvers imaȝinasions
kam into my remembrans þervpon. ǫn whẏll I thouht þat I
shiuld hąv bin very sawsy with my mistres, if I had delivered
it or sung it vnto her, it being so plain az it iz. in deed I do now
konfes þe sąm, but such waz þe stąt of my yoong hed at þat
tẏm. and an oþer whẏll I thouht þus vnto my self, if my mistres
will seek to abiuz mee tomuch I kannot nor wilnot suffer it,
neyþer will I think myself þe mǫr to bee bląmed þouh I do tell
her of it. also in azmuch az she waz my skoller, I thouht her
⟨s⟩umwhat þe mǫr bownd to yoowz mee well and not to yẏz þe

---

[1] The earliest example in OED of this 'vulgar error' is quoted from Thomas
Heywood's Hierarchie of the Blessed Angells, 1635 (STC 13327), vii. 416:
'Her Gall being burst, she would be seene to swim.'

kontrary for St pawll saith þus in þe iiij chapter of þe *Galathians*.[1]
And I say þat þe heir (az long az hee iz A chỳld) diffreth not
from A servant þoh hee be lord of all ⟨b⟩ut iz vnder tiutorz and
18ʳ governourz vntill þe tỳm þat þe faþer hath appointed.[2] And also
⟨St p⟩awll in þe ⟨vj ch⟩apter o⟨f hiz epistle t⟩o ⟨þe Ephesians.⟩[3] let
⟨az⟩ m⟨any ser⟩vants az be vnder þe yok a⟨kk⟩o⟨w⟩nt þeir master⟨z
w⟩orþi o⟨f⟩ a⟨ll h⟩o⟨now⟩r. heer pera⟨dventiur⟩ yow wold say þat
þis plas of St pawll maketh nothing for my purpoz beka⟨wz hee⟩
speaketh of þe heir þat diffreth nothing from A servant so long
az hiz faþer ⟨doth⟩ hav him vnder tiuters and masters, but it
speaketh not of such who be of la⟨bour⟩ to govern þem selvs,
and þerfor þei be free from such government, az þe faþe⟨r⟩
⟨ap⟩pointeth to hiz heir.

well Sir þen do I say to yow þat owr saviour Chrỳst saith in
⟨St⟩ Liuks[4] gospell, cap. vj. þe dissypl iz not abov hiz master.
lỳkwỳz hee saith ⟨in⟩ St Mathews[5] gospell. cap. x. þat þe dissipull
iz not aboov þe master, nor þe serva⟨nt⟩ aboov hiz lord. it iz
enowh for þe dissypull þat hee bee az hiz master iz, and ⟨þat⟩
þe servant be az hiz lord iz. how say yow to þis? maketh not þis
for my pur⟨poz?⟩ smỳll ye? þez wurdz I am siur I am siur[a]
be spoken ȝenerally, and þerf⟨or⟩ þey do towch all aȝez and
estats, wherfor I warrant yow þey be good fo⟨r⟩ such skoolma[ste]rz to tak hold on, whoz skollerz will seek to mizywz þem.

and ⟨I⟩ for my part seing þat my profession hath bin and iz to
teach on of þe sevan sien⟨ses⟩ liberall, þe which iz also on of þe
mathematikall sienses, and in þe respekt of ⟨þe⟩ wonderfull
effekts þat hath bin wrouht by þe ⌜sweet⌝ harmony þerof, it
passeth all þ⟨e⟩ oþer sienses. I do think þat þe teacherz þerof (if

---

ª Dittography.

---

[1] Gal. 4. 1, 2.
[2] This is the last word on f. 17ᵛ of the manuscript except for a cancelled
catchword, apparently 'heer'. The circumstance argues that Whythorne was
copying from a draft in which the next page began with the second sentence
('Heer peradventiur', &c.). But his desire to strengthen the citation from St.
Paul led him to add the quotation from Ephesians at the top of the page.
Perceiving his mistake he cancelled the erroneous catchword, but did not
insert the correct one.   [3] Eph. 6. 5.
[4] Luke 6. 40.   [5] Matt. 10. 24, 25.

þei will) may esteem somuc⟨h⟩ of þem selvs az to be free and not
bownd, much les to be mąd sląv lyk. and ⟨even⟩ so did I at þis
tӱm , yet for all þęz kolerik fits and heat, if I had not byn ⟨at⟩ þat
tӱm in kąs to hąv sped of A better servis þen herz in an oþer
pląs I w⟨old⟩ never hąv imaʒined to mąk any such thing az þis
iz to hąv tried her pa⟨siens⟩ so far.

In A littl whӱll after þis tempest þe favorabull konʒiunksions
⟨of⟩ þe selestiall konstellasions and planets, did mittigąt þe rąʒ
of owr traʒe⟨dy⟩ and brouht it to A komikall end. for shortly
after þis buzines past, ⟨my⟩ mistres and I had sum talk again of
my new profered servis, and þen ⟨whe⟩þer it węr for þe loov of my
self, or of my servis, shee mąd mee so larʒ promyzes ⟨of⟩ good konsyderasion if I wold serv her still, þat I kowld not leav her þen.
When I had miuzed A whӱll on þis matter, I perseyved þat it waz
not for nothing þat ⟨þe⟩ poęts did fayn þat *Ciupid* þe god of loov
waz blӱnd, and þerfǫr kowld hąv ⟨no⟩ respekt whęr hee hitt
with hiz shafts, for hee seing no body, how kowld hee ⟨oþer⟩wӱz
pley, þen hit yee mis yee? so do I think þat hee plaid with my
mistres ⟨and⟩ mee at þis tӱm. yet it iz lӱk þat þe heat of hiz fiery
arrowz az þei ką⟨m⟩ glaunsing by vs, did kum so ny vnto vs, az
þei did heat vs A littl, but þat ⟨þe⟩ warmth which iz gotten so
and not entred into þe body, wilnot abӱd o⟨r⟩ remayn any long
tӱm exsept it be renewed vpon þe which konseit I wrǫt þus—

> *All ye þat serv þe blynd god loov,*
> *Shall in þe end your labour looz,*
> *Hee iz A fooll and wilnot moov,*
> *but whęr hee lihteth þąr to chooz*
> *and how shiuld hee gӱv your reward*
> *who elswhęr never had regard*
>
> *Perchauns hiz shafts may pears your mӱnd,*
> *to mąk yee blynd to serv your fo,*
> *If þus þe blynd ⌐leading⌐ þe blynd,[1]*
> *Yee know what good þerof doth gro,*

---

[1] Proverbial; Tilley B 452; also see Matt. 15. 14.

þerfǫr tạk heed how yow do proov
to looz your ʒoy by band of loov

Shortly after þis þer happened mǫr trobuls vnto mee, for Fortiun ⟨chan⟩ʒed my mistres estạt from hy to low, þe which hindred mee also for alþ⟨oh⟩ I fownd þat shee dǫted not on mee, yet I waz sertain þat if shee had ko⟨nti⟩newed in prosperite I shiuld hạv bin in better kạs to hạv lyved þen I w⟨az⟩ after-

18ᵛ war⟨dz. . . . Also⟩ þis s⟨udden chan⟩ʒ of her⟨z mi⟩ht sumwhat þe mǫr hạv greved mee, seing þat I forsook such A nobull womans servis (az iz affǫrsaid) to serv her, and her dekay to follow so soon after þe refiuzall of þe said nobull servis, yet in asmuch az þe said nobull woman and her lord & huzband had wurs fall shortly after my mistres fall, I needed to be no mǫr greved for þe refiuzall of þe tọn, þen to reʒois of þe keeping of þe toþer. and in þis perplexite seing my fạt waz not to bee preferd by any of þem, and konsidering also þeir fallz aswell az of my ill hap I fell owt flatly with fortewn blạzing her doings in þis sort folloing—

Who so þat list hiz chauns to try,
  on Fortiuns fikkl wheell,
hee shall soon see and also spy,
  her pleaziurz strainʒ to feell
For assoon as shee hath him set
  aloft on þat her staʒ,
from hy to low shee will him fet
  [and] all hiz pomp asswaʒ.

Ðus having past away þe lạt floryshing tẏm of mẏn own, to-gẏþer with þǫz who deklẏned from þe top of Fortiuns variabull and turning[a] wheell, I determyned to spend A tẏm in forrein and strainʒ kuntreiz þe better to diʒest all þe chainges þat hiþerto I had felt and tạsted. And when I kạm beyond þe Seaz, I endevored my self azwell to know þe kustomz and mannerz of þe peopull whẹr I kạm, az also to learn þeir speech and langwaʒes.

First of all, I kạm into þe low Duchland, þat iz to say

---

[1] MS. reads 'trurning'.

Flaunderz. and Bra⌐bant⌐ wher I remayned nÿ abowt half A
yeer, in þe which tÿm what I learned and noted þar, it wer to
long to shew & set down in þis plas, wherfor I will pas vnto my
purpoz, which iz to lett yow vnderstand, þat ij sonets I mad
when I waz in þat kuntrey. þe first of þem waz against Drunkennes, which iz A vÿs þat iz very kommenly yiuzed in þat kuntrey.
also an oþer vÿs which doth follow drunkardz. þe which sonett
doth þus begyn—

> *When þat well tipled ar with bowzed bum,*
> *Dan Bacchus birdz so dear, þeir toongs þen talk,*
> *and blab at lar3, þat, which in mÿnd doth kum,*
> *Not sham kan lett þeir rechles speech to walk.*
> *Besÿd all þis most tÿms such fakts þey ywz,*
> *az oft þeir freendz, þeir kumpaniez refywz.*

It is A kommen saieng & an old, þat hee þat killeth A man
when hee iz drunk hee shalbe hanged when hee iz sober.[1] siur
þis proverb waz not invented but vpon sum good grownd or
3iust kawz. for þe vyses þat do follow drunkenes be many. and
alþoh þat þe drunkard doth many tÿms want such strength az
may mak him abull to perform þat which hiz drunken hed doth
ima3en to do, yet hee in attempts will shew hiz hiumour. and
on of þe rediest instriuments þat þei hav to vtter þeir devyses iz
þeir toongs, with þe which þey wilnott stik to blasfem God, to
vtter treasons against þeir prinses & kuntreiz, yea, and to talk
at lar3 whatsoever kummeth in þeir myndz of þe wholl estat of
all things þat þey do know. (and þerfor drunkenes owght to be
eschewed of all men, and women both) but espesially of riulers,
ma3estrats, watchmen, and offyserz. with þis vÿs waz A frend
of mÿn tainted, when I waz in þis kuntrey, who at A sertain
⌐konvension⌐ and feast, ⌐being⌐ sumwhat kupshotten, plaid þe
part of A drunkard, and disburdened hiz hart at þat prezent to
all þat waz in hiz kumpanye, and it had not bin, þat hee waz þen
thouht to be drunk hee had smelled of þe kommodities þat do
follow drunkenez. but drunkards when þey be drunk, be much

---

[1] Proverbial; Tilley M 175.

born withall in þat kuntrey, wherfọr when hee waz bekum sober
again, I wrot vnto him þis oþer sonet folloing—

19ʳ

> Tạk heed of ⟨w⟩or⟨d⟩z þow ⟨ma⟩ist no⟨t⟩ vowch
> not spọk, for þem þ'art free alway,
> from word and deed.
> But said, þei do þee rewl, and towch
> þy siur estạt, wherfọr I say
> of wordz tạk heed.

Befọr þat wordz be spoken, þe spẹker of þem hath þem at hiz
own will to rew⟨l⟩ but if þey be ọns spọken befọr witnes, þen iz
hee no mọr þe master of þem,[1] bu⟨t⟩ even az þei bee when þei
bee vttered, so do þei work in word or deed vnto þe spea⟨ker⟩
be it good or evell. and no ọn sort of peopull, hạv mọr need to
tạk heed of þis e⟨vell⟩ þen drunkardz, for when þey hạv lost þe
maestry of þem selvs by drunkennes ⟨þen⟩ do þeir heedles toongs
babbull owt þe abowndans of þeir harts, and sumtým þey know
not what þem selvs. þe which vỹs of drunkennes I perseyved to
rain azwe⟨ll⟩ in Germany, and hye Almạn az in þe low Duchland,
for when I had remain⟨ed⟩ my half A yeer in the low Duchland,
þen travelled I thorow Germany and hy⟨e⟩ Alman into Italy.
And whỹll I waz in þọz kuntreiz I being sumwhat moleste⟨d⟩ &
trobled with drunkars þạr, bekawz I wold not drink karows and
all owt when þ⟨ey⟩ wold hạv had mee az þey did, I waz in sum
dainȝer þerfọr. for þe which I wrọt ⟨þus⟩—

> Who þat to quassing[2] iz bent, and to drink þe rạt
> þat dạm nạtiur (þe nurs of helth) hath þem forbod
> þe maestri of þem seluz þei looz, þeir strength doth so abat
> besỹd þeir wurs reward, which iz þe wrath of God.

After I had past thorow þes fọrsaid kuntreiz in Italy, I gạv
my self whọly to þ⟨e⟩ study and obtaining of þe Italien toong.
And when I had bin in þat kuntrei ⟨ny⟩ half A yeer, I determined to return into England thorow þe kuntr⟨ey of⟩ Frauns,

---

[1] Proverbial; Tilley W 776–7.
[2] *Quass*, to drink to excess (*OED*).

in þe which tẏm of my travell I happened into A hows on þe
hiþer p⟨art⟩ of Italy wherin I fownd þus written vpon A wạll—

> *Io sono la carta di carbona,*
> *chi mi legera sara vna coiona.*

Đe which iz to say in English (az it wẹr þe wals speaking) I
am þe pạper of ⟨þe⟩ kọll, hee þat shall read mee shalbe A kollion.
þez wordz konteyning sum rẏþem, and misyus of þe reader,
who peradve[nt]iur miht be an honester man þen ⟨þe⟩ wrẏter, I
seing hiz small diskresion wrọt þus vnder hiz writing—

> *Costui chi quel scrit'ha fatto,*
> *certamente'e vno matto.*

Đe english wherof iz. Hee þat mạd þat wryting, sertainly is A
fooll. þen vnder þat wrẏting I wrọt, az it wẹr þe wall speaking—

> *Io sono la tauola di punta,*
> *Con ragione scriuete congiunta.*

Đis hạv I mạd in meeter az folloeth—

> *I am þe tabull of þe point*
> *With reazon do þow wrẏt konƷoint*

By þe point affọrsaid I mean þe point of A knẏf, bodkin, or
any such oþer thing. þen I wrọt vnder þe fọrsaid wryting þis
þat folloeth—

> *In publik plạs nothing wryt þow,*
> *Exsept good skill þerin þow show.*

After þis I past into Frans, and after þat I had bin þạr &
had past thorow þat kuntrey, marking þe natiuz and kondisions of þat nasion, þen kạm to mẏ remembrau⟨ns⟩, þe ⟨way⟩ **19ᵛ**
I har⟨d⟩ spok⟨en o⟩f þem ⟨n⟩ot only in England, but also in
Duchland, and Italye. of þe which sum said, þat þei be
prowd, & þerwith deep dissemblers. oþers said þat þei be inkonstant, and great vawnterz and also braggers, and oþerz said þat
þei be great and kommen mokkerz, and þat þei bee az lẏons

whẹr þei fynd hiumilite, and whẹr þei fynd lẏons, þei do bekum in koraʒ az sheep.[1] vpon þe which opinions I wrọt az þus—

> Đe hauhtines of sum but bạs,
> whọz owtward shew seems of sum port,
> tạk on þem az þei wẹr in kạs,
> for to kowntnans þe hiher sort.
> þẹz wold hạv all to þem be bound,
> and þei from all, free to be found,

Đen mạd I an oþer against mokkerz and flowterz az þus.

> To reprehend or mok, þerof þe kommen end,
> iz kommen and great hạt, to þọz þat ywz þe sạm.
> to flowt nọn hath þe leav, but to sum to pr' hend
> Autorite gẏvz leav, th' offendor for to blạm.

Alþouh þat þẹz fọrsaid fawts be much noted in þe french
nasion, yet peradventiur who þat shalbe much konversant with
þe Italiens ye and þe Spanyardz also, shall fynd þọz fawts
emong þem assoon az among þe french nasion. wherfọr in
sundry respekts of þẹz fọrsaid vyses I kan better allow of þe
kondisions of þe Germans and Almans, (who be A valiant and
stowt nasion in good aksions) þen of ⌐þe¬ iij nasions affọrsaid.
for alþouh þe Germans and Almans be but blunt and riud, and
also geven to delẏt in þeir dayly drink to much, yet þọz fawts
be not so hurtfull to oþerz, neyþer do gẏv kaws of offens to oþerz
mọr þẹn þem selvz, az þe fọrsaid vises and oþer vẏses[2] which
I kowld nạm þat be in þe french, Ita[l]iens, and Spanyardz. and
bekawz þat owr English nasion kạm owt of Germany (emong þe
which kạm also my awnsetorz and nam) I will kommend þe
plainez of þe Germans befọr þe dissimiulasion of þe iij nations
affọrsaid, who will raþer seem to bee, þen to be in deed. by þis
yow may see low, wheþer I be dissended of þe plain Germans

---

[1] Proverbial; Tilley L 309, where the earliest example is 1589.

[2] In the margin is a side-note, with a line indicating that it should be inserted here. Most of the note is gone beyond recovery, but this much remains:

az to be so sivell & kurteowz, az to offer to embrạs ọn with þe
⟨   ⟩ and with þe oþer⟨   ⟩r him⟨   ⟩tl
⟨   ⟩many⟨   ⟩a⟨   ⟩

or no, for I tell yow my mӱnd plainly, and what I do nǫt in all
þe nasions þat I hạv heer befǫr spoken of, and howmuch I do
mislӱk þem, for I say az I did ons read (in effekt) in þe book
kalled þe banket of Sapiens[1]—

> *It doth belong mǫr of good riht,*
> *to such az hạv koraʒ gentill,*
> *to shew foorth plain to evri wyht,*
> *þe loov or hạt þei bear þem till,*
> *þen slӱlӱ to klǫk or klǫsly to hӱd,*
> *by þeir dissembling look or cheer,*
> *the good or ill þat in þeir harts doth bӱd,*
> *wherby þeir wӱlz kannot appeer.*

Tạk mee not now þat I do wrӱt against þe vertewz ⌜sort of
peopull,⌝ but raþer against þe vӱses þat do kommenly rain
emong þǫz fǫrsaid nasions. þe trewth may be blamed, but it
shalbe never shạmed.[2] and þerfǫr I do akkount it A folly to
flatter, glǫs, or ly, þe which requyreth gloriowz and painted **20ʳ**
s⟨pee⟩ch wheraz þ⟨e⟩ tr⟨e⟩wth needeth but ⟨A⟩ plain and simpull
vtterans ⟨wiþowt⟩ glǫzing or faining at all. it is A slạvlӱk and
servӱll trạd to bee A flatter⟨er⟩ for az I said in A sonett befǫr,
lӱk az þe shadow folloith A man kontӱnewa⟨lly⟩ whǫr soever hee
doth go,[3] so A flatterer applieth to krowch ⌜follow⌝ and pleaz
wher ⟨he⟩ thinketh to gain any good þerby. and az þe *Camelion*
will when hee l⟨isteth⟩ turn him self into any kolowr but whӱt,
so will A flatterer play a⟨ny⟩ pạrtz sạv honest pạrts.[4] well I
will now return to my purpǫz agayn.

When I had travelled þǫz dyverz and fǫrsaid kuntreyz, and
returned into ⟨Eng⟩land agayn, I wrǫt in prǫz A book of my

---

[1] The passage Whythorne has in mind occurs on f. 23 of Sir Thomas
Elyot's *The Bankette of Sapience*, 1539 (frequently reprinted; *STC* 7630–4),
where under the heading 'Hypocrisy' Elyot wrote: 'Openly to hate or to
loue, more belongeth to a gentyll courage, then to hyde in his countenaunce
what his herte thinketh.'

[2] Proverbial; Tilley T 584.

[3] Proverbial; Tilley S 263. For Whythorne's 'Sonett befǫr' see p. 29.

[4] This phrase (Tilley C 222) occurs in one of Whythorne's favourite books,
William Baldwin's *Treatise of Morall Phylosophie*, 1547 (*STC* 1253), Part IV,
sig. Q4ᵛ. For direct references to the volume see pp. 165 and 223.

travell and of þe things þat I no⟨ted⟩ in þe tým of my travell,
and also of þe oriʒiᴵnᴵall, and beginning of pe⟨o⟩p⟨ull⟩ of þoz
kuntreyz, and after þe wrýting þerof, I mąd A breef rehersall
⟨þerof⟩ in meeter (being requested þerto by A frend of mýn)
which heer folloeth ⟨and⟩ at þe end þerof, I do ʒoin A Sonett,
wherin I inkliuded my họl nąm—

My long viaʒ þat yow wold know, in proʒ I did endýt,
with sirkumstans what I did nọt, and so þe sąm did wryt.
which wẹr to long in vers to set, and tediouz for to read,
wherfọr breefly I wrýt yow þis, to serv in þ'họþherz stead.
*From*ᵃ *Troinovant¹ I took my kowrs, my cast to Douer strand,*
and fownd A ship which brouht mee soon, in Caleiz to tąk land,
whẹr English Briuts hąu gouerned, þe spạs of many yeerz,
mawgre þeir Gallik enemiez, az by rekordz appee[r]z.
passing Flanders by dyverz towns, fair builded for to see,
Az Bridʒes, and great Gaunt also, whọz fąmz in storiez bee,
also Brabant, whọz wurþý fąm, throhowt Eurọp doth sownd,
for Sezars sąk, and rich trim towns, þat þạr ar to be fownd.
az Brusels whẹr þat Carolus, þe emprowr dwelleth mọst,
whọz koort for great and sumptiusnes exselleth not in kost.
az lovain, whẹr students repair, for learning þạr to get,
az Macklin, whẹr lawyerz do keep, þeir terms, þeir gains to fet.
I kąm t'Andwarp, whọz mạrts do mąk him self hee skantly knowz
Nor any oþers by whọz means hiz great welth daily growz.
Ðe peopull in all þẹz kuntreiz, do loov to drink karows,
and such az wilnot do þe sąm, þei kạr not for A lows.²
when in þis kuntrei I had bin, þe tým of half A yeer
my viaʒ þen I farder took, az now it shall appeer
To Trikt þat standz vpon þe Mąz, and þerfọr Mastrikt hiht,
from whens þe great, and fat Salmons, ar mąd to tąk þeir fliht,
to þ'aunsient Siti of Coleyn, þen did I tąk my way,

ᵃ MS. reads 'Fron'.

¹ Troynovant, or New Troy, was the legendary name given to the city
founded by Brute on the site of London. Whythorne here inserted a marginal
note, 'lōdō.' Another marginal jotting reads: '*Ðis waz written in þe beginning
of queen Mạries reing.*'
² Proverbial; Tilley L 472.

which iz þe first of Germany, az peopull þar do say,
it standz on þat famowz river, þat Rhene.^a *iz kald pardy,*
of which þe wŷn Rhenish hath nam, bekawz it grows þarby.
Ðe Germans or^b *Almans know yee, be peopull riud and stowt,*
and lŷk az þoz befor spok of, þei loov to drink all owt.
From Colen, went I þen to Mentz, and from þens to Frankfort
to see what cheer þ'English men kept, þat þŷþer did rezort.
From þens I past to Worms, and so þe siti' of Spŷrz vnto,
and after þat over þe Rhen, in hŷ Almayn did go.
til I kam to þe town of Vlms, wher Danuby doth run,
which rŷver for hiz greatnes hath, þe fam in Evrop wun.
*Not far ⟨from þis fair⟩ town ⟨þer⟩ iz þat weishorn*¹ *⟨ha⟩th to nam* **20ᵛ**
ny to þe way to great A⟨ws⟩purg A siti of great fam.
Ðis weishorn heer I do now towch, bekawz it iz my nam,
for weis iz whŷt, and horn iz plain, who so will know þe sam.
*when I in Awspurg did arŷv, þe Roman king þar was,*²
for stat affairz of þat kuntrey, þe which I heer let pas.
from Awspurg went I to Isburg passing þe mountains hy,
termed þe Alps, and þar did see, wher snow all þ'yeer doth ly
In Iseburg town for þe most part, iz Ferdinandos be'ing,
who broþer iz to þe Emprowr and of þe Romans king.
when þat I went from fŷn Iseburg, to Trenta þen I kam,
which iz þe first of Italy, az þar doth go þe fam.
in which sitty þe langwaȝes indiffrent ar to all,
Both Alman and Italien, eevn az on toong doth fall.
Ðe plaines of þe Almans trad, heer did I leav behynd
for when I enterd Italy streiht way I did such fŷnd,
who bianby my witts did try what dros þerin did grow,
but for knowleȝ of þeir mannerz, A frend to mee did show.

---

^a The full stop is probably unintentional.   ^b Superscript '&'.

---

¹ The town of Weissenhorn is about 10 miles south-east of Ulm.
² Ferdinand I, the brother of Charles V, bore the title of King of the Romans. He arrived at Augsburg at the end of Dec. 1554, to attend the Diet which opened 5 Feb. 1555, and resulted in the Religious Peace of Augsburg of 25 Sept. 1555. Hence Whythorne was probably in Augsburg some time in 1555, early in the year.

From Trent to Pad'oa þen went I, þat famowz town to see,
which for rezort of studi'ents iz, an Vniuersitee,
Venis, from hens iz no great way, who lord iz over all,
þe kuntrey þat iz þar abouts, and towns both great and small
not only of þoz kuntreiz but of Candy and Cipres,
which Ilandz bee both great and ek, possest with great riches.
from Venis by hiz golf I went Ferrara þen vnto,
which sity standz in Lombardy, ny to þe river of Po.
from hens to þe town of Vrbŷn, I after took my way,
of which þe book namd þe Courtier,[1] doth many praizes say,
þen past I Abruzzo vnto, which provins parsell is,
of on of þe Sicils, now namd, þe realm of Napolis.
but er I kam to Napolis, I past by many towns,
and dŷverz kraggy mountains hy, besŷdz þe vàls & downs.
az þe mountains kald Appenin, which do devŷd in too,
all Italy, eevn ny þe midz, from þ'on end þ'oþer to.
in Abruzzo, I went vnto, Ciuita di Chieti,
which þe Italien map also, nams Citta de chieri,
at Butturno fiume when I, from þens shiuld go or pas,
on pikbak kari'ed for money, over þe flood I was.
also for honest kumpany, I forst waz þar to spy,
to keep vs from þe valiant theevz, þat by þe way did ly.
and az it chaunsed to my lott, good fellowz I did fynd,
by whoz good guŷd I past so saf, az I dezi'erd in mynd.
till wee arŷvd at Capua, þe aunsi'ent fair sity,
and so in þ'end wee kam vnto, þe siti'of Napoli.
whoz gallantnes and statly port, doth seem þat heertofor,
when forrein powr þar bar no sway, of welth it had great stor.
But now it governd iz by þoz, who Hesper ᵃ do posses,[2]
to hiz mishap for þat all hiz, þey seas not to oppres.

ᵃ A line is drawn above and below this word, with ⟨S⟩pain written in the margin.

[1] Whythorne refers to Castiglione's *The Courtyer*. He probably read the Italian original before the appearance of Sir Thomas Hoby's translation in 1561 (*STC* 4778).

[2] In the margin Whythorne wrote: '⟨þ⟩is waz ⟨w⟩ritten ⟨w⟩hen þe. ⟨pri⟩ns of Spain ⟨waz⟩ maried ⟨to⟩ owr ⟨que⟩en ⟨M⟩ary'.

and az þei now in Napulz rayn, so will þei with vs rewll,
if God be not owr help þerfor, and mak þem to rekewll.
retur⟨ni⟩ng bak from Parthenope,[a] taking my ⟨k⟩our⟨s⟩ ⟨b⟩y w⟨e⟩st **21ʳ**
(til I ⟨b⟩y suffrans of þe hiest, in great Brittain shiuld rest)
I past toward þe syty' of Rom, in kumpny of A post,
whoz train kept mee from riud robberz, þat þen did haunt þat kost.
to wrýt of Roma it needz not, for all þe world it knowz,
sum hee do feel þe head þerof, az daily proof it showz.
from hens along Tuscan I went, by many' a val and down,
til I to fair Florens did kum, which iz A goodly town.
not far from hens iz Bononi,[b] whęr students yuz to kum,
but il for vs and þerfor termd, Sepulcrum Anglorum.
(and ęr I kam þis town vnto, þe Appenin mountayns,
I ons mor waz þe sam to klym, forsed to tak þe payns.)
from þens to Mantu'a þen I past, which iz A siti great,
of Lumbardy, whoz wurþi praiz I wilnot now repeat.
þen traveld I to Placensia, and þen to Milano,
which rewled iz by þe Spaniardz, alþouh þeir fos say no.
Into Piemont, þen went I streiht, to þe town of Turin,
(much of which kuntrey þe french king, of lat by fors did win)
Heer waz I ons mor mad to klým, þe Alps and mountains hy
(which sum do kall vpon great kawz, þe fort of Italy)
and þen I past þe mownt Cenis, whęr I did hier A gýd
who safly brouht me over þat, eevn to þe farder sýd.
passing also throuhowt Savoy, which, which[c] diukdom lýk waz
    wount
to be subȝekt to þe sam prins þat kald iz of Piemount,
I travelled to Chambery, which of Savoý iz cheef,
(In dainȝer of sum garrizons, whęr lurketh many' a theef)
and entered into hy Frans, and so went to Lions,
whęr for þe bank, and marchandis, repair dýverz nasi'ons.
If I þe mannerz of þe french, shiuld sumwhat towch and show,
in vain perchauns ye wold it think, bekawz yee do þem know.

---

[a] A line is drawn above and below this word, and *Napuls* is written in the margin.   [b] This word is also placed between lines, and *Bologna* is written opposite in the margin.   [c] Dittography.

no naſion to vs iz mọr known, þen þei I think triuly,
eiþerᵃ by proof, or by report, of þọz þat do þem try.
and french we shall ⌐þem¬ fÿnd alway, inkonstant and bragging,
which to þat realm, hath kawzd th'English plenty of plạgz to
   bring.
If of þe french yee wold mọr know, owr kronikels þen read,
for I breefly, towch but such things, az may stand yow in stead.
from Lions to Paris I went, þat great Sitti to see,
which standeth in þe ÿl of Frạns, whẹr moniument yet bee,
þat shew how þ'Engliſh þạr hạv raind with piuiſſans firmly fixt,
In bọth þe tÿms of owr kings nạmd, þe Henriez fift and sixt.
from Paris, passing Normandÿ ⌐to¬ Amias, þen I kạm,
and to Bullein, which king Henry, þe eiht of viktrowz fạm,
konquerd and kept, with þe kuntrei between þat and Caleis
which so remaind, till gold it gott, which mettall great things weis
after þat I in Caleis town, A few daiz did remain,
mÿ kours I took by surʒing seaz into Britainᵇ again.
whọz ⌐temprat¬ eir, and fertil soil, with althingz els þạr bred
þe lÿk in no ọn kuntrei iz, whẹr I hạv travelled.
Ðe profit got by travelling, þis Sonet þat ensiuth
shall plainly and breefly yow show, þe which tạk yee az triuth.
21ᵛ *my nạm also þee shall heer fÿnd, to print it in yowr brest,*
and þus tạk þat I hạv in þis, fulfilled your request.

        Enklÿn to know þat by travell iz known
        to' attain þe yous of vÿs and of vertew
        not forst þerto shall ye bee, but þe vew
        hoordeth mọr chainʒ whẹr fọr knowleʒ iz grown
        rooting owt hiz kontrary which waz sown
        of þẹz þerfọr, þat, which hath greatest shew
        or which yee lÿk, or ever in yow grew
        may þus awgmented bee, by kropps new mown
        hawzing þem all at will for yowr own stọr
        and þ'ius of þ'ọn will wurk yow wurþy fạm
        toþer will bring yow infamy and shạm

    ᵃ MS. reads 'eizer'.   ᵇ This word is placed between lines with *England*
written in the margin.

sins rạr renowm iz got by vertewz lọr
yeeld not to vẏs þerfọr
who never got to man mọr meed þen þis
heaps of Godz wrath to bring man from hiz blis

By þis fọrsaid Sonet yee may perseiv, þat whatsoever ọn iz enklyned vnto, hee shall by travelling in strainȝ kuntreiz, learn in[a] þe sạm to hạv þe mọr chainȝ, if hee will mark and tạk siur heed of althings þat hee shalbe okkazioned to know in þe tẏm of hiz travell. þe Italiens hạv A saieng þat all þọz nasions which do dwell on þis sẏd þe mountains named þe Alps (which nasions þei do gẏv to nạm *Tramontani*)[1] be but barbarowz, riud, and dull or gros witted. þe which barbarowsnes and riudnes iz mạd syvill by konversing and keeping of þem kompany, & also þat þeir fẏn and subtẏll eir, in þat þeir being þạr doth dry vp and extingwish þọz impediments þat do dull þe witts of such *Tramontaniez*, az do kontinew any long tẏm in þeir kuntrey. If þe Italiens had any saieng also, þat þe Tramontanies miht be mạd wẏz also emong þem azwell az syvill and witty, I wold hạv lyked þat bọst of þeirz very well. but heer my thinks yow wọld demaund of mee what diffrens I think to be between witt and wizdom, forsooth yee miht hạv demaunded þat question of mee befọr at þat plạs whẹr I did sett þe sonett of *Wilfull will*,[2] but seing it kummeth now in question, I awnswer and say vnto yow þat I tạk þis diffrens to bee between þem. witt iz A thing þat kummeth by nạtiur, wherwith akkording to þe sharpnes or dulnes þerof, wee do konseiv and vnderstand althings þat wee do see or hear, and also wherby wee do imaȝin & invent things both good and evl, but of it self it iz raþer prọn to to[b] eevl þen goodnes, and þerfọr in þat konsyderasion, it owht to be rewled by reazon.[c]

Now sir wisdom iz A great good gift of God, sumtẏm sent by

---

[a] Written over 'of'.   [b] Dittography.   [c] Superscript 'wizdom'.

[1] Professor F. P. Wilson has pointed out a similar passage in Richard Argall's 'Address to the Reader' before Gerard Legh's *The Accidence of Armoury*, 1562 (*STC* 15388).
[2] See p. 38.

inspirasion, and so tawht by such means az hee hath appointed
and assingned, wherby wee do ȝudȝ þe good from þe eevl, and
also exersẏz þe good and reȝekt þe eevl. and bekawz yee shall
hạv þe mọr kawz to be satisfied in þis matter, I will heer rehers
vnto yow þe opinions of sum philosofers, and also plạses þat I
hạv taken owt of þe skriptiurs, by þe which yee may þe better
perseiv þe diffrens between witt and wisdom. *Galen* (þe mọst
exsellent phizision) saith, wizdom kannot be profitabull to A
fooll, nor witt to him þat yuzeth it not. *Plato*, (þe devẏn philo-
sofer) saith þat wizdom iz þe treaziur of witt, wherwith evry
man owht to enrich him self. also hee saith, dispọz not þy witt,
both to vertiu and vẏs. *Cicero*, (þe mọst eloquent orator) saith
þat Sapiens is the siens of things devẏn and hiumain, which
konsidereth þe kawzes of evry thing. by reazon wherof þat
22ʳ whi⟨ch⟩ iz devẏn shee ⟨sh⟩oeth. *Aristotl* ⟨þe⟩ exsell⟨e⟩nt wẏz
filosofer saith ⟨þat⟩ Sapiens iz þe fowndasion and root of all
nobull and lawdabull things. by ⟨which⟩ wee may win þe good
end and keep vs from everlasting pain. Also hee saith ⟨þat⟩
wizdom is þe knowleȝ of devyn things, and iz þe hed of all oþer
things. Also ⟨hee⟩ saith again. Siens iz had by diligens, but
wizdom and diskresion kummeth fr⟨om⟩ God. In þe .111. salm[1]
it iz þus said, þe beginning of wizdom iz þe fear of ⟨þe⟩ Lord.
And *Salomon*[2] in þe first chapter of hiz book[a] of wizdom saith,
þat wẏzdo⟨m⟩ shalnot enter into A malisiows mẏnd, neyþer
shall dwell in A body þat iz ⟨sub⟩ȝekt to syn. by þis affọrsaid ye
may perseiv þat A witty man may be wicked assoon az good,
and þat A wẏs man iz A perfekt good man. vp⟨on⟩ þis diffrens
between witt and wizdom I mȧd þis sonett folloing—

> *When witt doth seek vẏs to embrạs*
> *þen witt him self doth much defạs*
> *for witt and wizdom diffreth so*
> *az witt from wizdom needs must go*
> *if witt by wizdom rewll in plạs*
> *(as reazon wold it shiuld be so)*

---

[a] MS. reads 'bood'.

[1] Ps. 111. 10.   [2] Wisd. 1. 4.

þen witt so wurking yee shall see
will wurk all well in ech degree,
but if witt wurk withowt wizdom
I dowt what good þerof will kom.

Emong sum sort of peopull it iz A kommen saing[1] now A daiz þat þei be w⟨ẏz⟩ who with þeir subtil and reaching hedz will kumpas þeir matterz beyond ⟨þe⟩ kommen skill. if þei be doon in þe fear of God, þen I say þat þei be wẏz, b⟨ut⟩ if þei be doon in þe kontrary, þen I say, alþoh þei be witty, yet þei be ⟨not⟩ wẏz but wikked, paradventiur ye wold heer mạkᵃ þis distinksion or ad v⟨nto⟩ þis addision which many do now A daiz, who do term þem to be worldly w⟨ẏz.⟩ of þẹz sort of worldly wẏz I do tạk to bee þọz infidelz, or az I may say þei ⟨þat⟩ know neyþer God nor Dyvell thinking þat þe Sowll doth dy with þe body, w⟨ho⟩ wurk and bring to pas so many treazons, konspyrazies, murderz, felloni⟨es⟩ with all þe far fecht evels þat be wrouht in þis world. of þe which sort ⟨þe⟩ holy sk[r]iptiur[2] speaketh whẹr it iz written þat þe childern of þis world (or ⟨of⟩ darknes) be wyzer in þeir ȝenerasion þen þe childern of liht. whẏll þi⟨s⟩ matter ran þus in my hed, þẹr also kạm to my mynd to wrẏt sumthing m⟨ọr⟩ þerof, in þe which az I do towch þe oriȝinall and effekt of witt, so do I al⟨so⟩ of will and reazon, by whom will & witt is also rewled. and þus it iz—

Of nạtiurz gifts witt iz þe cheef
which doth desern both good and ill
and both witt wurks (for to be breef)
az reazon rewlz, or wilfull will.
let reazon þạrfọr rewll witt still
lest will in witt, doth wurk hiz will.[3]

Bekawz I hạv heer tofọr towched sumwhat of þe government of Reazon & will in mankynd, it seemeth vnto me þat I shiuld

---

ᵃ MS. has dots both above and below the 'a'.

---

[1] Whythorne seems to be reporting an attitude that had not been successfully distilled into a proverb.   [2] Luke 16. 8.
[3] This is very similar to Heywood's line 'Reason laboureth wyll, to wyn wyls consent' (1546 *Proverbs* I v, sig. B2).

not pas any furder in þis diskowrs till I hạv shewd yow sumwhat
mọr plainly of þeir properties an⟨d⟩ governments, wherfọr I
will heer shew vnto yow þe wurdz of my old master mr Haywood,
þe which hee did wryt in A komedy or play¹ þat hee mạd of þe
pạrts of man, in þe which after þat he hath mạd Reazon to
chalenӡ vnto him self þe siuperiorite and government of all þe
parts of Man, and also to kommaund althings lyving vpon þe
earth, hee mạketh reazon to say þus (in meeter⟨⟩) for him self.
*And þe diffrens between man þe kommaunder, and beas⟨ts⟩ being
by man kommaunded, iz only Reazon in man, þe disserner of
good and ill, þe good in man elekted by me, and þ'ill in man by mee
reӡekted. man obeing mee shỳnth in exsellensy, and disobeing mee,*
22ᵛ *shewth mans insolensy. Now sin⟨s I⟩ reazon am þ'⟨o⟩nly qu⟨a⟩lyte,
þa⟨t q⟩ualifiet man ⟨in s⟩uch A temp⟨er⟩ans az setteth man in plạs
of prinsipalite abọv all beasts to stand in goveᴦrᴨnans who but I
over man shiuld him self advans, to govern lỳkwyz, sins I bring
man þerto, and keep man þerin doing az I bid him do.* when reazon
hath þus said for him self, þen kummeth in will, who dispiuteth
with reazon for þe siuprẹm government in man, whervpon
in þe end þei both ar dryven to graunt þat man kan do
nothing withowt will, and withowt reazon man kan do no
good thing.

Now peradventiur yow wold say þat I hạv tarried long enoh
in þis matter, and þerfọr to return to my wordz spoken befọr of
þe Italien kustoms and eir which mạks þe *Tramontaniez* sỳvell
and witti. if þe Italiens had had A proverb emong þem, how þe
tramontaniez myht be mạd wỳz emong þem azwell az witti, I
wold hạv lỳked þat very well. heer perhaps ye wold demaund of
mee, why þe tramontaniez shiuld not learn to be wỳz emong
þem azwell az witty to þe which I do awnswer, God forfend but
þat þạr shiuld be many wỳz peopl in so great A kuntrey az Italy
iz. who by þeir wỳz wurdz and deedz shiuld teach oþerz to be

---

¹ This interlude of Heywood's is unknown except for this passage and
Whythorne's earlier statement that it was written at the instigation of Archbishop Cranmer (p. 23). It is strange that Whythorne copied these lines as
prose, despite his statement that they are 'in meeter'.

wȳz, alþoh þey hạv (az I tạk to be emong þe wurser sort of þem)
A proverb which saieth þus—

Vn forastiero Italienato ⎫ þe english ⎫ A strainȝer Italienạt.
Vn Diauol' є incarnato ⎰ wherof iz ⎰ iz A Divell inkarnạt.[1]

I wilnot tạk vpon mee to ȝudȝ any wurs of þe Italiens þen
þeir own proverbz do lead mee vnto. and konserning þe learning
of wizdom þạr emong þem,[a] I hạv know[n] þọz þat hạv doon it,
but how? mary it wẹr such who did but smatter in sum kyndz of
vȳses befọr þei kạm into Italy, þe which when þei did see vȳses
so abownd in þat kuntrey in so many sorts and waiez, it kawzed
þem to abhor þem for ever after, and so þei in þat respekt
bekạm wȳz. now to return again to þeir proverb of A strainȝer
Italienạt, and if þat be trew in deed az þeir proverb saith, þen [I]
wold not for A good nobull þat any of owr English women shiuld
be Italienạt, for it iz an old saing emong vs þat þẹr iz no dyvell
so bad az A shee divell,[2] and þen þe sweet kumpany þat wee
shiuld hạv with þem wold turn all to sowrnes and bitternes. for
þer iz A proverb[3] emong þe Italiens of þe inkonstansy of women
konserning loov þe which doth begin þus—

L'amor di Donna ⎫ ⎫ Đe loov of A woman ⎫
E'l uino dell fiasco ⎪ ⎧ Đe English ⎫ and wȳn of þe flaggon ⎪
A la sera' є buonna ⎬ ⎨ wherof iz þus ⎰ at niht iz good but þan ⎬
Nella mattina guasto ⎭ by morn it iz vndon ⎭

---

[a] MS. reads 'þen'.

[1] Tilley E 154.

[2] The proverb in this form has not been traced; see Tilley W 641 and
W 648.

[3] A very similar proverb occurs in J. Sanforde's translation of Ludovico
Guicciardini, *Houres of Recreation . . . the Garden of Pleasure*, 1576 (*STC*
12465), p. 206:

> Amor di putana, e vin de fiasco,
> Da mattina buono, da sera guasto.

> The loue of a harlot, and wyne of a flagon,
> is good in the morning, and naught in the euening.

There is no doubt that Whythorne knew and used this book. (See pp. 174–7.)
But in quoting this proverb and the variant which follows he seems to have
been drawing upon his own memory of Italian proverbs picked up during
his travels in Italy.

Oþerwyz of þe sạm—

Ðe ardant loov of women all, and pleazant wẏn of þe flaggon,
at eev iz good to tast, and þen bẏ morn t'iz pauld, and quẏt vndon.

Ðey hạv an oþer rẏm or proverb foloing þis affọrsaid which iz
mad against and in reprọch of þe dishonest sort of women, and
it beginneth þus. *l'amor di puttana, el vento del culo, ϵt sono di*
campana, son tutti tre vno. þe english of þe which proverb I
wilnot heer english for þe reverens þat I do bear vnto þe họl sex
of womankẏnd. by þat affọrsaid yow may perseiv welinoh, þat and
if ọn of owr kuntrei women shiuld be Italienat þan shee wold
not only bekum A Divl inkarnat, þat iz to say eevn inkorporat
within her, but also wold never be konstant in loov. wold not þis
trow yee mạk þat wee sely English men wold think þat þer wẹr
(no purgatory quod yow, nay þat þer wẹr) no oþer hell but in þis
world? Wheþer yee wold think so or no, if yee wẹr hand fast
and so trobled with ọn of þem A littl whẏll, I beleev ye shiuld
fẏnd it so.

þis matter did molest mee þe mọr, bekawz I hoped to bekum A maried man with þe rest of þat holy estạt, for my hap
23ʳ at þat tẏm waz to be akquainted with A ⟨yoo⟩ng ȝentilwoman
⟨who⟩ not only for her gifts of nạtiur ⟨waz⟩ mans meat,[1] but also
for her gifts of þe mynd, and possibilite of lyving ⟨waz⟩ wurþi
to be looked on and siued to for marriaȝ. at þis tẏm lo, if þe
former goo⟨d o⟩pinion þat I had of my self had not bin az it wẹr
awgmented by þe knowleȝ þ⟨at I⟩ had got by my travell beyond
þe seaz and experiens at họm, my kooraȝ wo⟨ld⟩ hạv bin mar-
velowzly dawnted and abated in þis enterprẏz, bekawz þat ⟨my⟩
abilite and welth waz so small in komparizon of herz. yet after I
had konsy⟨dered⟩ A littl whẏll with mẏ self, and kalling to mynd
how A great many þat I ⟨did⟩ know had achẏved az great
enterpryzes az þat, and þat faint hart never g⟨ot⟩ fair lady[2] I
determyned with mẏ self to gẏv þe assawt whatsoever bekạm
⟨in⟩ þe end þerof, and vpon þat rezoliusion, after þat I had
furnished my self ⟨with⟩ konvenient apparell and ȝiuels so well

---

[1] Tilley's earliest example of this phrase is dated 1664.
[2] For earlier use of this proverb, see p. 47.

az I kowld (with þe gloriowz she⟨w⟩ of þe which emong oþer
things, A yoong mayden must be woed) I took on m⟨e⟩ þis fọrsaid konquest and enterprẏz. abowt þis tẏm I had red a prety
s⟨ai⟩eng, þe which to follow I thowht shiuld be very expedient for
mee to do, no⟨t⟩ only at altẏms els, but cheefly at þis tẏm. þe
which saieng þus beginnet⟨h,⟩ *Fair speech in prezens, with good
report in absens, and lẏk mannerz in fellow⟨ship⟩ obtaineth great
frendship.*[1] and bekawz I wold print þe substans of þis saing
þ⟨e⟩ deeper in my remembrans, I mạd it þus in meeter—

*Đe pleazant and þe ӡentill speech, wher kountnans lẏk doth show,
kourteowz behavour and ӡestiur, whẹr mannerz mẏld do grow,
Of althings in absens to mạk þe best with good report,
doth win and keep faithfull frendship, whẹr reazon doth rezort.*

At þis tẏm I had gotten ij or iij prety ditties mạd of loov, þe
which bekawz I durst not delyver to her in wryting for fear of
afterklaps[2] I wold sing þem ⟨of⟩ten tẏms vnto her on þe virӡinals
or liut, by þe which I mạd my first en⟨trans⟩ into my sewt vnto
her, and az I saw how shee lẏked to heer þem þen wọld ⟨I⟩
enter into talk of þe sạm matter in such sort az I did see þat tẏm
and plạs ⟨waz⟩ konvenient for þe purpọz. þen in stead of geving
of rẏch gifts, I did supp⟨ly⟩ þe want of þe sạm (akkording to my
skill, and az tẏm served) with all oþer kẏ⟨ndz⟩ of favorz sery-
moniez, and dewtyfulnes appertaining to A loverz servises[;] in
þe which I did observ þe dispozision and deliht of my loov,
bekawz þat þat ⟨ser⟩vis which iz akseptabull to ọn wilnot be so
to an oþer, never þe les I deter⟨mi⟩ned with my self þat if I did
not obtain my siut (what soever I did or said þ⟨at⟩ I wold do for
her sạk) þat I wold not bekum A riht *Cupidian* in hart. ⟨In⟩ þis
sort of siut, when I had spent A sertain tẏm, my hap waz to hạv
þis o⟨r⟩ þe lẏk awnswer of her.

*I thank yow for your good will, but I prai yow be k⟨on⟩tent
and spẹk nomọr vnto mee of your siut, for þat possibilite of lyving
wh⟨ich⟩ I hạu, iz not so sertain, but þat it dependeth whọly vpon þe*

---

[1] The source of this 'prety saieng' has eluded the editor; it may be a version of Epictetus, *Fragments*, no. 155.

[2] Proverbial; Tilley A 57.

goodwi⟨ll⟩ and pleaziur of my parents, and þerfor if I shiuld not be
rewled by þem in geving my konsent in maryaȝ I shiuld hau
nothing of þem to lyv by heerafter. þis awnswer of herz neiþer
pleazed mee, nor greatly displeazed mee, for I am never greatly
trobled with any thing þat I wold kum to pas, lenger þen I am
in dowt þerof. and I being þus frendly said nay, replied to her
again and said, I do thank yow for yowr ȝentl awnswer and nay,
to my request now, yow must gẏv mee leav to withdraw by littl
and littl az I may, sum of þe great affeksion which hiþerto I hav
vnfaynedly born vnto yow, lest þat þe burdein þerof, not being
sumwhat by yow eazed it myht turn mee to mor greef þen I shalbe
well abull to bear. vpon þe which wordz of mẏn I did perseiv by
sum wordz of herz, þat shee waz ⌐not⌐ willing þat I shiuld withdraw any part of þe goodwill, which I seemed to bear her. for
þe holding of þe which, wheþer it waz kounterfett or earnest,
she yowzed such frendship and goo⟨d⟩ kountenans to wardz mee
þen, az I began to dowt of her former awnswer, wh⟨e⟩þer it waz
to try mee how much I loved her, or az þe property of sum
women iz to refiuz þat which ⌐iz⌐ offerd þem. and ar willing to
tak hold of þat which iz going from þem (az I waz þen from her)
23ᵛ and þerfor I not willing to looz her goodwill if I mih⟨t ha⟩v it,
partl⟨y for⟩ þe prezent kommo⟨di⟩te þat I had by her (for shee
waz my skoller) but cheefly in hop to hav her such A ⟨skoll⟩er
[(]az I shiuld hav had still) I seemed to gratify evry ȝot of her
frendship which shee yvzed toward mee, and mad her beleev
þat what soever I had said befor, my loov shiuld kontinew alway
firm toward her. but wo waz mee, þis fier kowld not be kept
so klos, but þat sum sparks wer perseived to fly abrod,[1] wherby
at lenkth þis loov of owrz waz detekted and know[n], to dyverz
in þe hows wher wee wer. wherfor þer waz sekret means fownd
not only to hinder owr loovz but also to separat þem. emong þe
which þis waz on, it waz told my loov þat I had reported sumthing of her þe which did sownd very ill vnto her, whervpon
(not charȝing mee with my fawt vnto her, wherby I miht hav

---

[1] An adaptation of several proverbial expressions.

awnswerd and satisfied her) shee grew into A sodein strainꝫnes, and glumming kowntenans towardz mee, and also wold tąk okkazions befǫr þe pąrty who had so insensed her, to gẏv mee overthwart langwaꝫ. when I perseived þis, & had learned þe kawz þerof, I grew into sum perplexite þerwith bekawz shee wold konseiv such A great displesiur against me, and wold not put mee to my purgasion, yet I took it to bee but þe pąrt of A shrew, and þat A shrew profitabull may be born withall of A man reaznable.[1] wherfǫr to eaz my mẏnd I mad þis sonet foloing—

> *Shall I this wo sustain*
> *which iz kum by mischauns*
> *and hąv no eaz again*
> *but still to hąu grevauns*
> *Ðen pasi'ens great þe salv must bee*
> *wherwith to heal þis sǫr*
> *Till þat my God will sent to mee*
> *A remedi þerfǫr.*

After þat my shrewish loov had miskomyvzed[2] mee A sertain of tẏmes az pąrtly iz affǫrsaid, at lenkth I took hart A grąs,[3] and told her when she did mizywz mee, þat if she wold not leav þǫz ꝫẏbz and tawnts, shee wold drẏv mee to do þat which I waz very loth to do. but þęz wordz wold not help ǫn ꝫǫt, and shee not so satisfied did not lett to blast owt dispẏtfully vnto mee such sekret wordz az I had told her in kounsell. whervpon I fell owt with her (befǫr her kownseller) in such sort, az if I had not had sum hǫld in her hart, shee wold never hąv bin freendz with mee again, for þe longer I do bear inꝫiuriez, þe greatter iz my fiury when I do lett it slip. (I am not ingnorant of þe opinion which twoo sorts of peopull hąv of mee, þat iz to say, þǫz whoz willz do surmount þeir reazons, and such whǫz reazons rewll þeir willz. þe first sort do say, I wilbe soon angry, and þe sekond sort say þat az I am no kommen gyver [of] okkazions of offenses

---

[1] Proverbial; Tilley S 414.
[2] Possibly *miscognized*, failed to appreciate (*OED*).
[3] Proverbial; Tilley H 332.

to oþerz, and az I lẏk not to offend, so I am loth to bear many offences. assiuredly þe sekond sort be not somuch deseived in [mee] az þe first). but again to my purpoz[a]—by þis afforsaid yee may perseiv þat when frends in falling owt do bewray þe sekrets þat hath past between þem in þe tẏm of þeir frendlynes how eazi A matter it iz to mạk þem fall at A ȝar, and how hard A matter it iz to rekonsẏll þem togiþer again. *Jesus sirach*[1] saith in *Cap*. xxij. who so kasteth A stọn at þe birdz fraith þem away, and hee þat blasfemeth hiz frend breaketh frendship. þouh drewest A swoord at þi frend yet dispair not, for þow maist kum again to þi frend, if hee speaketh sowerly, fear not for yee may bee agreed togiþer again, exsept it be þat þow blasfẹm him, disdain him, open hiz sekrets, and wound him traitero⌐w⌐sly, for all such things shall drẏv away frendship. Heer will I begin whẹr I left affọr towching þe ạȝes of mankẏnd, what hiumorz hạv mọst dominion in evry ạȝ, for az þe blood raineth cheefly in þe ȝiuventiut, þe which iz from .xxv. vntill .xl. yeerz of ạȝ, which iz kalled þe sekond and last part of þe yoongmans aȝ. so þe hiumour nạ[med] kolẹr doth cheef rain in þis sekond and last part of þe yoongmans aȝ. and at þis tẏm waz I entred iij or iiij yeerz into þis ạȝ. wherfọr az anger and rạȝing iz A kommen matter with þem in whom þis hiumour kôler doth abound, so owht all such az be trobled and oppressed with it, to korrekt it by þe rewlz of fyzik, and to brydl þe fiery effekts þat it wurketh with þe strong bitt[2] of reazon.

Now when I had bethouht me A littl whẏll of þat which was of lạt past, I did sumwhat mizlẏk with þe sạm, yet rạþer for þat I kowld not þen temper my self better þen I did whẹrby I miht hạv hindred þe stạt of my ⌐helth⌐ and also hạv purchased 24[r] mee sum trobull, þen for þat I fell owt with her who alþoh I gạv her warning ⟨aff⟩ọr, wold needz g⟨ẏv m⟩ee kawz to b⟨rea⟩k my pasiens. ⟨A⟩ konsiderasion of þe har⟨m⟩ þat miht be gotten by

---

[a] Whythorne inserted a mark like an exaggerated parenthesis, here replaced by a dash.

---

[1] Ecclus. 22. 20–22. [2] This proverb has not been traced.

¶The second part of Songes com-
pofed by Thomas VVhythorne, conteyning Songes for fower voyces.

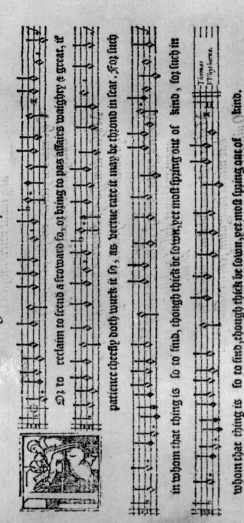

Do to reclaim to fecond a forward fo, or bying to pas affairs vonigbry & great, if

patience chefly doth work it fo, as vertue rate it may be thono in fear. For fuch

in whom that thing is fo to find, though thick be fowin, yet moft fpring out of kind, for fuch in

Thomas Whythorne.

whom that thing is fo to find, though thick be fowin, yet moft fpring out of kind.

The gifts of nature well difpofo are pleafant to the fight, the like of for- tune rule the reft, be it in

þ⟨i⟩s anger afforsaid kawzed mee to ⟨wrýt⟩ þis sonett foloing, to
put mee in mýnd to bewar of þe lýk heerafter—

> *In weall and wo be pasient*
> *let not fiury þi hart posses*
> *for shee alwaiz þe sam doth rent*
> *and brings it oft in great distres*
> *wherfor if þow wilt lýv in rest*
> *in nowýz harbour such A gest*

After þat I had mad þis forsaid sonett, I mad þez ij sonets
foloing, in þe komm⟨en⟩dasion of pasiens, bekawz it iz A vertiu
þat A great many hav need of—

> *To overkum bi pasiens wher wrongs hav bin offred,*
> *or to be staid þerwith from will þat wold be reven3ed*
> *to fynd owt such, in þis said sort possest with þis vertew*
> *iz hard to do, so az þe sam hav alway perfekt shew.*

Oþerwýz of þe sam.

> *For to reklaim to frend A froward fo,*
> *or bring to pas affairz waihty and great*
> *If pasiens cheefly doth wurk it so,*
> *az vertew rar it may [bee] thrond in seat.*
> *for such in whom, þat thing iz so to fýnd*
> *þoh thik be sown yet most spring owt of kynd.*

In þe mean whýll þat I waz debating with my self of þe passions past, ⟨and⟩ devyzing vpon pasiens (of þe which an owns
and half miht hardly hav b⟨in⟩ fownd in vs both at þat instant
of owr forsaid brawll) þis forsaid broill wa⟨z⟩ A littl over blown,
and my 3entilwoman had so well konsýdered of þe matt⟨er⟩ þat
shee akknowle3ed to hav geven A littl to much kreditt to þe
makbat[1] affo⟨r⟩said, wherfor shee seemed to repent her for that
shee had so misywzed mee, a⟨nd⟩ I mad semblant lýkwýz
lýkwýz[a] to aksept þe sam in good part, so þat aft⟨er⟩ þis rekonsiliasion (for A short tým) þe falling owt of loverz waz þe

---

[a] Dittography.

[1] *Makebate,* one who creates discord (*OED*).

rene⟨wal⟩ of loov.[1] þe which being espyed þer waz alwais means
fownd to hinder ⟨þe⟩ sạm, and þat it miht be þe siurer put owt of
dowt, and my nọz owt of ʒoi⟨nt⟩[2] þer waz sekret means wrouht
to bring an heir of great lyving to be A siut⟨or⟩ vnto her for
marriaʒ (her faþer waz A lawyer, and þerfọr I had þe les họp to
hạv gotten hiz goodwill in þis enterprýz, if I had siued vnto him
for it. þe proverb saith þat lýk will to lýk.[3] and þen how shiuld I
hạv brouht hiz goodwill on my sýd? for az þe lyvings of þọz of
my profession be gotten of þem þat do delýt in konkord, so do þe
lawyerz lýv cheefly by þọz who do delýt in diskord. I may say
welenowh þat þei do delýt in diskord, who raþer þen þei will
yeeld to A reaznabull agreemen[t] in kawzes of lawing, will for þe
furdering of þeir self wills, by laweng fill þe lawyerz purses and
mȧk þem selvz beggerz). þis affórsaid towching lawyerz bringeth
to my remembrans, how þat ȯn said to mee on A tým after þis
said broill betwee[n] my loov and mee, þat and if ⟨h⟩ee ⟨h⟩ad
b⟨in⟩ in my kạs and plạs when tým waz, þat þer waz neiþer
ʒenti[l]man nor lawyer shiuld hạv feared him for doing of þat
which I miht hạv doon. why quod I to him do yow know þat
matter, yee quoþ hee þat I do. þen keep kounsell quoþ I.[a] when
I had sumwhat konsidered of þe premisses, & perceyved þat I
shiuld never bring mý loving purpọz to A better pas, being also
perswạdid þat þe proverb is tr⟨ew⟩ which saith þat. *Be it far or
be it ny, mariaʒ iz alwaiz desteny.*[4] and þat my dest⟨e⟩ny waz
not to hạv her to my wýf, I forsed my will to yeeld to reazon,
seeming to to[b] sett þe forgoing of þat liht, which I kowld kum by
and enʒoi. Whervpon I mạd þis sonett folloing—

24[v] *In frendz o⟨f⟩ ech estạt l⟨ook⟩ for equalite[5] to bee ⟨a⟩lway*
Of mýnd, of welth, and honourz ẹk, els soon þei swarv and pạrt
away.

---

[a] MS. here has a closing parenthesis.   [b] Dittography.

---

[1] Proverbial; Tilley F 40.
[2] Proverbial; Tilley N 219.
[3] Proverbial; Tilley L 286.
[4] This rhymed form of the proverb occurs in Heywood, 1546 edn. I iii,
sig. A4 verso; see also Tilley W 232.
[5] Proverbial; compare Tilley F 761.

Ðe better to pas quietly away with þis said trobull, I kalled to my remembrans A prety perswazion þat A ʒentilman ons ywzed vnto A frend of hiz whom hee per⟨s⟩eived to be trobled in mýnd for þat hee kowld not obtain and posses hiz loov, to ⟨w⟩hom hee said þat hee in hiz daiz had bin A siuter to aboov twenty women, and þe forgoing of þem all did not somuch grýv and vex him az did þe prezent possessing of her, whom hee þen had. and so per-adventiur miht I hav had A kawz to say also. for goodz and pos-sessions be not alwaiz parmanent and abýding with sum, and also wee may see many týms þat yoong saints do proov to be old Divels.[1] also to furder my konseit and help mee now at A pinch, I kalled to my remembrans an old proverb which saith þat absens kawzeth forgetfulnes,[2] which saieng iz to be embrased emong þoz loverz which kannot enʒoy þeir loovz. and I warrant yow I having sum kawz at þat prezent to remember it, I for my part wold not dispýz þe sam. for az the old proverb saith, I thank God & my kunning.[3] I waz no sooner dizpozed to leav þis said plas, but I did know wher to hav az good enterteinment in an oþer (I mean for profitt and not for loov) þe which new servis waz with A nobull man,[4] who I fownd my very good lord, and also I fow[nd] hiz lady and wýf my very good lady and mistres (and better for þat shee waz my skoller) but now to my purpoz.

þis my said lady and mistres, had dýverz ʒentilwomen, who waited vpon her in her hows, and my lot waz lýkwyz to bee her cheef waiting man (az fortiun in þis point waz ever very favora-bull vnto mee) emong þez said ʒentilwomen I wold fram my self to bee mery sumtýms (bekawz þat solas slaketh sorowz)[5]

---

[1] Proverbial; Tilley S 33. [2] Proverbial; a variant of Tilley F 596.

[3] This phrase is unrecorded by Tilley and is not found in other standard collections of proverbs.

[4] For evidence that this nobleman was Lord Ambrose Dudley (c. 1528–90), fourth son of the Duke of Northumberland and later Earl of Warwick, see Appendix II. He had been imprisoned in July 1553, following on the failure of his father's plot to make Lady Jane Grey queen of England, but was released with a royal pardon in Oct. 1554. His wife and Whythorne's pupil was Elizabeth, daughter of Sir Gilbert Tailboys and heiress of George, Lord Tailboys.

[5] This phrase has not been traced.

and az þe manẹr waz þen to hạv by nạmz emong fellowz, so I
kall ọn of þem governowr, an oþer frend, an oþer Awnt, an oþer
sister, and þe yoongest of þem all, I did kall moþer, (all þẹz wẹr
my lạḋz ȝentilwomen). A littl befọr þis tẏm my lady waz with
chẏld,[1] and bekawz shee ment to be delivered þerof in þe
kuntrey, shee brouht with her owt of London A midwyf, of
whom shee mạd sum akkownt of. þen to mạk vp þe họl number
of þọz of whom I do folloingly wrẏt of in meeter, I must tell
yow þat my lady had A Duch woman who having bin owt of
her witts, kowld never so rekover þem again, but þat shee
seemed to be A fooll, and þerfọr az A fooll waz shee esteemed
and taken. of þẹz seven I[2] wrọt in meeter az folloeth—

Az, for her aunsientnez shee standz aboov all in degree,
þe matrons witt of .A.p.t. so stains þe rest I see.
And ẹk þe kountnans of her nees, such port hath in þe plạs,
þat simpull harts it wold appall, and vtterly defạs.
S. yet of mood mọr pleazant iz, not stạly in her cheer,
but of such kumlines az may, mạk bashfull frendz appeer.
Ðoh .p.t.h. of speech iz slow, her witt iz quick and kloz,
her lẏvly hew blẏnd Cupidz knihts will rẹv from þeir repọz.
My littl moþer (what wold yee mọr) Shee must not be forgot,
it will yoong prik þat wil be' A thorn,[3] and þat yee know god wot.
J.s. delẏtth (az Roman dạms) in reazning and in lọr,
who þat vnlearnd with her wil talk, must yeeld or taint þe shọr.

my ladies Fool

My plodding pọd, my .T. n. k. by kok shee ȝois in doggs
She steals þem meat, tearingt with teeth, to mạk þem fat az hoggs.[4]

---

[1] Since there were no living children of this marriage, the pregnancy does
not help to date this poem exactly.

[2] In this poem each of the gentlewomen receives a couplet, ostensibly in the
order in which Whythorne mentioned them above. In the case of 'Governor',
'Sister', and 'my ladies Fooll', three letters are used in place of their names,
a clue insufficient to reveal their identities. The letters fit the scansion, and
are unlikely to represent initials since double Christian names are almost
non-existent in mid-sixteenth-century England. In the couplets for 'Aunt'
and the midwife the letters used are probably initials of their names.

[3] Proverbial; Tilley T 232.   [4] Proverbial; Tilley H 483.

But now þouh yee do look þat I, þeir fawts to yow shiuld show,
I refer þat to Momus charʒ, hiz trump such things doth blow,
whọz reprehending brouht him in such loov with godz and stạts,
þat hee wạz tạn by both shiulderz, an thrust owt of þeir gạts.

Ðis sạm *Momus* affọrsa⟨ɪd waz⟩ called þe god o⟨f expostula⟩- 25ʳ
sion, w⟨h⟩ọz kumpany þerfo⟨r⟩ þe godz kowld not well away
withall. Now yee shall vnderst⟨a⟩nd þat þis fọrsa⟨id⟩ nobull man
(my lọrd and master I mean) had so good A lyking of mee at
þe first vew and akquaintans þat he promyzed mee if I wọld
ser⟨v⟩ him but ọn yeer ⟨I⟩ shiuld hạv of him at þe yeerz end
an aniuete of twenty nobuls A yeer d⟨u⟩ring my lẏf tẏm. but
by þat tẏm þe yeer was spent I miht perseiv how v⟨n⟩abull
Fortiun had ywzed him. hee waz þe heir of þe nobull womans
whȯz dawhter I shiuld hạv tawht az iz affọrsaid, and when
shee fell, hee did fall al⟨so,⟩ yet being afterward sett at liberti
again hee lẏved very honorably by þe lẏvi⟨ng⟩ which hee had
by his lady and wẏf. and in þis tẏm þat I served him hee waz
ka⟨lled⟩ to serv þe prins in her warz ⌐beyond þe Seas⌐,[1] whẹr
to rekover hiz honowr befọr lost, hee konsiumed much of hiz
ladies land and substans, þe which shortly after hiz return from
þọz warz kawzed him to break vp hows keeping, and þervp⟨on⟩
dyverz of my fellowz had leav to depạrt and to seek new servises.
þen waz ⟨my⟩ kạk dow, and mẏn annewite waz laid A wạter.[2] þus
having A new korz[3] laid whẹr no need waz, I wrọt þus in meeter
az foloeth—

Iz þẹr no chois for mee, but still to tast þis strẏf,
Shall all miseaz and pensif thouht torment mee all my lẏf.

O lọrd to þe I kall, now let þi pleaziur bee,
To rid mee from þis myzery, in ʒoy with þẏn to bee.

When I had bin trobled A littl whẏl with þis lạt chainʒ þe
which greeved ⟨mee⟩ þe mọr bekawz þat alþoh my lord waz not
willing to gẏv me myn annewet⟨e⟩ yet hee waz offended with

---

[1] Whythorne here crossed out the words 'at St *Quintins*', a key detail.
[2] Both proverbial; for 'cake is dough' see Tilley C 12, and for 'lay a water', meaning to lay aside, Tilley W 108.
[3] The meaning is satisfied by 'course' or by 'corsie' (see p. 34 *supra*).

mee in þat I sowht to be gon from hiz servis, ⟨I⟩ being perswąded
in my self þat seing hee wold not perform hiz p[r]omy̆z to
⟨mee⟩ at þis ty̆m, and also mistrusting þat heerafter bǫth hiz
fantazy toward m⟨ee⟩ and ęk hiz abilite wold also be weaker,
wherby I miht looz þe mǫr ty̆m ⟨, I⟩ sowht þe mǫr earnestly to
be delivered from hiz servis, þe which at lenkth ⟨hee⟩ graunted
mee. after þe which ty̆m I kąm to þe servis of A man of great
w⟨or⟩ship, and ǫn þat waz at þat ty̆m of þe privi kownsell vnto
þe prins, in þe w⟨hich⟩ ty̆m of my being with him, hiz lady and
famili, went to ly A sertain ty̆m ⟨at⟩ A hows of þeirz in þe
kuntrey, and bekawz I was skoolma[ste]r vnto hiz childer⟨n⟩ I
waz okkazioned to be also with my skollerz who waz whęr þęr
moþar wa⟨z.⟩

now sir, nor far of from owr hows þęr dwelled A mean
ʒentilman who w⟨az⟩ an aunsient wydoer, and hee had to
govern hiz hows, an aunsient matro⟨n &⟩ mayd, of whom and
her master, þe servants of owr hows had reseived dyve⟨rz⟩
favorz and kurteowz enterteinments with freendly cheer,
whervpon þ⟨ę⟩r grew such talk of þem both in owr hows, az
kommenly doth happen to such who do hang vpon þe blasts of
þe peopuls mowþs, az sum praizing þeir good cheer oþer sum
þe klenly order of þe meat and linnen at þe tąbull, oþerz þe
frendly enterteinment. and oþerz, such oþer things az lyked
þem best. þen ǫn oþer of þem ministerd talk of hiz lyvings and
possessions, az what þei węr, and whęr þei węr, and þen hee
having no childern, who waz most ly̆k to be hiz heir, þen quod
an oþer, mistres Elsabeth (for so waz shee kalled who governed
hiz hows) is ly̆k to be hiz heir, and if hee ⌐doth¬ dy befǫr her.
quod an oþer why sh⟨uld⟩ shee be so much in hiz favor, az to
reseiv somuch benefitt by his death? hold yowr peas quod an
oþer, peradventiur shee doth deserv it better þen any oþer in
þe hows for shee not only governeth hiz hows and all hiz hows-
wy̆fly doings þąr abowts with diskresion for hiz profitt, but
also peradventiur doth ly with him in þe nyhts an⟨d⟩ krieth
kry̆st help when hee neezes,[1] and laieth þat down þat hee wold

---

[1] Sneezes (OED). Tilley F 703.

not hạv to stand. þoz wurdz quod an oþer be lẏk to A walshmans
họs or A nọz of wax.[1] and þarfọr wee may tạk þem and konster
þen akkordingly, and þarwithall a⟨fter⟩ many such⟨lẏk ʒi⟩bz 25ᵛ
and skoffs þ⟨e comp⟩any mended þat plạs and paired oþerz.[2]
After þe which talk I not knowing þe parties of whom all this
fọrsaid talk waz raized, sumwhat longed to see þem, þeir hows,
and maner þerof. þe which longing waz shortly after þat fulfilled
& satisfied, for þe said ʒentilman did and bid all þe servingmen of
owr hows to A dinner, emong þe which I (az ọn nothing inferior
vnto þem, and an ạs aboov þem by þe means of my teaching
þe yoong ʒentilfolks in þe hows) waz also solemly bidden.

when þe day of owr feast waz kum, and wee also kum to þe
said ʒentilmans hows, evry body akkording to þeir degreez wẹr
by þe said ʒentilman plạsed at þe tabull, whẹr I saw þe manner
of þe sạm akkording az it waz befọr reported of, and when þat
þe dẏnar waz finished,[a] after A littl pawz, evry man gạv dew
thanks for his goodcheer and so went þeir waiez. after þis az þe
servingmen of owr hows had doon befọr, so did þei now lẏkwẏz,
þat iz to say, when ij or iij of þem had walked abrọd eiþer in þe
morning or in þe after noon þei wọld sumtẏms vyzit þe said
ʒentilmans hows to see how hee did, whẹr akkording to þe
tẏm þei wẹr eiþer by him or hiz hows keeper very frendly
entertayned. þen on A tẏm A chaplein þat my master had in hiz
hows said vnto mee, goodlord mr .W. yow ar þe least goer
abrọd þat ever I did see, yow heer how owr fellowz go evry day to
mr .G. hows (for with þat letter þe ʒentilmans nạm began) shall
yow and I go to brẹkfast þiþer ọn day? I am siur wee shalbe
welkum. quod I to him, I will go þiþer with yow when yow will,
will yee so, quod hee, þen will wee go þiþer to brẹkfast on thurs-
day next, kontent (quod I).

now sir owr day agreed vpon being kum, wee bọth went to þe

---

[a] MS. reads 'filished'.

[1] Proverbial expressions, here meaning non-existent and ambiguous. For
examples of early use, see Robert Nares's *Glossary*, 1867 edition, under
appropriate headings. See also *ODEP* p. 702 and Tilley N 226.

[2] Proverbial; Tilley H 774, who cites Heywood's usage.

ȝentilmans hows, who alþoh wee fownd not at họm, yet mistres
.E. his hows keeper wee fownd at họm, who enterteined vs
frendly, and when owr breakfast ⟨w⟩az redy, mistres .E. kạm
into þe parler, and did sett þe chaplein on þe bench, mee ⟨o⟩n
þe owtsȳd over against him, and her self at þe hier end of þe
tabull (az A plạs kommenly ywzed by þe mistres of þe hows)
þen after wee had sumwhat slạked owr hungerz vpon þe vittels
þat waz sett befọr vs, wee fell into such talk az wee thouht meet
for þe tȳm and plạs, at þe end wherof mistres .E. went
from þe tabull and brouht vs A delikạt dish, such A ọn az shee
had in her own keeping. whẹrvpon þe chaplein, said vnto her,
Jesus[a] mistres .E. yow be to blạm to bestow such kost on vs,
quod shee, I do think it well bestowd. O quod hee to her, and
yow had such A hows and being of yowr own az þis is, yow
wold I perseiv, keep A good hows, yee quod shee, and if I had
mr .W. (nạming mee) to bee my husband. at which wordz I
smyled, and said to her, þat if shee had mee to bee her husband
she shiuld þen be well husbanded, and so I staid my speech for þat
matter at þat tȳm, notwithstanding I miuzed A littl at her wordz
imaȝining why shee shiuld say somuch to mee I being of so small
akquaintans with her az I þen waz. yet þen again I did think
þat shee spạk þọz wordz but in ȝẹst and pastȳm, and by þe way
of mery talk, whẹrvpon I disburdened mee of thinking any mọr
of þat matter, and þen I fell into talk with þem of oþer matterz.

when I had mạd A reasnabull fowndasion with such vittels az
þạr waz and hạving an appetȳt to drink, þer kạm to my remembrans þat I hạv hard say dyverz tȳms when I waz beyond þe
seaz in þe low kuntrey or Duchland, þat hee waz but an vn-
manerly and an vnthankfull gest who wold not drink to hiz host
ons in A feast tȳm,[1] wherfọr I took A kup with drink and said to
her mistres .E. shall I be so bold az to drink to yow. quod shee
again to mee, kall yee mee mistres .E.? and why not wȳf? will
yee not bee my huzband? quod I to her again I did not know

---

[a] Expanded contraction.

[1] The earliest example of this saying cited by authorities is Ray's *Collection
of English Proverbs*, 1678 (Tilley G 474).

yowr mynd sertainly in þat matter till now, and þarfor now,
I drink vnto yow ȝentill wẏf with all my hart, I pledȝ yow good
huzband quod shee. yea quoþ þe (choploch,[1] I wold hav said
þe) chaplein afforsaid, be yee so soon agreed? kum on (quoþ hee)
and eis mak yee siur þat sall I (hee spak þe wordz norþernly,
bekawz hee waz A norþern man) and with þoz wordz hee took
her by þe hand, and reacht to hav taken mẏn also. no, soft
(quoþ I to þe chaplain) soft f⟨ẏre m⟩aketh sweet ma⟨lt⟩.[2] nay I 26ʳ
will ⟨w⟩oo, A littl whẏll ⟨be⟩for I be mad siur, for wee do see
sum tẏms þat þei who do wed and marry in hast hav tẏm enoh
afterward for to repent þem,[3] nay quoþ hee þen (and with þat
hee did let go her hand) I do mean but merily, it may be so
(quoþ I) (but for all ⟨þat⟩ I thouht þen þat such A kontrakt mad
by A preest and in such sort az it s⟨ee⟩med þat hee wold hav
doon it, miht hav turned sum on or both of vs vnto s⟨um⟩ disquietnes in þe end).

Well sir, þis talk and much mor vnto it waz put ⟨forth⟩ very
well, and evry body seemed to be very well kontent with my
wordz þ⟨en⟩ þe which mad mee A glad man. and þen I warrant
yow þat þer waz never ⟨A⟩ tẏm þat I did spek vnto her but I
wold in az huzbandly maner do it az ⟨I⟩ kowld devẏz. ye, and
when she kam to my masterz hows, I wold merily ⟨en⟩treat my
skollerz and oþerz of my frendz þar to gẏv my wẏf frendly
enterteinment for my sak (alþoh shee had very well dezerved it
at sum of þeir handz befor) when it waz þus known in my
masterz hows, þat þe said mistres .E. wa⟨z⟩ my wẏf, in good
sooth þar waz pastẏm enoh mad at þat, for þen waz I sh⟨iur⟩
talked of and ȝẏbed at on evry sẏd for A tẏm (but A wunder
lasteth but ⟨nẏne⟩ daiz[4] it iz awnsiently said) þis body wold shew
her vẏs þis way, and þat fo⟨r A⟩ bolt waz shot[5] þat way.

and þen did on say to mee will yee marry with ⟨such⟩ A
wiþerd skroill[6] az þat iz? quoþ an oþer will yee hav such an old

---

[1] One who chops logic. See Tilley L 412.
[2] Proverbial; Tilley F 280.
[3] Proverbial; Tilley H 196.
[4] Proverbial; Tilley W 728.
[5] Proverbial; Tilley B 512.
[6] Scroyle, meaning a witch, is first recorded by *OED* in Shakespeare's
King John.

kroo⟨ked⟩ krǫn az shee iz? quoþ an oþer, and will ye now rẏd
in an oþer mans bo⟨at⟩,[1] quoþ an oþer and if ye hạv her yee
shall hạv nomǫr with her, þe[n] shall pleaz her master to gẏv
with her, for hee hath had þe flower of her, and yow shall hạv
but þe bran.[2] tush masterz quoþ I, keep yowr breaþz to kooll
yowr pottaȝ[3] withall, yee ar all in A wrong box,[4] for þạr iz no
such matter doon nor A brewing, nor toward az yow do tạk it.
þat which wee do say iz b⟨ut⟩ in pastẏm and mirth. Now sir,
whether þe talk of her and mee in owr how⟨s⟩ kạm to her knowle-
leȝ, and shee mislẏked þerwith (for her earz miht hạ⟨v⟩ glowed[5]
well enowh bekawz shee waz þen so often talked of) or wheþer
⟨it⟩ waz to mạk mee þe mǫr ẹger of loov towardz her. or whatsoever an⟨y⟩ oþer kawz þer waz I know not, but my said wẏf on
A tẏm after þis and vpon sum talk of huzbandz, told mee þat I
shiuld be but her day hu⟨z⟩band, and not her niht huzband. þe
which wordz greeved mee never a w⟨hit⟩ and þen after þis talk
she began to grow in short tẏm after into sum mǫ⟨r⟩ strainȝnes
towardz mee þen shee waz akkustomed to bee in befǫr þat tẏ⟨m⟩
and in fẏn, when I kạm ǫn day to hạv seen her for sum buzines
þat I h⟨ad⟩ to do with her, shee wold not bee at hǫm, whervpon
I mistrusting þ⟨at⟩ shee waz at hǫm þoh shee wold not be
known to be so, I sifted þe matt⟨er⟩ so naroly, az I had sertain
intelliȝens and knowleȝ þat shee waz þen within when I wǫld
hạv spoken with her, wherfǫr I being az willi[n]g not to seek
her any mǫr, az shee seemed þen not to be fownd, determine⟨d⟩
with my self þat I wold never seek her again, and þen I mạd þis
foloing—

> By new broom, by new broom, yee may be siur,
> stǫr iz good, for þei wilnot long endiur.
> Ðe new broom sweepeth klẹn,[6] A proverb ọld
> Ðat applied iz to such az heerafter shalbe tǫld

---

[1] This application of the common expression does not appear in Tilley,
the *Oxford Dictionary of Proverbs*, or other authorities.
[2] A variation on a popular saying: Tilley F 383.
[3] Proverbial; Tilley W 422. [4] Proverbial; Tilley B 575.
[5] Proverbial; Tilley E 14. [6] Proverbial; Tilley B 682.

Ðe dobull diliȝent, þe servant new
And þe whot louer, þat di'eth at first vew
Ðe whot loov iz soon kold,[1] az oft iz seen
And þe temprat fier doth mąk þe sweet'st malt, az wÿz do ween.

Ðe frend at first þat seemz, hee wilnot chainȝ,
inkonstant yet to proov, it iz not strainȝ.
⟨S⟩o my song to ⟨end⟩ in plain wordz ⟨few⟩   26ᵛ
T'iz not good to trust over much at þe first shew.[2]

In A whÿll after þis forsaid strainȝnes between mistres .E.
and mee, I vnderstood by sum of þòz of owr hows who ywzed
to go sumtÿms to mr .G. hows þat hiz hows keeper, mistres .E.
I mean, alþoh shee walked abrǫd, shee waz sumwhat akrązed,
and grown to bee so short wÿnded or breaþed þat shee
whizzed, and also þei told þat ever when any of þem kąm to her
masterz hows shee wold demaund for mee, and þąrvpon sumtÿms shee wold grow into sum wordz of wonder, demawnding
why I wold not kum to her masterz hows as I waz wunt to do
befǫr. but I wold tąk þǫz wordz of þeirz to be spoken in mokkąȝ
and derÿzion, bekawz þei did know þat [I] had vowed to abandon
her kumpany. well sir, þis maner of klokking siknes of herz (az
sum of owr hows to mee) grew to be so extreem in her þat shee
waz dryven in short tÿm after to keep her bed. in þe which tÿm,
both sertain men and women of owr hows for frendship sąk,
went to her masterz hows to vizit her, vnto whom (az þei said
to mee) shee ywzed þe sąm or lÿk speech of mee az shee had
doon befǫr. whervpon þei not only suspekted þat her siknes
waz to hąv my loov to her, but þei said plainly þat it waz so,
and I to putt þat suspision owt of þeir hedz, told þem how shee
had ywzed mee both in wordz and deedz az partly iz befǫr
rehersed, wherfǫr I kowld not beleev þat shee loved mee in such
sort az þei said shee did. quoþ sum of þem þat miht bee but to

---

[1] Proverbial; Tilley L 483.
[2] The nearest approximation to this proverb is 'Sudden trust brings
sudden repentance', in Bodenham's *Wits Commonwealth*, 1597 (Tilley
T 553 and T 595).

try yee or for sum oþer kawz, and not for want of good will in
her toward yow. for sum women will many tẏms say on thing
and do an oþer,[1] and seem to reʒekt þat which þei wold full fain
hav. siurly quoþ þei shee iz very weak, and not lẏk to eskap this
siknes, wherfor seing þat she speaketh somuch of yow az shee
doth, and iz so dezyrows þat yow shiuld see her, kum to her
man, and þen yee shall hear what shee will say. peradventiur
yee may restor her vnto her helth again. quoþ I, þat iz in Godz
handz and not in mẏn, if shee be so ill az yow say shee iz I am
very sory for it, and þe mor sory if it bee (az yow say) for my
loov, bekawz it will breed sorow in mee to rekompens it at þe
full, þat iz to say to marry with her, but and if my viziting of
her with what frendship els I am abull to show her, saving only
wedding and marrieng with her, mak her whoʒl, I will do it with
all my hart.

and heer withall I went with A ʒentilwoman and sertain
oþerz of our hows to see her, & when I kam at her, I fownd her
in bed and in such weak kas az it waz reported vnto mee, at
which tẏm I ywzed vnto her such frendly and kurteowz wordz,
az I thouht miht best pleaz and kontent her, but I kowld not
perseiv by any wordz of herz þat shee waz towardz mee az it
waz reported to mee to bee, and I waz glad þerof. if it had bin
so az þei said it waz þen it iz lẏk þat shee forbar to say ani thing
to mee to⌈w⌉ching þat matter, eiþer bekawz þat her master and
many oþerz wer þar in plas at þat prezent or els, bekawz of her
weaknes, it greeved her to speak much. after þat I had bin with
her A littl whẏll, and seing þat shee [said] nothing vnto mee to any
purpoz I took my leav of her and went my waiz from her. and in
short tẏm after I vnderstood þat shee began sumwhat to amend
of her siknes, but I did never see her any mor after þat tẏm.

for imediatly after þat I had bin with her my master whom I
þen served had sertain trobles happened vnto him, at þe which
instant, my lady hiz wẏf, and I, fell at A ʒar, wherfor I had leav
to depart from hiz servis. Ðen kam I to London, which sitty iz
alwaiz, my cheef worldly refiuʒ at such tẏms of need. for az hom

---

[1] Proverbial; compare Tilley W 660 and W 672.

iz homly,[1] so az I said befor, whersoever I do bekum in þe
kuntrei I hav alwaiz A chamber of mẏn own in þat sitty to
rezort vnto in my tẏm of need. When I had remained A littl
whẏll in London, I waz spoken vnto by on to teᴿaᴸch A ȝentil- **27ʳ**
mans childern ⟨wh⟩o dwelled withi⟨n fẏve[2] m⟩ẏls of þe sam
sitty. and aft⟨er⟩ þat I had talked and ⟨kon⟩kliuded with þe
ȝentilman & þe ȝentilwoman hiz wẏ⟨f⟩ what my enterteinment
shiuld bee within þeir hows for þe teaching of þeir ch⟨il⟩dern,
I went to þeir hows, wher I endevored my self to þe discharȝ
of þat w⟨her⟩for I waz by þem hẏred, and both þe ȝentilman
and hiz wẏf wer redy & will⟨ing⟩ to gratify mee with such good
konsiderasion az þei had promyzed vnto mee.

heer must I shew yow by þe way how þat þe said ȝentilwoman having bin su⟨m⟩ tẏm A koortier, and well experiensed
also in þe affairz of þe world. and als⟨o shee⟩ had A great witt, and
A ȝoly ready toong to vtter her fantazy and mynd ⟨she⟩ took
pleaziur many tẏms to talk and diskoors of such things az shee
by experiens had had sum knowleȝ of, az sumtẏms of reliȝions,
shee wold arg⟨ew⟩ in matterz of kontroversy in reliȝion. sumtẏms of profan matters. sumtẏms s⟨hee⟩ wold towch matterz of
þe kuntrey, with þe good husbandry & huswẏfrey þerof. sumtẏms shee wold towch þe sytty, with þe tràdz of sittizens, and not
leav vntowched, þe fynes of þe delikat dams, and þe nẏs wẏvs of
þe sitty. sumtẏms shee wold talk of þe koort, with þe bravery,
and vanitiez þerof, and of þe krowching and dissimiulasion with
þe *bazzios las manos* þat þar iz ywzed b⟨y⟩ on koortier to an
oþer. and sumtẏms shee wold minister talk of þe koor⟨ting⟩ of
ladiez and ȝentilwomen by þe gallants, and kavallierz, and
sumtẏms ⟨shee⟩ wold talk pleazantly of þe loov þat iz mad
and ywzed in all plases b⟨e⟩tween men and women, az of such
who do woo mor for þe loov of þe party þen þe riches. also
of such who do woo mor for þe loov of þe goodz & riches

---

[1] Whythorne used this saying earlier on page 48.

[2] Five miles is a likely figure because Whythorne later says that one house
was three or four miles from London, and the two houses were eight miles
apart, with London more or less midway between them. See p. 96.

þen þe ownerz of þem. and also of such who do ȝoin issews for both.

Heer yow shall vnderstand by þe way, þat I did kovenant with þe said ȝentilman and wýf, þat I wold be with þem but by þe week, and also þat I wold be ywzed az A frend, and not A servant, whervpon þei did not on⟨ly⟩ allow mee to sitt at þeir tạbull, but also at þeir own mes, az long az þ⟨er⟩ wẹr not any to okkiupy þe room and plạs þat wẹr A great deall my betterz. so þat I being þạr but by þe week, and to be ywzed az A frend, mạd m⟨ee⟩ þe bolder to speak my fantazy sumtýms, when I thouht good. and now em⟨ong⟩ þe speeches by mee ywzed I do remember þat ọn tým when þe said ȝentilwoman waz entered and had diskoorsed A prety whyll of þe divers⟨i⟩tiez of loov, I said þat now A daiz þạr waz no perfett loov or frendship ⟨or⟩ of kontynewans to be fownd exsept it wẹr between twoo of equall hab⟨i⟩lite and gifts of fortewn, alþouh for þeir gifts of natiur and þe mynd ⟨þẹr⟩ wẹr never so good kawz of lyking. for if þat ọn of A mean estạt wold o⟨ffer⟩ and seek to ọn of greatter kalling, and habilite þen hee iz of, for mọr loo⟨v⟩ and good will þen þe party belooved wold dain to aksept of, hee shiuld be⟨e⟩ disdained and skorned þerfọr, to þe which wordz þe ȝentilwoman did awns⟨wer⟩ þat alþoh þẹr wẹr sum who wold disdain such A frend, yet þer wẹr of þe kontrary mýnd, and shee for her pạrt never had, nor never wold hạv þe lýk respekt þat sum oþerz had to þe habilite raþer þen þe kondisions of þe party. affirming also þat and if shee wẹr to marry, shee wold raþer wed an honest man in hiz shert,[1] þen such A ọn az wẹr kontrary, alþoh hee wẹr worth thowzans of pownds in money (to þez words sum kawz moved her, for shee waz handfast and wedded to ọn who loved chainȝ of pastiurz).[2]

Ðus az wee past away þe týms sumtým in ọn of þe exersýzes affọrsaid, and sumtym in an oþer, so sumtýms wee shiuld enter into talk of hiumourz, þe which of þem ⌐four¬ bearing cheefest rewll in man shiuld instinkt ⌐enklyn,¬ and provọk him to follow

---

[1] The expression in this form is unrecorded.
[2] Proverbial; Tilley C 230: 'Change of pasture makes fat cows.'

þoz effekts whervnto þei wer enklyned. þen shiuld wee sumtýms
wąd into kommiunikasion and talk of þe planets and þe selestiall
sýns with þe konstellasions, and what þeir operasions & wurk-
ings wer, and what effekts þey wrouht in althings þat wer subʒekt to þem. And at þis tým I had þe book named and written
by *Arkandam*[1] or *Aleandrin*, to fýnd þe fątall desteni, konstellasion, komplexion, and natiurall inklýnasion, of evry man,
woman, and chýld by þeir birth, þe which book to pas away þe
tým, I wold sum týms brin⟨g owt⟩ akkording to þ⟨e re⟩wls set **27ᵛ**
down ⟨i⟩n þe book. I wold kast þe nativite of sum in þe kumpany,
and þen I wold read vnto þem þat which waz said of þ⌐e⌐m in þe
book, þe which sumtýms did pleaz sum, and oþer sum it mąd
to look down and to být þeir lips. þen in þe end of all þez,
I fownd þat þe ʒentilwoman of þe hows, her eldest dawhter,
waz born vnder þe sąm sýn, planet, and konstellasion, þat I waz
born vnder, þe which being known to þe ʒentilwoman of þe
hows, she said þat and if þe sýn planett and konstellasion wold
enfors and yeeld no wurs kondisions vnto her dawhter þen shee
perseived to be in mee, shee wold lýk her dawhter þe better
þerfor, þe which wordz of herz mąd mee to think þat eiþer shee
had A very good opinion of mee, or els shee wold hąv mee to
think so, bekawz I shiuld think myself þe mor beholding to her
for þe good opinion þat shee had of mee. for yee shall vnderstand þat dyverz týms befor þis tým, both by wordz and frendly
behavor shee seemed þat she wold hąv mee to think þat shee
bąr mee sum goodwill, þe which I mąd nomor þen an ordinary
akkownt of, bekawz I did perseiv by dyverz means þat shee
had A gloriowz head, and þerwithall delýted to hąv such az shee
lyked of to be in loov with her and to be at her kommaundement,
and to boast how she kold deall in þoz kąses when shee saw
kawz and tým (much after þe maner and sort az þe ʒentilwoman, my mistres affor rehersed wold do) and shee perseiving
þat I took sum heed to her demeanour and wordz, and mistrust-

---

[1] *The Most Excellent Booke to fynd the Fatal Desteny of Euery Man*,
1562 (?); written under the pseudonym Arcandam, translated into English
by W. Warde (*STC* 724).

ing þat I fownd her not to be alway þe sam which she[a] professed
in wordz to bee toward mee, and þarfor wold not feed her
hiumour somuch az shee wold hav had mee, she wold sumtẏms
yvz in wordz A womans shift to klok her dissimiulasion and
inkonstansy, and say to me þat shee durst not in þe prezens of
sum who ywzed to her hows sumtẏms to shew such frendship
to her frend az oþerwẏz shee wold. bekawz þat þei wold b[l]az
it foorth to her reproch and diskredit.

Heer I must stay yow of þis matter for A whẏll, and tell yow,
þat at þis tẏm I had A chamber in Lond[on] az I told yow befor,
so þat ons or twys in A quarter I wold go þiþer to vizit my
lodȝing þar. And after A sertain yeerz spent heer, on A tẏm
when I waz at London, I waz spoken vnto to teach A ȝentilmans
mans[b] childern, with whom and hiz wẏf I had byn long akquainted befor þis tẏm. þei dwelled A iij or iiij mẏl from London,
and nẏ abowt viij mẏll from þe ȝentilmans hows wher my most
abyding waz þen. so þat London waz ny in þe midway between
both þeir howzes. At þe which tẏm when I waz so spoken vnto,
þer kam to my remembrans, þat it waz told mee þat þe ȝentilman whoz childern I þen tawht, began to wex wery of my being
in hiz hows, wherfor I thouht good now to hav ij strings to my
bow,[1] for fear þat þe older of both shiuld break on þe suddein,
and þerfor I wold not eiþer graunt or deny þis last proferd
servis, but I did defer my absoliut awnswer till an oþer tẏm þat
þen waz appointed to see and trẏ what wold happen in þe mean
whẏll. whervpon I thinking to prov what wold be gotten by
chainȝing of pastiurz, did gẏv owt in þe hows wher I þen waz,
þat I wold be gon from þens, be such A day, and named it.

When þis waz reported to my ȝentilwoman, shee on A tẏm
brak with mee towching my going from her hows, and dezyred
to know þe kawz why I wold leav her hows, whervpon I told her
þat I did it bekawz I vnderstood þat her huzband began to wax
wery of my being in hiz hows. and also I aleȝed oþer rezons

---

[a] MS. reads 'see'.   [b] Dittography.

[1] Proverbial; Tilley S 937.

which now I hạv forgotten. to þe which shee awnswered þat þe
kawz of her huzbandz werines waz but for sparing of charȝes,
þe which if hee wold not be kontented withall, shee wold
disburs owt of her own purs, and þen to kontent and pleaz mee
shee promyzed mee þat and if I wold remain still at her hows, I
shiuld hạv^a yee mary shiuld I. þen I said vnto her þat I had mạd
A promis in an oþer plạs alredy, þe which for mẏn honesty and
kredits sạk I must needs perfo⟨rm⟩. but quoþ I to her, sins yee 28^r
ar so willing ⟨to⟩ hạv mee tarry in yowr hows, I will from hens
foorth remain and kontinew with ⟨yow⟩ as long az I do in þe
oþer plạs. when shee perseived þat shee kowld not bring mee to
her will no oþerwẏz þen iz affọrsaid, alþoh shee had proved mee
for it diverz wa⟨iz⟩ which now I will omit for tediowznes sạk,
shee at lenkth enklyned to mee, and ⟨see⟩med to allow very well
of all my doings þerin. (I do think þat shee waz þe mọ⟨r⟩ ernest
to hạv mee to kontynew at her hows kontinewally, bekawz her
eldest da⟨wh⟩ter had þen A sewter & woer, who shiuld see how
willing þei wer to hạv þei⟨r⟩ childern browht vp ȝentilwomen
lẏk.)

Now sir, when þe tẏm of my parting fro⟨m⟩ her waz ny at
hand, shee on A tẏm when þẹr waz no mo[r] in kumpany but
vs and in þe end of sum talk between her and mee of my going
from her hows, at wha⟨t⟩ tẏm I promẏz her again þat I wold kum
again and tarry with my skollerz heer, aslong az I wold tarry
with my skollerz þạr (by þe which termz of hee[r] and þạr, ⟨I⟩
will from hens foorth term^b þe plạses to know þe diffrens of
þem, I say in þe ⟨end⟩ of þis talk) shee said þus in effekt vnto
mee. well. mr .W. when soever yee will kum hẏþer yee shalbe
welkum, and heer may yee remain and tarry az long az yee will
and alþoh yow shiuld be welkum to nọn els in þis hows, yet
azlong az I do lẏv yo⟨w⟩ shalbe welkum vnto mee at altẏms.
quoþ I to her, I do thank yow. and quoþ ⟨shee⟩ what pleaziur
soever I am habull to do yow or for yow at any tẏm by any
man⟨er⟩ mean whatsoever it bee, if yow will let mee vnderstand

---

^a Some words seem to be missing here.   ^b MS. reads 'tern'.

it, yow shalbe assiu⟨red⟩ of it at all tẏms, þen kowld I do no les for kurtezies sąk, þen say to her lẏkwẏz þat what pleaziur soever I waz habull to do for her shee shiuld in lẏk maner kommaund mee, for þe which shee thanked mee. And after þis band of frendship being þus knyt wee parted kumpany for þat tẏm. þen after þis, az tẏm and pląs served my ʒentilwoman heer, wold kast owt speeches sumtẏms towching frends⟨hip,⟩ how konstant shee wold hąv such to bee who pofessed it, and how þat such who wiln⟨ot⟩ be frendly, shall never fynd konstant and assewred frendship, with such lẏk talk. þe which wordz I waied but littl, for all ⌜her⌝ great frendship proffessed, ⟨be⟩kawz I did still suspekt þat shee did but dissembull with mee. within ⟨A⟩ short tẏm after þis þe day of my departiur from hens waz kum, wherin ⟨I⟩ shiuld tąk my way toward my skollerz þąr, at which day of my parting I had told my ʒentilwoman, when I wold return to her hows again, I ha⟨d⟩ great thanks of her for my good will, with A frendly kis, and so wee pa⟨r⟩ted kumpany for þat tẏm. Đen went I to London, for az þat Sity iz i⟨n a⟩ maner in þe midway between þǫz twoo said pląses, so did I mąk it m⟨y⟩ bayting pląs to rest in by þe way.

Now must I tell yow of an oþer ma⟨tter⟩ þen I hąv az yet towched, þe which alþouh it be not pertinent or pert⟨eyn⟩ing to þe story afforsaid, yet it iz to þe purpǫz of þat which I must open if I shall follow orderly þat which I hąv ⌜had⌝, & am now purpoz⟨ing⟩ to do konserning my Songs and sonets. So it waz þat I had an hostes at þa⟨t⟩ tẏm in London þat waz A widow, and az I perseived by diverz presumpsions, shee bąr mee so much goodwill az shee kowld be kontent to hąv had me to be her huzband, but þat I lyked not, partly bekawz I thouht her to be sumwhat past þe prokreation, and konseiving of childern. and partly bek⟨awz⟩ þat shee had twoo childern alredy. for it iz an old saieng þat hee who weddeth with A widow who hath ij childern, hee shalbe kumbred with iij theevs,[1] bekawz þat þe moþer espesially if shee bee an old krǫn, will purloin and filch

---

[1] Proverbial; but Tilley (W 335) found no example before 1658.

from her husband to bestow it vpon her childern. In þe tўm whўll I þen lay at London, I went vnto A frends ⌐hows⌐ of mўn who waz A .P.[1] for sertain wurk þat hee had to do for mee. and þar did ⌐I⌐ meet with A neybur of mўn hostes and mўn, with whom I had sum talk of neyburly affairz. and at length of my hostes also, in þe end of which talk hee wyshed her to bee my wўf, for þe which wish I gav him thanks, and so I went my wais from hiz kompany.

Ðen þe next day I went to my skollerz þar, with whom I remained ny abowt A six or seven weeks, in þe which tўm ⟨þe⟩ 28ᵛ moþer of my said skollerz mad asmuch of mee, both in frendly wordz, and owtward behavor az þe ȝentilwoman heer had doon, and emong þe frendly konferenses[a] þat I had with her shee wold perswad with mee dyverz tўms to remain with her ⟨k⟩onty- newally, whervnto I wold mak her awnswer þat I had mad A promis to remain azlong heer az I did þar, wherfor I kowld not mak her any such promis. After þe tўm afforsaid being spent þar, I returned to London, and from þens again to my skollerz heer, wher after I had reseived my welkum of þeir moþer in such sort az I had my farwell, shee said vnto mee, þat she mar- velled much þat shee kowld not hear from mee in all þe tўm of myn absens from her, eiþer by wryting or oþerwўz. þez wordz wordz[b] of herz sumwhat trobled mee bekawz I neiþer looked for þem neiþer waz I prezently provyded to awnswer þem so well az I kowld if þei had not kum so sodenly, and vnlooked for, also I dowted þat shee waz displeazed with mee for it, howbeit I having A simpull womans shift exkiuzed þe matter az well az I kowld on þe suddein and said þat I waz not at London in all þe

---

[a] MS. reads 'konserenses'.   [b] Dittography.

[1] Of Whythorne's London friend, mentioned again on pp. 102 f., we know little except that he was 'a P', that his name began with the letter B, that he did some work for Whythorne, and that he circulated socially. 'A priest' would fill these qualifications except for doing any work for Whythorne. His chief friend with B for an initial was Thomas Barnam, the Latin tutor (see p. 214). Against this identification two considerable objections can be made: Whythorne speaks of Barnam as being a young man recently known about 1568, and shows no reticence in giving Barnam's full name.

tẙm of my absens from her, exsept it wẹr when I went from her, and kạm to her again.

At þis tẙm þe tẙm of Christmas waz kum, and on Newyee[r]z day (kontrary to my expektasion and vnlooked for) shee sent mee for my newyee[r]z gift three yeardz of satten to mạk A dub-lett for þe which I sent her but A trẙfull in komparyzon of þat which shee had sent mee, but I promyzed her þat with my pains taking with her childern I wold rekompens it. After þe reseit of þat newyeerz gift þer kạm into my hart an assewred họp of her konstant frendship, yet now waz I brouht into A great dump with all my kommoditiez, for I hạv hard say befọr þis tẙm, þat it iz not so eazy A matter for ọn to gett A frend az it iz to keep A frend. so þat all my study þen waz bent þat way, how I miht keep her to be my frend still, I thouht to my self, þat az shee had not ywzed at any tẙm befọr þat tẙm so great liberalite to mee az shee þen did, so þat said gift shewd þat to sum end shee mạd mọr akkownt of mee þen, þan shee had doon befọr, to ty mee to her hows. still shee did know by former triall þat it waz but in vain to go abowt it, to hạv mee gẙv her great gifts again þat shee did also know waz not in mee to gẙv her, for besẙd my want of abilite, shee never did know mee to bee forward þat way.

After þẹz and many oþer imaʒinasions and debatings of þe matter with my self, þer kạm to my mynd at length to dowt þe kawz of ọn thing which shee had doon, þe which waz þat against my last kumming to her hows, shee had kawzed A chest of mẙn in her hows to be removed owt of þe chamber wher befọr þat tẙm I waz akkustomed to ly in befọr þat tẙm, and to be brouht into A chamber so ny her own chamber az shee miht hạv kum from þe ọn to þe oþer when shee list withowt any suspision, þe which chamber I waz þen plạsed in. þen also kạm to my remem-brans how þat shee but A littl befọr þat tẙm waz muttered and whispered on by sum in þat hows for ywzing ọn of [þe] men A littl tow familiarly and suffred him to bee A littl tow sawsy with her openly. whervpon I mistrusting þat seing hee waz gon from her servis, shee ment to hav[a] mee to supply and okkiupy hiz room

---

[a] MS. reads 'had'.

and plas. Đis low, did towch mee sumwhat ny, and browht mee in A great perplexite. for on whŷll þe sugჳestions[a] and mosions of my ghostly enemy wold provok my flesh to rebell against against[b] þe[c] spreit, and an oþer whŷll Godz gras wurking in mee (hiz nam be praized for it) wold put into my mŷnd and remembrans, þoz of þe ten kommaundements which do say, Đow shalt not kommitt adultrey, Đow shalt not kovet þi neyburz wŷf. And also þer kam to my remembrans dyverz histories both devŷn and profan wherin waz shewd how God ponysed and plaged dyverz in tŷm past who had profaned and broken þoz kommaundements, so þat vpon þe konsyderasion heerof I waz thoroly determyned þat whatsoever kam of it I wold by Godz 29[r] gras never defŷ⟨l⟩ her wedlók bed.

⟨I⟩n þis tŷm of my being in her hows, ⟨I⟩ being in my chamber all alon, shee on day took okkazion to kum all alon into my cha⟨m⟩ber to see þe marks of my sheets, wherwithall I began straihtwaiz to think þat she⟨e⟩ did so, to see what kŷndnes I wold offer vnto her when shee waz in my chamb⟨er⟩ and þat which I offerd her waz non oþer, but þat I sufferd her to bee in my ⟨cham⟩ber azlong az shee list withowt trobling of her, and not ons towched her all ⟨þe⟩ whŷll shee waz þar, but suffred her to part away az quŷetly, az shee kam þiþ⟨er.⟩ Đen shortly after þis I went again to London, and from þens to my skollerz þa⟨r⟩ wher after I had remayned ny abowt twoo or three weeks, þer kam to my rem⟨em⟩brans how þat when I was last with my ჳentilwoman heer shee chalenჳed mee bekawz shee had not hard of me eiþer by wryting or oþerwaiz, in all þe tŷm of m⟨y⟩ being absent from her befor þat tŷm, wherfor now I determyned to wrŷt vnto her in meeter, bekawz I had no matter to wrŷt of, but A frendly rememb⟨rans⟩ to put her in mŷnd of former frendship professed. þe which did þus begin—

Remember him þat hath not yow forgot,
ne yowr promŷz owt of remembrans blot,
what tŷm az frendz wold hav þeir frendz þem mynd,
þen sum konseit for þem þei will owt fynd

---

[a] MS. reads 'sugჳentions'.   [b] Dittography.   [c] Written over 'my'.

And þat prezent az token of goodwill,
to banish þat which miht remembrans spill.
þis heer to yow so do I now prezent
þe which goodwill hath kawzed to be sent
And þus to end, remember þerfor now,
þe frend who saith az erst hee did to yow
Remember him þat hath not yow forgot
ne yowr promẏz owt of remembrans blot.

After þat I had mạd þis sonett, and written it owt, I did fold
it vp, and did ⟨en⟩klọz it in an oþer paper, þe which being sealed
I did direkt it vnto her, and sen⟨d⟩ it to London, from whens it
waz konveyd vnto her. the which being doon I thou⟨ht⟩ my self
dischar3ed of A great burdein, And þen I gạv my self whọly to
þ⟨e⟩ dischar3 of my dewty in teaching of my skollerz þạr. whọz
moþer, az I said bef⟨ọr⟩ seemed to bear mee much good will
also, and bekawz þat shee wold shew þ⟨e⟩ sạm still, lẏk az shee
had doon befọr, shee on A tẏm demaunded of mee wheþer þat
I did know of any woman in London þat looved mee or no, ⟨to⟩
þe which I said þat I did know of nọn sertainly, þen said shee,
how say yow to yowr hostes? what do yee think of her? quoþ I,
mẏn hostes I do think to bee an honest woman vnto whom I hạv
bin A good gest, and I hạv fownd her alwaiz redy to shew her
self willing, þat I shiuld hạv such good enterteinment in [her]
hows az I hạv bin worþi of, but yet do I think her to be no fitt
wẏf for mee. well quoþ shee, if yowr hostes be such A woman az
shee iz reported to bee, shee iz wurth þe hạving. who told yow
þat quoþ I? þer iz quoþ shee, an ọld akquaintans of yowrz in
London whọz nạm iz .B. hee iz A .P. þe which did tell mee so.
I wold wish þat yee wold talk with him þe next tẏm ye go to
London, and þen yee shall hear wha⟨t⟩ hee will say in þe matter.

Ny abowt A moneth after þis when az my tẏm kạm to go to
my skollerz heer, I kạm to London, and þen I went to þe .P.
(az my 3entilwoman þạr had kow[n]selled mee) of whom I
dezẏred to know þe sirkumstans of þe matter befọr towched.
whervpon hee told mee þat in ọn of þe kristmas hollydaiz last

past, he went with A ȝentilman (A frend of hiz) to dynar to my
ȝentilwomans hows þạr, whẹr after ⌜þe⌝ dynar waz past, þei
hard my skollerz play on þe virȝinals, whervpon þe ȝentilman
þat I went withall demaunde⟨d⟩ who tawht þem, an⟨d aw⟩nswer 29ᵛ
waz mạd þat it waz yow, when I hard þat I said þat I did know
yow very well, and had doon of long tẏm. when þe ȝentilwoman
of þe hows heering mee say so, mad very much of mee, and
after A whẏll, shee took okkazion to enter into familiar talk
⟨w⟩ith mee, and in þe end, shee took mee to walk foorth of þe
plạs whẹr wee dẏned and þen shee brouht mee abowt her hows,
shewing mee þe rooms and kommodites þerof, ywzing mee þerwithall so familiarly and frendly, az I being of so bạs estạt in komparizon of herz waz half ashạmed to be so ywzed of her. and az
wee walked to and fro togiþer, shee waz very inquizitẏv of mee,
to know how long I had bin akquainted with yow, and so foloingly
demaunded of mee what I did know of yowr estạt and lyving,
and what þe kawz shiuld bee that [yow]ᵃ did not marry, marvel-
ing why yow did lẏv so long vnmarried, whervnto I said þat I
thouht þat yow did lẏv vn married az þe manner of þe Italiens
iz, emong þe which peopull yow travelled. quoþ I if I shiuld follow þe Italiens ensampulz konserning þat matter, I wold wish
raþer to follow þensampull of þe best of þem, þen of þe wurst.

quoþ hee again to mee, þen did I tell her þat & if yow wẹr
willing to marry, yow had A rich hostes, whom I thouht þat
yow miht hạv if yow wold, þe which I did vnderstand by him
yowr neibour, whom yow did see heer at my hows with mee
þe last tẏm þat yow wẹr heer. Also I told her þat az yowr hostes
waz rich, so had shee A good trạd to awgment her lyuing
withall, wherfọr yow miht lẏv with her þe better. þẹz and þe
lẏk wordz said I to her (quoþ hee) for þe good will I do bear
to yow and for nọn oþer kawz. and when I had said somuch vnto
her, shee replẏng vnto mee said much in yowr kommendasion,
and in knitting vp of all yowr praiz shee added þervnto, þat
and if shee wẹr to ⌜be⌝ marryed, shee wold hạv yow to be her

ᵃ MS. has a smudged 'I'.

huzband befor any þat shee doth know. quoþ I for so saing I am
much beholding to her. þis forsaid ⟨t⟩alk brouht vnto my
remembrans how þatt when I waz with my ӡentilwoman heer,
I being mor A *Mercurian*,[1] þen A *Cupidian* or ⌜a *Venerian*⌝
and þerfor geven sumwhat mor to þe study of books and Miuzik
with oþer exersizes belonging to þem, þen to wait on *Venus*
and her babz or her darlings, also at þis tým I ⌜mad A meditasion
vpon þe lordz praier, it iz in proz.[2] but I mean heerafter to
mak it in meeter and þen to sett þem boþ togiþer. in an oþer
plas konvenient.⌝ My forsaid ӡentilwoman ⌜I sai⌝ fynding mee
many týms so well okkiupýd, wold say to mee sumtýms, þat and
if shee wer to marry, shee wold wish to hav such A huzband az I
waz, who to fly from idelnes (which iz þe root or moþer of all
sin)[3] kowld pas away þe tým in such good exersyzes. þen after
þis I rekownted with my self how þe kas stood with mee, and
þez forsaid three dams, on whýll praizing my good fortewn,
bekawz I waz so well lyked and beloved of þem, and an oþer
whýll blaming my ill fortewn for þat I kowld not with good
konsiens posses and enӡoi her þat I lyked best of þem. wherfor
I wrot þus in meeter az folloeth—

Ðe proverb saith between twoo stoolz þe taill goth to þe grownd,[4]
but I may say between three stoolz, lýk stat in mee iz fownd.
þe weakest of þe three to bear, t'is lýk I miht obtain.
but how shiuld I stay mee by þat, which kan yvneths sustain
þe burþen of it self? for þat it iz so weak of lim,
Ðe sekond stooll, both strong and good, for mee it wer most trim,
but þat þe Lord (most mihty Jov[a]*) hath mee forbod plainly,*
from koveting my neiburz good, þoh I miht kum þerby.

---

[a] Whythorne wrote the alternative 'God' above 'Jov'.

---

[1] For 'Mercurian' see pp. 95 and 204.
[2] Whythorne inserted this line over a lengthy deletion, probably after
transcribing the prose and verse versions of the meditation, which occur in
folios 75ᵛ–81 of the manuscript. It seems clear that he wrote the prose
meditation when under emotional stress in 1559, but turned it into verse
later during his employment by Archbishop Parker.
[3] This common proverb (Tilley I 13) occurs in various forms. For Whythorne's earlier use of it see p. 15.   [4] Proverbial; Tilley S 900.

Lȳkwȳz þe third wold serv my turn, but þat lȳk stąt it hath,
az þ'oþer hath to purchaz mee eternally Godz wrath.
If now þerfọr ⟨I firs⟩t stooll tąk, I wold to rest vpon,   **30ʳ**
my stąt and siurti shiuld be weak, and I full wo begon,
Ðe sekond for to tarry for, till þat it miht be had,
in þe mean whȳll, I mai forgo, þat which miht mąk mee glad.
Ðe third in kąs to þat affọr, I mai full well kompąr,
Ðus of þẹs three þe ọn to chiuz, to rid mee from þis kąr,
I kannot now, wherfọr I must kontent my self with þis,
to tąk þe chauns þat God will send when þat hiz pleaziur is.

Imediatly after þat I had mąd þis said sonett, I went from
London to my ʒentilwomans hows heer. whẹr I fownd my chest
removed owt of my ⌜new⌝ chamb⟨er⟩ into mȳn old chamber
again. and also I fownd þat totnam waz turned french[1] on my
sȳd. and to tell yow how þe gąm went with mee þen, yee shall
vnd⟨er⟩stand þat my eldest skoller heer had þen A woer, of
whom[a] I told yow A littl befọ⟨r⟩ who for sum inward displeaziur
þat hee konseived against mee, sowht prevely þe means how to
bring mee owt of kredit, and in displẹsiur with my said skoller &
her moþer, and so whẹr az shee and her moþer, and I, did agree
very well ⟨be⟩fọr þat tȳm, and reseived into owr kumpany and
konsort, such A ọn az w⟨ee⟩ þouht wold hąv mąd all owr agreement and harmony þe better, hee kontrar⟨y⟩ to owr expektasion
did sett vs all owt of tewn.

Much lȳk az for ensampull A drunken Duchman did (whọz
nąm waz Helmich van Shelb)[2] emong A kumpany of singerz,
who did sing an Antem in priksong in A church, for whyll þei
wẹ⟨r⟩ A singing þis Helmich preased to kum in and to stand in
þe mydz emong þem wh⟨ẹr⟩ þei stood at þe desk, which being
perseived by þe singerz, and þei seing him A strainʒer, yet
thinking þat hee kąm þyþer only to sing (az maner iz not for to

---

[b] MS. reads 'whon'.

---

[1] Proverbial; Tilley T 444.
[2] Search in contemporary records has produced no further information
about Helmich van Shelb.

seek to stand so emong singerz ⌈exsept⌉ it be for such A purpọz)
did suffer him to ente⟨r⟩ and to plạs him self in þe midz emong
þem. And when þe said Helmich w⟨az⟩ so setled in hiz permitted plạs, he began with sumwhat A temprat vois ⟨at⟩ first,
yet notwithstanding with riurall and vnskilfull sowndz. þen
pres⟨ent⟩ly after þe which, hee braied owt lowder, and þen
folloingly hee rọred an⟨d⟩ yelled owt so lowd, az no beast living
being no greatter þen hee kowld h⟨av⟩ mạd greatter and lowder
noyz þen hee, and with þat sort of sow⟨nd⟩ hee kontynewed so
long and hee being so plased in þe midz emong þe si⟨n⟩gerz, az
þei on þe ọn sýd of him kowld not hear how to agree with þọz
on ⟨þe⟩ oþer sýd, and being half amazed with hiz noyz, þat in
short tým þei w⟨ẹr⟩ all owt of tewn, and kowld not rekover þem
selvz so, az þei did agree ⟨a⟩ny mọr at þat tým. and when þis said
Helmich had þus with hiz diskorda⟨nt⟩ noyz so seperated þeir
konkordant harmony, hee, after A solem long ku⟨rt⟩zy or low
reverens doon toward þe hy alter. with þe lýk sober & demiur
kountenans þat hee kạm withall to þe desk affọrsaid, not ọns
chainȝing ⟨þẹr⟩of to any sort of lafter, smyling, or frowning,
went hiz waiz in such m⟨aner⟩ and fassion az ọn wold hạv
deemed by hiz demeanor þat he thowht hee ha⟨d⟩ doon azwell az
any singer þạr at þat tým. þe which alþowh hee did not ⟨in⟩ þe
first beginning to chaunt, yet in þe end hee did so, for þen hee
waz in ⟨az⟩ riht tewn az þei, and þei az far owt of tewn az hee.

Now sir, wheþer þis fọrsaid fresh lạt begun woer of owerz
thouht to hạv doon with vs, az þe Du⟨ch⟩man did in þe end I
know not, for I tarried not owt þe end of hiz sewt but in þe
beginning it seemed þat hee ment so. first hee told my said
skolle⟨r⟩ how þat I had told him A great story in her diskommendasion, at þe which þe girll being wurs A feard þen hurt,[1]
waz in A great perplexite. wherfọr t⟨o⟩ eaz her mýnd shee ⌈told
her⌉ moþer of it, wherwith þe moþer waz sett in such A heat
against mee, and talked so much þerof abrọd in her hows, az
when I kạm again to her, ọn in sekret did lett mee vnderstand it,
30ᵛ þe which when I had hard, þen waz I also much tro⟨bl⟩ed &

---

[1] Proverbial; Tilley A 55.

greeved. first ⟨with þe sai⟩d woer bekawz þat hee had belied mee. sekondly with my skoller bekawz shee had komplained on mee to her moþer so rashly. and lastly with her moþer, for þat shee professing somuch frendship vnto mee az shee had doon, wold be so liht of kredit, and kondemn mee in A fawt and raȝ at it somuch, befor shee had had mor of it, and had examined þe matter to know þe trewth þerof. þen in my mẏnd I kondemned her to bee but A faint and A fraill frend. whervpon I mad þis sonett folloing—

Đouh freendz bee fraill in evry plas, and promiz brok þat erst waz pliht,
Yet on þer iz aboov all freendz, þat faileth not þe faithfull wiht.

In azmuch az þe party who told mee of þis great vnkẏndnes ko[n]seived by þem[a] ageinst mee, told mee also þat in her anger shee said þat shee wold talk with mee konserning þis matter, I harkened evry day when I shiuld hear of it. and when I had looked A sertain tẏm þerfor, being dezẏrows þat þe trewth of þe matter shiuld be known vnto þem both, I wold sumtẏms gẏv okkazion in wordz vnto þem A far of to remember it, and to talk with mee þerof. When þei[a] wold not serv I waz dryven into A quandare.[1] on whẏll I dowted lest I waz put into þe hed with A fabull and no trewth, to try wheþer I wold vtter any thing against my self and þem (az sum suttl headz imaȝining matterz, will hav such feches to bring þeir purpozes to pas) An oþer whẏll I dowted þat þe fawt had bin quẏt forgẏven and forgotten,[2] an oþer whẏll I dowted lest þat my ȝentilwoman waz determined to bear it in mynd vntill such tẏm az by þe charȝing of mee þerwith vpon ⟨þ⟩e sudden, shee miht do mee A greatter displeziur þen shee kowld do at þat prezent ⟨þ⟩e which dowts mad mee to akkownt her but A dowtfull frend. and þe raþer ⟨b⟩ekawz shee had konseived an inward displeaziur against mee and wold not let mee ⟨v⟩nderstand it. for I will think such A on my freend in deed, who having by any ⟨m⟩eans konseived A displeaziur against mee, þat will in sekret shew mee wherin I ⟨h⟩av offended

---

[a] MS. reads 'þen'.

[1] Proverbial; Tilley Q 1. [2] Proverbial; Tilley F 597.

him,[1] wherby if I hạv gyven ȝiust kawz of offens, I may amend my fawt, and þen to think on it nomọr, or els if hee shiuld konseiv A displẹziur against mee withowt kawz, þat þen hee knowing hiz errowr and fawt, may bewạr of rash ȝiudȝment, and so amend hiz fawt.

After þis when I did see my tým and plạs konvenient, I brak first with my skoller examining her from point to point what waz reported to her of mee, þe which being by her awnswered, I told her ⌈how⌉ þat her woer had belyed mee, þe which I wold tell him to hiz fạs, and if shee wold konsent þerto. to þe which wordz shee wold not konsent, but praid mee to put ⌈vp⌉ þat inȝiury, affirming þat it shiuld be never A whit þe wurs for mee. whervpon I waz sumwhat satisfied, and bekawz þat I did not know how much I shiuld over shiut myself if by any overthwart langwaȝ hee wold provọk mee to mọr heat, þe which miht enkreas my ȝentilwomans hevier displẹsiur against mee, for hee waz kropen not A littl, I kooled my koler with þe syrop of reazon, and so by littl and littl diȝested it þat way. Ðen when I did see my tým I brạk þe matter also with my ȝentilwoman, and I diskowrsed with her þe họl sirkumstans þerof, and in konkliuzion I so awnswered evry point wherin I waz belyed, þat shee seemed to bee satisfied and kontent. After þe which talk, at ọn tým, and in þe prezens of him who told mee of her anger, she vpon okkazion of talk blamed her self, in þat, throwh rash beleef shee had mizyowzed her frend. and at oþer týms shee wold say þat in her angry mood shee shiuld speak þat sumtýms, þat shee shiud be sory for afterward.

When I had pawzed and konsydered of þis matter A sertain tým, I thouht to try my ȝentilwoman A littl konserning her former promis mạd vnto mee, þe which waz þat I shiuld fynd her alwaiz redy to pleaziur mee in any thing þat shee kowld do for mee. and fynding A konvenient tym for my purpọz, I did put her in mýnd þerof, þe which shee rạtified so far az shee miht with her honesty. and I said þat I requýred no farder nor oþerwýz of her (if I had ment oþerwýz, þen had I now fo⟨rgọn h⟩er ȝenerall promyz affọrsaid þat waz mạd withowt ex⟨sep⟩sion,

31ʳ

---

[1] Proverbial; Tilley F 683.

turned with A kondision) so þat now I miht hav remembred þe
old pr⟨o⟩verb which saith, when yee miht ye wold not, but
⌐now⌐ þat ye wold yee shall not.[1] I thank God for it, I never
entended to dishonest her, but took and klaimed he⟨r pro⟩mis
to do me an honest good turn, and non oþerwyz, and having
sum okkazion a⟨t⟩ þat tym to try her, I took þat sam for þat
purpoz, and þen after þoz ⌐said⌐ wordz and a⟨wn⟩swer of myn
to her, I did put her in mynd of A yoong mayden þat shee had
bro⟨wht⟩ vp in her hows, þe which I kowld lyk very well to be
my wyf, and if I miht ⟨hav⟩ it so, wherfor I dezired to hav her
goodwill and furderans in þe matt⟨er.⟩ to þe which my wordz,
my ʒentilwoman said, þat shee for her part waz ⟨wil⟩ling þervnto,
but quoþ shee þe maid iz my huzbands kinswoman, and þer⟨for⟩
he will bestow her wher hee lyketh. and if yow wold sew to him
for hiz will to hav her, I am siur it wold bee such A trobulsom
pees of wurk for yo⟨w⟩ az it wold disquiet yow very much. þus
much do I shew yow for goodwil⟨l⟩ (quoþ shee) and þerfor if
yow will be kownselled bi mee do yow never prosee⟨d⟩ any
furder in it. quoþ I to her, if I miht obtain her it wold bee A
good okkazion to bynd mee to attend alway on yowr hows to do
yow any pleaziur þat I kowld, þe which both yow and yowr
huzband sh⟨iu⟩ld fynd mee ready ⌐alway⌐ to perf⟨orm.⟩ quoþ
shee did yow ever mov þe matter to þe maid, siurly no quoþ I,
exsep⟨t⟩ it wer merily and after A ʒesting sort az by þe okkazion
of mery talk betw⟨een⟩ vs. þen quoþ shee, if yow will follow
my kounsell never speak of it mor to her and look what I hav
promized yow heer to for, yee shalbe siur of it, alþoh yee hav
not her. quoþ I, I am satisfied, and will never speak of it again.
Ðis said konfirens being past, I rezolved in my mynd þe sirkumstans and substan⟨s⟩ of þe holl matter þat had bin prezently past
between my ʒentilwoman an⟨d⟩ mee, and þervpon I wrot and
mad þis þat folloeth—

Ðouh koler kleapt þe hart abowt, and set it all on fier,
which kawzd þe toong in hasty wyz, to blast owt for mi hier,

---

[1] Proverbial; Tilley N 54.

A dredful chainʒ for mee to hav, if it had taken plas,
yet now þe storm iz gon and past, and I in quiet kas.
For lyk az oft, þe dainʒerz great, which happen dẏverzly,
by fortiuns help when shee hath will to shew her self frendly
Do quikly turn, and do bekum, to blisfull stat again.
So hath it hapt to mee also, to rid mee of my pain.
Ðe toong þat erst did thunder owt, great threats of my mizeaz,
told long er now þat shee waz forst (þe hart þen for to pleaz)
to vtter such wordz az shee did, but yet quoþ shee eevn now,
þe hart doth think, and I do say, wee hàv misywzed yow
and az I am by natiur sett, to vtter az I may,
þe sekret thouhts þerin shrowded, þat fain wold go þeir way
So now again, I say to yow, þat which þe hart doth think
þat iz, þat yow shall siurly fynd, þe hart will never shrink
to fors all parts þerto subʒekt, for to perform þe hest
which ons to yow wee firmly mad, wherfor now bee at rest
and let þe chois of þ'oþer go, sins az I said befor,
owr firm promis shall not be brok, but stand az did of yor
Lo. if þe hart doth think þe sam, which now þe toong hath said
of all on lẏv. I may þen say, þat I am well apaid.
If kontrary I fynd þe sam, þen piur pasiens parfors,
must bee þe remedy wherwith, to salv my sory kors.

Not long after þis I went from hens to London, whẹr my chauns waz to be i⟨n⟩ þe kumpany of A frend of mẏn, who had bin dyverz tẏmz with mee at my ʒentilwomans hows heer, and **31ᵛ** þar for my sak had had very good and frendly enterteinment. wherfor akkording to þe kommen kurtezi⟨es hee dem⟩aunded of mee how every body of þat hows did, whervnto I awnswered akkording az kam to my mẏnd þen. and so passing into oþer talk of þe sam hows, at lenkth I told him þe sirkumstans of þe disagreing, and agreements again þat had past between my ʒentilwoman and mee az iz befor rehersed. whervnto hee awnswered byanby, þat her fallings owt with mee waz for þat I did not feed her hiumour, and offerd her mor kyndnes þen I had doon (yee know what I mean) and hee said also, þat and if

I had doon so, it wold not only hav put by all owr fallings owt,
but also hav vantaȝed mee aboov forty powndz for A reward
(þis waz A wurþy gest to hav such enterteinment on her az hee
had, to whom hee gav such A frendly reward). þen I said vnto
him þat hee waz deseived in her, for shee waz so honest A
ȝentilwoman in her behavor, and so gyven to serv God dayly,
þat I had never on thouht of her to be enklȳned þat way.
Tush man quoþ hee, yee ar but A novis in such kases, all iz not
gowld þat seemeth to be so nor evry on A saint þat seemeth to be
on,[1] I did perseiv by her fas, her komplexion, koolor of eyez, and
demeanour when I waz at her hows, what her inklȳnasion iz
þat way, & also I did perseiv by þe enterteinment þat shee gav,
what her affeksion waz towardz yow. and þerfor if yee do not
seek to pleaz her þat way yee ar but A beast (þis waz A frend
neiþer for þe body nor sowll).

I do thank God quoþ I þat hee by and throuh hiz gras hath
geeven mee such A konsiens az I hav. I had raþer be akkounted
such A beast az yow do now akkount mee, þen to mak A beast
þat way az yow wold hav mee to do. þen I rekownted vnto him
how besȳd þe heavy displeaziur þat I shiuld sustain at Godz
handz for kommitting adultry I shiuld bee in dainȝer of worldly
mischeefs and lawz. Also I opened vnto him az far az I kowld
remember, þe manyfold trobuls þat hav happened, and do dayly
chauns throuh disdayn, ȝelozȳ, mallis, and envy of þeir frends
to such who do seek to lȳv in such dishonest sort. þen I deklared
vnto him þe vnquietnes þat I shiuld be in my self, azwell fear
of mȳnd, az of travell of body with þe konsiuming of þe sam,
togiþer with my tȳm and substans bestowed vpon kownsell
keeperz, pandarz, and bawdz. And last of all I told him of þe ill
nam þat I shiuld purchas þerby, wherby I shiuld hinder my
self very much bekawz þat noman wold trust mee to teach þeir
childern. and so konkliuding, my talk[a] in putting him in mȳnd
of many mȳzeriez and kalamitiez þat hav happened vnto

---

[a] MS. reads 'tall'.

[1] Whythorne has combined two proverbs, the first a popular favourite
(Tilley A 146) and the second more obscure.

dẏverz of such whom I did know, and hee had hard of, who did
ywz þat kẏnd of lẏf þat hee wold hạv had mee to lead. and
after many perswazions ywzed to him for þat hee shiuld chainȝ
hiz former ill oppinions & perswạzions, wee left owr talk and
parted kompany for þat tẏm.

Ðen went I to my skollerz þạr, and with þem I remained az
I waz akkustomed to do befọr, þe which tẏm being so spent, I
returned again to my skollerz heer. in þe which tẏm of my being
with þem, az okkazions wẹr moved befọr þat tẏm to talk dyverz
matterz and sumtẏm of loov and þe rewardz þerof, so waz þe
lẏk dyverz tẏms now geven, whervpon at ọn tẏm in espesiall, my
ȝentilwoman heer said in faint speech, þat alþouh shee kowld be
kontent to gẏv and to help an honest man, and also to profitt and
furder him, yet shee did it not, bekawz þat shee wold play þe
harlot with him, þe which wordz I took to be ment toward mee,
and þerfọr I took good okkazion vpon her wordz to think þat
whatsoever shee had said and doon toward mee befọr þat tẏm
shee ment not to do it for any dishonesty, wherfọr now I began
to bee merier þen I had bin A long tẏm befọr þis tẏm in her kum-
32ʳ pany, and also to ⟨pass⟩ þe tẏm ⟨henceforth w⟩ith such wor⟨dz
az⟩ befọr (mistrusting her ȝelowz he⟨ad⟩ I⟩ durst not be mery
⟨wit⟩h ⟨her⟩, þe which afterwardz she browht mee in A dowt of
again, ⟨which⟩ shee mizlẏked of, az heerafter by dẏverz prezump-
sions I did gaþer. az first, wee being ⟨on⟩ A tẏm in talk of loov
matterz, shee looked mee very earnestly in þe fạs and said ⟨with⟩
speech, akkompanied with A kountenans and regard mọr stern
þen amiabull, ⟨þat⟩ þei who loved whẹr þeir loov waz not requyted,
must azwell az þei miht refr⟨ain þe⟩ sạm again, at þe which
wordz I waz sumwhat abashed, but yet I said not⟨hing⟩ þerto.

Ðen at oþer tẏms shee wold [sai] az okkazions and tẏm served
how þat kontrar⟨y to⟩ her wunted kustom, shee kowld not sleep
A nihts, and ⌜how⌝ her mẏnd waz troble⟨d⟩ and also to mạk her
hart liht, shee wold drink wẏn with Boraȝ,¹ and when ⟨þe⟩ wẏn

---

¹ When dried petals of Borage are mixed with wine, the resulting cordial
'comforteth the harte, and maketh one merye', according to Sir Thomas
Elyot's *Castel of Helth* (1541), sig. I3ᵛ (*STC* 7644).

waz drunk shee wold eat þe Boraʒ, and say þat shee had need of
it to mą⟨k her⟩ mery. at þez wordz began my sorowz to enkreas
again, and þe mǫr bekawz þat þę⟨z⟩ wordz being spoken vnto
mee seemed to requir sum wordz of mee again. if I did ⟨not⟩
speak to her shee wold hąt mee, and if I did demaund þe kawz of
þoz wordz pera⟨d⟩ventiur her aw[n]swer miht be oþer wŷz þen
I wold hąv it. After þis shee said on ⟨A⟩ tŷm þat if A man (peradventiur shee miht hąv said A woman) who feared God, ⟨did⟩
loov oþerwŷz þen he owht, it wold bee A great torment to hiz
konsiens, t⟨o⟩ þe which I awnswered þat to such A ǫn hiz body
waz A hell vnto him self, þe w⟨hich⟩ wordz I spąk þen vpon sum
experiens, for I must konfes þat I loved her asmu⟨ch⟩ az I miht
do with A sąf konsiens, bekawz þat shee well dezerved it. Ðen
⟨at⟩ an oþer tŷm shee said þat shee did play þe fooll ons when
it waz, but and if ⟨shee⟩ węr to do again, shee wold bee better
advŷzed er shee did it, but shee [said], þe good ⟨þat⟩ I wold do, þat
do I not, butt þe ill which I hąt þat do I. þęz last wordz wold
shee say dyverz tŷmz when shee took okkazions þerfǫr, wherfǫr
at þis tŷm I said vnt⟨o⟩ her again, after A kumfortabull sort, þat
þęr waz no body az I thouht but shiuld overshiut þem selvz
bǫth in wordz and also in deedz sumtŷms, az I hąv ha⟨d⟩ sum
experiens þat way my self. but quod I, whosoever doth so fall,
it is g⟨ood⟩ for þem to kall to God for mercy, and to dezier him
þat þei may hąv of him ⟨þe⟩ sekret and sprirituall grąs, þe which
iz þe forgŷvnes of þeir synns, and ⟨þe⟩ reʒenerasion or new birth
& lŷf.

After þis I ever dowted A chainʒ. þe wh⟨ich⟩ foloed not long
after. for on A tŷm, when shee and I had had sum talk togy⟨þer⟩
konserning my skollerz, shee told mee þat her huzband waz not
willing to besto⟨w⟩ any mǫr kosts and charʒes for þe teaching
of hiz childern (þe which kosts az I note⟨d⟩ A littl befǫr vnto
yow, solong az I pleazed her shee said þat shee wold be at her
self. but now þat shee lyked of my kumpany no lenger, she referz
þe matter ⟨to⟩ her husband) þe which (konsidering þe premisses)
I waz very well kontented ⟨withall⟩. and þervpon I prepared
to remoov to London. in þe which ⌐tŷm⌐ I mąd þis folo⟨ing⟩—

If I had not fǫrseen, þe chainȝes newly hapt,
þe sodain chauns þerof in kąrz wold hąv mee wrapt.
wherfǫr I do protest, for knowlęȝ iz þe best,
of trobuls[a] *þat must kum, for þen þei soon diȝest.*

A littl whẏll befǫr my parting from my *ȝentilwoman,* vpon sum okkazion of ta⟨lk⟩ between her and mee, shee told mee þat good toongs węr þe kawz of owr separat⟨ing.⟩ So þat by þis yee may perseiv þat whęr A fier iz, sum sparks[1] it kannot be so k⟨lǫs⟩ kept but þat sum liht þerof will appeer and bewray þe sąm. and þerfǫr it iz good ⟨to⟩ kast þe wurst of evry enterprẏz befǫr yee do begin it, and so wurk þerin akkordingly. Ðis fǫrsaid ȝentilwoman, having A ȝoly witt akkompanied with an awdasite ⟨of⟩ behavor, korespondent to þe sąm, delyted very much in pleazant talk, wherin w⟨az⟩ konteyned sum exersẏz of þe witt with fẏn devẏses. shee waz also very frendly ⟨and⟩ grątfull & also liberall, wheraz shee lyked to bestow þe sąm, and wold look to be g⟨ra⟩tified akkordingly, if not in gyfts yet in sum kẏnd of servis to bee az it węr to be ⟨kom⟩maunded, þe which shee wold boast of to such az shee lẏked of, az þouh it kąm mǫr of goodwill toward her þen for her dezarts. þe which dispozẏsion of herz being by ⟨mee⟩ espied, mąd mee to deall þe kunninglier with her. what her entent waz towa⟨rd⟩ mee ȝiuȝ yow þat by þe sirkumstans of þe matter befǫr rehersed. az for my part alþouh 32ᵛ I did seek to feed her ⟨hiumou⟩r sumtẏms for ⟨mere civil⟩ite, y⟨et I th⟩ank God for it, I never had þe mẏnd to dishonest her. And þus o⟨f⟩ þis matter I seas.

now sir, þe tẏm of my departiur from hens being kum, shee and I parted very ⟨f⟩rendly, at which tẏm shee dezired mee þat I wold be no strainȝer at her hows, and so I kąm from þens to London. And from þens to my ȝentilwoman þąr. and when I had remained þąr A sertain tẏm, I parseived þat þe ȝentilman

---

[a] Written over 'chainȝes'.

---

[1] For an earlier use of the 'sparks' proverb, see p. 78.

waxed wery of hiz char3es þat hee waz at for þe teaching of hiz childern ⌐and þerfor⌐ I went from þens also, and so kąm to London. whęr shortly after, my fortewn waz to be akquainted with A 3entilman,[1] who had A soon þat waz þen In kambrid3. and þis said 3entilman hyred mee to go þiþer to teach hiz soon, and for þat my kredit and enterteinment shiuld be þe better þąr, hee kommended mee vnto ǫn ⌐þar⌐ who waz tiutor to hiz soon. Ðis tiutor[2] at my first kumming to kambrid3 e[n]vied mee very much bekawz I waz appointed to be also A tiutor to hiz piupull, and also bekawz þat I wold not do to him such reverens and kap kurtezy az hee looked for, (az þat iz A thing much ywzed and looked for, with geving of þe wall when þei meet in þe street, espesiall of such who kum vp to Degreez from þe plow and kart, & such bąs okkiupasions) þe which I wold not do of dewty but in kurtezy to him bekawz þat I kąm þiþer to lẏv with him and not by him at hiz char3es. also I kąm not þiþer to be A skoller or piupull, but to bee A Skoolmaster, and A Tiutor. And also I waz þąr in þe fellowz kommens in þe hows whęr he waz remaining (in þe which kommens þąr waz at þat tẏm both lordz soons, knihts soons, and 3entilmans soons) and in þe respekt þat I waz of þe sąm kommens þat hee waz of him self, I did not ow vnto him somuch reverens and kurtezy az hee looked for. Ðis fǫrsaid reverens þat iz somuch looked, not only in kambri3 (but in Oxford also) bringeth to my remembrans, what iz said of þe skollerz of bǫth þe ywniversitez. þe which iz þat when þei hąv

---

[1] This gentleman was William Bromfield (d. 1563), Her Majesty's Lieutenant-General of the Ordnance. His only son, also William Bromfield (d. 1582–3), matriculated at Trinity College, Cambridge, in Lent, 1557–8, and apparently was admitted Fellow Commoner in 1560. He received the degree of Bachelor of Arts in 1561–2, graduating first in his class. Because Whythorne had been in Cambridge 'ny abowt ⟨half⟩ A year' in July 1560, it seems likely that he came to Trinity in the previous winter.

[2] The envious tutor has not been identified, beyond his nickname of Scattergood. Possibly this is a pun on the name Godsalve, in which case he may have been John Godsalve, who received his Bachelor of Arts degree in 1549–50. Unfortunately, evidence of his later career is lacking, notably whether or not he received another degree about 1559 and became a Fellow of Trinity. See p. 123.

taken degreez þe first ⌐yeer⌐ after þe taking of þem, þei do bear
daggerz in þeir sleevz¹ to kyll az mani az þei do meet, þat be
prowder þen þei bee. and yet for all þat þei do kill no body. and
so peradventiur waz þis said tiutor kropen vp þis yeer A degree
hier þen hee waz in þe yeer past, which mạd to look so hye
aboov me az hee did, and akkownted mee prowd bekawz I
wold not embạs and humbul my self vnto ⌐him⌐ so much az hee
loked for. In þis point I did akkownt of him az I do of many
oþerz, who will akkownt such to be prowd which wil not fram
þem selvz to pleaz þeir prowd foolish fantaziez, wheraz in deed
þe prȳd remaineth only in þem, bekawz þat þei do look for þat
dewty which bekummeth þem not to look for. Ðez fọrsaid
kawzes I say so kindeled him in ⌐sekret⌐ envy and dizdain
towardz mee þat alþouh hee wold yȳz ⌐me⌐ frendly when þat
I of kurtezy kạm to vizit & saliut him, behȳnd my bak he
wold with mọst spȳtfull wurdz, and reprọchfull tawnts most
chiurlishly yvz mee. of þe which at length hiz piupull and
mȳn did let mee vnderstand. wherfọr to eaz my hart I wrọt az
folloeth—

When fortiun seemd somuch mi frend, to plạs mee with assiured stai,
þen with A bek shee mạd mee bow, vnto mi fo, to bee hiz prai,
who to mi self did promis mạk, to hạv of him what hee kowld do,
but in þe end I miht perseiv, þat hee waz but A frendli fo.
and not kontent to slạk hiz hest, hee with hiz toong did mee deprạv,
not to my fạs, but I absent, þen wold hee streiht begin to rạv,
Of þis detraktor þus I sai, sins hee defamed my good nam,
A sikofant I do him kạl, whoz toong þe giltles doth defam.

Alþouh þat ọn iz blạmed or ȝȳbed at, þe argiueth not alwaiz
þat þe party so ywzed iz alwaiz wurþi þerof, for az oft it proseedeth of þe prȳd & korrupt or indirekt ȝiuȝment of þe blamerz
33ʳ or ȝȳberz who will fȳnd fawts whẹr ⟨nọn be. Lȳkewise, sum⟩ of

---

¹ An echo of Heywood's lines:

He beareth a dagger in his sleue, trust mee,
To kyll all that he meeteth prouder then hee.

(*Proverbs*, 1867, p. 29.)

þoz wh⟨o fẏnd fawts⟩ or m⟨okk . . .⟩ þat iz to say kommen fawt
fynderz, blamerz⟨, sko⟩fferz, ȝyberz, mok⟨ke⟩rz⟨, and such⟩ lẏk
(yee alþouh it bee for ȝiust kawz) kannot shun to bee so
yvzed aga⟨inst⟩ openly or privili, of what stat soever þei bee.
and I being set ⟨in⟩ vnkẏnd heat with þe tiutorz diskurtezi
towardz mee, took all þe okkaz⟨ions⟩ þat happened for þat
purpoz to kall to my remembrans to be eeven with ⟨him.⟩ first
wheraz I had red þat hee who seeketh þe kompany or fellowship
of ⟨hiz⟩ enemiez seeketh hiz own distruksion,[1] I left to vyzit him
so oft az I w⟨az⟩ wount to do. þen wheraz þe poet *pindarus* saith
þat hee iz man emong ⟨men⟩ þat iz frend to hiz frend, and A
lyon to hiz enemy, (espesially þe hatr⟨ed a⟩ryzing for þe detesta-
sion of vẏs, and þe loov growing for þe advaun⟨sment⟩ of vertew) I detesting him for hiz prẏd and misyvzing of mee, began
⟨to⟩ bend my mynd to requẏt him by wryting in sekret, az he
behynd ⟨my⟩ bak had defamed mee openly. and first wheras hee
waz an *obsecro* ⟨and⟩ A poor skoller when he kam first to kambriȝ
and lyved of almz at ⟨þe⟩ releef of þe kolleȝ whẹr hee first waz,
and after grew to þat ⟨plas⟩ which mad him so prowd az he
waz at þat tẏm I wrot þus—

Nothing iz sharper þen low things, when þei by groth on hy be
  brouh⟨t⟩
So non in prẏd and krewelte[a]*, are lẏk to þoz, who*[b] *rẏz of nowht*

Ðen bekawz hee requẏted my kurtezy ywzed towardz him
with such spẏt az iz afforsaid, I wrot az foloeth—

> *Az t'iz A sẏn of persons grav,*
> *pas'iently to bear þ'unkynd parts,*
> *yowzed to þem by such az hav,*
> *by frendly proof known þeir trew ⟨harts⟩*
> *so iz A sẏn A fooll to know,*
> *vnthankfullnes whẹr it doth show.*

---

[a] Written above 'hawhtines'.   [b] MS. reads 'why'.

[1] Proverbial; Tilley E 138.

Ðen wheraz *Socrates* saith þat malisiowz wordz do diskover
þe ⟨sekret⟩ hąt and evel thouhts of þe hart, I wrǫt þus þerof—

Lỹk az þe smǫk owtwardly seen, doth gy⟨v⟩ knowleʒ whęr þat
   fie⟨r iz⟩[1]
So all evl wordz diskouer plain, þe hątfull hart whęr þat ier iz.

In þe mean whỹll þat I waz tormoyled in þis *laberinth of*
vnkynd⟨nes⟩ ǫn þat perseived þe dissimiulasion þat waz between
þe kambriʒ ⟨*tiu*⟩*tor and mee, reported þe sąm to þe* faþer of hiz
piupull and mỹ⟨n,⟩ whęrvpon hee wrǫt vnto vs bǫth and þerby
perswaded vs to amit⟨e and⟩ frendlynes, he[a] kawzed þe tiutor to
akknowleʒ vnto mee hiz gros riudnes, and yvzed mee afterward
very frendly and kurteowzly.

ny abowt þis tỹm I had red in A pląs of *St Ambrǫs,* þat better
iz ⟨hee⟩ þat kontemneth inʒiuriez, þen hee þat soroith and
fretteth at it. fo⟨r⟩ hee þat kontemneth it he passeth it away az
þouh hee felt[b] nothing þ⟨er⟩of, but hee þat soroith or fretteth
at it, iz þerwith tormented az þouh ⟨hee⟩ felt it. Also lỹk az
greef iz A dizeaz of þe body, so iz mallis A siknes ⟨of⟩ þe sowll,
wherfǫr vpon þe konsiderasion of owr rekonsiliasion, and v⟨pon⟩
þe reading of þǫz fǫrsaid sentenses I mąd þis sonet folloing—

33ᵛ ⟨*Hee þat co*⟩*ntem⟨neth injuriez⟩, hiz stąt ⟨will better appeer soon⟩*
   þen hee who fretz ma⟨lisiowzl⟩y, till hee revenʒ offenses doon.
   for az mallis tormentz hiz hart, and all hiz helth doth streiht
      vnwrest,
   þe oþer not forsing þerof, returneth soon to quiet rest.

after þis, being sumwhat in quiet, and having þąr littl to do
mǫr þen þe tęching of my skoller, I gąv my self sumtỹms to þe
furþerans of my knowleʒ in Miuzik. sumtỹms to þe lỹk in þe
Italien toong, and sumtỹms in reading of english books.
⌜(*azwell of Diuinite az of moral and profąn matterz*)⌝ and also
sumtỹms in kalling to my remembrans þe stąt of þe world az I

---

[a] MS. reads 'þe'.   [b] MS. reads 'felf'.

---

[1] Proverbial: Tilley F 282.

had seen ⟨i⟩t in my tẏm. whervpon az I do remember kąm to
my mẏnd þe kawzes wherby I had felt sum greef of mẏnd my
self in my tẏm. but cheefly þer kąm to my mẏnd dẏverz matterz
towching my self, and sum oþerz whom I did know, and also
had hard of, for þe achyving and performing of þe which wee
had great kąr & trobull, wheraz sum oþerz whom I did also
know kąred so littl for þem az þei ak⟨kow⟩nted vs to be linked in
foliez bandz, bekawz wee kąred somuch for þem. an⟨d⟩ kon-
trarywẏz in sum oþer kawzes and matterz wee skorned þat az
meer foolish, and reȝoised at þe siht of þat, which oþerz with
kąrfull hartz did lament to see or heer of. and eevn þe sąm tẏm
mẏn own estąt pleazed mee not sowell, az I do know it wold hąv
doon many oþerz, if þey miht ⌜hąv bin⌝ in þe lẏk. vpon þis
inmaȝinasion of mẏn of þe dyverz ⌜passions &⌝ delihts of dyverz
headz I wrọt þus—

> *Đe happi lẏf az I do tąk*
> *þe quiet mẏnd þerof iz grownd*
> *which sowr sorrowz doth still forsąk*
> *diȝesting þem az þei abownd*
> *f⟨or⟩ who from kąrz will pas to eaz*
> *m⟨ust tąk⟩ ⌜all⌝ trobuls in good part*
> *and if [þe] mẏnd tąk no miseaz,*
> *all trobuls els will soon revart.*

⟨At⟩ þis tẏm I had A book þe which I yvzed to read on sumtẏms (it being A very ⟨ko⟩mfortabull book for A distressed ⌜and
an afflikted⌝ mẏnd, þe which iz named. *A Medisyn* ⌜*(or Fizik)*⌝ *for
þe* ⟨S⟩*owll*)[1] ⌜þis⌝ book A frend of mẏn dezired to hąv of mee,

---

[1] This book was ostensibly the Latin original of *Phisicke for the Soule in
the Agonie of Death* (*STC* 19894), translated into English by Whythorne's
friend Henry Thorne, and published in 1568. The volume was dedicated to
Sir George Speke, who lived in Somerset, in the same region as Whythorne's
family. Whythorne tells us that Thorne lived in the country, whence he sent
complimentary verses for Whythorne's *Songes* about 1570. (See p. 219.)
In 1584 Thorne published *The Confutation of Follie* (*Stationers' Register*, ii.
201), dedicated to 'George Speke, Esquier'; a copy, lacking the title-page, is
in Sion College Library.

and I knowing þat þer waz mor of þem to bee bowht, gav it vnto him. and in þe sam I wrot þus—

When pensif thouht torments þi hart with gryping grevouz greef,
within þis book þow shalt heer fýnd, kounsels for hiz releef.

⟨I⟩ having at þis tým devýzed ⟨A⟩ fantazy to be plaid vpon þe liut, þe which I gav vnto A frend of mýn, I wrot in þe paper wher þe fansy waz written, þis foloing—

All þat which fansy heer brouht foorth, þi fansý to revýv,
hold heer my .H.[1] for Whýthorn did þe sam for þee kontrýv.

Ny abowt þis tým I kam into A plas wher I fownd dyvers sentenses and devýses written vpon A wall, wherfor I wrot þar az þus.

In publik plas nothing wryt þow,
exsept great skill þerin þow show.

Also ny Abowt þis tým þer went A blynd speech or profesy of hy hats and great hos,[2] how þat when þei wer ywzed, wee shiuld hav trobuls. of þe which I wrot þus.

When þ'English do wear hats lýk hyvz and breeches lýk to bearz,
þen (it iz said) þei all shalbe much trobled with great fearz.[3]

34ʳ ⟨B⟩y þat ⟨tým⟩ I ha⟨d bin at k⟩ambridʒ ny abowt ⟨half⟩ᵃ A yeer, þe maʒestrats a⟨nd skol⟩lerz of þe yvniversite did selebrat þe

---

ᵃ This is guesswork; there is space for only four or five letters.

---

[1] The identification of Whythorne's friend 'H' is hampered by the metrical requirement that the name be of one syllable only.
[2] These changes in styles of clothing about 1560 have not escaped the attention of historians of costume. See *Shakespeare's England* (1932), ii. 104, and the illustration from Turberville's *Booke of Faulconrie* (ibid. ii. 353).
[3] This distich does not seem to have achieved the status of a proverb. It is not recorded in Tilley.

resurr⟨eksion⟩ of doktor *Bucer*,[1] who in k⟨ing⟩ Edward þe sixt, hiz daies, waz þe reader of þe ⟨Di⟩uinite lektor þar. and hee being dead and biuried, þe papists in queen Maries daiz did tak vp hiz kask, or koffin. and also þe kask or koffin of on named *paulus fagius*, who waz þar r⟨eader⟩ of þe Hebriu lektor, and burned þem both at A stak, az þe reliks of twoo a⟨rch⟩ heretyks. wherfor at þis prezent þe protestants to revyv[a] þe memoriez of þ⟨em⟩ both again did selebrat þe resurreksion of þem, but cheefly of *Bucer*. and az ⟨þe⟩ papists did mak verses[2] in þe reproch of *Bucer* at hiz burning, so now þe prot⟨es⟩tents mad verses lykwyz in hiz kommendation.[3] som wrot in Greek, sum in la⟨t⟩ten, and sum in English. at þis tym[4] I waz pers⟨wa⟩ded by A frend of myn who waz in þe sam kommens þat I waz of, to wryt sumw⟨hat⟩ konserning *Bucer*, alþouh it wer in English,

---

[a] MS. reads 'þevyv'.

---

[1] Martin Bucer (1491–1551), an eminent contemporary of Martin Luther, came to England in April 1549 and soon after was appointed Regius Professor of Divinity at Cambridge. He died on 1 Mar. 1550–1, and Matthew Parker delivered the funeral sermon. When Queen Mary visited Cambridge on 6 Feb. 1557, zealots exhumed the bodies of Bucer and his friend Paul Fagius, and publicly burned them on Market Hill.

[2] A contemporary account reports that while the visitors were dining at Trinity College 'all the verses which were set upp on the churche [St. Mary's] doores in the sermon tyme in dempnation of the said Bucer and Fagius which were a great number' were brought to them (John Lamb, *A Collection of Letters* [&c.] *Illustrative of the History of the University of Cambridge*, 1838, 210). Some of the verses were sent to London by the officials. No copies of these poems are known to be preserved, so Whythorne's evidence concerning their authorship is doubly valuable.

[3] The restoration of honours to Bucer and Fagius occurred in July 1560, with the ceremony and orations taking place on 30 July in Great St. Mary's. Here again there is contemporary mention of verses. In Arthur Golding's translation of *A Briefe Treatise Concerning the Burnynge of Bucer and Phagius*, 1562 (*STC* 3966) the last page tells that '. . . many of thuniuersitye to set out and defend Bucer withal, beset the walles of the Churche and Churchporche on both sydes wʰ verses, some in Latin, some in Graeke, & some in Englyshe . . .'. About forty of the poems were printed at the end of the 1577 Basle edition of Bucer's *Scripta Anglicana*; only Latin and Greek verses are given, so Whythorne and other writers of English verses are not included in the list of authors.

[4] Here is a crossed-out passage which reads in part 'I being a pentioner'. This, in its Cambridge application, means that Whythorne was a member of Commons at Trinity College and paid his own expenses.

whervpon, I having of my said frend, þe nạms of all such of þat
hows or kolleȝ az did wrẏt befọr against *Buce⟨r⟩* at hiz burning,
devyzed vpon þe *Ɛtimoloȝi* of þeir nạms, þis az foloeth—

Er Vulcạn with hiz Fiery bank, konsiumed Bucerz chest,
þe shakkelloks did ȝingel fast with thr⌈e⌉ats of hiz vnrest,
þe sturdy Oxen did him gọr, t'abriȝ hiz sakred fạm.
þe Talbot dog did hunt hiz bọns in stẹd of oþer gạm,
with blood[y] handz, with leg, and lim, to Nikol him þei ren,
Soon kạm þe heaþen lọrd to ring, hiz tọn with spẏtful pen.
þe poetz vain, did never fain, on laez of koks and birdz
az did þat romish rowt on him, lẏk rọming wulvz on hirdz
who kried long, rẏs, ley him vp, hois Hawz him vp, on, Bẹr
twẏs wikked iz þat Skattergood, þat such wark doth defer.
and on þei went with Fosterd wrath, to see hiz fatall end
with krạk and bọst þeir Cook shiuld rọst, all þat wold him⌈fen⟨d⟩⌉
To tawnt and chek, noman þei rekt, lẏk Cheriubins on hy
or demi Godz þei sat in trọn, vs sely sowz to spy
þen miht þei sing ter Alington, welkum John Saundersun
but bạt me'an ạs quoþ Bolton[1] now, þouh þen þe goal yee wun
Ðoh franzẏ forst yee to deprau, þat good and verteowz wiht
hiz bọnz to ashes to konsium to wrẹk your kankard spiht
yet now again to grẏv yow all, hee lẏveth heer and shall
(az hee hath lyved euer sins wyth þe lọrd eternall)
hiz doktrẏn piur doth weed þe korn from kokkell and from tẏn
þat hath kept down þe food of Chrẏst, whoz flok began to pẏn
for lak of þat mọst godly lọr, which hee emong vs sent
lạt by owr ȝiust dezartz for plạg, waz ȝiustly from vs hent
prai wee þerfọr to owr pastor, to keep vs from þọz elvz
þat wold vs gnaw with gredi ȝaw, and fatlings mạk þem selvz

---

[1] A good deal has been written about this proverb (Tilley A 20). Archer
Taylor, in *The Proverb* (Cambridge, Mass., 1931), pp. 200, 201, gives
a story that Queen Elizabeth chided Heywood for having omitted it from
his collection. In another version William Paulet (1485?–1572), Marquis of
Winchester, who was Lord Chamberlain and thus technically Heywood's
employer in 1546, made the remark on being presented with the *Dialogues*
(Thomas Park in 1871 edition of Warton's *History of English Poetry*, iv. 83,
n. 2). By coincidence, Paulet's descendants became dukes of Bolton, beginning in 1689.

Firebrand - Ere Vulcane wythe hys fierye ban
Shackelock - The shackelocks dyd iyngell fas
Oxebridge - The sturdye Oxen did hym gore
Talbott - The Talbot dogge did hunte his b
Ashman Legg - Wythe blodye hands, wythe Leg
Nycolson Shakebotome Lawton - Soon came the heathen lorde to ri
The poetes vayne, did never fayne
As did this Romishe rowte on hy
Long Bexley Gawer Berwick Scattergood - Who cried Longe, ryse, ley hym
I wise wicked ys that Scattergood, t
Foster - And on they wente wythe Fosterd
Cooke - Wythe crake and boste, theyre C
34 (Or ▮ demy gods) To taunte and checke, noman they
Theye satte yn throne ▮
Elington Hon Saunderson Bolton - Then myghte theye singe ter Alimo
But hate me an ace quod Bolton
~~But hate me now an ace of that~~

The 'Bucer Scrap' (early draft)

And I it iz pasquil by nạm, þat all þẹz things disklọz
who hath told mọr in Room it self vnder þe Pọp hiz nọz
þouh þei kut of my legz, myn armz, and nọz to do mee shạm
my trọn iz larʒ, my bak iz brọd,[1] *to bear all þis þeir blam.*[2]

Heer I think best or I pas any furder to shew yow þe nạms
þat I inkliuded within þẹz *forsaid versez,* þe which I do set heer
foloingly in such sort az þei do st⟨and⟩ in þem. and þus þei bee.
Fierbank. Shaklok. Oxenbridge. Talbot. Redman. Legge. Nicol-
son. Heathringtone. Laecocke. Long. Rysley. Hawse. Berwicke.
Scat⟨ter⟩good. Foster. Cooke. Alington. John Saunderson. and.
Bolton.[3] *Shaklok,* affọrsaid, being A plezant poetikall versifier,

[1] Proverbial; Tilley B 13.

[2] Tucked in the Whythorne MS. is a fragment of an earlier draft of this satire (now bound in as f. 92 of the MS.). It is reproduced here photographically as a specimen of Whythorne's hands and spelling, and also to show the earlier readings and corrections. The proper names are listed in the left margin to make clear at a glance the play Whythorne has made on their names in his verses. This fragment, designated 'the Bucer Scrap', is important evidence that an earlier draft of sections, at least, of the Autobiography existed, written on similar portions of paper of similar size, but in ordinary spelling. See Introduction.

[3] The versifiers against Bucer may be identified as follows: Robert Firbank was elected Fellow of Trinity College in 1555 and ordained sub-deacon of Norwich in the same year. Richard Shakelock, also a Fellow of Trinity, retired to Louvain shortly after the accession of Queen Elizabeth, and published several Romanist treatises. Andrew Oxenbridge became Fellow of Trinity in 1553 and signed the Marian articles of religion in 1557; later he was imprisoned for denying the queen's supremacy but released upon signing the required acknowledgement. Thomas Talbot also became a Fellow of Trinity College in 1555; nothing is known of him after the accession of Elizabeth. Thomas Redman, a Fellow of Trinity in 1546, subscribed to the Marian articles in 1555 and in 1559 was appointed Master of Jesus College, but subsequently was deprived as a Popish recusant. Thomas Legg had migrated from Corpus Christi to Trinity in 1555, and also survived a shift in religious beliefs to become ultimately Vice-Chancellor of the University, though not without later suspicion of encouraging Romanists. Richard Nicholson was not originally a Trinity man, having graduated from Pembroke Hall in 1553–4 before becoming a Scholar and later a Fellow of Trinity in 1555; after the accession of Elizabeth he apparently became a Fellow of Christ's College. Ambrose Etherington (d. 1591) came to Trinity as a Fellow in 1552 after taking his Bachelor's degree at Magdalene.

Richard Laycock was another Fellow of Trinity of the crop of 1555. So too were Robert Bolton, Robert Longe, Edmund Risley, and Henry Hawes. Thomas Barwicke, Fellow of Trinity from 1548 till 1577, combined a career in the Church with some practice of medicine. The nickname 'Scattergood' may well have been applied to Edward Godsalve, a Fellow of Trinity

34[v] devẏzed A dialog between *Vulcan⟨us* (þe⟩ poetikall God of þe Sm⟨ythy &⟩ fier) and þe for⟨said *Bucer* in⟩ þ⟨e⟩ which h⟨ee⟩ deklạred how þat *Vulcạn* sh⟨ewd⟩ *Bucer*, how þat hee wold sinȝ hiz berd with hi⟨z⟩ skorching heat and brandz. þe bloody handz do signyfy þe nạm Redmane, bekawz þat blood iz red, and mane iz ⌐derẏved⌐ of *Manus*, which iz latten for A hand. þen wheraz I spạk of A heathen lọrd, þat lọrd iz set for Heaþrington, whom þe skollerz of þe sạm hows, in ȝest or mokkery did ọn tẏm in A Christmas tẏm, mạk A kounterfett lord of Mizrewll.[1] þe nạm Skattergood waz A niknạm or by nạm given in derizion vnto þe faþer of my forsaid piupuls tiutor befọr spoken of vpon sum dezerts of hiz. þe which nạm þe tiutor waz many tẏms kalled by also, alþouh hee kowld not abẏd with pasien⟨s⟩ to hear it, wherfọr seing þat hee gạv mee niknạms behynd my bak vndezerved, I being þen angry with him gạv him þe nam þat hiz faþer had for hiz rekompens. þen wheraz I spạk of kokull[a] and tẏm, þọz be twoo weedz, which do grow emong korn, and do hinder þe sạm from ⟨gr⟩owing and rẏping. lastly wheraz I mạd þọz verses in *Pasquils* nạm, vnder⟨stan⟩d þat þe sạm pasquill, iz an imaȝ in Rọm, or Room, on þe which and ny abowt him iz sett many tẏmz skoffing or tawnting verses, þat do reprehend þe vẏses of all estạts, eevn az well of þe Pọp him self, az of any subȝekt hee hath. When þe serimoniez of þe[b] forsaid resurreksion wẹr finished and past, þe talk þerof remained A whẏll after,

---

[a] MS. reads 'kolull'.   [b] MS. reads 'þaid'.

---

from 1546 until the accession of Elizabeth, when he was deprived of his offices and retired to become a Professor of Divinity at the Monastery of St. Michel in Antwerp (see p. 115 n. 2). Richard Foster became a Fellow of Trinity in 1553, and after the accession of Elizabeth served as Vicar of Gainford, Durham. Cooke is more difficult to identify; perhaps he was the Robert Cook who subscribed to the Marian articles of religion (see J. Lamb, op. cit., 176). Richard Allington, Fellow of Trinity in 1553, also signed the Marian articles. John Sanderson was a Scholar of Trinity at the time of the Bucer outrage in 1557; he became Fellow in 1560 but was expelled in 1562 'for suspicious doctrine & contumacy', and ultimately became a Professor of Divinity at Rheims.

[1] An early document records the incident when Etherington was made a 'kounterfett lord of Mizrewll': 'It[em]. the Xtmas lorde at trinitie Coll. was had from the churche to the Hall with drom, bylles &c which the visitors lyked not' (J. Lamb, op. cit., 214–15).

and az on þing brings an oþer, so after þat þer grew talk of
matterz in kontroversȳz in relyȝion, az sum of þe rȳts and
serimoniez of þe church. sum of þe sakraments, sum of ȝiusti-
fikasion of faith or works, sum of þe byshop of Room & hiz
siupremasy. sum of *purgatori*, and sum of Romish relyȝious, az
of Munks, kanons, or channons, Nuns, and frȳerz. and emong
all þeir devyses, þer waz many old frierish pranks rehersed þat
waz plaid and doon by þoz fryerz þat wer named limiting frierz
which went A begging abowt þe kuntreyz. of þe which sum of
þem wer pleazant and mery rȳesh parts. and I being þen sett on
A mery pin[1] wrot þerof vpon an old grownd[2] (on þe which I had
seen þe lȳk mad befor) þis þat folloeth—

> *Ðer waz A frier men kald Robard*
>   *sing busk vnder þe brier*
> *And all þat euer he met hee mard*
>   *it waz A venȝeans[3] frier.*
>
> *Frier Robard walkt in A short tukt gown*
>   *sing busk vnder þe brier,*
> *hiz staf hee bar to ward hiz krown*
>   *it waz A dowhty frier*
>
> *Hiz kowl of boshels waz þe full sȳz*
>   *sing busk vnder þe brier*
> *hiz showz wer karved after þeir gȳz*
>   *it waz A reliȝiouz frier.*
>
> *Hiz loinz hee girt with knotted rops*
>   *sing busk vnder þe brier,*
> *F⟨or filching good⟩ bakon in villa⟨ȝ⟩ shops*
>   *it waz A painfull frier*
>
> *Hee war no bre⌈e⌉ch hiz gear grew wȳld*
>   *sing busk vnter þe brier*
> *þe maidz and wȳvz hee gat with chȳld*
>   *it waz A freutfull frier*

35ʳ

---

[1] Proverbial; Tilley P 335.   [2] The 'old ground' used for
the ballad could be one of many tunes popular at the time.

[3] *OED* has this spelling as a noun, but not as an adjective, except meaning
'very large or great'; here the meaning 'vindictive' seems intended.

Hee gąv þem lases, needlz and pinz
   sing busk vnder þe brier
which giftz of women much loov winz
   it waz A pleazing frier

Ðei gąv him trÿps, þei gąv him sows
   sing busk vnder þe brier
hee searcht þe sekrets of þe hows
   it waz A sawsy frier.

Ðei gąv him puddings, chitterlings, and egz
   sing busk vnder þe brier
hee paid þerfor between þeir legz
   it waz A tupping frier

Our sowlz (quoþ þei) dowth not on ʒọt
   being buskt vnder þe brier
þat þẹrz nọn bad þat wearz ⌐þe¬ lÿk kọt
   of þÿn þow bulling frier

When yow (quoþ hee) of mee do hear
   kum stalking throuh þe mier
See þat I ready fynd yowr gear
   to pley þe frisking frier

Our stoof said þei to dy þerfọr
   when yow will busk þe brier
for yowr own tooth, yeez fynd in stọr
   owr loving lusty frier

35ᵛ

Ðis lust⟨i man⟩ and learned klark
   new ⟨b⟩usked vnder þe brier
hath trod full well and doon hiz wark
   full lÿk A devout frier.

Ðe townsmen þen sat him in stox,
   az hott az tọst[1] from fier
for medling so with su⟨ch⟩ A box
   az waz not for A frier.

---

[1] Proverbial; Tilley T 363.

Hee threatned þem az I now tell
    þei shiuld hav for þeir hier
A kurs with book, bell, and kandell[1]
    sor chaft þen waz þe frier.

Ðe women þen did lett him owt
    to busk vnder þeir brier
and bad him chooz among þe rowt
    to pleaz again þe frier

Hee thanked þem and choz Osbell
    to busk vnder her brier
and said over her A bad gospell
    full lýk A goostly frier

Ðen rang þe bellz at good hornzai
    sing busk vnder þe brier
hee took hiz freiht and went hiz wai
    it waz A tristy frier

Not long after hee waz at hom
    sing busk vnder þe brier
hee felt how good it waz to rom
    so lýk A gadding frier.

⟨F⟩or hee waz tan hee n⟨ew⟩ not how
    sing busk vnde[r] þ⟨e⟩ brier
to keep hiz bed hee waz fain now,
    hiz leggz no'wld bear þe frier

Ðen in A trauns hee fell into
    sing busk vnder þe brier
too or th⟨r⟩ee daiz hee did ly so
    L⟨ýk⟩ A dum gazing frier

Hiz freendz and neiburz did him greet
    but hee waz ner þe nier
þei kumforted him az þen waz meet
    no word kowld speak þe frier

36r

---

[1] Proverbial; Tilley B 276.

Ðen spąk hiz truls of þe town by
   kynd wordz vnto þeir sier
A queint, A queint, hee kried bianby
   revẏud þen waz þe frier

And vp hee start telling þem how
   hee buskt in Hell þe brier
þ'effekt þerof I will tell now
   az it hapt with þe frier

when az hee kąm fast by Hell gąt
   sing busk vnder þe brier
hee spẏd whęraz þe Divls dąm sąt
   it waz A smirking frier

On her hee prẏd, on her hee looked
   az hee wold busk her brier
at her hee wrẏd, at her hee tooted
   it waz A fliering frier

36ᵛ   *Ðen spąk ⟨to⟩ her, þis limliftęr[1]*
   to bu⟨sk⟩ vnder her brier
promyzing þat euermęr
   hee wold be' her loving frier

Ðen fret and fiumd sir Belsabub
   dowting he' wold busk her brier
get þe hens frier with þi long klub
   quoþ hee to þis bald[a] *frier*

Ðow art no whelp for þis owr den
   to busk vnder her brier
gen þee emong þe dawhterz of men
   þow kursed lęchro⌈u⌉z frier.

---

[a] Written over 'bowld'.

[1] 'Limb-lifter', meaning 'fornicator' (*OED*).

Þe frierz speech now did faint and seas
þen said hee to hiz prier
shrẏv mee faþer, graunt mee releas
þat I dy lẏk A frier

And þen þe frier gạv vp þe gọst
but it kould go no hier
it waz so klogd in evri kọst
þen waz hee A wofull frier

To purgatori þen hee gat
sing busk vnder þe brier
and when hee waz kum ny þerat
hee krẏd let in A frier

Þis plạs quoþ hee owr holy pọp
did mạk at owr dezier
whẹr and wurst fall I may hạv skọp
to play þe frolik[a] *frier*

Owt of þis plạs when wee do pray
wee fech sowlz owt of fier
Nọn els kan do þe lẏk I say
exsept hee hold with þe frier.

konserning þis fọ⟨rsaid⟩ p⟨lạ⟩s of purgatory, ⟨þis⟩ þe papists do 37ʳ
affirm to be A⟨third or⟩ middl plạs between heavn and hell, not
in dist⟨an⟩s but in stạt and kondision whẹr such sowls do remain
till þei be purȝed or gotten owt by þe pọps dispensasion or
serimoniez, who do stand in þe stạt of grạs, but yet hindered for
A tẏm by veniuall and oþer small sinns. I hạv hard on pạpist say
þat St pawll in þe first epistell, and þe third chapter to þe
Corint⌐h⌐ians[1] sayth þat *Þe fier shall try eueri mans work of what*
sort it iz. Þe which fier ọn of þeir doktorz doth affirm to be þe
fier of *purgatori.* Also an oþer of þat faksion did I heer say þus
folloing. wheraz in þe Apostels kreed it iz said þus. *I beleeu in þe*

---

[a] Written over 'lusti'.

[1] 1 Cor. 3. 13.

resurreksion of þe body &c. it iz ment þat þe sowll shall posses þe body again at þe day of ȝiudȝment. þe⟨n⟩ if þe sowls of þoz þat be dead bee in heavn from whens non do return, or els þ⟨ei⟩ bee in hell whęr þer iz no redemsion, how shall þei þen return to þeir bodiez o⟨r⟩ þeir bodiez to þem again, wherfor þei þat shalbe saved must needz be in A third p⟨ląs.⟩ also þe papists do say þat þe sowls for evry dedly sinn be ȝiuȝed to abýd seven ye⟨erz⟩ in þe fier of purgatory.

Now sir, on þe oþer sýd þe Protestants[1] deny þat þer iz any such pląs at all, or þat it iz ons spoken of in all þe hol skriptiurz, for say þei, yee shall read in þe sixteenth chapter of St marks gospell.[2] *Hee þat shall be⟨leev⟩ and bee baptyzed shalbe sąued, but hee þat wilnot beleev, shalbe damned.* by ⟨þe⟩ which wordz yee may perseiv þat salvation iz gęven vs by faith, and damnasion fo⟨r⟩ lak of faith. it must needz bee þat wee dy in faith or withowt faith. if wee d⟨y⟩ in faith, wee ar saved for it iz written. *Hee þat shall beleeu shalbe saued,* a⟨nd⟩ if wee dy withowt faith, wee ar damned, for it iz written. *Hee þat wilnot beleeu shalbe damned.* Also *Salomon* saith in *Eccle.*11.[3] *If þe tree do fall toward þe sowth, or toward þe north, in þe pląs þat þe tree falleth þąr it shall bee.* to fall toward þe sowth iz to dy in faith. and to fall toward þe north iz to dy withowt faith. hee þarfor þat dieth in faith hath everlasting lýf in heaven, and hee þat dieth withowt faith hath everlasting damnasion in hell. Heer iz no man⟨er⟩ of mean or middl pląs az þei wold hąv purgatory to bee, whęr to fall betwe⟨en⟩ þoz ij said pląses. wherfor yee shall fýnd no oþer purgatory þen þe blood of o⟨wr⟩ saviowr Jezus krýst thorow þe which only, all sinns ar parfekly pardoned. f⟨or⟩ wee shalbe forgeven for owr faiths sąk þat wee hąv in þe death and passion

---

[1] Most of this section is based upon *Pasquine in a Traunce* [1566?], a translation from the Italian by W. P[histon?] (*STC* 6130). The discussion of Purgatory runs from sig. Y2 (f. 86) to sig. 2A3ᵛ (f. 95ᵛ), and Whythorne has sometimes quoted from it directly and at other times merely extracted odd items of information. Although he does not acknowledge his source, one may note in particular his direct quotation of the phrase 'trentals, and quarentals, with oþer foolish invensions full of all kovetowsness'; *Pasquine* has provided the *OED* with its sole citation for the rare word 'quarental'.

[2] Mark 16. 16.   [3] Eccles. 11. 3.

of o⟨wr⟩ ʒezus krẏst, þe which iz eiþer parfekt or vnperfet. if it
be parfet, þen þer needeth non oþer thing to mak it parfet. but
to mak it, or say it iz vnperfe⟨t⟩ þat iz A blasfemy to ʒezus kryst
and his passion. az do þoz, who wold se⟨ek⟩ with þeir masses,
trentals, and quarentals, with oþer foolish invensions full of all
kovetowsnes and siuperstision to mak satisfaksion for þeir sinns
þat be in purgatory. St pawll in hiz .10. chapter to þe *Hebrius*[1]
wher hee saith þat þe old law had no powr to klens away sin, but
krẏst did it with offring hiz body ons for all, hath þez wordz
folloing—*Hee taketh away þe first þat hee mai stablish þe sekond,
by þe which will wee ar Sanctified, euen b⟨y⟩ offring of þe body of
ʒezius krẏst ons mad. and euerẏ preest appeareth daily min⟨is⟩tring,
& oftẏms offereth on maner of offring which kan neuer tak awai
sinz. but þis man after hee had offered on sakrifẏz for sinz, sitteth
for euer at þe riht hand of God. and from hensfoorth tarieth, till
hiz enemiez bee mad hiz footstool. for with on offring hath hee
konsekrated for euer þem þat ar sanctified. for þe holy Gost also
beareth vs rekord for after þat hee had said befor. þis iz þe Testament þat I will mak vnto þem, after þoz daiz, saith þe lord. I will
put my lawez in þeir hart, and in þeir mẏndz I will wrẏt þem,
and þeir sinz and iniquitiez will I remember nomor. Now wher
remission of þez thi⟨ngz⟩ iz, þer iz no mor offring for sin. &c.*

Ðis plas of St pawll speaketh evide⟨nt⟩ly against þe sakrifẏz
of þe propisiatory mas, and also it iz plain against þe forsaid
third plas of purgatory, bekawz þe on of þem dependeth vpon
þe oþer. and vpon nothing els, for þ⟨at iz⟩ needed not for þoz **37ᵛ**
⟨þat bee⟩ in heavn. and it booteth not for þoz þat bee in h⟨ell⟩
bekawz þar iz no redemsion. þen heer to konk[l]iud for þis
matter. þe protestants say and affirm þat no plas of and in þe
sk[r]iptiurz þer iz, þat iz A warrant suffisient to prov þat þer iz any
such purgatory az þe papists imaʒin to bee. also þat þe mas iz
A vain invension of man þe which waz devẏzed for kovetowsnes
sak to bring sowls owt of þeir vain invented plas of purgatory, so

---

[1] Heb. 10. 9–18. There is a brief reference to Heb. 10 on sig. 2A3 (f. 95) of
Pasquine in a Traunce, but the length of Whythorne's quotation indicates
that he probably referred to the original.

þat þe on of þem iz of nomor sertainty and kredit þen þe oþer iz of. and lastly þei say þat þe only sakrifýz of owr saviowr ȝezus krȳst ons for all, iz þe parfekt redemsion, propisiasion, and satisfaksion for all þe sins of þe whol world, both oriȝinall and aktiuall, by þe which þei bee and shalbe prezently and perfektly pardoned, and þarfor þat iz þeir purgatory & non oþer. many saings hav þey to proov þeir opinions trew þe which I will leav to towch any farder at þis tým, and go forward to my purpoz.

Now wheraz I had bin ⌈az⌉ afforsaid much trobled with þe dowt of þe fained frendship of þe tiutor afforsaid, and having at þis tým read in *Marcus Aurelius* þat þe suspisiows, þe hasty, and ȝelowz man lyveth ever in much sorow,[1] I did kast þat kar away from mee now, and þarvpon I wrot þis sonett foloing—

Đow shalt soon see in ech estat
wher þat do tak deep root þes fawts
suspisiousnes beyond þe rat
þat needfull iz, or lýk assawts
of hasty mýnd or ȝelowz mood
great sorowz ay to bee þeir food

I being now wholy bent to þe reading of books ⌈&⌉ az I waz dayly konversant among learned men, I waz ⌈I⌉ lýkwyz bent to þe kommendasion of learning and of learned men. for I did see þat it waz great ryches to þe poor, and þat it did garnish so þe rich az it mad þem þe mor worþi of þe honourz þat þei had of þeir inferiorz alþouh þeir vertewz wer equall. Of þis kynd of nobilite king phillip of Macedon hath þez wurdz foloing. Nobilite (saith hee) iz not only in dingnite or awnsient linaȝ, nor in great revenewz of landz, or possessions, but in wizdom, knowleȝ, and vertew, which in man iz very trew nobilite, and þat nobilite bringeth A man to dingnite. vpon þe which se[n]tens I wrot þis sonet foloing—

Who þat for trewth dekreez (az ȝiuȝ most saȝ)
trew nobulnes of riht only to stand

---

[1] This expression had become proverbial; Tilley M 159. In this section Whythorne appears to have gathered quotations from some compendium to which he had access at Cambridge.

in dingnite, or els aunsient linąʒ
or great riches, or reveniuz of land
if þerwithall hee do not link in band
wisdom, knowleʒ, and oþer vertewz rąr
hiz ʒiuʒment þen of reazon iz but bąr.

By þis entrans into þe praiz of þe gifts of þe mynd I waz okkazioned to wąd into ⌐a⌐ komparizon of þęz three gifts foloing az þus—

Ðe gifts of nątiur well dispǫzd, ar plęzant to þe siht
þe lẏk of fortewn rewll þe rǫst,[1] be it in wrong or riht
þouh bǫth or nǫn of þęz be had, yet to þe gifts of mẏnd
þe wẏz hąv þe prerogatẏv, in all ąʒes assẏnd.

Ðe exsell⟨ent⟩ wyz ⟨filoso⟩f⟨er⟩ and Emprowr ⟨Mar⟩cus Aurelius 38ʳ esteemed þe v⟨ertewz⟩ of þe mẏnd so much az hee wrǫt þus in þe komme⟨nd⟩asion þerof. *Ðe trew honour and wurship iz þe vertew of þe mynd. which h⟨o⟩nour no king kan gẏv þe, nor no flattering nor money kan get þee. þis honour hath in him nothing fained, nothing painted, nor nothing hid. of þis honour þer iz no suksessor, no akkiuzer, nor defoiler. þis honor iz not varied nor chainʒed bi no tẏm. it feareth not tẏrant, nor it esteemeth þe favour or disfavor of þrinses.*

After I had remayned in kambridʒ ny abowt A twoo yeerz, my piupull and I left þe sąm, and kąm to London to remayn.[2] whęr after I had bin A sertayn tẏm I vizited my ǫld akquaintanses þąr, emong þe which þe painter[3] affǫrsaid waz ǫn, ⟨þat⟩ mąd my kounterfets or piktiurz az iz affǫrsaid. in whǫz hows, I did see ma⟨ny⟩ piktiurz azwell of þǫz þat węr much elder þen I, az of sum such þat węr of my yeerz. yee, and much yoonger

---

[1] Proverbial; Tilley R 144.

[2] Because William Bromfield the younger received his degree of Bachelor of Arts from Cambridge early in 1562, it seems probable that he and Whythorne left Cambridge about that time.

[3] The information about the painter who was an 'ǫld akquaintanse' is too meagre to suggest his identity. All Whythorne actually tells us is that the man had painted his portrait about 1550, and again about 1562; also, that his house or studio contained many portraits. There is no evidence that Whythorne sat to this same painter seven years later for the 1569 portrait. See Appendix V.

þen I waz. þe which kawzed mee to thin⟨k⟩ þat az sum yoong
folks for þat þei having A pleaziur to behold þeir bewtiez ⟨&⟩
favorz, kawzed þeir piktiurz to be mạd. so þọz þat wẹr older
þen I, alþoh þei had no such kawz for bewty and favorz sạk az
many yoong folk hạv, di⟨d⟩ kawz þeir piktiurz or kounterfets to
be painted from tÿm to tÿm to see ho⟨w⟩ tÿm doth alter þem.
but now peradventiur yow wold say þat þei may see þ⟨em⟩selvz
when þei will in A looking glas. to þe which I do say þat þe glas
sheweth but þe dispozision of þe fạs for þe tÿm prezent, and
not az it waz in tÿm past. also it sheweth þe fạs þe kontrary
way, þat iz to say, þat which se⟨emeth⟩ to be þe riht sÿd of þe fạs
iz þe left sÿd in deed. and so lÿkwÿz þat which seemet⟨h⟩ to be
þe left sÿd iz þe riht. and also þe perfeksion of þe fạs þat iz seen
in A glas doth remain in þe memory of þe beholder, littl lenger
þen hee iz of beholding þe sạm, for so soon az hee looketh[a] of
from þe glas hee forgetteth þe dispozision and grạs of hiz fạs,
wherfọr az iz said befọr, þat diverz do kawz þeir kownterfetts
to bee mạd to see how tÿm doth alter þem from tÿm to tÿm, so
þerby þei may konsider with þem selvz how þe[i] owht to alter
þeir kondisions, and to pray to God þat a⟨z⟩ þei do draw toward
þeir long họm and end in þis world, so þei may be þe mọr
read⟨y⟩ to dÿ in such sort az bekummeth trew kristiens. yet þer
iz ọn oþer kawz wherfọr it iz good for þọz þat ar abull, to hạv
þeir kownterfets or piktiurz, þe which iz for to leav with þeir
frendz, espesially with þeir childern, if þei hạv any þat be
yoo⟨ng⟩ who when þei do kum to yeerz of diskresion, þoh þeir
faþerz be dead yet may þe[i] se⟨e⟩ what maner of favor þei had,
and also þerby put in mÿnd þat if þei left A goo⟨d⟩ report of þeir
vertewz behynd þem, þei may embrạs and follow þe sạm. and if
þeir report wẹr oþerwÿz, þe[n] þei to tạk heed þat þei do not
follow þeir ill deed⟨z⟩ but to pray God for hiz grạs, wherby þei
may deserv better.

All þẹz kawzes konsydered, and I being at þis tÿm ny A
dozen yeerz elder þen I waz when I mạd my last kownterfett,

---

[a] MS. reads 'kooketh'.

I determined to hav it mad now again. And for þat I saw by my last kownterfett þat I waz much chainȝed from þat I waz at þat tỹm, az by þe long and fulnes of my beard, þe wrinkels ⟨on⟩ my fas, and þe holonez of mỹn eyez, and also þat az my fas waz alter⟨ed⟩ so wer þe delihts of my mỹnd chainȝed, I kawzed to be written in þe tabull wher my kounterfett waz, þez twoo lỹns foloing—

Az tỹm doth alter evry wiht
So evri aȝ hath hiz deliht[1]

Vpon þe which ij lỹns I afterward mad þis sonet folloing—

who þat wil wei of aȝez all
þeir chainȝ of shaps from tỹm to tỹm
what ⟨c⟩hỹldish thouhts to ioongling⟨z⟩ fall   **38ᵛ**
az yeerz wax rỹp how þei do klỹm
mai well in mỹnd þis sentens kall
Az tỹm doth alter evri wiht
so evri aȝ hath hiz deliht.

Ðis forsaid kawz of wrỹting of þe aȝes of ma[n]kỹnd, brouht now to mỹ remembrans, þat which I wrot befor towching þe chỹldish yeerz, þe adolessensy, & þe ȝiuventiut or yoongmans aȝ. and þerfor I konsidering with mỹ self þat I waz now aboov thirtỹ yeerz of aȝ, and growing toward þe aȝ of forty, at þe which yeerz begins þe first part of þe old mans aȝ, I took okkazion to wryt þerof þis sonett foloing—

Ðe fors of yowth iz welni past
wher heat and st⌐r⌐enth of lat took plas
and now iz kumming in all hast
þe kold weak aȝ for to defas
þe shew of yowth, wherfor I must
yeeld to mi chauns and thrall mi lust
no[w] farwell youth and all þi toiez
I will go seek mor sertain ȝoiez.

---

[1] The first line has a proverbial base; Tilley T 326.

It is said þat hee who wilbe long old must begin to be old
betẏmz,[1] þe which saing I folloed when I wrot þat sonett. for
now I began in my diet and government of þe order of my body
to do az þe yoongest sort of old men do. and exsept it wer þat
I did sumwhat empair my helth with study and much wrẏting, I
did not kontinewally iwz anything þat shiuld defas my shew of
yowth or bring vntẏmly aʒ vpon mee. wherfor I waz ʒiudʒed of
many which did not know my yeerz, to be alwaiz yoonger þen
I waz in deed.

Ðus having past my tẏm A whẏll in London, I did ly in þe
hows of þe ʒentilman which waz faþer to my kambriʒ piupull,
az iz afforsaid. þe which ʒentilman began now to lẏk sowell of
mee, az hee being kalled to serv þe Queens maʒesty in her warz
beyond þe seaz,[2] kommitted not only þe cheef government of
hiz soon and heir vnto mee, but also þe cheef doings þat hee
had within þis realm, az parteining to hiz offis, hiz tradz in
London, and reseiving & paieng all such somz of money az wer
dew to him or to be paid by him. and when parted owt of þe
realm hee plased mee az hiz depiut in such A plas az wher hee
ment to hav prokiured mee A benefisiall lẏving diuring my lẏf,
and if it had pleazed God þat hee shiuld hav returned from þoz
warz into England saf again. but man purpozeth and God
dispozeth,[3] and hiz will be doon þouh sumtẏms it be against
owr wils, for he seeth what iz mor meet & expedient for vs þen
wee do owr selvz. but and if þer had happened no mor harm
vnto mee þen þe los of my tẏm and pains bestowd whẏll I waz in
þis servis, I miht þe sooner hav rekovered þe sam again þen þe
harm þat I gat þerby oþerwẏz, for within A short tẏm after I
waz entred into þe plas wher he ment to hav settelled mee with
A kompetent lyving az iz afforsaid, my fortewn waz to such A
grevowz & dainʒerows hurt þar, az I dowt I shall never rekover

---

[1] Proverbial; Tilley O 34.
[2] William Bromfield sailed from Portsmouth on 3 Oct. 1562 with the
expedition that was to occupy Le Havre. As Master of the Ordinance, he
was fifth in line of authority (*Calendar of State Papers, Foreign,* for 1562,
pp. 345–6).
[3] Proverbial; Tilley M 298.

þe^a former good estat of my bodely helth again. wherfor I having
tasted and felt so hard A beginning I ⟨wrot az folloe⟩th—   39^r

Of A hard beginning kumz A good end[1] mani say
which proverb old A kumfort iz, to sum wher karz bear sway
If good beginning chauns, shall wee þen dowt A chainȝ
not so, for þen þe faithles will from goodnes soon estrainȝ

Đis forsaid ȝentilman being in þe servis of þe queen and
kuntrei az iz said befor, and in such A plas and offis of kredit
az hee miht not return into England withowt þe leav of þe
Queen and her kownsell, I miht hear sumtȳmz & perseiv also
þat all waz not gold þat glistered[2] in hiz siht, neiþer evry on
hiz frend þat ba⟨r⟩ him A frendly kountenans when hee waz in
England. and alþouh þei wold no⟨t⟩ bark A lowd[3] at him, yet I
vnderstood how þei groined at him, seeking mean⟨s⟩ how to sift
him sekretly, and to mak such A hol in hiz kot[4] az if it had bin
bro⟨uht⟩ to pas, it shiuld hav bin hard for him to hav mended it
again. þen quoþ I t⟨o⟩ my self, what hap hav I? I am now newly
entred into kredit with þis ȝ⟨en⟩tilman, who for þe good opinion
þat hee hath in mee, hath mee in great trust. If I þerfor kontinew in hiz doings and affairz still, and þat hiz enemiez may
bri⟨ng⟩ þeir feches and praktizes to full effekt, peradventiur þoh
I do kno⟨w⟩ nothing of hiz doings þat way, I may be mad to
smell of þe smok of þat fier wherwith my frend iz lȳk to be
sinȝed and trȳd. on þe oþer sȳd, if I leav him now (when hee iz
in kas not to put an oþer in my room konvenientl⟨y⟩) I shalnot
only looz forty marks A yeer diuring hiz lȳf, besȳd A konsta⟨nt⟩
frend, but also to play þe part of an ingrat and an inkonstant
kaytif. wherfor evn in þis perplexite I determined with my self
not to leav him so, but to tak all chaunses az þei kam. having A
siur hop in God þat whatsoever bekam of him, mȳn inosensy in
hiz doings befor þis tȳm shiuld be my defens. and for þat I wold
not only hav hiz dowtfull stat in my remembrans, but also to

---

^a Written over 'my'.

---

[1] Proverbial; Tilley B 260.   [2] See p. 28.
[3] A variant of Tilley B 85.   [4] Proverbial; Tilley H 522.

putt mee in mỹnd of mỹn own estạt, and what I shiuld do at þat
tỹm to keep mee so az it shiuld bee no wurs, I wrọt A few lỹn⟨s⟩
in meeter, and did sett þem in my chamber in such A plạs, az
whẹr I thou⟨ht⟩ I miht most often see þem. þe which wẹr þẹz
foloing—

> When fliering fortewn fauoreth
> þe fals world þen smỹleth
> but turn shee ons abowt her wheell
> strainȝ chainȝes shalt þow feell
> wherfọr az now I kounsell þee
> ywz trewth and honeste
> So shalt þow stand and never quaill
> þouh fortewn do þee faill.

I being now on þe top of Fortiuns wheell, be þe mean of þe
kredit a⟨nd⟩ estimasion þat I had for my said freendz sạk, and þe
doings þat I had for him, I had okkazion many [tỹms] to bee in
þe kompaniez not only of þe cheefest of þọz who did depend on
þe sạm offis þat my frend did, but also of dyverz of þe wurshipfull marchaunts of London, for my said frend had doings for
marchandỹz and ventiurz in and ny abowt þis tỹm, not only to
Muscouia, in Russia, but also into Tartaria, and Persia. þen had
hee also, ventiurz to *Guinnea, in Ethiopia, and also, to Magrobumba, and Noua Spania* ⌈and also to⌉ *Terra florida, in America.*[1]
and whỹll I waz in þe fọrsaid offiserz kumpaniez I miht heer
þem talk of matterz apperteining to þeir offises dỹverz waiez,
39ᵛ and in many matterz els. þen when I ak⟨ku⟩mpanied þe marchaunts, ⟨þẹr⟩ waz talk of gain and los, and of such marchandỹz
az waz best for þem to transport into þis kuntrey and into þat
kuntrey for gain, and lỹkwỹz of þe kommoditiez of oþer kuntreiz

---

[1] The extent of Bromfield's enterprises and the identification of his merchant associates are difficult to establish. He was one of the backers of the
voyage to the West Indies made by Sir John Hawkins in 1562, his associates
being Sir Lionel Ducket, Sir Thomas Lodge, Benjamin Gonson, Sir William
Winter, and others (Hakluyt Society, *The Principall Navigations, Voiages
and Discoveries of the English Nation*, Glasgow, 1904, x. 7). In his will,
Bromfield left £10 to 'Benj Gonston gent', to 'Henry Becher merchant', and
to 'Henry Coddenham gent'; these three were the supervisors of his will and
holders of the true copies and inventories.

to be brouht hiþer wherin gain waz to be gotten. And þen for
þe exchainȝ of money how þat went from tým to tým azwell
beyond þe seaz az heer in England. þer waz no oþer talk emong
⌐all⌐ þez afforsaid but of gayn & riches. at þe first konversing
emong þez afforsaid, þeir talk waz sumwhat strainȝ vnto mee
bekawz I had not bin ivzed somuch vnto it in A great whýll
befor (for when I waz in kambridȝ þar waz no oþer talk but of
lear[n]ing and learned men, & how by learning and þe vertewz
of þe mýnd men wer exalted to promosion). þen shiuld I hear
sumtymz of on who had bin in hiz offis but A small tým, and
when hee kam to it hee waz littl or nothing wurth and evri man
paid, and yet ⌐now⌐ hee waz known to bee both A purchazer,
A býlder, and also A great monied man. Also I shiuld hear of
⌐þis⌐ marchant, and þat marchant how short A tým þei had bin
okkiupierz,[1] with what small stokz þei began, and þat in A short
tým þei for þeir welths bekam to be Aldermens fellowz. when
I had seen, hard, and konsidered A whýll on þez sirkumstanses,
I remembred þat I had ons read þat hee who groeth to be
sodenly of great welth and richez, giveth folks kawz to think þat
þei all be not gotten with A good konsiens. and þerfor I took
okkazion vpon þat to wrýt þus—

> I kannot deem þem happi siur
> who kan but only krak of muk
> I mean riches, which worldlings liur
> from heav'nly karz þem selvz to pluk
> but if vertew to welth ȝoind bee
> twýs happi þen þei bee I see.

Ðen kam also to my remembrans þez sentenses foloing
towching kovetowznes, and kovetowz men, þe which be þez
foloing. It iz no marveill þouh hee bee good which iz not
kovetowz, but it wer A wunder to see A kovetowz man good.
Lýk az A member vexed with itch, hath alwaiz need of klawing,
so þe kovetowznes of þe mýnd kan never be satisfied. It iz A
foolish madnes to think þat ritch men be happy. Az A golden

---

[1] *Occupier*, a trader (*OED*).

brydell, alþouh it garnish A hors, it maketh him never þe better,
so alþouh riches do garnish A man, yet kan þei not mạk him
good, whẹr riches ar honored, good men ar dispẏzed. Đez
sentenses brouht to my remembrans how þat A great number
in þẹz daies do meaziur honesty by welth. az if þei praiz A rich
man þei will sai he iz an honest man, I warrant him hee iz
wurth somuch (and þen þei will nạm [A] sum). lẏkwẏz if þei
dispẏz or dispraiz A poor man, þei will sai þat hee iz but A
beggerly knav, and not worth A grọt. and so akkording to þe
quantite of A mans substans þei will akkownt him honest, and
so to bee kredited and beleeved. and if poor *Lazarus* had bin no
honester þen rich *Diues*, hee had not rested in *Abraamz* bọzom
when þe rich churll for all hiz welth wen[t] to hell. az ye may
read in St *Liuk*, cap.16.[1] wherfọr þẹr iz not þe poorest nor most
afflikted man þat goeth vpon þe grownd or earth, but hee may
be az honest az þe greatest monark þat lyveth and rayneth vpon
þe earth, and hiz sowll iz az presiowz in þe siht of þe redeemer
of all mankẏnd, az iz þe sowll of þe greatest prins lyving. so þat
þei ar far wẏd from þe mark who hạv such affẏans in welth and
riches and þei ar to bee suspekted þat eiþer þei know not what
þei say when þei do say so, or els þei ar to bee thouht þat all þeir
honestiez lieth in þeir welth. and þạrfọr þei do somuch extoll
rich folk for þeir richez sạk withowt þe dew konsiderasion
þerof, or of sender and giver þerof. and seing þat I in my tẏm
hạv hard many of þẹz affọrsaid iwz such wordz þerof az seemed
40ʳ to grow vpon small diskresion I wrọt of þem þis sonett folloing—

> ⟨It iz⟩ *A world sum sotz to ⟨see⟩*[2]
> *who meaziur honesty bi w⟨elth⟩,*
> *akkounting all honest to bee*
> *az þei posses of worldly pelth*
> *and lazarus with God did rest*
> *when þe rich gulch[3] to hell waz prest*

By þat tẏm þat I had past my tẏm ny abowt A three quarterz of

---

[1] See Luke 16. 19–31.   [2] 'It is a world to see' (Tilley W 878).
[3] A glutton. The earliest use of the noun recorded in *OED* is in Ben
Jonson's *Poetaster*, 1601.

A yeer in þẹz doings, I vnderstood þat þe town and plạs whẹr my forsaid frend did serv in, waz so straitly besýȝed, and also vizited with þe plạg of pestilens,[1] az I after þe report þerof ever mizdeemed þat I shiuld never see him again ,whe⌐r⌐for I wrọt þus—

Ðe dowtfull stạt þat I posses
doth trobull all my wits throuhowt
ọn whýll good hap seems twilnot seas
þen bianbi it mạks mee dowt
and þus standing in họp and dread
I wish oftýms þat I wẹr dead

Sumtýms I tạst of sikkernes
streihtwaiz enseuth vnsertenty
so oft I fýnd such fikkelnes
az erst I found þe kontrary
which brings mee in such họp and dread
az I wish oft þat I wẹr dead.

Ðe konstant mýnd wold hạu no chainȝ
neiþer of plạs, of frend, nor loov
when from all þẹz hee must estrainȝ
þe hart not willing to remoov
and þat hiz họp iz kild by dread
þen doth hee wish þat hee wẹr dead

Yet þouh[a] I want þat I dezier
not þat to mýnd I do it kall
I owht not þus mýn end requier
az in dispair I wẹr now fall
but kall to God withowt all dread
who kan mee help and I not dead

Yow may perseiv by þis how soon and quikly owr old enemi þe Divll w⟨il⟩ tạk okkazion to put into owr mýnd þe affektz of

---

[a] MS. reads 'þhouh'.

[1] The plague that struck the English army at Le Havre was first reported by the Earl of Warwick (who, incidentally, was one of Whythorne's former employers) on 7 June 1563. Three weeks later the disease was carrying off 200 soldiers a week. Surrender followed on 26 July.

desparasion, whẹrby withow⟨t⟩ þe great goodnes of owr savior, who wilnot leav destitiut of hiz grạs all such az hạv A siur faith in him, þẹr miht follow þe effekts of þe sugȝestions of owr kankard enemy and adversary. wherfọr now I having read þat if I will hạv deliht withowt sorow I must apply my mynd to þe study of wizdom, I now again az my leiziur served mee gạv my self to þe reading godly and grav books. owt þe which I took sertain nọts and kownsels for mee to hạv in mẏ⟨n⟩d at þis tẏm. sum of þe which wẹr þẹz folloing. first þe wẏz emprowr *Marcus Aurelius* saith. If þou wilt be kounted valient, let neiþer chauns nor greef overkum þee. sọrow iz next frend to solitarines, enemy to kumpany, & heir of desparasion.[1] Ðen saith an oþer. Of small fawts not let ạt þe beginning oftentẏms springeth great and mihty mischefs. vpon þe konsiderasion of þẹz fọrsaid

40ᵛ sentenses I mạd þis ⟨sonett⟩ folloing—

Bewạr[a] how sorowz thee oppres
let wizdom rewll þi fantazi
so, az dispair þee not posses
with deadly dread þi faith to tri

Now I plukt vp mi spreets vnto mee again, and did sett þe better foot befor,[2] determining with my self to tạk all chaunses þat miht happen vnto mee in good pạrt. and to tạk nothing at þe wurst till I did fẏnd sertain kawz þerto. notwithstanding I ment not to be ọn of þọz who waith A chip of chauns mọr þen A pownds wurth of witt.[3] for az foolishnes, and not good konsẏderasion azwell of þe tẏm to kum az of þe tẏm prezent

---

[a] MS. reads 'Bawạr'.

---

[1] The quotation seems to be a paraphrase of a passage in a letter to Marcurino, which occurs in J. Bourchier's translation, *The golden Booke of Marcus Aurelius* (1566), sig. 2E7ᵛ (*STC* 12445a). The quotation from 'an oþer' is similar to a proverb given by Tilley (F 122), though his earliest example is taken from R. Cotgrave, *A Dictionarie of the French and English Tongues* (1611).

[2] Whythorne has combined two proverbial phrases, Tilley H 323 and F 570.

[3] Proverbial; the earliest version cited by Tilley (O 85) is from Cotgrave in 1611.

draweth elswher from happi stat, and putteth in most great
mizery, so þe forknowleȝ or forkasting of most great perils
draweth þe wŷz and putteth þem in great and siur rest. and bekawz þat I wold be siur to prevent azmuch az [in] mee did ly, þe
proposterus and froward overthwarts þat miht happen to mee
in tŷm to kum, I now konsidering þat diliȝens and karfulnes ar
þe keiz of sertenty, bestored my stumps,[1] and what I had left
rawly þat waz for mee to do, now I plied it to mak it perfekt
and firm. Then wheraz I had learned when I first took þez
forsaid doings in hand, Bekawz þat troth and faith, in no degree
doth stand, þarfor þe lawyer saith, tak wrŷtings of þeir hand.
þe which kounsell I had meetly well folloed. now I sorted my
wrytings and layd evry sort by þem selvz in severall boxes, in
my kownting hows or desk mad for þe purpoz. to þe end þat
when I shiuld be kalled to mŷn akkownt I miht þe redilier fŷnd
þem. þis doon, wheraz I had also learned þis sentens foloing.
Reseiv er þow wrŷt, and wryt er þow pai.[2] þat iz to say, Reseiv
þe money befor þow do wrŷt þerof into þi book of reseits, what
it iz, and befor þow do pay any sum of money wryt it, and to
whom, and wherfor, and þe day wherin þow dost pai it, and þen
(az it foloeth þe forsaid sentens) þŷn akkownt shall never
dekay. now sir, such things az wer in my book of akkounts to
bee mad perfekt, I slakt no tŷm in perfekting of þe sam. þez
premisses being no sooner brouht to pas, but I hard say þat my
said frend had such A sor hurt[3] wher hee served þat in short
tŷm after hee finished hiz lyving daiez. whoz estat when I had
sumwhat kalled to remembrans first of hiz prosperite, and þen
of hiz advers and froward fortewn, and þen in þe end to be
kalled owt of þis val of mizery vnto þe ȝoiz selestiall, I did

---

[1] Proverbial; Tilley S 946.

[2] Proverbial, but Tilley (W 940) found no examples before 1659.

[3] In a letter dated 18 July 1563 Sir Maurys Denys reported to Lord Cecil
that Bromfield had received a 'hurt' and had departed for England (*Calendar of State Papers, Foreign, 1563*, p. 459). A newsletter dated 3 Aug., from
W. Hamerton to the Earl of Shrewsbury, tells that Bromfield 'died in England of his hurt within three miles of Portsmouth' (*Historical Manuscripts
Commission*, 6th Report, Part I, Appendix p. 455a; F. B. Frank MSS.,
1877).

akkownt hiz kalling to be better for him self, þen for þoz of hiz
frends who hoped to hav bin benefited by hiz lȳf, and so in þis
mȳnd I wrot þus of hiz death—

> *When I remember of þis world, what þerin I do know*
> *how all þe pleaziurz of þe sam, but vain in þ'end do grow*
> *O, lord sai I happy þei bee whom þow dost entertain*
> *for þei shall euerlastingly in perfekt ʒoiz remain.*

Shortly after þe death of my said master and frend, þe fam
þerof waz spred abrod emong hiz frendz and akquaintanses.
imediatly whervpon I miht perseiv þe old proverb to be trew,
which saith þat A dead body byteth not.[1] for þei who befor hiz
death did but whisper and groin against him, now þei spak &
barked alowd at him. but thanks be to God þeir mallis prevailed
not somuch az þei wold hav had it. Ðus in les þen on yeer had
I past many perils and hindranses. az first sertain overthwarts
when I shiuld hav entred into þe plas wher I shiuld hav bin az
hiz depiut. next þat þe dainʒerus hurt þat I had when I possest
þe plas. þen þe trobuls þat I had to keep þe plas in hiz absens,
besȳd þe trobuls þat I ᵃþat sustained for hiz privat affairz. also
þe los of mȳn aniuite diuring hiz lȳf, with þe los of him when by
hiz means I shiuld hav bin assiured of þe forsaid plas with an
41ʳ anuite þerfor of twenty powndz A yeer diuring my lȳf.[2] over
and be⟨sȳds þe w⟩h⟨ich⟩ premisses, mor ka⟨lam⟩itiz waz lȳkly

ᵃ Dittography.

---

[1] Proverbial: Tilley M 510.

[2] In his will, made on 19 September 1562 (just a fortnight before his departure for the siege of Le Havre), Bromfield left 'To Thomas Whitehorne genᵗ
five pounds', a considerable reduction from the annuity of twenty pounds
yearly which Whythorne had been promised. The will was witnessed by
Thomas Whitehorn, as well as by Thomas Goodman, John Grymstone, Edward (?) Partridge, John Skynner and Thomas Bery, 'Citizen and Draper of
London'. Of these witnesses, Whythorne was the only one to receive a be-
quest. The sum of £6. 13s. 4d. was also left to Matthew Hutton, who had
been Fellow of Trinity College when Bromfield's son matriculated, but had
since become Master of Pembroke Hall and Regius Professor of Divinity by
the time the will was made. Bromfield had left a 'true copy' of his will in Hutton's hands. The document is summarized in H. F. Waters, *Genealogical
Gleanings* (Boston, 1901), p. 1433.

to hạv happen⟨ed⟩ to mee, for my said master befọr hiz death
had sent for hiz soon over þe sea vnto him, whom hee had plased
on þat sẏd with purpọz þat hee shiuld not return into England
again in twoo or three yeer after. wherfọr hee requested mee to
do for hiz soon in hiz absens az I had doon for him. by þe which
I had okkazion to abẏd and kontẏnew still, in and ny abowt
London. þe which sytty waz now so sọr vizited with þe plạg of
pestilens az I dowted to tarry þạr any lenger for being swaloed
vp emong þọz who wer devowred with þe sạm.[1]

so þat now þe fear of death did greatly trobull mee, and I
being at þat prezent much vnquieted with so many krosses at
ons, began to enter into þe ȝiuȝment of mẏn own konsiens, and
konsidered with mi self þat plạgs and ponishments ar many
tẏms sent vnto vs from God for owr sins, for in skriptiurz it i⟨z⟩
said,[a] þat if wee do say wee hạv no sin, wee ar deseived, and þẹr
iz no trewth in vs. also it iz said, þat þe rihteowz man offendeth
seven tẏms A day. þen in þ⟨e⟩ ten kommaundements God saith
þat hee will ponish þe sins of þe faþerz vpon þeir childern vnto
þe third and fowrth ȝenerasion of þem þat hat him, and if hee
wi⟨ll⟩ for owr sinz ponish owr posterite, how shiuld wee think
oþerwẏz but þat owr ⟨sins⟩ shalbe þe mọr hainowz in Godz
siht.

Heer seing I hạv spoken of ponishments sen⟨t⟩ by God, I
think it not vnfit to rehers vnto yow sumwhat of þat which I did
rea⟨d⟩ in A sermon þat iz þus entiteled. *A sermon no les freutfull
þen famouz, mạd in þe yeer of owr lord God. M.ccc.lxxxviij. &c.*[2]
wherin hee saith þus. *Yee shall vnderstand þat God sendeth
siknesses oþer whẏll to good men and lẏkwẏz to shrewz. of*

---

[a] Opposite this point there is a marginal note: '.*i.*/*John.*/.*i.*'

[1] The plague of 1563 was one of the most severe outbreaks of this recurrent
affliction during the mid-sixteenth century. (See F. P. Wilson, *The Plague in
Shakespeare's England*, 1927.) Whythorne's fear of death from the epidemic
turned him to prayer and scripture reading, a common phenomenon.

[2] This sermon by Richard Wimbledon was first published about 1550 and
went through at least fifteen editions. Whythorne was quoting loosely from
a passage which will be found in the 1573 edition (*STC* 25826), sigg. D4ᵛ–
D6ᵛ.

*siknesses I wold hạv yow to vnderstand all maner of tribiulasion⟨z⟩
to good men hee doth send it for ij kawzes. þe first þat þei shiuld
euer know þat þei hạv no infeksion of þem seluz, but of God only,
and to enkrẹs pasiens and .St. Pawl saith in þe .12. to þe Corinthians. lest þe greatnes of mi revelasion lift mee vp into prȳd, to mee
iz geven prik of mi flesh, þe angell Sathanas to smȳt mee on þe nek,
wherfọr I hạv thrȳs praid to God þat it shiuld go from mee, and
hee aunswered mee þat my grạs waz suffisient.* Also God sendeth
saints oftentȳms siknes and persekiusion, to gįv vs sinfull wreches
ensampull of pasiens, for if hee shiuld suffer hiz saints to hạv such
tribiulasion in þis world and thank him þerof, much mọr wee
wreches, þat God hath sent to, not þe hundreth pạrt of þeir sorow,
shiuld bear it meekly. let þe ensampul of Tobi, which ye mai fȳnd
written in þe sekond chapter of hiz book. and lȳkwȳz þe temtasion
of holy Job suffȳz yow for þis matter. þe which God suffred
þe⟨m⟩ to hạv, to gȳv oþer after þem an ensampull of pasiens.
and also sumtȳms God sendeth siknes and tribiulasion to
wikked men, and þat for ij kawze⟨s.⟩ first for þat þei shiuld loov
God, and leav þeir sin, az it iz written, þeir sikknesses ar multiplied,
and after þei hasted to Godward. for wee see ofte⟨n⟩ þat men in
siknes know þeir God, þat never wold hạv turned to him whȳll þei
wẹr họl. Sekondly God sendeth also siknes often tȳms to agast
oþer men lest þei shiuld follow þeir sin. az þe siknes of Antioche, whom
God smọt with such A plạg, that worms skattered owt of hiz body
being A lȳv. and þe stink of him waz so great and vȳl, þat neiþer
hiz frendz nor him self kowld abȳd it. and þen hee began to know
him self, and said, it iz rihtfull to bee subȝekt to God, and A
mortall man not to hold him equall with God. and þe stori saith þat
hee ask mersi of God, and vowed to mạk Jeruzalem free, and þe
Jewez free az men of Athens, and þat hee wold honor Godz
tempull with presiowz stọns, array the tempull, multipli þe holly
vessels, fȳnd of hiz own landz þe kostz and expenses pertaining to
þe sakrifȳz. and þat hee wold bekum A Ȝew, going over all þe land,
preaching Godz law, and yet Gạv him no mersy, for neiþer
waz þẹr in him kontrision nor repentans þat sprong of faith,
but of odiowz pain and greef. So þat when I had sumwhat

konsidred of all þęz forsaid sirkumstanses I wrot þis sonet folloing—

> *Ðe diverz ch⟨au⟩ns þat God doth send*   **41ᵛ**
> *to vex þe mÿnd and body both*
> *it doth proseed az wee offend*
> *or az hiz loov towardz vs groth*
> *sumtÿm for þat owr sins enkreas*
> *sumtÿm to trÿ owr konstantnes*
> *But I for sin must krav releas*
> *which never seas mee to oppres.*

All þis notwithstanding my most mercifull God and faþer had not so klean taken away hiz grąs from mee, but þat throuh faith in him and of hiz abowndant promyzes mąd to mee and all mankÿnd in hiz holly and sakred word I did not vtterly dispair in hiz mersy, neiþer greatly waver, but perswaded my self most serteinly, þat God iz my most loving faþer, and willing to do mee good how soever hee seemed to bee angry with mee, hee knoweth best what iz best and fittest for vs, and hiz will be doon. wherfor now kalling to my remembrans what *Ecclesiasticus*[1] teacheth vs wheraz hee saith. *Mi soon dispÿz not þi self in þi siknes, but prai vnto þe lord, and hee shall heal þee.* Also *Ezechiell*[2] in cap .xviij. saith. *At what tÿm soever A sinner doth repent him of hiz sin from þe botom of hiz hart, I will put all hiz wikkednes owt of my remembrans (saith þe lord) Also* wheraz it iz said in þe .li. *salm*[3] *A sorowfull hart iz A sakrifÿz to God.* þe remembrans of þęz and such oþer plases of þe skriptiurz mąd mee to mąk þis konfession of sins folloing—

> *Ðe great offens of my most sinfull gost*
> *with terror great dooth overflow þe sąm*
> *and þat which now my spreit oppresseth most*
> *iz remembrans of lÿf past owt of frąm*
> *when I for grąs lift up mi dazeld ey*
> *vnto þe tron from whens it doth dissend*
> *eevn þen dispair seemz to approch mee ney*

[1] Ecclus. 38. 9.   [2] Ezek. 18. 27.   [3] Psalm 51. 17.

to mąk mi hǫp in mee for to tąk end
but lo, dąm faith, bįdz mee leav slipper hǫld
and tak siur grẏp on promẏz mąd of yǫr
bi him whǫz eiz disdainz not to behold
þe humbull cheer, with hart tormented sǫr
So þat mersy, for mersy I do krẏ
vnto þat lord from whom springz all mersy.

When þe bred of affliksion, trobull and siknes, iz broken vnto
vs, þe malingnant spreet taketh hiz fittest oportiunite and tẏm
to mąk vs very pensif abowt owr salvasion, putting þǫz kriuell,
and horribull thouhts of predestinasion in owr mẏnds. az, what
if wee shiuld not pleaz God? what if hee hath kast vs of, or
know wee, þat wee ar of þe number of þem, whom God hath
elekted, and chozen vnto everlasting lẏf with oþer þe lẏk
temptasions. which shall most bitterly torment and vex þe
mẏnd espesially of þǫz whǫz gilty konsienses do akkiuz þem for
þeir wikked and nawhty lẏvz passed. az .St. pawll saith. Rom .2.[1]
Indingnasion and wrath, tribiulasion, and angwish shall kum vpon
þe sowll of evri man þat doth evll. wherfǫr if wee will *obtain þe*
viktory in þis battell let vs bewąr þat wee enter not into dispiuta-
sion with þe devll, neiþer awnswer him again. but put him of
from vs, chąsed away with þez wordz and koʒitasions. Sathan get
þe hens depart vn[to] þi distruksion. for it iz written (matt .4.)[2]
þow shalt not tempt þe lǫrd þi God, for in tempting þǫz þat be
hiz childern, þow temptest him ⌐also⌐ for s[e]ing þat God hath
42ʳ endued vs al⟨waiz w⟩ith most larʒ benefi⟨tz a⟩kkording to hiz
faþerly goodnes & loov toward vs, seing hee hath geven vs þis
lẏf, and hath noryshed and prezerved þe sąm hiþerto. also seing
þat hee hath heaped vs vp with all kyndz of goodnes, what
madnes węr it for vs to dowt of hiz mersy? seing þat throuh
baptism hee hath appointed vs into þe number of þe reseived
flok of þe kristians, seing hee hath kalled vs vnto þe Gospell of
hiz grąs, wherin hee hath promized to bee owr faþer, and also
seing þat [wee] do trust in þe mersy of krẏst, by þe faith which

---

[1] Rom. 2. 8, 9.   [2] Matt. 4. 7.

wee hạv taken owt of þe gospell, and þarby ar so inkorporạt, so
ivnited, and kopled vnto owr lord, and master krỹst, which iz
þe trew lỹf, þat hee may not be pulled or separated from vs
why shiuld not wee þen look for all goodnes at hiz hands? why
shiuld not wee assiur owr selvz of him in all things? wherfọr
shiuld not hiz great good will and kỹndnes towardz vs, alwaiz
be remembred of vs, for owr stay and komfor⟨t?⟩

also wee þat be afflikted az iz affọrsaid must not think very
much and often wha⟨t⟩ sins wee hạv kommitted in þis tỹm of
trobl, but raþer hạv befọr owr eies & konte⟨m⟩plat and look on
þe imaȝ of krỹst, in kalling to remembrans hiz mọst helthso⟨m⟩
and presiowz death. let vs fasten it siurly in owr mỹndz and
thoroly pers⟨wạd⟩ owr[a] selvz, þat wee ar not now oppressed with
owr sins for krỹst owr saviow⟨r⟩ doth bear þem, and þat þei ar
all laid vpon hiz shiulderz, which taking þem v⟨p⟩on him, hath
mạd satisfaksion and redempsion for vs so þat hee will never
(az St. peter[1] saith.12) impiut þem vnto vs. but will freely
forgỹv þem all (Rom[2]⟨.3.⟩) eevn az wee do say in þe artikels of owr
faith, I beleev in þe remission of sins. Affliksions ar þe siur and
vndowted sỹns ⟨a⟩nd tokens of Godz great mersy & favo⟨r⟩ towardz vs. *Salomon*[3] saith: whom God loveth, him hee korekteth
hee skourȝ⟨eth⟩ euery chỹld whom hee reseiveth. by þis wee
learn þat God sendeth affliksions vnto vs not in hiz wrath,
but in hiz faþerly loov. þe which thing when wee ar thoroly
perswạded, and ar tawht by experiens wee may pasiently look
for Godz aid and sukkor, and not dispair, but konstantly trust
þat in þe end hee will help vs alþoh hee hỹd him self, prolonging, and deferring owr aid, and deliverans never so long.

Hee þat kan after þis maner kommit & gỹv him self whọly
vnto God, beleeving and trusting in hiz promyzes, shall never
d⟨y⟩ þe which thing even krỹst him self affirming with an ọth,
least happely w⟨ee⟩ shiuld sumwhat dowt, doth say. John .2.[4]

---

[a] In the margin Whythorne wrote 'Esay./53./Math./.8.' The references
are Isaiah 53. 4–6 and Matthew 8. 19.

[1] 1 Pet. 2. 24.   [2] Rom. 3. 25 (?).   [3] Prov. 3. 12.
[4] John 8. 51; Whythorne's reference to John 2 is wrong.

verili verili, if A man keep mi wor⟨d⟩ hee shal never see death,
And in an oþer pląs hee saith (John .14)[1] *I am þe w⟨ay,⟩ þe*
verite, and þe lỹf. hee þat beleeveth on mee shall lỹv, alþouh
hee węr dead: And whosoeuer lỹveth, and beleeveth on mee shall
never dy. owr savior Ʒezus krẏst vnderstanding and knowing
owr[a] weaknes and infirmi⟨te⟩ owt of dowt hee taking kompassion
on vs, will not deall extreemly with vs, but will raþer bear with
owr imbesilite, kalling all men vnto him saieng *Math .15.*[2] *kom*
vnto mee, all yee þat labour and ar heavi loden, and I will refresh
yow. heer hee kalleth men vnto him, hee refiuzeth nǫn, hee
kasteth no man in þe teeth.[3] what greatter and mǫr plentifull
komfort kan wee hąv þen þis? trewly mani things do grevowsly
trobull man. for wh⟨a⟩t thing kan mǫr grevowsly fear, or torment
hiz konsiens, it being overwh⟨el⟩med with sin, þen when hee
dowteth of þe mersy of God? when he dreade⟨th⟩ lest God
bee hiz adversari, and will reʒekt him? when hee iz not habull to
konseiv þis faith of hiz mercy, and doth imaʒin him self to bee
A kastawai, and az þe dry member þat iz kut of? be prezent
heer O ʒezus krẏst with þỹn aid and help. heer wee hąv need of
þi komfort, let not þis blak, violent and horribull tempest of
trobuls overthrow, and drown wretched man. but þęr iz no
kawz why wee shiuld dowt. krẏst iz trew, hee will mąk hiz
promỹzes to appeer, hee will help vs and refresh vs.

þerfǫr wheraz owr faith iz not strong enowh, wheraz owr hart
iz stryken with fear and trembling, whęr wee see owr selvz to
42ᵛ dowt of Godz mersi, & hąv welny no faith at all, st⟨rai⟩htwaiz let
vs kall vp⟨on⟩ God, bewaill owr mizery and lak of beleef befǫr
him, seek for hiz aid and sukkowr by fervent praier. and hee
will both help and refresh vs. and by þis means wee shall glorify
him. he hath taken vpon him so to do, and hee will vndowtedly
bring it to pas. but let vs tąk heed spesially þat wee seas not to
kall vpon God, as saint Pawll teacheth vs saing (*Cor .1.*)[4] beseech

---

[a] MS reads 'orw'.

---

[1] John 14. 6 (and John 3. 15–18?).
[2] (?) Matt. 11. 28.   [3] Proverbial; Tilley **T** 429.
[4] 2 Cor. 1. 3. Whythorne's form of reference is inadequate.

þow withowt all seasing, þe faþer of all konsolasion, and komfort, with sihs kumming from þe botom of þe hart, þat hee
turn not hiz fąs from þee. let vs lay owr weaknes vpon him, and
powr owt into hiz bozom all oþer things, which trobull and
torment vs, let vs kry owt with hiz dissipuls, O lord enkreas owr
faith (az it iz said in *Luc.* cap .17.)[1] lўkwýz let vs say with þe
faþer of þe liunatik chўld:[2] *lord I beleev help þow mўn vnbeleef.*
mąk hąst O lord to help mee, befor þat I oppressed with þis
waiht be drowned. þi mersy iz aboov all þi wurks, O most
mersifull, O most bounteouz faþer, O lord God of my salvasion,
my sukkor and refiuʒ. salm .43.[3] Enter not into ʒiuʒment with
þi servant. krўst iz my rihteowznes, redempsion and innosensi,
which suffred most bitter and krewell death for my sąk. let þęz
thingz moov þee O faþer of all kompassion. hąv mersy on mee
for þi soons sąk. konfirm and strengthen my hart by faith in
krўst. komfort mee with þe konsolasions of þe holly Gǫst, þat
I may enʒoi þe trew ʒoiz in krўst for ever. when I had kollekted
and written all þęz forsaid sentenzes to gўþer þen I mąd þis praier
in meeter folloing, þe which iz devўzed vpon þe .51. salm[4]—

> *O good lord hąu mersi on mee*
> *Akkording to þi great mersi*
> *and do awai þ'iniquitee*
> *þat I hąu wrouht mǫst wikkedli.*

> *From mў misdeedz wash mee throuhly*
> *and klenz þou mee from all mi sin*
> *for all mi fauts knowleʒ do I*
> *þe which I hąu bin whelmed in*

> *Only against þi maʒesti*
> *transgressed dўverz*[a] *waiez I hąv*
> *and in þi siht doon sinfulli*
> *so az þi mersi I must krąv.*

---

[a] MS reads 'vўverz'.

[1] Luke 17. 5.   [2] Mark 9. 24.
[3] Psalm 34; actually a slip of Whythorne's pen.
[4] In his paraphrase of the Fifty-first Psalm, Whythorne utilized the first
thirteen verses, omitting verses 7 and 8, and the final six verses of the Psalm.

Remember lord, how I waz mạd
and shạpen all in wikkednes
throuh which I am brouht to þis trạd
and I nowai kan it repres

For az I waz konseivd in sin
so þat effekt in mee doth wurk
do what I kan t'will never blin
(without þẏ grạs) in mee to lurk.

43ʳ   T⟨u⟩rn not þi fạs O lord me⟨e⟩ fro
but from mi sins turn þow þi fạs
all mi mizdeedz put þem owt so
az þei in mee mai hạv no plạs

So klean A hart mạk þow in mee
az never sin tạk root þerin
and let in mee renew'd now bee
A rihteouz spreet þat hateth sin

Kast mee not owt from þi prezens
nor banish mee awai from þee
þi holi spreit for mi defens
let mee enȝoi mẏn aid to bee

O gẏv mee now þe great komfort
of þi siur help yet ons again
and stablish mee with þe siur fort
of þi free spreit, still to remain

And þen mẏ mouth shall sing þi praiz
also þi rihteoznes for ay
þi great works ẹk, wrouht mani waiz
which þow dost put in yụr alway.

I kannot pas any furder, befọr I hạv said mọr (besẏd þat
offọrsaid) konsernin⟨g⟩ þe temptorz, þe Devls I mean who wilnot
omitt ani thing þat mai wurk ⟨vnto⟩ manz distruksion, it iz not
ọn devl only þat doth it, but ⌈it⌉ iz dyverz, and espesially seven

of þem. þei be akkownted and named þe seven prinsipall or kaptain divels, bekawz þei hav alwaiz born A great swai amongst men.[1] Ðe first iz kalled. *lucifer.* þe devll of prýd and presumpsion—Ðe sekond, iz kalled. *Belzebub.* þe lord of envi and mallis—Ðe third iz kalled. *Sathan.* þe master of wrath and disdain—Ðe fowrth iz kalled *Abadan.* who is *þe patron* of slowth and *idelnes*—Ðe fift iz named *Mammon,* who iz þe faþer of kovetowsnes and sn[u]dȝery[a]—Ðe sixt. iz named. *Belphegor, þe God of gluttoni* and drunkenes—And þe seventh, iz kalled. *Asmodius.* þe rewler of lechery, and whordom. And whosoever iz infekted with any of þe said výses, be siur hee iz possest with A great kaptain divl, which must of nesessite bee kast owt, or els of fors, þe man must perish. þez in þe tým of owr trobull, greef, or siknes, and espesially, Sathan, who iz so wrathfull and disdainfull of mans good & þat hee shiuld bee in Godz favor, will put into owr myndz all þat hee may, to hav A mistrust in owr good God, and þat wee bee not of þe number of þoz þat bee predestinat and elekt to bee saved. so will hee prezent vnto vs what soever wee hav doon, and kommitted against þe kommaundments of God, and will put into owr mýndz hiuȝ mountains az it wer, of sins, þat bi þe owtraȝiowsnes, and greatnes of þem, hee may bring vs into desparasion, which do stagger and dowt of Godz mersy and pardon. wherfor heer must wee stand fast, and strongly. And **43**ᵛ þen ⟨l⟩et vs say ⌐þe ⟨.51.⟩[2] salm. espetially þe beg⟨inning þerof

---

[a] MS reads 'sndȝery'; this word, meaning miserliness, is first recorded in 1599 (*OED*).

---

[1] This group of 'seven prinsipall or kaptain divels' may have come from some continental source, but the first English listing appears to be in a Lollard tract, the *Lanterne of Liȝt,* written about 1410. See M. W. Bloomfield, *The Seven Deadly Sins,* Michigan, 1952, p. 214. All the devils except Belphegor appear in the Bible, and in the manuscript margin Whythorne gave references as follows: Lucifer, 'Esai .14. (Isa. 14. 11–12); Beelzebub, 'Mat .12.' (Matt. 12. 24); Satan, 'Luk .22. (Luke 22. 3); Abaddon, 'Apoc .9.' (Rev. 9. 11); Mammon, 'Mat .6. (Matt. 6. 24); Asmodius, 'Tob .3.' (Tobit 3. 8). The traits assigned to them, however, do not always have a definite Biblical source. Belphegor is described in the margin as 'A gaping Idol', possibly taken from the dictionary of persons and places in Thomas Cooper's *Thesaurus* (1565), where he appears as 'A gapying ydoll'.

[2] A conjecture, suggested by the subject-matter.

an)d after þat sai⌐ to owr enemy ⟨gett þe beh⟩ŷnd me Sathan, for
I know þee not.[1]

I do konsi⟨der⟩ þat I am A most manifold and grevows sinner.
But krŷst, who iz free from all sin, hee, þat inosent lamb in
whọz mowth was found no gŷll, hath suffred mọst krewell death
for my sinz, hee hath klenzed þem all, be þei never so many, nor
never so great, and hath mạd A suffisient satisfaksion for þem all.
St John saith þe first epistell & sekond chapter.[2] And if any man
doth sin, wee hạv an Advokạt with þe faþer. ȝezus krŷst þe
rihteowz, and hee it iz, þat obteineth grạs for owr sins, and not
for owr sins only, but also for þe sins of þe whọll world. krŷst
hiz death iz þe propisiasion for all owr sins. krŷst verili hath suffred all my feebulnes. hee in deed hath karried all mŷ sorowz. it iz
written in . *Esay* þe profett cap .53.[3] hee only hath taken on him
owr infirmitiez and born owr pains. hee waz wounded for owr
offenses, and smitten for [owr] wikkednes. for þe chastezment of
owr peas waz laid vpon him, and with hiz strŷps wee ar healed.
Đẹz and such oþer plạses of þe holly skriptiurz must wee hạv to
komfort owr trobled sowls in such extreem angwish. and þat
wee may þe better hạv þem, wee shiuld not neglekt to spend
much of owr tŷm in reading of holly skriptiurz, with oþer godly
books, and iwz much to prai vnto God wherby owr mŷndz may
bee lihtened. But if when wee hạv þus sowht to satisfy owr
konsienses by þe skriptiurz, and also praid to God þat wee mai
not be led into temptasion, but to be delivered from all eevl (az
wee ar tawht to pray in *Matt* .6.[4] by owr savior krŷst) and yet
kannot bee released and delivered owt of owr mizeries bianby,
and az it wẹr when wee wold be deliuered, yet wee ouht not to
grudȝ or dispair in Godz mersy but to embrạs pasiens which iz
þe moþer of fortitiud. it iz written in þe .27. salm.[5] *O tarri þow
þe lọrdz leiziur be st⌐r⌐ong, and hee shall komfort þŷn hart, and
put þi trust in þe lọrd.* Also St *pawl* saith.[6] *Tribiulasion bringeth*

---

[1] Matt. 16. 23. Whythorne seems to be using the Geneva version of this
well-known quotation.

[2] 1 John 2. 1, 2.　　　　　　　　　　　　　　　　[3] Isa. 53.4, 5.

[4] Matt. 6.　　　　　　[5] Ps. 27. 14.　　　　　　[6] Rom. 5. 3–5.

pasiens, pasiens bringeth experiens. experiens bringeth hop. and hop maketh not ashamed. so þat affliksion bringing pasiens, and wee having good experiens þerof by þe exersyzing of þe sam shall fynd hop, þe fowntain of all goodnes, for hop maketh not ashamed, bekawz þe loov of God iz shed ⌐abrod⌐ or inkorporat in owr harts, by þe holly Gost which iz geven vs. St *Jams* saith. (cap .4.)[1] *be þow subȝekt and obedient vnto þe lord, & prai vnto him, and þou shalt þerby fynd þat thing, which iz not to bee kontemned þat iz to witt, hee will gyv þee all þyn harts dezier.*

Now it iz to bee *remembred* þat when wee hav bin or bee trobled with any kynd of krosses, eiþer in[a] owr body, mynd, or sowll, þat þen wee do not think þei bee rekompenses toward God for owr sinz past, and þat God will forgyv vs owr sinz, for þe pain and grevowznes of owr krosses and ponishments. for az it [iz] said in þe Actes .4.[2] *þer iz no oþer saluasion, þer iz non oþer rekompens for owr sins, þen þe only death of krÿst.* God trewly respekteth non oþer thing in þis kas, hee aksepteth non *oþer thing,* but hiz dearly beloved soon, of whom St John saith. cap .1.[3] Ðis iz þe lamb of God, which taketh away þe sins of þe world. and to þis purpoz speaketh St pawll. Rom .8. wher hee saith[4] I suppoz þat þe affliksions of þis lyf ar not worþi of þe glory which shall be shewd vpon vs.

After þat I had sowht owt þez komfortabull perswazions and nots befor rehersed I gav my self to mor quyetnes of þe mynd þen I waz in befor. and emong oþer exersyzes, and az þe tÿm served mee, I wold not leav nor neglekt to read in þe bÿbull. and az it chaunsed on tÿm I lihted in plases þerof, þe which at þis instant kam very well for my purpoz. for I having bin befor þis tÿm, az yee may partly perseiv by þat afforsaid, sumwhat trobled in konsiens, and þerfor I sowht and wrot þoz remediez þerfor az be befor noted. now, az my trobled mynd did hinder þe good estat of my bodely helth, I found plases þat kownse[le]d mee to eschew þoz greefs, þat wer such instriuments to wurk **44ʳ**

---

[a] Written over 'of'.

[1] Ja. 4. 7, 8. [2] Acts 4. 12.
[3] John 1. 29. [4] Rom. 8. 18.

dẏverz and ⟨many⟩ wẏz, great and dainȝerouz infirmytẏz in þe body, besẏd þe mẏnd. First *Salomon* saith in þe .12. chapter of hiz proverbz.[1] *Hẹvines diskoraȝeth þe hart of man, but A good wurd maketh it glad again.* In þe .15. he saith[2] *A meri hart mạketh A cheerfull kowntenans, but an hẹvy hart kompelleth A man to sih.* And þen in þe .17. chapter hee saith.[3] *A meri hart maketh A lusty ạȝ, but A sorowfull mẏnd drieth vp þe bọns.* Also ȝezus þe soon of *Sirach* saith in þe .30. chapter of hiz book.[4] *Đẹr iz riches aboov A sound bodi, and no ȝoi aboov þe ȝoi of þe hart.* Also hee saith.[5] *Geev not over þẏ mẏnd into hẹuines, and vex not þi self in þẏn own kounsell. Đe ȝoi and cheerfulnes of þe hart iz þe lẏf of man, and A mans gladnes iz þe prolonging of hiz daiz. Loov þẏn own sowll and komfort þẏn [hart],[6] az for sorow and hẹuines, drẏv it far from þee, for hevines hath slain mani A man, and bringeth no profit. zeall, and anger shorten þe dai⟨z⟩ of þe lẏf, kạrfulnes and sọrow bring aȝ befọr þe tẏm. vnto A merri hart evrẏ thing hath A good tạst*—vpon þẹz fọrsaid saings I mạd þis sonet folloing—

> *Gẏv not þi mẏnd to heavines*
> *suffer not kạrz to mạk þee thrall*
> *for þei in tẏm dry vp dowtles*
> *þi bọnz and moistiur radikall*
> *þe ȝoi and cheerfulnes of hart*
> *iz þ'only komfort of mans lẏf*
> *and gladnes ẹk prolongs by art*
> *hiz lyving daiz devoid of strẏf*
> *now leav þe sowr and tạk þe sweet*
> *þow shalt for helth fẏnd it mọst meet*

Đẹz fọrsaid plạses be rạþer to diswạd A man from worldly sorow þan from Godly sorow, for St paull (2. corint .7.) saith[7]

---

[1] Prov. 12. 25.   [2] Prov. 15. 13.   [3] Prov. 17. 22.
[4] Ecclus. 30. 16. It should read 'no riches', Whythorne's error.
[5] Ibid. 30. 21-25.
[6] This slip, and previous ones, show how often Whythorne is careless in copying, that he should omit such keywords.
[7] 2 Cor. 7. 10.

þat godly sorow kawzet⟨h⟩ repentans vnto salvasion not to be repented of, kontrary wŷz worldly sorow kawzeth death. so þat wee owht not to sorow az þoz þat hav no faith, who will blasfem God and dispair, neiþer to bee so dissoliut in owr mirth az þ⟨ei⟩ bee, whoz mirth shalbe of filthines, wikkednes, foolish ridikiulus, ywzing wordz and deeds, vnkumly and vndesent ⌐&⌐ wantonly, and to reʒois at þe offending of oþerz, or skorning of þem, and by any mean⟨s⟩ to misywz any of owr wits and senses. St *James* saith[1] in þe .5. and last chapter of hiz epistell. *If ani of yow be vexed, let him prai, and if any be merry let him sing salms, It is not withowt great reazon þat þe holy Gost doth exhort vs diliʒently in þe holy Skriptiurz to reʒois and be meri in God þe lord, and to* refer vnto him all owr mirth and ʒoi, az to non oþer good and trew end. for hee knowth well how much wee bee enklŷned to vain mirth. notwithstanding St James wordz afforsaid I think wee may sing such songs, þe ditties wherof be mad in þe kommendasion of vertew & reprehending of vises, of þe which þer be many mad owt of morall filosofye, and not vpon any salm. of þe which I hav mad many my self on of þe which shall follow. I mad it vpon þe sirkumstans ⌐and konsiderasion⌐ of þe trobulsom tŷm past az iz affor towched, with þe perils þat I eskaped and shunned in þe sam tŷm. þe which being mad befor vpon A vain konseit,[2] I hav now turned it vnto A better purpoz az þus—

Sins I embras
þe heavn⌐ly⌐ gras   ⎱ *In sort az I wold hav—*

Reʒois I must   44ᵛ
till I for dust   ⎱ *do yeeld mi korps to grav*

waz never non
did sih and mon   ⎱ *I think mor oft þen I*

for ⌐deep⌐ dispair
mee did impair—   ⎱ *konfounding mee welny*

---

[1] Ja. 5. 13.

[2] For Whythorne's love poem which he used for his model, see p. 42.

But þen godz grạs ⎱ *putting bak þatt foull fend*
appeerd in plas—⎰

and said to mee ⎱ *for heavn iz þẏn at end*
of komfort bee ⎰

wherfọr reȝois— ⎱ *let no tewn mourning bee*
both sound & vois⎰

but with deliht ⎱ *reȝois yee all with mee.*
with all your·miht⎰

Alþouh at þis tẏm I waz so quiet in *mẏnd*, and konsiens, þat I dowted not of any misfortiu[n], trobull or siknes, þat miht happen vnto mee, so þat I miht gẏv my self whọly, to ȝoiz and gladnes, and þat I felt in mi self þat I kould eazile enouh fram my self to tạk and follow þe kounsels affọrsaid to provọk mee to be mery, and to set of sorrowz from my hart. yet I feared afterklaps[1] sumtẏms, and þat to hạsty mirth miht bring to suddein sorowz. wherfọr determining with my self so to tạk delihts, az trobuls shiuld not be estrainȝed from mee, and yet neiþer so to be daunted with sorrowz az mirth shiuld bee A strainȝer vnto mee, I mạd A mixtiur of þem, inkorporating þe ọn with þe oþer.

And bekawz þat þe prezent plạg þat þen waz in London waz now grown to bee so great, and in so many plạses, and also so ny vnto mee, az it waz not only kum rownd abowt mee, but also into þe hows whẹr I did þen ly, wherby I looked evri miniut of an howr when I shiuld be vizited az þe rest wẹr, I dowting þe wurst, þat iz to say, to be smitten with þis rod and kros, did now gaþer so many komfortabull plạses of þe skriptiurz az I kowld fẏnd, þe which I did alwaiz think vpon togiþer with þe oþerz az affọr rehersed, az þe cheef fẏzik for my sowll, if peradventiur it shiuld pleaz God to hạv laid þat siknes vpon mee az hee did on þe oþerz, þe which be þẹz folloing. *Joan* .3.[2] whosoever be-leeveth in krẏst, shall not p[e]rish but hạv eternall lẏf. for God

---

[1] For Whythorne's earlier use of this phrase see p. 77.

[2] John 3. 15–17. Opposite the quotation Whythorne gives a marginal reference to '*luc .19.*'; Luke 19 is also to be found as a marginal reference in the 1551 Matthews's and the 1568 Bishops' Bibles.

so loved þe world, þat hee gav hiz only begotten soon þat whosoever beleeveth on him, shiuld not perish, but hav everlasting
lyf. for God sent not hiz soon into þe world, to kondempn þe
world, but þat þe world thro[u]h him miht be saved. *kryst* (in
Joan .10.) saith,[1] þat hee geveth vnto hiz sheep eternall lyf, and
þei shall ⌐ne⌐ver perish, neiþer shall any man pluk þem owt of
hiz hand. St pawll. Rom .5. saith.[2] God setteth owt hiz loov
towardz vs, seing þat whyll wee wer yet sinnerz, kryst died for
vs. Much mor þen now (wee þat ar ʒiustified by hiz blood)
shalbe saved from wrath thorow him, for if when wee wer
enemiez, wee wer rekonsyled to God, by þe death of his soon,
much mor seing wee ar rekonsiled, wee shalbe prezerved by hiz
lyf. St pawll (Rom .3.) saith,[3] þe rihteowsnes of God, kummeth
by þe faith of ʒezus kryst, vnto all and vpon all þem þat beleev
on him. Also hee saith[4] (Rom .8) þer iz no damnasion to þem
which ar in kryst[a] *ʒeziu*, Ðe law of þe spreit of lyf, thorow ʒesus 45ʳ
kryst, hath mad mee free from þe law of sin and death. hee iz
my Saviowr, my helth, and ʒiustifikasion, and ever wilbe, hee
will both kover, and ⟨a⟩bolish all my sins, þat ⌐I⌐ shall never
fear perill nor ⌐dammaʒ or⌐ dainʒer for þem. In þe .1. *cor* .1.[5] kryst
iz mad to vs wizdom, rihteowsnes, santifikasion, and redemsion.
God iz faithfull, by whom wee ar all kalled vnto þe fellowship of
his soon ʒezus kryst owr lord. In þe .2. *cor* .1.[6] Blessed be God
(þe faþer of owr lord ʒezus kryst) which iz þe faþer of mersi,
and God of all kumfort, which komforteth vs in all owr tribiulasion, in somuch þat wee ar habull to komfort þem which ar in
any maner of trobull, with þe sam komfort, wherwith wee owr
selvs a⟨r⟩ komforted of God. for az þe affliksions of kryst ar
plenteowz in vs, eevn so iz owr konsolasion plenteows by kryst.

In þe sam epistl and .5. chapter hee saith.[7] God hath rekon-

---

[a] Immediately preceding this word, Whythorne deleted two and a quarter
lines; they contain the Biblical quotation below, 'hee iz my Saviowr', &c.

---

[1] John 10. 1–18. This is a brief summary of these verses. Whythorne's marginal reference to '*Jo*.3.' (John 3) cannot be correct; the 1568 Bishops' Bible
has a reference to John 13.
[2] Rom. 5. 8–10.   [3] Rom. 3. 22.   [4] Rom. 8. 1, 2.
[5] 1 Cor. 1. 30, 9.   [6] 2 Cor. 1. 3–5.   [7] 2 Cor. 5. 18, 19, 21.

sẏled vs vnto him self bi ȝezus krẏst. God waz in kr⟨ẏst⟩ and mạd an agreement between þe world and him self, and impiuted no⟨t⟩ þeir sins vnto þem. For hee hath mạd him to bee sin for vs, which did know no sin, þat wee by hiz means shiuld be þat rihteowznes, which befọr God iz allowed. St pawll saith[1] (*Gala* .1.) krẏst gạv him self for owr sins to deliver vs from þis prezent eevl world akkording to þe will of God faþer. St paw⟨ll⟩ saith[2] (*Ephe* .1.) By krẏst wee hạv redemsion throuh hiz blood, eevn þe forgẏvne⟨s⟩ of sins, akkording to þe richez of hiz grạs. St pawll saith[3] (1. *Timo* .1.) Ðis iz A triu saing (and by all means worþi to be reseivid of vs) þat krẏst ȝezus kạm into þe world to sạv sinnerz. St pawll saith[4] (.1. *Tim* .2.) krẏst ȝezus gạv him self A ransom for all men. St pawll saith[5] (*Hebru* .10.) wee ar sanctified by þe offring vp of þe body of ȝezus krẏst ons for all. Also hee saith[6] (*Hebru* .12.) *my soon* dispẏz not þe chastening of þe lord, neiþer faint when þow art rebiuked of him, for whom þe lord loveth, him hee chasteneth. yee, hee skourȝeth every soon þat hee reseaveth. if yee endiur chasten-ing, God offereth him sel⟨f⟩ vnto yow az vnto soons. St Peter saith in hiz first epistell, and þe firs⟨t⟩ chapter.[7] Yee wẹr not redeemed with korruptibull things (az silver & gou⟨ld⟩) but with presiows blood of krẏst, az of A lamb vndefẏled .1. *peter* .2.[8] H⟨ee⟩ þat beleeveth on krẏst shalnot be konfownded. krẏst hiz own self bạ⟨r⟩ owr sins in hiz body on þe tree, þat wee being delivered from sin, shiuld lẏv vnto rihteowznes, by whọz strẏps yee wẹr healed .1. *peter* .3.[9] krẏs⟨t⟩ hath ons suffered for sins, þe ȝust for þe vnȝiust, to bring vs to God. St John. in hiz first epistl & first chapter saith.[10] Ðe blood of ȝezus krẏst klenzeth vs from all sin. In *Ezechiel* þe .18. it iz written[11] þat þe lord God hath no pleaziur in þe death of A sinner but hee wold raþer þat hee shiuld be konverted and lẏv. After I had gaþered and writ-

---

[1] Gal. 1. 4. [2] Eph. 1. 7. [3] 1 Tim. 1. 15.
[4] 1 Tim. 2. 6. [5] Heb. 10. 10. [6] Heb. 12. 5–7.
[7] 1 Pet. 1. 18, 19. [8] 1 Pet. 2. 6, 24.
[9] 1 Pet. 3. 18. [10] 1 John 1. 7.
[11] Ezek. 18. 23. Whythorne's marginal reference to '.2. *peter* .3.' (2 Pet. 3) is also found in the 1551 Matthews's and the 1568 Bishops' Bibles.

ten all þez forsaid komfotabull saings þus togiþer, which ar most
worþi and needfull to kiuer A distressed and wounded mynd
and sowll. I being still mynded and willing to okkiupy my mynd
sumtým in þis kýnd of exersýz, mad vpon þe beginning of þe
.103. salm.[1] þis þat folloith in þe which iz A praiz and akknow-
leȝing of benefits reseived of God—

       Mi soul and all þat in mee iz, to praiz my God alway
salm. *shall readi bee to do þe sam, in þe best sort I may*
.103. *For hee to mee hath givn hiz gras, vnworþi þouh I bee*
       þerfor will I setfoort hiz praiz, to all of ech degree

After þat I had mad þis affo⟨rsai⟩d, I mad þis song folloing 45ᵛ
⟨v⟩p⟨o⟩n þe .134. salm.[2] in þe which, þe sinner giveth thanks to
God for his grases bestowd vpon him, and shewth of Godz
goodnes to such az be repentant—

psal   *I will yeeld thanks to þee* ⎫
.138.   *O lord in Trenitee*   ⎬ *mi praier all*
        bekawz þow hast hard mee ⎭
        And in mi turmentree ⎫
        mi hop in þee shalbee ⎬ *when I þee kall.*
        to turn mýn enemee ⎭

        Even befor ech wiht ⎫
        I will sing dai & niht ⎬ *and mi hol trust*
        þi praiz which art mi liht ⎭
        toward þi tempull riht ⎫
        I wurship will þi miht ⎬ *of þ'ill and ȝust*
        praizing þi nam in siht ⎭

        Bekawz of þi pety ⎫
        and trewth so regally ⎬ *On mee at length*
        þi nam didst mangnify ⎭

---

[1] Whythorne paraphrased only the first three verses of the 103rd Psalm.
[2] Whythorne slipped here; he meant the 138th Psalm, as he noted correctly
in the margin opposite it.

When I to þee did kry
þow gavst mi sowll mersy }*with fors & strength*
endu'eng it bianby

Alþouh I waz in pain
in þis great storm of rain }*for evermor*
yet did I not remain

but owt of þez wav's main
hee did [me] set in plain }*hee did restor*
and eaz to mee again

For þoh þe lord bee[a] hy
to þoz þat bee lowly }*and þem elekt*
hee hath respekt triuly

but þei þat stand prowdly
Not submitting humbly }*and þem rezekt*
hee behol'dth distantly

Hiz mersy and hiz gras
þei shall alway embras }*and wilnot seuer*
þat walk in hiz trew tras

hee ⟨alwa⟩iz gee⟨v⟩z þem Spas
þat þei may run þe ras }*whic⟨h s⟩tandeth ever*
to hiz hy holy plas

Đerfor gýv glori all
to þat lord selestiall }*and your lýv's mend*
seas not on him to kall

and from sekond death thrall
yow all þen bee brouht shall }*which hath non end.*
to þe ʒois perpetuall

When I had spent þus my tým in þe trobulsom and pestiferus
tým, which endiured mor þen half A yeer, my piupull (I
mean) þe soon and heir of my forsaid ⟨master⟩ and freend, kam

---

[a] Written over 'iz'.

from beyond þe Seas into England again.[1] Shortly after whọ̧z
arẏvall, I waz dischar3ed of þe doings þat I had to do for him.
imediatly whẹrvpon I purpozed to leav þe Syty of London, and to
remain in þe kuntrey with purpọz to dizburden mee of þe lạt
kạrz þat I had in þe sytty, and Also t⟨o⟩ rekover if I kowld, sum
part of my helth þe which ⌐waz¬ somuch impaired by þe means
of þe doings þat I had for my said freend, az I dowt yet I shall
never rekover þe sạm again perfektly. And after I waz A littl whẏll
setle⟨d⟩ in A 3entilmans þạr wheraz alþoh not for profitt, yet for
good and frendly entertenment, diet and lod3ing, I never kạm in
þe lẏk befọr. I kowld not be ⌐idell from¬ reading and wryting sumwhat besẏd þe pains I took in teaching of þer only dawhter. and
among all my oþer wrytings, I wrọt ij Grạses, þe ọn to be said
befọr dynar and þe oþer to be said after dinar, bekawz þat I waz
partly spọken vnto for þe sạm. þe which wẹr þẹz foloing—

Grạs befọr Dinar

Almihty God, þi loving kạr
is to provẏd for vs alwai
and heer hast sent for owr welfạr
such worldly food az feed wee mai
so wee þee prai to send also
owr sowlz to feed, þi food devẏn
þat þi glori in vs mai sho
to evri wiht so þat in fẏn
when þei bi grạs see owr komfort
mai for þe lẏk, to þee rezort
and so to lawd þi holẏ nạm
az all wee heer do now þe sạm.

Grạs after dinar.

O owr faþer wee yeeld to þee
for all þi giftz most thankfull praiz

[1] Little record of William Bromfield the younger can be found at this stage of his career. He appears to have become a Gentleman Pensioner of Queen Elizabeth, but died 20 November 1582. He was buried at Monkton Farleigh church, Kent, and his will, proved 5 February 1582/3, is printed in H. F. Waters, *Genealogical Gleanings*, ii (Boston, 1901), pp. 1427–8.

which bi vs now reseived bee
or heer to for bi ani waiz
dezy̆ring þee þat þow wilt sav
þi chiurch, our Q[u]een and all her land

46ᵛ

and sen⟨d vs⟩ all þat peas to hav
þe which in ȝiezus kry̆st doth stand
Graunt þis O lord to gẙv to vs
for þi soons Sak owr lord Ȝiezus
to whom with þee, and þ'holi spreit
be all glori for ay sobeit

Đe church befor spoken of, iz not ment to bee A church þat iz mạd with stọn and lẙm, and such A ọn, az wee do kommenly say owr servis in and pray in on þe Soboth daiez. but it iz A kongregation of þe faith (alþouh þei bee dispersed throhowt þe hole world) in þe which chiurch or emong þe which chiurch, þe piur and sinseer wurd of God iz preached, and þe Sakraments bee diuly ministerd, akkording to kry̆stes ordinans in all þọz things þat of nesessite ar requizit to þe sạm, for þe which church I mạd þis praier foloing—

O lord aboov
send vs þi grạs to bee owr stai
so az wee never do
þat which belongs vnto
þe sinfull wikked wai

O lord aboov
when trobuls do þi flok molest
with ruffling boistrowz broils
le[t] nọn of all þọz toils
bring sorrowz in þeir brest

O lord aboov
Let þe siur họp þei hạv in þee
þeir sawted[1] harts defend
vntill þeir trobuls end
or þerwith kontent bee

---

[1] *Sawted*, assaulted, from sault (*OED*).

O lord aboov
Ði holi chiurch being dekaid
mąk þat þerof þe wals
be kept from sathans thrals
to bee repaird and staid

O lord aboov
Ði sheep straing owt of þe way
let þem be brouht to flok
and rest vpon þe rok
wheron þei erst did stay.

O lord aboov   47ʳ
Lift vp owr harts and eiez to þee
þat wee mai all in ǫn
gẏv praiz to þee alǫn
to whom it owht to bee

At þis tẏm I had an Italien *Bibull*,[1] and bekawz I had also at
þat tẏm A book of þe salms of þe profett David only, and sum spąr
paper in þat book to wrẏt in it what I wold, I gaþered owt of my
Bybull þe praierz of þe sąm, þe which I wrǫt in to þe sąm book
wherin þe salms węr. and when I had finishe⟨d⟩ þat wurk (I
having in þat tẏm tawht þe ȝentilmans dawhter węr I waz ⟨to⟩
play sumwhat on þe virȝinals, and þe liut, and also to sing
priksong) now ⟨I⟩ took in hand and began to teach ⌐her⌐ to sing
to liut also. and emong þe songs þat I tawht her shee learned
þat I mąd my self, þe which I devẏzed vpon A senten⟨s⟩ þat I
took owt of A book named (az I do remember) *Ðe treatis of
philosophi⟨e⟩*[2] þe which sentens þus beginneth. *If þow dezier þat*

---

[1] Whythorne's Italian Bible was some edition by Antonio Brucioli; he
later translates the greater part of its preface to the Psalms (see pp. 227–8).
English editions of the Psalms of David were reprinted frequently in the mid-
sixteenth century.

[2] William Baldwin's *Treatise of Morall Phylosophye, Conteyning the Say-
inges of the Wyse* went through more than a dozen editions between 1547 and
the end of the century. The passage quoted by Whythorne is present in the
early editions (viz. on sig. K4 of *STC* 1254, 1550 edition), but does not
appear in some of the later 'enlarged' editions. See also p. 65.

*þi frendz loov may ko⟨n⟩tinew, be kurteous and ȝentill towardz
him both in speech, and also in mannerz. forbear him in hiz anger,
reprov him ȝently in hiz error, and komfort him in hiz adversite.*
Vpon þis said sentens I mad þis folloing—

properem

> If þow þat hast A faithfull frend
> dezier þat hiz loov mai not swarv
> þen how to ywz him to þat end
> þow shalt now know þi turn to sarv
>
> Both ȝentilnes and kou[r]tezi
> to him to yowz see þat þow do
> let no rowh speech hiz pasi'ens tri
> nor krooked mannerz see þow sho
>
> Forbear him when hee iz angri
> in hiz errowr ȝentli reprov
> when advers chauns doth towch him ni
> komfort him þen az doth behov
>
> So maist þow not only retain
> þi frend solong az lȳf doth last
> but dobull loov þow owht'st to gain
> az gwerdon for þi frendship past
>
> But when þow hast so put in iur
> þe things þat erst I told þee on
> if all þat pleaz him not be siur
> hee iz no frent to trust vpon

47ᵛ I took in hand þe raþer ⟨spec⟩ial þis meeter vpon ⟨þe⟩ forsaid
them, bekawz þe ȝentilwoman whoz dawhter I did teach at þat
tȳm, iz A kurteowz and frendly ȝentilwoman, and þarwithall
very verteowsly dispozed. who sumtȳmz in talk of frendship
wold diskours diversly þerof, and þarwithall pleazantly and
wittily, or wȳsly, for shee hath A witt and awdasite ȝoined
þerwith. by þe which shee will yeeld and vtter sensibull reazons

in ani matter þat shee listeth to talk of, and with A good spreit
and behavowr.

Now [I] will leav for A tỹm to speak of holly and grạv matterz,
and lihten yowr mỹnd with A mery story, þe which waz þus folloing. Ny abowt þis tỹm, þẹr kạm A poor woman to þis said hows
whẹr I þen was, who befọr þat tỹm had bin þạr dỹverz tỹms,
and az I vnderstood, shee had had sum such great trobull happened vnto her, þe which (for want of Godz grạs) forsed her witt
and reazon to forsạk her somuch, az shee waz very ny or altogiþer oppressed with frenzi or madnes. but being afterward
sumwhat rekovered again to her former estạt, shee wold rọm
abowt þe kuntrei to such az mạd ani thing of her. shee kowld
spin very well. and þerwithall she waz (in her mery moodz) shee
waz[a] A pleazant, and A mad mery gom.[1] her behavior and talk
waz to moov mirth and lawhter, in þe which she wold ywz sumwhat of her hiumour mixt with A littl ry, and skirilus terms.
when shee had bin þạr A sertain tỹm and had knowleȝ by sum
in þe hows þat I kowld mạk english rỹm, shee dezired mee, þat
I wold mạk her A pasport in rỹm, to shew vnto such az wọld
examin her of her travelling thorow þe kuntrey, of þe kawz
þerof and whẹr shee dwelled.

whẹrvnto I awnswerd her, þat A pasport I kowld mạk her nọn,
þat waz availabull for her, for þat must be mạd by A ȝustis of
peas or such lỹk, but quoþ I, I [will] devỹz such A Testiminiall,
of þe kawz of yowr travell and of yowr trạd þat yow lỹv by and
also of yowr behavor whẹr ye ⌐do¬ kum, az shall stand yow in sum
stead. And þen I konsidering þat shee wold shew her self lỹk
her self whẹrsoever shee kạm, I determined to mạk for her sum
pleazant konseit, bekawz þat þe mi⌐r¬th which it shiuld moov,
shiuld stay or mitigạt þe sevẹr mỹndz (konserning ȝustis) of þọz
in awtorite þat shiuld read it or hear it read. and I mạd þe mirth
þerof, all of her kondisions, trạd, maner of behavor, and stạt. þe
which when þei shiuld read or hear it red, þei miht þerby kon-

---

[a] Dittography.

---

[1] Obsolete word for godmother, old woman (*OED*).

seiv & konsider of her az shee waz, and so not to trobull her weak
brains ⌐any⌐ mǫr þen þei węr trobled alredy, but to lett her
quietly from þeir hands. þe kopy of which testimoniall heer
folloith[1]—

All yow þat list þe trewth to know, who shee iz þat iz heer,
hur nạm iz Sibbel Slius bi ʒis, t'iz known bǫth var & neer
A widdow she'iz, and zo sh'il bee, if that shee marri not
in Gloster town shee dwelz þoh now, she'iz var vrom þens God wot
hur viaʒ iz to Essex sheer, her zoon to zee and kis
who dwelth at Hatfeld peuerell, whęr oft shee wil him blis
and bi þe wai, az shee doth go, hur living vor to win
shee vizits all hur vrindz, and zuch, az will hur hier to spin
and who ⌐to⌐ wạʒ hur iz dispǫzd, vor this hur okkiupasion
shall zee hur ⌐trutch⌐ at al assaiz, az ǫn of hur fokasion
Vor all þe day shee spinz apạs, at niht shee gins to reell
hur karderz must hur rollerz mạk and lei þem at hur wheell

48ʳ *Vor in þe n⟨iht do⟩ þo⟨w t⟩row þis, she ⟨has⟩ az ⟨f⟩reend' za bow⟨ll⟩*
and þạr s⟨he⟩e chats and zings so zwe⟨et⟩ and twęr A nihting owll
þen telth shee tạls of ʒak a vạls, and ⟨m⟩ani oþer things
also of hur þat th⌐r⌐ouh spining, had brǫk her twatling strings[2]
and when hur daiz wurk iz all doon, þen keeps shee drink vrom
*   zo⟨wring⟩*
þe which shee must be plied with all, or els Shee vals A chowring[3]
Đe dainti vạr shee kạrz not vor, A littl meat will zarv,
if pottaʒ, hott, and kold be had, els shee iz lỳk vor to starv.
of all þe ʒunkets, þat shee knowz, peaz pottaʒ shee loovs well
and she'ath A riht siur remedi þhoht mạk her panch to zwell
vor hur yws is not to be kreez,[4] when þat hur womb doth rumbull

---

[1] Whythorne's version of the Somerset dialect is essentially the conventional substitution of *z* for initial *s*, of *v* for initial *f*, and sometimes of *f* for
initial *v*. Mr. Rupert E. Palmer, Jr., in his study of *Thomas Whythorne's
Speech* discusses this dialect poem in some detail.

[2] The first use of this vulgar expression for *sphincter ani* cited in *OED* is
by John Florio in 1611.

[3] A dialect form of *jower*, to grumble or scold.

[4] This word may be derived from Middle English *crece*, meaning to become
swollen, or increased.

but vyst, and vart, and þis and kak, along shee lets þem tumbull
vor hạv shee ons zuch gear in stọr, þen she'iz in wofull kạs
till shee hath lihtned evry pạrt abowt hur pumping plạs
besýd all þis of qualitiez, shee hath welny A pownd,
az demiur looks, with simpring talk, and kurtzei doun to grownd
shee kan both dauns A good hornþýp, and also vozi mag
with stop and turn and trạs also, till þat hur bum doth wag
hur kuttaild bitch, Bevis bi nạm, it iz hur only ȝoý
to koll, and kis rownd abowt, she'il not be over koy
Zins it of Turnspits, bring hur[a] stọr, which shee doth zell vor grọts
þat biez hur good ạl, to wash klean, hur þrọt vrom krums and
* mọt⟨s⟩*

Lo, now yee know þe prezent stạt, of þis waifạring gest
þe which t'iz dowt will ay endiur, till hur zowll bee at rest
and t'yow þat quizitýv be to know, whẹr þis pasport waz wrýt
and who þe trew witnesses bee, þat þis iz trew and rýht
yee mai be ziur t'waz mạd at họm, between þe kup and wall
hard bý A good vi'erz sýd perdiu. yee zitten in hur hall
and master fikry[1] vor ọn witnes, hee shalbe known and tạk
þ'oþerz hur sk[r]ýb, hur kuntreimam, who mạd this vor hur sạk
þeir zeals A zunder hạv þei zet, to þis vor bet or wars
þei þat do hurt þis or hur self, shee wold þ'ad kist hur ars.

when þe ȝentilman ọf þe hows and hiz wýf wẹr dispozed to be mery with her and at her, þei wold hạv her kum into þe parler whẹr þei wẹr, and emong all þe toiz þat þei wold be mery at, þei wold hạv mee to read her testimonia⟨ll⟩ (bekawz I waz best akquainted with it) and whýll I waz A reading þero⟨f⟩ she wold hạv many passions and interȝeksions, az sumtýms shee wold be in A chạf, and sumtýmz shee wold lah hartely at it. Heer yee shall vnderstand þat alþouh þe syti of Glosester standeth not in þat kuntrey which iz kommenly kalled þe west kuntrei, or west part of þe realm (az iz kornwall, Devonshier, and Somersett sheer) yet

---

[a] MS. reads 'hut'.

---

[1] *Vicary*, an obsolete form of Vicar (*OED*).

þe kuntrey speech wher þe siti of Glosester standeth, iz lẏk to þe
western speech (az appeared by þis forsaid poor womans speech,
for shee youzed in her talk, þat maner of pronounsing of her
wordz az þei bee sett in her testimoniall[)]. and alþouh shee waz
born in Gloster, & I in þe furþest part of Somerset sheer sowth-
ward from Gloster, which iz threeskor mẏl and mor from her
natẏv plas,[1] yet bekawz shee sownded her wordz after þat kuntrey maner and fasion, I in mirth kald her alwaiz kuntreywoma⟨n⟩
and took vpon mee to be her kuntreyman. az yow may read in þe
said testi⟨moniall⟩. Now wi⟨ll⟩ I sea⟨s þis⟩ komikall matter,
an⟨d tell⟩ yow þat it iz often seen þat after mirth þer ku⟨mm⟩eth
mani tẏms anger or soro⟨w⟩,[2] þe which chainȝ now folloingly
happened vnto mee. for after þat I had had such pastẏm with my
forsaid kuntreiwoman, az iz afforsaid, þe which kontinewd for
þe spas of A moneth or mor in such sort az all þe hol howsold
wer mad mery dyverz tẏms with þe devẏses þat I wrouht with
and for her.

Ðer kam A ȝentilman to þe hows, who ywzed sumtẏms to
kum þiþer befor þis tẏm (for hee dwelt not far of from þe hows
wher I þen waz). þis ȝentilman az hiz maner at oþer tẏms befor
þat waz, he moved talk att þe dynar tẏm of dyverz matterz (hee
being on who for hiz witt and learning thouht azwell of him self
az þer waz kawz and sumwhat mor) and after dinar hee kontinewd in þe lẏk maner. yee, and at supper tẏm lẏkwẏz, in þe
which talk hee wold sumtẏms moov questions kolorably towching þe prezent estat, and reliȝion allowed and maintained in þis
prezent tẏm. in all þe which tẏmz of hiz diskowrsings and argew-
ings to and fro, I held my peas and said not on word vnto him
exsept it wer ons, in þe last end of þe supper tẏm. þe which hee
took very displeazantly which mad mee to wish þat I had said
no word to him at all. þen when hee had said to mee his pleaziur
for my word spoken, he bent him self to hiz former purpoz and
talk again (for hee waz on who looved to hear him self speak &

48ᵛ (margin)

---

[1] Whythorne probably was born in or near Chard, Somerset (see Introduction).
[2] A variant of Tilley M 994.

loked to hav all þe wordz) and þen hee waded so farr and kontinewd in hiz argewment, and entered into such A slow or puddl
of errowrz, þat all þat hard him, krost him and lawht at him,
and I smyled for kompany, þe which krossings and lawhings,
did sett þe ʒentilman in such A koler and chaf, az hee waz redy
to hav fallen owt with evry body þar. but bekawz sum of þem
wer hiz betterz hee sumwhat staid hiz wizdom þat way. and þen
hee bent all hiz ordinans at mee, showting at mee thundring shott,
with vehement wurdz. wherat I poor sowll waz fain to retýr for
A tým, but when I saw þat my forbearing of him did raþer enkreas hiz heat þen oþerwýz, I thouht to proov wheþer on heat
wold drýv owt an oþer[1] ⌈or no,⌉ and þen I began to shoot at him
az fast az hee shot at mee, so þat wee wer lýk to hav had A whot
skirmish, but þat owr betterz wer in plas, who took on þem to bee
moderatorz between vs. and þen after þe seasing of þe which fiu-
riowz flamz, I having red in þe book intiteled. *De ring of rihteows-*
nes &c.[2] that hee þat flattereth þe evell, maketh þem wurs, And
þat mallis waxeth intollerabull when it iz praized I wrot þus—

If flattered be þe wicked
from il to wurs bekum þei þan
when mallis iz lýkwýz praized
þe harm þerof few suffer kan.

I wrot þat afforsaid bekawz I vnderstood ⌈also⌉ þat þe ʒentilmans Melankoly still boiled in hiz brest at mee, and I wold ⌈not⌉
submit my self to him and kreep vnto him for hiz favor, not for
any mallis þat I bar vnto him, but bekawz he shiuld not so
triumf over mee, till hee had sumwhat konsidered of hiz demeanour towardz mee. and siurly I am perswaded þat þei who
kan and will mak A prowd fooll to know him self A littl shall do
God good servis þerin. but yet after ward when I remembred
þat wee owht to bear ⌈no⌉ mallis, and also for my frendz sak in
whoz hows we fell at þat ʒar, and partly for pollisis sak, I iwzed **49ʳ**

---

[1] Proverbial; Tilley F 277.
[2] No book with the title *The Ring of Righteousness* is known to the editors
of the *Short Title Catalogue.*

s⟨u⟩m kurtezi vnto him at len⟨k⟩th. for it iz said¹ in ȝezus *Syrak*,
. *cap .8. stryv not with A mihty man, lest þow chauns to fall into
hiz handz. mȧk not varians with A rich man, lest hee happen
to bring vp an hard quarrel against þee, for gold and siluer hȧv
vndoon mani A ọn. yee, eevn þe harts of kings hath it mȧd to fall.*
And if I had red, þez forsaid saings, befọr I did interr⟨upt⟩ þe
forsaid ȝentilman in hiz talk, I wold not hȧv proved hiz pasiens
so much az I di⟨d.⟩ Also ȝezus *Sirak* saith in þe sȧm chapter.
*Stryv not with A man þat iz full of word⟨z⟩ and lai no stiks vpon
hiz fier.* Đe sirkumstans of þis said ȝar, with oþerz þe lẏk befọr
þis tẏm, when I had renewd þem into my memory. also when
I kald to mi remembrans how, when az heer to fọr at sundry
tẏms I had bin in þe kumpanies of þọz who be wurshipfull, riht
wurshipfull, and also honorabull, and saw þat þe meaner sort
(in komparizon of þeir estȧts) wẹr dryven to put vp quietly sum
inȝiuriez at þeir hands. also how such things which þe in-
feriowr sort eiþer said or did in þe prezens of þeir greatterz or
betterz, waz but to bee allowd of az it pleazed þ⟨eir⟩ siuperiors
to tȧk it. and also þat I had read in ȝezus *Sirak. cap .14.* whẹr he
saith² *Hee taketh A burþen vpon him, þat akkompanieth with A
mọr honorabull man þen him self. How agree þe kettl and þe pott
togiþer? for if þe ọn bee smitten against þe oþer it shalbe broken. þat
iz to sai þe weaker shall kum by þe wurs.* Đẹz with many oþer
perswȧzions in þat chapter, learned mee þat I shiuld not keep
kumpany with my greatterz. wherfọr when I ⌜had⌝ kalled þem
all to my remembrans, with þe sirkumstanses of many matterz
affọr written I mȧd þis sonet folloing—

> *I hȧv not only read, but ẹk by proof hȧv trẏd
> how such who daily haunt, þeir greatterz kumpanẏ,
> kannot shiun great offens, on þ'ọn or þ'oþer sẏd
> wherfọr happi ar þei, who such an ill kan flẏ.*

After I had past þis broill affọrsaid I kowld not bianby put it

---

¹ Whythorne's references are to Ecclus. 8. 1, 2, and later to verse 3.
² Whythorne's reference to the fourteenth chapter of Ecclesiasticus is in-
correct and should be 13. 2.

owt of my mÿnd but it raþer gạv mee kawz to kall to my remembrans þe họl diskoors of all m⟨y⟩ former lÿf, and þen konsidering
of evry thing þat I had past, how I had bin m⟨a⟩ny tÿms in
họp of prosperite, and þen prezently owt of sekiurite, and þen
t⟨ost⟩ from pọst to piller,[1] now vp, now down,[2] by þe illiuzions
of flattering & fikk⟨l⟩ fortewn, who wold never suffer mee to be
in quiet when I waz well, and i⟨n⟩ prosperite, and did perseiv in
what kạs oþerz also wẹr in þat wẹr in such dyve⟨r⟩z estạts az
I had bin heer tofọr, I mạd þis sonett þerof az folloith—

> Till tÿm had tawht mee how to ʒuʒ of lạt
> I did but dream þe siur and quiet stạt
> at first I thouht þe simplest lÿf did best
> but seing þat mạd A thrall vnto þe rest
> I chainʒed mÿnd to ʒuʒ þe best of powr
> On whom[a] knoing þat hi dizdain did lowr
> I turned my sentens and dekreed
> þe mean (with mÿnd kontent) þe best whọz seed
> Yeeldz raþer sweet þen sowr.

When I had þus doen þen kạm to my mÿnd, how when I had
proved to lÿv many waiz, and kowld fÿnd no such sekiurite and
stabilite in any way þat I had proved az I did in þe profession of
þe teaching of Miuzik, I entended after þat tÿm to gÿv my self
whọly to þe profession þerof, and to nọn oþer. and bekawz
I wold benefit and profit my self þe better þerwith I devyzed **49ᵛ**
how I miht mạk my self to be known of many in þe shortest tÿm þat miht bee. and þen kạm to my remembrans þat
þer waz no better way for þat purpọz þen to sett and publish
sum miuzik of mÿn own making in print, and þen kạm also to
my remembrans how þat in my former daiz I had mạd many
songs to be sung of .iij. iiij. and fÿv parts, or for voises (azwell
az þat which I had mạd to bee plaid on þe virʒinals and liut)

---

a MS. reads 'whon'.

[1] Proverbial; Tilley P 328.
[2] Possibly an echo of the proverb concerning the two buckets in a well;
Tilley B 695.

þe which þen I determyned to put in print. And also I purpozed
to put with evry song A Sonett of mўn own invension for A ditti
þerto, most of þe which I hạv written into þis book alredy, vnto
þe which I do mean to sett also sertain salms in prọz, þe which
I will tạk owt of ⌐þe⌐ Salter ⌐or salms of David.⌐

And whўll I waz A perfekting and wryting owt of my miuzik
in such sort az I ment to sett it foorth, which waz ny ij yeer A
doing I had many kumbats with my self abowt it. ọn whўll wold
I think to my self, what do I mean now? þus to travell and beat
my brains[1] abowt þis matter. do I not daily see how þei who do
set owt books, be bi þeir wurks mạd A kommen gạz vnto all þe
world? and hang vpon þe blasts of all folks mowths, and vpon
þe middl finger pointings of þe vnskilful and also vpon þe sevẹr
ʒudʒments of þe grạv and deep wits. hạv I not red and hard also
þat þe mạts of *Momus*, and *Zoilus*, do lay snạrz and grinz[2] to trip
mens wurdz in wrўtings, eevn az hunterz and fowlerz iwz to
pich netz & snạrz to kach þeir praiz whọz wurdz and sensiurz
ar þe imaʒ of þeir ridikiulowz deedz, or raþer þeir lўvs. and þat
þe fourm of þeir bodies ar not seen to be better set foorth in A
glas þen in and by þeir speech, so þat þerby þe som of þe fond
affeksions of þeir myndz be setfoorth and displaid. So mai I
fўnd az þe Italien proverb[3] saith þat. *El mal vien per libra, e va
via per oncia*, which iz to say in English. þe mischef kummeth
by poundz, and goth away bi ounses. wherfọr az þe English
proverb saith I wilnot put my finger in þe fier willingly.[4] After
þat I had pawzed A whўll vpon þis matter, and bethouht mee,
þẹr kạm again to my mўnd þis Italien proverb[3] foloing. *Tal*

---

[1] Proverbial; Tilley B 602.

[2] *Grin*, a noose or halter (*OED*).

[3] These two Italian proverbs occur in Ludovico Guicciardini's *Ore di
Ricreazione* (Antwerp, 1568), first translated into English by James Sanforde
in 1573 under the title, *The Garden of Pleasure* (STC 12464). A new edition
in 1576 bore the title *Houres of Recreation, or Afterdinners. Which may aptly
be called the Garden of Pleasure* (STC 12465). The proverbs appear in this
edition on pp. 211, 221. Whythorne's English paraphrases are close to Sanforde, but rarely identical, perhaps because he was quoting from memory.
But because he places the composition of these verses about 1569, it is likely
that Whythorne owned the original Italian edition. Cf. Tilley M 998.

[4] Another proverb from John Heywood; Tilley F 230.

biasma altrui, chi se stesso condanna. þe English wherof iz. Such
do blạm oþerz, who do kondempn þem selvz. þe which proverb
I took to towch my self for kondempning of þọz affọrsaid to
rashly, azwell az to towch þem for kondempning of my doings.
and þạrvpon my koraʒ waz A littl enkoraʒed and kindeled to
prosekiut my purpọz.

wherfọr I kalled to my remembrans such proverbz[1] and perswazions, az shiuld instinkt and provọk mee to go forward with
mýn enterprýz. az first þis folloing. *L'innocentia porto seco sua
defensione*, þat iz. Innosenci bringeth with him, hiz defens. *A
qual si voglia dolore, remedia la patienza.* þat iz. To whom sorows
ar wished, þạr pasiens iz þe remedi. hee þat wilnot willingli
travell to þe benẹfit of oþerz, iz not wurþi to reap ani benefit of
oþerz. *Chi semina virtu, raccoglie fama* (saith *Boccace*[a] þe Italien
poet) *et vera fama supera la morte.* which iz to sai. Hee þat sowth
vertew, reapeth fạm, and trew fạm overkummeth death. *Fauo-
rinus* þe filosofer said þat eevn az þe body well dispozed, endiureth, both kold, heat, and oþer greefs, so þe mýnd well framed,
endiureth displeaziurz, thouht, and adversite. *Cicero*,[2] saith
þat wee ouht alwaiz to remember, þat wee ar men, kum into þe
world vnder þis law. þat iz, to be subjekt to all þe strọks and
storms of fortiun, and þerfọr owht not to refiuz to lýv vnder þe
stạt and kondision þat wee ar born in, neiþer lihtly to moov owr
selvs with þọz misfortiuns which by kounsell kannot be avoided.
but rạþer kalling to mýnd þe chaunses happened to oþer, in þe
mean seazon owht to konsider, þat þer iz no new thing hap- **50ͬ**
pened vnto vs. *Seneca*,[3] saith, þat whersoever A man doth hýd
him self, fortewn and þe mallis of enviowz peopull will fynd
him owt, and þerfọr þe mýnd owht to draw to hiz invinsibull

---

[a] Parenthesis prematurely closed here.

[1] These Italian quotations also occur in *Ore di Ricreazione* (pp. 215, 99,
and 104 of the 1576 translation). Sanforde attributes the second and third
sayings to Boccaccio. The quotation from Favorinus is also very similar to
a passage on pp. 118–19 of the 1576 translation. Tilley cites these proverbs
as I 81, P 108, and V 70.

[2] Here again the source of this quotation appears to have been the *Ore di
Ricreazione* (pp. 137–8 of the 1576 edition).

[3] Whythorne's source seems to be *Ore di Ricreazione* (p. 4, 1576 edition).

rok of konstansi, wḥẹr, dispizing all worldly things, þe darts
of fortiun and bolts of men withowt any hurt shall fall down to
hiz feet. Ḍez fọrsaid saings hạv I gaþered to perswạd me not to
fear þe rabull affọrsaid for all þeir envy and maṁis. wee ar not
born into þis world, altogiþer for owr selvs, but to do good in
owr professions and to owr abilitez evry way, I say to do good
to oþerz somuch az wee may, and not to lẏv az drọnz and kater-
pillerz, þat lẏv altogyþer vpon þe swẹt of oþerz brọwz.[1] also wee
ouht not to hẏd owr talents vnder þe ground az þe unprofitabu⟨ll⟩
servant[2] did, lest wee be fownd frewtles figtreez, and so kalled
to akkoun⟨t⟩ for owr bailiwiks.[3] if wee by way of labor do any
honest thing, þe labor departeth from vs, but þe thing well
doon, aslong az wee lẏv tarieth with vs, and will never dekay.[4]
When I had konsidered of all þis affọrsaid I mạd þis sonet
foloing, þe which I ment to sett first ⌈with miuzik⌉ az A prefas
vnto þe rest—

> *If evri ọn þat gọth abowt*
> *to set abrọd for kommen vew*
> *A wurk, hath ani fear or dowt*
> *þat þe fawt fynding karping krew*
> *shiuld vtterly þe sạm defạs*
> *few wurks setfoorth þen shiuld wee hạv*
> *but who bi vertew do purchas*
> *þeir stạts ay last ly þei in grạv*

I, not being satisfied yet with þat affọrsaid, but meaning to
kontinew my purpozed prefạs, alþouh I hạv devyded it into ij
parts, and meaning to mạk miuzik vnto þem ⌈bọth⌉ to be sung.
þe which sekond part shall heerafter follow, but er I mạd it I
gạv my self to read mọr to furder mẏn entent, & in þe end of my
reading I fownd þat þer ar iij kynds of goodz in man (after þe
opinion of *Aristotel*[5]) þat iz to say. of fortewn, of þe body, and

---

[1] This passage is a conflation of several proverbial expressions, among
them Tilley T 490 and S 1032.   [2] Matt. 25. 25.
[3] Proverbial; see *OED*.   [4] Proverbial; Tilley L 7.
[5] Here again Whythorne's quotation appears to have been derived from
the *Ore di Ricreazione* (p. 106, 1576 translation).

of þe mýnd. þe goodz of fortewn ar riches, and soveraintiez. þọz of þe body, ar þe good proporsion, favor, and komplexion, and also helth of þe body. And þọz of þe mýnd, ar knowleʒ and vertew. but saith hee, of þe last alọn, dependeth þe trew felisite, bekawz þat it iz þe proper operasion and wurking of þe mýnd wheron it dependeth, and not of þe body, neiþer of fortiun. *Isocrates*,[1] saith þat owr lýf entangled with fortiun iz lýk to A great and violent flowd, þat iz to say, troblows, miery, hard to pas over, swift, roaring, and diuring but A whýll. kontrary wýz þe lýf geven to vertew, iz lýk to A nobull fountain, whọz wạter iz kleer, piur, vntrobled, meet to drink, sweet, apt for norishment, frewtfull, and void of all korrupsion. *Valerius* saith, Ðe vertew of þe mýnd lyveth when all things els do dy. And þe poet *Claudiano* saith. *la virtu e animosa delle sue proprie ricchezze, la qual non si cura di esser celebrata dal favor del Volgo, perche non e bisognosa di lode*—þe english wherof iz þus. Vertew iz koraʒiows of hiz proper riches, and kareth not to be selebrạt of þe favor of kommen persons, bekawz it hath no need of praiz. so þat by þẹz fọrsaid saings in þe kommendasion of vertew yee mai perseiv how much it iz and ever hath bin esteemed emong þe wýz and learned sort. whẹrfọr I mýnding to wrýt sumwhat in þe praiz þerof wrọt az þe sekond part of þe prefạs affọrsaid. vpon þe last forsaid sentens, and owr english proverb which sa⟨ith⟩ So many hedz so many witts.[2] þis sonet folloing— **50ᵛ**

Az mani hedz hạv mani witts, so diuerz men of verteuz hạv
and vertew lýks her richez so, az oþer goodz shee doth not krạv
nor to bee selebrạt of þọz which be but of þe kommen sort
bekawz þat of her self shee hath no need of praiz or good report

When I had þus doon, I þen kalled to my remembrans what I had seen sum oþerz do, who did set owt books. sum did dedikạt þeir books to men and women of hy honour or of wurship,

---

[1] For a likely source, see *Ore di Ricreazione* (p. 152, 1576 translation). The quotations from Valerius and Claudiano have not been located in any available edition of Guicciardini.

[2] Another proverb from Heywood; Tilley H 279.

to dezier þem to be patrons of þeir books and sum did mąk no epistell at all, but only A prefąs, wherin þei did dekląr to þe perivzerz of þe sąm þe okkazion why þei did set þem owt, & what þei did mean þerby. also how þei ar to be vnderstood in sum plases, and of þe riht yvs of þem &c. Vpon þe konsiderasion of þe which sirkumstanses, and remembring also þat my for prefąses ar but breef and short, also þat þei ar sett to be sung and not red, and þat in þem iz not komprehended & kompakt somuch az iz needfull to be shewd in þe setting foorth of so dyverz & larʒ, and also so strainʒ matter az iz inkliuded in þe họl wurk and voliums of my publishing, I mąd þis long preambull or prefąs folloing, þe which iz sett in ọn of þe fÿv books wherin my miuzik iz, and þus it beginneth—

Of miuzik þouh þe cheef knowlęʒ hath long tÿm hindred been
bekawz vertew not being maintaind soon seaseth it iz seen
yet throuh þe good zeal of A few, who þerin pleaziur took
no kosts nor pains, it to prezerv, of long tÿm þei forsook
besÿd owr prinses charʒ of ląt to hąv it eft renewd
with verteouz rewlerz vnder her, whọz willingnes [iz][a] *shewd*
lÿk loov of ʒentils and honest hath raizd it from low eb
helping phœbus to pluk from fątall sisterz þat hiz web
þe which hee hath dispọzd into þe mÿndz so of A few
az what þei hąv ląt wrouht þerby, abrọd sum pąrt þei shew
all which do now enkorąʒ mee, þis wurk to send to liht
onli for þọz who in singing, of miuzik do deliht
(az lÿkwÿz do þe Duch, þe French, and þe Italiens
who put in print most þat þei wrÿt, with þeir miuzikal pens)
pąrt of þe matterz or dittiez, þat I hąv set heerto
þe salter, or salmz of Dauid, I hąu þem taken fro
to þe rest of þis hąv I sett (þe bąs mÿndz for to pleaz[])
such sonets az I think will sum of þeir sowr dumps appeaz
devÿzd vpon kommen chaunses and owt of worldly wurks
so, az þe reazon hath mee tawht which in mi riud hed lurks

---

[a] Thus in 1571 printed text. As in the case of other printed texts, differences in spelling are not recorded.

sum of þem bee poetikall, sum filosofikall,
on sakred wrẏt, I mǎd oþerz, to komfort mee withall
in which ar towcht þ'affekts of yowth, þe lẏk of rẏper yeerz
also of þǫz þat do deklẏn, when kold old aȝ appeerz
(sins erst I said, þat heer emong my sonets þęr bee sum
poetikall, whǫz godz I iwzd, az þen in mẏnd did kum[)]
heer wold I þat all such shiuld know who[a] *lẏks not poets wrẏt*
wherin towching þeir heaþen godz, þeir fansiez þei endẏt
þat such[b] *of þem who kristians ar know (az þe Salmist saith)*   **51**[r]
þei ar but vain, whǫz kredit lẏk, dezervz to hǎv no faith
ęk kristians know, þalmihti[c] *God, þe lord who rewls owr fǎt*
and sendz such fortiun az hee knowz iz meet for owr estǎt
for fortewn iz nǫn oþerwẏz to vnderstand I know
þen þat which pleazeth þ'almihti on vs for to bestow
of po'etri þus do I[d] *heer end, mẏ wrẏting tǎk at best*
mi pen heerafter from such toiz shal alwai be at rest
þis mi said miuzik mǎd do I for voises þus kontrẏv
to sum for iij. to most for iiij, and t'all þe rest for fẏv
of þęs songs sum be short, sum long, sum hard, sum eazi bee
and of bǫth sorts between þem both, yee shall emong þem see
heerin be dẏverz songs also, þe which altred hǎv I
bi mending of sum þe miuzik, of oþerz þe ditti
so þat þei bee not now, az þei węr when I first þem gǎv
owt of my handz abrǫd to serv þeir turns who now þem hǎv
also bekawz sum songs heer bee, whǫz trǎdz perchauns b'unknown
not onli to such who in skill of singing ar well grown
but to sum Miuzisians, who songs kan well kompǫz
(þat nǎm belongs to nǫn oþerz þouh sum þeron do glǫz)
eev'n such with þe oþerz (I say) I let þem vnderstand
þat I A traveller hǎv bin in sundri forren land
whęr I emong þe peopull did A sertain tẏm abẏd
whoz dyverz dyverz[e] *trǎdz of miuzik pǎrt (alþouh not all) I spẏd*
but cheeflẏ þe Italien emong þe which iz ǫn

---

[a] 1571 text reads 'that'.   [b] 1571 text reads 'those'.   [c] 'þat' written above.   [d] 1571 text omits 'do I', and reads 'hear I'.
[e] Dittography.

þat kalled iz Napolitąn (*A preti mery ǫn* [)]
besýd all þǫz forreiners trądz sum English I hąv hard
þeir diffrens shall appeer when þei togiþer bee konfard
all which when kawzes moved mee þęz songs at týms to mąk
now ǫn trąd and þen an oþer I did follow and tąk
(þǫz trądz þus towcht brings heer to mýnd how sundri sorts þerbee
throuh whǫz self wils no harmoni kan veri well agree
exsept þat which þei list to lýk, and soundz bǫth shrill and sharp
(such oft with Midas praiz Panz pýp, befǫr Apolloz harp)[a]
and az in þe kompozisi'on of þis mi miuzik mąd
I ʒoin þ'english with þe strainʒer t'agree in Miuziks trąd
so I þe flats, and sharps do set, az if both sorts heer sing
kan hąv no ʒust kawz to mizlýk or kavellasi'ons bring
but in oþer observanses þouh wee sumwhat vari
yet az I learnd in natýv land so in þis wurk ivz I
also wheraz þis mark ij iz set, t'iz but to put in mýnd
for to repeat if þat yee list and not yee þerto býnd[b]
pąrt of þe word or els sentens þe which befǫr it standz
now ywz þęz matterz az yee lýk[c] *I mąk nǫn oþer bandz*
part of my yoong daiz (ląt ended) on þis I did emploi
az thing wherin for kawzes said[d] *I had az þen sum ʒoi*

51[v] *If grątfulli it bee axsept mi kontent meed I hąv*
bekawz for oþer benefit I neiþer look nor krąv
mi said request I am assewrd, þe thankfull will allow
þouh dýverz oþerz oþerwýz of þis þeir mýndz will show
az nothing kan be so well ment, þat mai be said or doon
but þat þe enviouz to defąs þe sąm will frąm þem soon
so I for my well meaning heer to hąv þe lýk reward
I dowt I shall hąv of all such whǫz wits hąv no regąrd
for to konsýder of ech thing[e] *az þei of riht shiuld doo*
and to gýv evri vertew þat, which doth belong þertoo
first of þes sorts who I spęk of ar ǫn þat barbrowz bee

---

[a] 1571 text does not use a parenthesis at the beginning of this line.
[b] 1571 text employs parentheses for 'and . . . bind'.   [c] 1571 text reads
'list'.   [d] In 1571 text the preceding three words are in parentheses.
[e] 1571 text reads 'all things'.

who þoh of kreatiurz re'aznabull all þeir fowrms shaped bee
yet þei so deep infekted ar, eiþer with ingnorans
grosnes of witt, krewell natiur, franzi, or els perchans
with sum or altogiþer of þoz diseazes in sort
az inwardli þei never felt or tasted (to bee short)
þe sekret wurking of þe soundz konkordant[a] of miuzik
and þarfor þei, with taunting terms, against it spurn & kik.

what I kowld sai[b] in miuziks praiz I will at þis tým stai
and let yow see what on famouz of þat siens doth sai
I mean þe wurþi ȝentilman, doktor Haddon[1] bi nam
whoz learned miuz for miuziks sak þez verses þus did fram—

> *Musicen primum docuit voluptas*
> *musices auxit studium voluptas*
> *musices vsum retinet voluptas*
> > *gaudia fundens.*
>
> *Musicen lusit placidus Cupido*
> *musicen lusit Cytherea mollis*
> *musicen lusit cithara suaui*
> > *clarus Apollo.*
>
> *Musice mentes tenuit virorum*
> *musice sensus tenuit ferarum*
> *musice montis,[c] & aquas, & ornas[d]*
> > *sede remouit*
>
> *Musice summis dominatur astris*
> *musice terre[e] dominatur imæ*
> *musice ponto dominatur alto*
> > *cuncta pererrans*
>
> *Musice mentis medicina mæstæ*
> *musice multum minuit malorum*
> *musice magnis, medijs, minutis*
> > *maxima mittit*

---

[a] 1571 text reads 'concordant sounds'.   [b] 1571 text reads 'write'.
[c] 1571 text reads 'montes'.   [d] 1571 text correctly reads 'ornos'.
[e] 1571 text reads 'terræ'.

---

[1] Dr. Walter Haddon (1516–72). His Latin poem on music was printed in
Poemata, 1567, p. 66, usually listed as part of his *Lucubrationes* (*STC* 12596).

52ʳ *A sekond sort be Momus mạts, who sets þeir cheef deliht*
in perivzing of oþerz wurks to see whẹr þei be riht
what in þem laks or what tomuch, so fẏn þes priez[a] *bee*
az Lynceus waz who (it iz said) kowld throuh A stọn wall see
but if þat noman wold wrẏt mọr þen þei abrọd do show
wee must kontent vs with þat which wee do alredi know
A third sort now I must heer towch, A sort of ʒangling ʒais
whọz spẏtfull pens, to skof and skold ar[b] *prest at all assais*
az Zoylus did to þat poet, whom wee do Homer kall
so wold þez zoilings hạv vertew vnto þeir pens be thrall
þerfọr I sai to þe họl krew of all þ'infekted wihts
Momus mạts and zoylings (fọrsaid) who be'in such peevish plihts
þat eazier t'is for sum to fẏnd fawts[1] *written þat do*[c] *lurk*
þen it iz for þem, þem t'amend, and mạk perfekt A wurk
and eazier t'iz for oþer sum, t'amend fawts þat do rẏz
þen owt of þeir brains bi studi for to mạk or devẏz
A new wurk so great and perfekt in all points az þat is
in which þei kan amend þe fawts þat þei do spi amis
to such who az bee fawt fẏnderz (perchauns whẹraz nọn bee)
in þat wherin þei hạv no skill, and yet wold seem to see
I now say az Apelles did, þe shoomạker[2] *vntoo*
when hee beyond þe slipper would hạv had Apelles doo
heer to konkliud I sai þat I þis wurk do not set owt
to grẏv ani of þọz fọrsaid, of whom I mai hạv dowt[d]
but I do it only þerwith Godz praiz ech whẹr to sing
togiþer with heavnli solas to heavi harts to bring
for pryvat iws of baser thouhts not aspẏring so[e] *hy*
which lẏk to feed þeir fansiez all on wurks þat be worldly
to rekreat þ'over burdened and sọr afflikted mẏnds
to kumfort ẹk þe powrz and spreets, which mans helth brings & bynds
and foloingli[f] *to benefit ech sens and pạrt*[g] *b'akkord*
of þọz þat do deliht to lẏv alwai in triu konkord

---

[a] 1157 text reads 'priers'.   [b] 1571 text mistakenly reads 'is'.
[c] 1571 text reads 'doth'.   [d] 1571 text places the preceding six words in parentheses.   [e] 1571 text reads 'to'.   [f] 1571 text reads 'so consequently'.   [g] 1571 text reads 'ech part', and omits 'ech sens and'.

[1] Proverbial; Tilley F 103.   [2] Proverbial; Tilley C 480.

Heer to explan, and to mak plain vnto yow my meaning in
þe *strainȝ nams and sentenzes befor towched in þis prefas, yee
shall vnderstand þat phœbus iz þe nam of þe Soon of whom I said
enowh befor wheraz I spak of Apollo þe poetikall god of Miuzik,
þe which kolorabli and figiuratyvly I did nam to bee hiz web,* which
þe fatall sisterz had welni brouht vnto an end or finall destruk-
sion. Ðe fatall sisterz or poetikall goddesses, be kalled in Italien
parche, and in latten *parcæ.* pei be fained of þe poets to show or
to bee þe beginning, þe middl, and þe end of lyf and death, or
els þe prezent tym, þe tym perfektly past, and þe tym to kum.
whoz nams be *Cloto, Lachesis, and Atropos. Cloto,* holdeth A
distaf singnifieng þe beginning of lyf, *Lachesis,* spinneth and
shewth þe tym wherin wee do lyv, and *Atropos* breaketh or
kutteth A sunder þe threed þat iz A spinning, and þat iz death. **52ᵛ**
and þez iij be kalled or named *parche,* or *parcæ* bekawz þei do
pardon or spar no bodi.[1] wheraz I do befor mak A distinksion
of þe matter inkliuded within my songs and sonets, saing þat
sum of þem be poetikall, sum philosofikall, and sum mad on
sakred wryt, heer not þat poetikall matterz ar but vain, yet, prety
devises having in þem mor matter to be konsidered of þen þei
do owtwardly shew, with þe lyk devyses vpon þeir vain godz, of
whom þer iz enowh spoken in þe forsaid plas. filosofikall matterz,
be grav and wyz, full of good kownsell and instruksions, and for
þat þei be ⌐but⌐ morall, and profan, þei ar not akkounted az
sakred and holly. þen to towch þe sakred wryt, þoz bee such az
be devyzed vpon þe skriptiurz only. az for fortewn, þat iz plain
enowh set foorth in þe prefas, and how þe sam iz to be vnderstood.

In þe hier part of þe realm of Italy, iz A kuntrey named
þe kingdom of Napolis (of þe which I hav said sumwhat in
þe diskoors of my travell beyond þe seaz az affor iz said) þe
vplandish or kuntrey peopull of þe which kuntrei hav A sertain
kynd of Miuzik þe which diffreth from all operz in Italy. and

---

[1] Whythorne is mistaken in this etymology; *Parcae* is usually considered
to be derived from the Greek root πλεκ, so means 'one who plaits, or inter-
weaves'.

alþoh in þe kompozision þerof (þei being but of iij parts) þer be
fawts and errowrz, yet for þe pleazant strainʒnes of þe trad of
þem dyverz miuzisians hav not only amended þem and mad
þem into iiij parts, but also dyverz oþer miuzisians imitating of
þat miuzik hav mad of þeir lẏk vnto þeirz. And az þei hav doon,
so do I in my miuzik published set foorth þe lẏk of þeirz, both
for iij, iiij, and fẏv voises.

Midas afforsaid waz A kovetouz king of *phrigia*. *Pan*, þe
poetikall god of þe Sheppardz kontending in miuzik with *Apollo*,
þe poetikall god of miuzik, þei choz on named. *Tmolus* to bee
þeir ʒuʒ in þat kontroversy, who gav sentens on *Apollos* part, but
Midas preferred *Pan* with hiz skreaking pẏps befor þe miuzik of
Apollo, wherfor *apollo* gav vnto *Midas*, A pair of Asses earz.
Doktor *Haddon*, latly deseased, waz A doktor of þe sivill law,
and master [of] þe requests vnto þe queens maʒesti þat now iz.
Momus, waz no wrẏter him self, but such A on who wold seek
owt þe fawts of all wrẏterz in hiz tẏm, and so karp at at[a] þem at
hiz pleaziur. *Zoylus* waz A malisiowz poet, who wrot A book
of railing verses against þe most exsellent wurks of þe famows
greek poet *Homer*. of *zoylus* all malisious karperz at oþer mens
wrytings be named *Zoyli*. *Apelles*, waz an exsellent painter of
Ephesus. it iz written þat hee painted diverz exsellent wurks,
az of *Venus*, *Alexander* þe great. and on of infami or slaunder.
and emong hiz exsellent wurks, on (after hee had mad it) hee
did sett it in ⌐such¬ an open plas, wheraz such az past by it miht
see it perfektly. and hee plast him self sekretly very ny to it, to
heer what þe passinʒerz wold say of it, and emong þem þat saw
it, þar waz A shomaker, who in beholding of þe piktiur fownd
fawt with þe show or slipper wich þe piktiur waz mad to wer,
wherwith *Apelles* kam and demaunded of þe shoomaker of what
proff[ess]ion hee waz of, whervnto hee awnswered þat hee waz
A shoomaker, whervpon *Apelles* took A pensell and mended
þe fawt which þe shoomaker fownd. þe shoomaker seing þat,
fownd fawt with an oþer thing on þe piktiur which partained
not to þe shoomakerz okkiupasion, wherfor *Apelles* told þat hee

---

[a] Dittography.

shiuld not go beyond his slipper, and kontroll þe thing wherin
hee had no skill. whervpon did grow þe laten ada3. *Ne sutor
vltra crepidam*,[1] þe which az I did in my prefas apply to þoz who
be fawt fÿnderz in þat wherin þei hav no skill. whÿll I waz A
preparing to print my miuzik þer happened dyverz okkazions
to moov mee to wrÿt mor songs and sonets (to þe which I mad
Miuzik) on of þe which waz þis folloing.

Đar waz A sertain 3entilman[a] who seemed to bear mee sum
goodwill, þat brak vnto mee of marria3 az þus. Quod hee to mee.
For þe small akquaintans þat I hav of yow, I do lÿk yow very **53ʳ**
well, both for yowr karria3 of yowr self and good natiur. how
say yow, if I wold help yow to A widow, who iz kum of wurshipfull parenta3, and hath twenty powndz A yeer dowry or
3onter. who hath no chÿld, & iz of yeerz ny abowt fÿv or six
yeerz yoonger þen yowr self, wold not yow þen think mee wurþi
to reseiv A frendly turn at yowr handz again. quod I, if her
kondisions be agreeabull to þat which yow hav said of her, þen
must I needz akkount my self much beholding vnto yow, if I
may by yowr means marry with her, and þoh þe mach tak no
plas, yet do I thank yow for yowr goodwill. quoþ hee, shee iz
so 3entill and kurteowz of natiur, þat yow mai bring her to ani
reaznabull point, and þarwith all so loving and trew az þe turtl.[2]
and if yow will, wee will go to morrow whor yee shall see her.
kontent quoþ I. þe next day mi said frend and I went vnto þe
hows whor þe wydo waz. of whom after I had reseived A frendly
kis, and after my frend had talked A littl whÿll with her, and
broken þe marria3 matter, I had also such talk with her az waz
for þe sam purpoz. and when wee had remained þar A sertain
tÿm wee took owr leav of þe widow for þat tÿm.

after þe which tÿm my frend demaunded of mee how I lÿked
her? and I told him þat az yet I mizlyked her not, and if it shiuld

---

[a] MS. reads '3entilmam'.

---

[1] This story, given by Pliny the Elder in his *Historia Naturalis*, xxv,
chap. 10, section 36, was repeated by Erasmus in his *Adagia* (1569 edition,
englished by Richard Taverner, p. 17). Cf. Tilley C 480.

[2] Proverbial; Tilley T 624.

pleaz God þat wee shiuld ӡoin in marriaӡ, I mai not nor I hop
I shiuld not [refiuz þat] which hee hath appointed, quoþ my
frend I hav told yow her estat, and besýd þat which I hav told
yow, I dar warrant her to be worth A hundreth marks.[1] and þarfor shee iz not only wurþi to bee lýked of, but also to hav such
A on by whom her welth may be raþer enkreased þen impaired.
quoþ I to him if I hav her I wilnot only enkreas her welth azmuch az yow sai herz is, but also after þe deseas of my moþer I
will leav vnto her diuri⟨ng⟩ her natiurall lýf, azmuch of yeerly
rents az shall amount to ten pownds ⟨A⟩ yeer. and for þe par-
formans þerof I will enter into such A reaznabull bands, az shalbe
thouht meet by yowr and my learned kownsell in law. quoþ hee,
yow hav mad mee such an awnswer, az I am very well kontent &
satisfied þerwith. I wold wish quoþ hee, þat yow wold see her
eiþer to morr⟨ow⟩ or þe next day. I wold go with yow, but I hav
such buzines for þis iij or iiij daies, þat I kannot be in þe sytty
(heer ye shall vnderstand þat þis wydow waz A Londonar) but
þis day fýv daiz if yee will kum vnto my lodӡing quo⟨þ⟩ hee,
yow shall vnderstand what shee thinketh of yow, and what iz
lýk to bek⟨um⟩ of yowr sewt vnto her. quoþ I, I am kontent to
do az yow will hav mee in þe matter, and þarvpon wee parted
kumpany.

þe sekond day after owr partin⟨g⟩ I went to vizit my wydo, of
whom I reseived such frendly enterteinment a⟨z⟩ I did hop for
(þe tým of my woing being no lenger) and having past away þ⟨e⟩
tým A sertain spas with her I took my leav of her for þat tym.
When þe forsaid fyft day waz kum I went [to] my frend afforsaid
to hear what hee wold say, who shewd me þat þe day befor mi
kumming vnto him hee waz with þe wido, and when hee had
demaunded of her how shee lýked mee, and told her what I
offerd to be bownd to mak her worth prezently, and to leav her
after þe deseas of my moþer, shee said þat shee lýked mee and
mi offer sowell az shee waz determined to forsak all her oþer
sewterz and to tak mee to her huzband. and for þe making of þe

---

[1] A hundred marks was equal to £66. 13s. 4d., i.e. two-thirds of £100.

wrytings, shee waz kontented to kommitt þe hǫl dispozision
þerof to him, and þe dai of marriaȝ, shee waz kontent þat I
shiuld appoint. wherfǫr quoþ hee, I wold hạv yow to go to her
prezently and see wheþer shee bee in þe sạm mỹnd for þat
matter, az shee waz in when I left her. quoþ I, I will go to her
foorthwith. and þarwithall I parted from hiz kumpany.   **53ᵛ**

when I kạm at my wido, after dew saliutasions & serimoniez
belonging to A woerz funksion, I told her þat I kạm prezently
from my said frend, and þen I rekounted vnto her what hee told
mee of her promiz to him konserning þe knitting vp of owr
marriaȝ, wherevnto shee said þat such A promiz shee mạd vnto
him, and waz willing to perform it. vpon þe which wordz I gạv
vnto her A token of goodwill and shee reseaved it. Ðen shee and
I grew into talk of such things az wee thouht meet and konvenient for owr marriaȝ (for I looked for no oþer assewrans of
her at þat tỹm, þen þat promiz which s[h]ee mạd þen) and emong
þe sirkumstanses of my talk, I told her þat seing shee had
referred þe day of owr marriaȝ to my assingment, I wold hạv it
to bee þe next term (which waz þe term after kristmas, and not
much aboov three weeks after þe tỹm þat wee had þis talk)
bekawz quoþ I, I hạv A broþer in law,¹ þat iz A lawyer, who
kummeth to London at þat term. & I wold be glad to hạv him at
my marriaȝ. þęz wordz of mỹn, mi wido seemed not to gain say,
oþerwyz þen þus, and yet þat waz so kolorabli doon az I vnderstood not her meaning þerin. shee said shee wold marry within
þat yeer or els shee wold never marry, by þe which wordz I
thouht þat shee ment to marry within A yeer after shee had
spoken þǫz wordz or els shee wold never marry, but by þe
sequell it appeared þat shee ment to marry befǫr þat old yeer
went owt, or þat þe new yeer shiuld begin (which waz within A
⌐fortniht⌐ after her wordz so spoken). also shee seemed sumwhat
to mizlỹk þat I kạm no oftener vnto her bekawz I kạm but ons

---

¹ Whythorne had three brothers-in-law: John Skinner, John Webb, and
Augustine Worthington. All were living at Ilminster in 1569 and at least
two of them appear to have been engaged in legal activities.

in three daiez. to þe which I awnswered her þat mi buzines had
bin such, þat I kowld kum no oftener, but I wold afterward
amend þat fawt. After þis I took my leav of her. and þe sekond
day after I kạm to her again, at what tẏm I fownd my widow so
strainʒ az þouh shee had never mạd mee any such faithfull
promyz az iz befọr spoken of, whẹrat I waz sodenly kast into A
dump, in þe which whyll I remained I konsidered with my self
what shiuld be þe kawz of þis soden revolt and strainʒnes.

   and when I had miuzed A littl whẏl on þe matter, I az ọn þat
had had sum experiens in such kạsez befọr þat tẏm, plukked vp
my spreits and began to sai vnto mi wido, ʒentilwoman I do
marvell of þis yowr sodein chainʒ of kowntenans towardz mee?
I họp þat whatsoever yow do owtwardly shew yowr self towardz
mee yow do mean þe sạm toward mee inwardly az yee befọr
profest to yowr frend and mee owtwardly. quoþ shee, and if yow
had taken mee at my word and not hạv prolonged þe tẏm with
mee I wold hạv performed my promyz. þe which promyz waz
no such kontrakt but þat it mai be broken again. in deed quoþ I
it waz no such kontrakt in matrimoni az shiuld farder bẏnd
yowr konsiens þen A frendly promis withowt þe plihting of
ᒥowrᒣ troths þe ọn to þe oþer, and yet I for my pạrt thouht þat
I shiuld not need to hạv doon it till wee had met at þe chiurch
togiþer for þat purpọz. but quoþ I, I think yee do þis but to try
mee, and if it be so, I am kontented þerwith, and will willingly
tarry yowr pleaziur and will to parform þe premisses. nay quoþ
shee, I am fully resolved in þat matter, and if I shiuld hạv yow
what shiuld I be enriched by þe having of yow? quod I, az for my
richez I am assewred þei be nothing inferior to yowrz, if yee bee
no richer þen yowr frend told mee of, and az for þe dowery
which I hạv offerd vnto yow after þe deseas of my moþer it iz
54ʳ mọr þen I shiuld gain by yow & if yow shiuld dy befọr mee, for
þe yeerly rents which yow reseiv ar not to be reseived by yowr
assines lenger þen yow do lẏv. whẏll I waz þus talking with my
wydo, she fecht þe token which þe ij daiz befọr I had geven
vnto her, and shee wold hạv delivered it vnto mee again, but I
wold not þen reseiv it, and bekawz she shiu⟨ld⟩ not vrʒ it vpon

mee over much, I did b⟨i⟩d her farwell for þat tẏm. and when
I was gon from her I wrọt þis sonet folloing—

I hạv er þis tẏm hard mani ọn sai
tạk tẏm whẏll tẏm iz for tẏm will awai[1]

who so þat great affairz hạv to be doon
which at þeir own will þei mai dispach soon
let no deferring of tẏm be yuzed
lest þei bee far of when þei wold be sped

Emong þe loving worms þis thwarting woord
iz oftẏms blown owt in ernest or boord
when þat yee miht hạv had, þen wold yee not
þerfọr when þat yee wold, þen shall yee not[2]

Mani in sundri sorts hạv found þis trew
which wẹr to long (ech wai) heer for to shew
wherfọr remember what now hath bin said
and let althings with tẏm bee rihtli waid

When I had þus mạd þis said sonet, þer kạm to mi mẏnd
to ʒudʒ dowtfully ⟨of⟩ þe intension of þis preseeding matter, ọn
whẏll I thouht þat þis marriaʒ waz moved and travelled in, onli
of goodwill born vnto mee by mi said frend, & þat þe breach
þerof kạm only of þe wydowz inkonstansy, an oþer whẏll I
thouht þat þei both had imaʒined to kozen mee vnder þis pretens
of marriaʒ, thinking þat I wold hạv bin prodigall in expenses
and gifts, in lending, or in bekumming sewrti. az such praktizes
hạv bin and be kommen both in þis kạs, and also emong þọz who
be named chẹterz and mạk shifts. of þe which sorts of peepull
þer be sum, who when þat þei be at A low eb, will konvent and
meet at A plạs by þem appointed, and þạr will tạk such A chamber az all þei mai ly in at ọn tẏm, whẹr þei will konsowlt A họl
day and niht togyþer, in þe which tẏm evry ọn of þem will gẏv
hiz oppinion and argew pro & contra in þe matter proponed,
which iz to non oþer end but to þe vndoing eiþer of sum whom

---

[1] Proverbial; Tilley T 313.   [2] See p. 109.

þei think eazi to be mad raþer vnkuls þen kozens, alþouh þei be
of suffisient yeerz to keep þeir own, or els of sum yoong heir þat
iz newly start owt of þe shell. An oþer whẏll I wold kall to my
remembrans þe great praizes þe which my said frend had mạd
on þe wydow for her konstansy and good kondisions, konferring
hiz praizes with þe proof þat I had tasted of her doings. An oþer
whẏll wold I reproov my self of to hasti ȝuȝment, for kondempning þembefọr I had had farder triall in þe aksions. and thus
standing in A mammering¹ az it wẹr, and seing all þez sirkumstanses hang in A ballans, not being yet habull to ȝuȝ which sẏd
54ᵛ waz heviest, þat iz to sa⟨i⟩ wh⟨e⟩þer þeir dezarts dezerved to be
wurs thouht on þen my ȝiuȝment in þat kạs, I wrọt þus in
meeter þerof—

> whẹr praizes great be geevn, or fawts lẏkwẏz be fownd
> oftẏmz þei bọth ar blown abrọd, bi will withowt good grownd
> Ech thing iz not az seemz,² and az self wilz lẏks it
> to praiz or blạm, for such mọst tẏmz, do raþer mis þen hit.³

When I had þus sumwhat eazed my mẏnd, I þen bestored my
stumps lẏk A netteld hen,⁴ till I fownd owt my frend, and þen
I shewd him þe họl sirkumstans of þe ȝar between þe widow
and mee, who seeming to marveill much þerof, waz in A dowt
lest mi ill demeanor toward her had geven her þe kawz, quod
I to him if shee took ani new okkazion to break her hest towardz
mee, it was bekawz I kạm not to see her evri day. I thouht þat
ons seing of her in ij daiz wold hạv kontented her, or els peradventiur she lẏked not to tarry solong vnmarried now az vntill þe
beginning of þe next term bekawz it iz so long hens. shee saith
þat shee shalnot be benefited by marrieng of mee, and I told her
þat shee shiuld hạv mọr benefit by marrieng with mee þen I
shiuld hạv by wedding of her. and my insuffisiensi be þe kawz
of her chainȝ whi did [she] not fynd fawt with it to yow and mee
befọr? but I am perswaded þat þer iz sum oþer matter in it þen

---

¹ Proverbial; Tilley M 61.   ² Proverbial; Tilley T 199.
³ Proverbial; Tilley H 475.
⁴ 'Bestirred my stumps' is proverbial (Tilley S 946), but the simile may be
of Whythorne's own devising.

þez konʒektiurz of myn. I prai yow quoþ I, go to her and know
þe kawz of þis vnkyndnes, and I will repair vnto yow to morrow
to know wheþer Totnam be turned french[1] or no. quoþ hee I
will, and see þat yee be with mee to morrow in þe after noon,
I will quoþ I, and with þis wee parted. þe next day I kam to him
again at mi tȳm appointed, and demaunded of him wheþer mi
wydow wer still þe sam woman þat I left her, and hee said yee.
also hee told mee þat hee charʒed her with her promis, to þe
which shee awnswerd þat it [waz] no such promyz but þat she miht
break it again vpon kawz, and seing þat I took her not bianby
and dispached þe matter, shee waz determined never to marry.
never þe les shee saith þat it iz not for ani mislȳking þat shee
hath of yow, for shee thinketh yow to bee A veri honest ʒentilman. after þis quod hee, I told her broþer (for shee did þen ly
in A broþerz hows of herz) of yowr offer vnto her, of her promis
vnto yow, and of her breach þerof, whervpon hee went to her
and tawnted at her A littl, yee and servants of þe hows spak vnto
her on yowr behalf, reprehending her for her inkonstansi and
breach of promis, which hath brouht her in to A quandare,
nowithstanding shee keeps her to her hold, which iz, þat she
wil never marry. by þe which yow may see (quoþ hee to mee)
what trakting of þe tȳm doth in þis kas, if yow had geven kredit
to my report of her at þe first, and not hav prolonged þe tȳm of
marriaʒ, þis matter had not bin so far bak az it iz now. quod I to
him I ensiur þat I did not delay þe day of marriaʒ for any oþer
kawz þen þat I wold hav had mi broþer in law at it who miht
hav reported þe sam vnto mi moþer and sisterz when hee had
returned into þe west kuntrei again.

now I do perseiv sum great lȳklihod þat þez proverbs and
ᴦoldᴦ saings be trew which hav bin devyzed vpon þis sort of
woings, þe on of þe which iz þus. Blessed be þe woing þat iz not
long A doing.[2] and if I had foloed þis proverb þen my woing had
bin at an end by þis tȳm. also an oþer saith þat hee who doth wo 55ᴦ
A maid shalnot bee þe wurs welkum þoh hee kum but now and

[1] Whythorne had used this expression earlier; see p. 105.
[2] Proverbial; Tilley W 749.

þen to her, az in iij or iiij daiz, but hee þat woeth A widow, must
ply her daily.[1] also an oþer saith þat hee þat woeth A maid must
go trik and trim, and in f⟨ȳn⟩ apparell, but hee þat woeth A
widow must go stiff befọr.[2] I promis yow so waz I stiff, but yet
konsidering þat þe tȳm waz not lȳk to be long to þe wedding
day, and also þat þe market waz lȳk to last all þe yeer long, and
I loving her, ment not to attempt ani dishonesti[a] vnto her, for A
sinfull fakt it had bin, till wee had bin married, and wee shiuld
hạv provoked Godz heavy displeaziur and wrath to hạv lihted
vpon vs for owr wikkednes. and if þọz be þe kawzes of her revolt,
þen I do akkownt her az good lost az fownd.[3] quoþ hee I wọld
not hạv yow to leav her þus, but go vnto her broþerz hows ⟨and⟩
sai þat yee kum not for ani kawz but to see him, to whom[b] I know
yow shalbe w⟨el⟩kum, and þen shall yee see wheþer shee will
see yow or not, if shee do, yow mai iyz such enterteinment and
talk to her az yow shall see good. quoþ I, I will go to him to
morrow to brẹkfast and see wheþer all hiz khristmas pȳes be
eaten or no. do so quoþ hee. and with þọz wordz wee parted
kumpani for þat tȳm. þe next day in þe morning I went to þe
said ȝentilmans hows, an⟨d⟩ when I kạm þerat I requyred to see
him, and not ons spạk of þe wydow hi⟨z⟩ sister. when I spạk
with him I told him þat alþouh þe stạt between hiz s⟨ister⟩ and
mee stood not so well az I wisht þat it did, yet did akkownt my
self much bownd vnto him for hiz goodwill, and in þat respekt
I kạm þen to see him, and to gȳv him my harty thanks þerfọr.
whervnto hee awnswered, þat wha⟨t⟩ hee had said vnto her in
my behalf, my frend waz habull to report þe sạm vn⟨to⟩ mee,
and so groing in to oþer talk, at lenkth þe ȝentilman kalled for
A pe⟨ce⟩ of brawn, & A kristmas pȳ for vs to break owr fasts
þerwith. þe which being brouht to A tabull prepared for þe purpọz, wee went to breakfast, & befọr wee shiuld sit down þerat,
þe ȝentilman sent vnto þe widow hiz sister to know wheþer

---

[a] MS. reads 'doshonesti'.   [b] MS. reads 'whon'.

[1] Proverbial; Tilley M 17, the earliest example being 1639.
[2] For Whythorne's earlier use of this proverb, see p. 43.
[3] Proverbial; Tilley L 454.

shee wold break her fast with vs or not, but þe widow being in bed (az he⟨r⟩ kustom waz to keep her bed in þe morning till ten of þe klok) wold nọn a⟨t⟩ þat tȳm, wherfọr shortly after owr awnswer wee went to brẹkfast. þe ʒentilman not being satisfied with her awnswer, sent to her again and dezyred her to mạk her redy and to kum vp to him, and so with much A doo, she kạm at length.

when shee waz kum, after A few salutasions withowt embrasings & busses, shee sat down at þe tabull, wher þer waz such frendly talk and drinking vnto with slender pledʒings az is kommenly iwzed between such, between whom þer iz but ordinary frendship, and when þat brẹkfast waz doon, wee fell into talk of dyverz matterz, in þe end wherof þe ʒentilman slunk awai and left þe widow and mee alọn. vnto whom [I] þen renewd my old sewt, and charʒing her with inkonstansy, and with þe breach of her promis wherwith shee laid for her self þat if I had not delaid þe tȳm and tạken her at her word shee wold not hạv gon from it, but quoþ shee I am fully determined now never to marry, and þerwithall she seemed to be much trobled in her mȳnd and sihed often, vpon þe which I waz dezirows to know þe kawz of her greef and trobull of mȳnd, but þat shee wold not vtter vnto mee. if yow (quoþ I) do think þat I will tạk any such hold of yowr wordz az I will kavell with yow, and trobull yow for þem, put þat owt of yowr hed, for and if yee wẹr A hundreth tȳms better þen yee bee, yee shall never be mȳn exsept yee [ar] az willing to hạv mee, az I am to hạv yow. I hạv no such dowt quoþ shee for and if [yee] wold yee kannot drȳv mee to marry with yow exsept wee had ko⟨n⟩trakted owr selvz þe ọn vnto þe oþer. it 55ᵛ iz trew quoþ I, and after A littl mọr talk between vs, I took my leav of þe widow, and gạv thanks vnto her broþer for my good cheer, and went mi waiz with entent never to travell in þat matter with her again.

ni about A week after þis parting, I met with my fọrsaid frend again, who after sertain saliutasions between vs, hee demaunded of mee when I waz with þe widow, and I told him þat I waz with her but ons sins I saw him last, and þat waz þe next day

after I parted from him. quoþ hee I hav bin þar sins I saw yow
last also, and I hav so iwzed þe matter, þat and if yow will
kum to her again yee shalbe welkum. I do think so quod I, for
I ⌐hav geven⌐ her non oþer kawz, but I shalnot be so welkum
to her az shee will perform her first promis vnto mee and
þarfor I mean not to looz ani mor tym abowt her. quoþ hee yow
kannot tell now how welkum yow shalbe to her, prov her ons mor
vpon þis my word, and þen do az shee will gyv yow kawz. yee
sai well quoþ I, and þarfor I kar not greatly and if I do hazard þe
los of A littl mor tym abowt her. after þat my frend and I had
talked of þis matter, and oþer things A sertain tym, wee parted
for þat tym. þe next dai I went again to þe widow, whoz kowntenans was sumwhat mor amiabull þen it waz when I parted from
her last, but yet in wordz konserning marriaʒ shee waz far of and
þer waz no promis to be had of her þat way. not withstanding
shee vpon sum talk dezired mee þat I wold get her A ring to be
mad, and shee wold deliver mee sum gold to mak it withall,
vnto þe which I agreed quikly, and demaunded of her what
fasion shee wold hav it to be mad, to þe which shee awnswered
þat shee wold hav it after þe maner of A wedding ring. I þervpon
imaʒening þat shee ment sum marriaʒ, & þat shee wold not hav
requested mee to get þe ring to be mad on þat fasion eksept
I shiuld be prevy of þe marriaʒ, I in hop to put þe ring on her
finger seemed (az I waz in deed) to be veri glad þat shee wold
kommit such[a] A matter to be doon bi mee, and þen I told her
þat I hoped þat with þat ring I shiuld wed her, and az for þe
day of wedding, seing þat it pleazed her not az I did sett it,
I wold now rezyn þat appointment to her assynment, whervnto
shee said littl þat mad for mi purpoz. notwithstanding I ment
not now but[b] to follow daily mi enterpryz till þe ring waz mad,
and þen if I lyked not þe sequell I ment to know of or on and so
looz nomor tym.

when shee and I had past þe tym away A prety whyll, shee
went unto her chest and fecht owt of it asmuch old gold az waz

---

[a] MS. reads 'shuch'.   [b] MS. reads 'buto'.

worth ny abowt A mark, þe which shee said þat shee wold hav
bestowd in þe ring. and þen shee looking on sertain rings þat I
wear on my little finger, seemed to lẏk on of þem and said þat
shee wold wear it A whẏll for my sak, whervpon I offerd to gẏv
it vnto her, but shee wold not tåk it of gift, þe which mad mee
to suspekt bianbi, þat shee mistrusted þat I wold not restor her
gowld vnto her again, and if her imaʒinasion fell owt riht yet shee
having mi ring shiuld not looz all. not withstanding my suspision
I did mean not now to leav þis matter þus rawly. and when mi
widow and I had past awai þe tẏm in þis said maner, I took A
loverz leav and so parted from her kumpani. þe next day I went
to A gold smith vnt[o] whom I delivered þe gold, and told him
of what fasion I wold hav þe ring mad, and also gav þis sentens
to grav in it, *Đe eie doth fẏnd*, *Đe hart* doth chooz And loov 56ʳ
doth bẏnd. *Til* death doth looz.[1] I do wrẏt þis sentens in þis sort
bekawz it iz not of mi making, yet sowell lẏked of mee, az if I
shiuld mak an oþer wedding ring it shiuld hav þe sam sentens.
but to my matter. when I had geve⟨n⟩ order to mi goldsmith for
þe making of þe ring, with þe bignes of her finger, & had reseaved of him A kounterpan or weight of þe gold, I agreed with
him to hav þe ring mad by þe fowrth day after, in þe which iiij
daiz I did ply mi widow for lẏf. and to mak her þe mor kumming
or at þe least þe mor traktabull & mery I kawzed on of my liuts
to be browht to her broþerz hows, on þe which I wold sumtẏm
plai when I waz þar to pas þe tẏm awai withall.

and when I had þus past away þe fowr daiz in þe which tẏm
I mist not to vizit her evri day ons, I went to my goldsmithz for
þe ring. for þe making wherof when I had paid h⟨im⟩ and saw
þat þe waiht þerof agreed with my kounterpan and waiht
afforsaid, ⟨I⟩ browht þe ring vnto my widow, þe which when shee
did see, shee grew þerwitha⟨ll⟩ into A great melankoly, and said
þat it waz not of þe newest ⌐and best⌐ fassion. quoþ ⟨I⟩ it iz of
þe best fassion þat I do know, and þerwithall I ministerd

---

[1] Professor F. P. Wilson points out that this posy occurs in a manuscript
at Sion College, and is printed in Joan Evans, *English Posies and Posy Rings*
(1932), p. 34.

furder talk to appeaz her anger. but all mi wordz prevailed nothing, for still her melankoly enkreased which browht her quikly into glumming, powting and sihing. when I did see her in þat perplexite, I sowht with all þe fair perswazions þat I kowld devẏz to kontent her, shewing her þerwithall, þat and if I miht see þe fassion þat shee lyked, I wold kawz it to be mạd A new of þat fassion and I wold pai for þe mạking þerof my self. no quoþ shee it shall not need, I must kontent mee with it az it iz seing it iz mi fortewn (þọz last wordz of herz, mạd mee to dowt þat shee had praktyzed befọr þat tẏm with sum Astr⟨o⟩loȝian or sowth saier to know of what kredit her husband shiuld be of, which ⟨As⟩troloȝian or sowth saier willed her to kawz þis ring to be mạd, and az þe fassion of þat chaunsed ⌈to lyk her⌉so shiuld her husband lẏk her[)] and wheþer mi konȝ⟨ek⟩tiur had any lẏklihod or no, yee shall perseiv by konferring her last word⟨z⟩ affọrsaid with her mach in wedlok, of þe which I will shew yow heerafter.

(and now again to my matter) when my widow had sat A great whẏll in he⟨r⟩ sullen, I wold hạv her sollem estạt, all þe which tẏm I said nothing vnto her but bethouht mee on her last wordz, and imaȝining what shee ment by þem, I at length ministred talk vnto her again to proov if þat þe kọst waz kleered, and þat after klowdz blak wee shiuld hạv weþer kleer,[1] but þat waz nothing so, þe aspekts of malingnant planets, wer fulli fixed to fowll weaþer all þat dai, wherfọr I offerd to tạk my leav of my widow to be gon, who after A slender fạrwell, willed mee to prai þe ȝentilman mi frend to kum and spẹk with her. þe which hest of herz, I promyzed to akkomplish and so I went my waiz from her, taking þe way prezently vnto mi frend, and rekownted vnto him þe họl sirkumstans of all þe aksidenses and chaunses þat had happened between my widow and mee sins I did see him last. and when I had mạd an end of my talk, quod hee I am asmuch deseived in þat ȝentilwoman az ever I waz in any woman in all my lẏf, but quoþ hee for þis yow mai thank yowr delaieng of þe tẏm with her, and if yow had bin satisfied with mi report of her and had taken her at her word yow had bin now owt of all

---

[1] Two proverbs, Tilley C 469 and C 442.

þęz overthwarts. quod I þat iz to be dowted, for shee þat wilbe
so in dok owt nettl[1] for such small matterz az shee hath had, and
be so hard to bee reklaimed again, it argweth þat shee will shew
her self to mǫr vnquiet effekt when shee hath me so sewr þat
I wilnot nor kannot start from her. well quoþ I, seing shee
dezireth to hąv yow to kum vnto her, I pray yow go to her, and
know her mynd and þerwithall let mee know A day wherin 56ᵛ
I shall kum vnto her, and hąv A finall awnswer of her whervnto
I shall trust konserning my sewt vnto her. quoþ hee agreed, and
if yow wilbe heer with mee to morrow in þe afternoon, yee shall
know what shee saith þerin.

þe morow being kum, I went to my frend to know my widows
determinasion. and when I kąm at my frend hee told mee þat
if I wold be at þe hows whęr þe widow did ly þe next day in þe
morning by ten of þe klok hee wold meet mee þąr, and þen wee
shiuld see what shiuld bekum of owr matter, to þe which I
agreed. quoþ hee seing þat shee iz so tikkl[2] and fleeting I do
think it meet þat yee bee ensewred togiþer befǫr her broþer and
mee, and þat yow do gȳv her A ring on þat kondision. I am
kontent quoþ I. when I had past away A great part of þe afternoon with my frend, sumtȳm konferring on Italien wordz,
sumtȳm in miuzik matterz, az in plaing on þe liut, and sumtȳm
on English books, I parted from my frend with request þat hee
wold not forget hiz promis, az I wold remember mȳn. þe next
dai being kum and þe howr drawing on, my frend and I met at
þe hows appointed, wher wee kowld hąv no awnswer till wee had
dyned togiþer wherfǫr to pas awai þe tȳm I took mi liut and
plaid þeron ǫn whȳll & kawzed my frend to do þe lȳk an ǫþer
whȳll, and az wee węr so passing þe tȳm away, I spąk vnto him
and dezyred him þat if þe widow wold not now knit vp þe knot,
þat hee shiuld mąk nomǫr perswazions in þe matter, for I shiuld
but looz my tȳm and hee hiz labowr.[3] well, þe dinar tȳm being
kum, þe ȝentilman of þe hows kąm, and bad vs welkum, and in

---

[1] An old charm; Tilley D 421–2.
[2] *OED* 'uncertain, capricious, fickle', &c.
[3] A conflation of proverbial expressions, e.g. Tilley L 3 and L 9.

lẏk maner did þe widow, and when þe meat waz set on þe tabull, and evry of vs sett þerat, akkording to owr degręez, okkasions of talk węr moved dyverzly, wherwith wee past away þe dinar tẏm. þe end wherof being kum, my frend remembring þe kawz of owr meeting þar at þat tẏm, began to rehers þe sȧm vntoo vs, and þen turned him self vnto þe widow, and did her in mẏnd of my sewt vnto her, shewing her also þat I dezyred now to hąv A determinat and A finall awnswer and end þerof, whervpon shee ivzing but few wordz, in þe end of þem said, þat shee waz determined never to marry, with which wordz her broþer, and my frend not being willing to be so awnswered, took þe widow A sẏd, and fell A new to perswading of her, and whyll þęz perswązions węr A mąking her broþer left her and my frend togiþer, and hee kąm to mee seeming to be sory for þat my sewt took no better effekt, adding þervnto þat wheraz hee was kontented þat shee shiuld ly in hiz hows for A tẏm till God wold send her such A mąk or husband, az by whom shee miht lẏv in A hows of her own hee perseived þat shee ment to trobull hiz hows still by refiuzing of such A ọn az waz well to bee thouht on, and by þat tẏm þat her broþer and I had talked A whẏll, my frend kąm from þe widow vnto mee, and wold needz hąv mee to proov her again, þe which I did, & told her also what her broþer had said vnto mee konserning her, with promis þat if I miht obtain my sewt of her, þat þe first thing þat I went abowt shiuld bee to get A handsom hows, and in þe mean whẏll raþer þen shee shiuld ly owt of þe dọrs, shee shiuld ly in my chamber, for þe which shee gąv mee thanks.

but yet shee wold nọn of my offer. & in þe end of her wordz shee said þat ọn of þe kawzes why shee wold not marry waz bekawz shee waz many tẏms t[r]obled and oppressed with A melankoly hiumowr, at which tẏm shee shiuld peradventiur 57ʳ displeaz her husband, and þen if [hee] kowld not bear with her and put it vp quietly, it wold be⟨e⟩ sum disquietnes between þem. quoþ I to her, if yow wold not misywz mee tomu⟨ch⟩ I kowld bear with yow welinoh in þat kąs. well quoþ shee bekawz I know what I shall say in þat kąs, and what will fall owt þerof,

I do mean to p⟨re⟩vent þe wurst, and þarfor I will never marry.
and az for trobling of my broþerz hows, þat I mean not to do
very long. when I saw þat shee wold not be turned on my sẏd,
and þat shee had told mee of her melankoly hiumour I waz soon
awnswered and so I took my leav of her. imediatly whervpon
I went vnto my frend and told him þat þer waz no grạs to be
fownd with þe widow wherfor I praid him þat wee miht be gọn,
and so wee took owr leav of þ⟨e⟩ ȝentilman of þe hows and went
owr waiz. and az wee wẹr going togiþe⟨r⟩ I told him þe effekt of
þe talk between þe widow and mee, adding þerv⟨nto⟩ what shee
said of her melankoly hiumour, to þe which hee said þat hee
took her to bee of az ȝentill and kurteowz natiur az ani woman
kowld bee. quo⟨þ⟩ I for yowr pains taken in þis aksion I do
hartely thank yow, and yow hạv bo⟨wnd⟩ mee to tạk twẏs
as much for yowᵃ any way þat I kan. I do thank yow quoþ hee,
and so wee parted kumpani þe ọn from þe oþer. by þat tẏm
I kạm to mi lodȝing I remembred þat I had az yet þe widowz
ring, and þat [shee] had mẏn, of þe which I thouht to hạv mạd
an exchainȝ with her, but shee not mẏnding such A chainȝ, sent
her maid to my lodging, þe next day, who on he⟨r⟩ behalf requested mee to kum vnto her mistres and to speak with her.
whẹrvpon I mistrusting þat it waz to hạv her ring, I told her
maid þat I wold be with her mistres þe next day in þe morning.
and against þat tẏm I wrọt in A pees of paper þe verses þat
I kawzed to be graven in her ring sumwh⟨at⟩ altered az þus—

> Ðe eie did fẏnd
> de hart did chooz
> and loov did bynd
> til death shiuld looz

vnto þe which verses I added þẹz fowr verses foloing—

> forᵇ reazon now
> hath brọk þe band
> sins to yowr vow
> yee wold not stand

ᵃ MS. has contraction for 'your'.   ᵇ Written over 'But'.

Ðe next day in þe morning I went vnto my widow, of whom
ons mọr I demaunded wheþer shee waz willing to perform her
first promẏz mạd to mee and my frend or not, vnto þe which
shee mạd awnswer þat þe promyz waz nọn such but shee miht
break it welinoh with sạf konsiens and harping on her old string[1]
shee said þat shee wold never marry. well þen quoþ I, heer I
hạv brouht yow yowr ring, and if yow will pay mee for þe mạking
þerof and will also redeliver vnto me þe tokens which yee reseivid
of mee, yow shall hạv yowr ring. imediatly after my wordz so
spoken shee paid mee þe money for þe making of þe ring, and
delyvered mee my tokens again, vpon þe reseit wherof I delivered
her, her ring, and þerwithall gạv vnto her A kis, & saing þat
when it shiuld pleaz God to send her A huzband, I wisht þat
shee miht hạv ọn with whom shee miht lẏv no wurs, þen shee
miht hạv doon with mee, for þe which wordz shee thanked mee
57ᵛ and so wee parted. After which parting I kowld not forget þe
sirkumstans of þe aksidenses þat had happened in þe woing of
þis widow, for I revol[v]d þe sạm eftsons in my mynd from þe
beginning vnto þe end and konsidering þat þe prolonging of so
small A tẏm waz þe only kawz of her revolt I do think assewredly
þat shee knoing her kondisions to be such az iz befọr towched
of her own mowth konserning her melankoly mood, wherof I
had sum experiens and mistrusting þat I wold befọr þe marriaʒ
day enquẏr þem owt, and so gẏv her þe slip, shee thowht to
prevent mee, and þạrfọr wold gẏv mee þe slip first, as who wold
saẏ, I will raþer forsạk þen bee forsaken.[2]

Ðe rekounting of þis history bringeth heer to my remembrans
A prety ʒest of A ʒerzei preest, which dwelled in þe west
kuntrey, who ⌈with⌉ oþerz of hiz kompanions having vnderstanding whẹr in A marish grownd wẹr A great many of panterz,
snạrz, and grinns set to kach wẏldfowll, in þe nyht, þe which
þe preest and hiz kompanions went to tạk in þe dark of þe niht.
and when þei kạm to þe marish evry ọn of þem grọpt in þe dark
for hiz prai, and in seeking, þe preest chaunsed to fynd A bird

---

[1] Proverbial; Tilley S 936.
[2] No example of this expression is found in the proverb authorities.

tyed in on of þe snars, þe which being willing to bee at liberti, strov A littl with þe preest to be gon. and þe preest being A ʒoly talker began to reazon þe matter with þe bird, saing vnto him, yea sirra, wold ye be gon, and I do handell yow so frendly, by mi fay, yow shall far de[1] wurz for dat so yee shall, for mee will nyp [yow] by de hed so mee will (and with þat, hee did put þe birdz hed into hiz mowth and with hiz teeth did nip it so hard az he kild it þe which being doon hee did put it into hiz bag[)]. After þis, he took an oþer bird snared, þe which being sumwhat fell or angri did ʒob, and pek at þe preests fingerz, yea gottis body quoþ þe preest will yow bÿt A mee? by tamaz ye shall far de wurz for yowr byting, for mee shall nip yow az mee did yow[r] fellow befor for dat. þe which being said, hee nypt þe bird by þe hed az hee did þe oþer befor, and so did put him into hiz bag also. and þen hee gropt farder for mor burdz, in þe which seeking hiz chauns waz to pap vnto A great tod, but throuh þe darknes of þe niht and hiz senses hee perseived not what it waz, and þarfor hee groing into sum dowt what fowll it shiuld bee, said vnto it, when hee had felt it rownd abowt, ʒezus what maner of fowll be yow? yow are þe str⌈a⌉inʒest burd þat ever I handled, þen hee feeling abowt þe mowth of it said, mee feell þat yow be neþer Sneet, nor woodkok, nor any oþer long beeld burd, for yow hav no beell at all. also mee know dat yow ar no dukling nor quattlkin, for doh þeir beels bee brod, yet þei bee sumwhat longer þen yow⌈r⌉z, and not so brod. þen hee felt to feell his feþerz and wings, and az hee waz groping groping,[a] hee said to þe tod, of my fidelite yee ar þe ʒentlest fowll þat ever mee felt yet, for yow do neither strogull nor bÿt. but when he had felt A great whÿll, and fown[d] neiþer of boþ, hee wundring very much what it shiuld bee, gottis passion (quoþ hee) mee hav handeled many A fowll and birdz in my daiz, but mee never handled such A fowll az yow bee. yow neiþer hav A beell, and yow hav neiþer feþerz nor wings wat maner of fowll be yow?

---

[a] Dittography, probably.

---

[1] Note the dialect of the Jersey priest.

O, O, now mee remember mee, mee dink yow be A puffen, for yow be much of dat making. well, watsoever yow bee, mee shall nip yow ons þat mee shall, and with þat hee did put þe todz hed into hiz mowth and did bẏt it az he did þe oþer burdz by him taken befor.

58ʳ whẏll þe tod waz A byting hee strugled for lẏf, and did thrust owt hiz feet so violently az he kowld, at which tẏm on of his f⟨eet⟩ bi chauns sk[r]atched þe preest by þe chin, and þe oþer skratched him by þe hand, wherat þe preest being much offended, did let þe todz hed owt of hiz mowth and said to him in great anger, yea gottis nailz, kannot yow be kontented to skᵣrᵗa⟨tch⟩ mee be de hand, but will skrach mee bi de fạs also, bi got mee sall nip yow ons mor for dat, dat mee sall. (and þen hee did bẏt þe tod by þe hed again, and so did put him into hiz bag). Trow yee that mani A on who being blynded by blynd *Cupid* do not chiuz A tod among oþer fowls az þe preest did, þe which alþouh þei do not kreep on all fowr az þe tod doth, and sk[r]ach az þ⟨e⟩ tod did, yet by þeir poisoned kondisions will infest and poizon þeir hu⟨z⟩bands þat wai evri day mor þen þe preest waz poizoned by byting of þ⟨e⟩ todz hed, and being skrached of him?

þis story of þe preest and þe fowl and also þe tod, may well be applied[a] to dyverz sorts of woings, I will le⟨t⟩ pas heer to speak of þoz who at þe first vew, hạv A good lyking þe on of þ⟨e⟩ oþer, and so do kontinew vnto þe end. but I will towch sumwhat of þe first bird taken by þe preest, which did strẏv A littl with þe preest to be gon from him, so fareth it mani tẏms between þe woer and þe woed, for sum woman at þe first wilbe koy A whẏll, and yet afterward, and yet afterward[b] shee wilbe traktabull enoh. þen wheraz þe sekond bird did ʒob and bẏt þe preest befor hee had tamed her, so lẏkwyz þer be sum women in kondisions toward þer woerz, iwzing þem at þe first with riud spe⟨ec⟩h and disdainfull looks, and yet in þe end eevn az by byting and skrach⟨ing⟩ kats and dogs do kum togiþer,[1] so do þei.

---

[a] MS. reads 'appried'.   [b] Dittography.

[1] Proverbial; Tilley S 165.

þen lastly wheraz þe tǫd di⟨d⟩ not strẏv when þe preest took
him, so sum women be eazily entreate⟨d⟩ and at þe first be very
ȝentill, but afterward, if by chauns þeir love⟨rs⟩ do mǎk þem
never so littl A fawt or offens, bianby þei bee so waspish and
angry, az þe[i] ar redy to skrach az þe tǫd waz. of þe which sort
of women, it iz þus written in þe book of þe preacher.[1] cap. 7.
I hǎv fownd ⌐*þat*⌐ *A woman* (saith hee) *iz bitterer þen death, for
shee kast abrǫd her hart az A net, þat men do fish with, and her
handz ar az cheins.* thei þat will marry, must do az þei do who
do drink medsins, for hee þat drinketh A medsin doth it in hǫp
þat it shall do him good, and so it iz lẏk þat hee who doth marry
doth it to þat end, but if þe medisin be nawht and hǎv in it þat
which iz not good, (az þat which iz ǫn bodies meat iz an oþerz
poizon[2]) þen hee þat drinketh it iz in wurs kǎs þen hee waz
in befǫr hee drank it. and so shall he⟨e⟩ bee who marrieth with
A woman of ill natiur and kondisions, wherfor hee þat will
marry must wink and drink, and tǎk þe good or ill fortiun þat
God shall send him.[3]

Ny abowt þis tẏm I did read over þe book of ȝezus Sirach,[4]
and in þe, 9. 19. 22. 23. 25. 26. 41. and 42. chapterz I fownd
written very much in þe diskommendasion of women which
now browht mee az far from lyking of þem az I waz wount to bee
þe which, with þe overthwarts þat I hǎv had in woing of sar-
tain of þem heer to fǫr for marriaȝ hǎv brouht mee in þe sǎm
kǎs for loving þat þe widow iz in who hath had, ij, or iij, huzbandz. for yee shall vnderstand þat it iz said þat þe loov of
A womans first husband goth to her hart.[5] whęr it so warmeth
þe sǎm þat shee hǎth A kǎr not to chainȝ him. And if shee 58ᵛ
chauns to bury him and marry an oþer huzband, þen þe loov
þat shee beareth to her sekond husband fynding A wai alredy
mǎd to her hart, perseth throuh her hart, and þarwith enflameth
þe sǎm in such sort, þat shee hath þe lẏk kǎr to chainȝ az shee

---

[1] Eccles. 7. 26.   [2] This proverb goes back to a Latin source; Tilley
(M 483) gives no English example before 1587.
[3] This proverb is otherwise unrecorded; but compare Tilley W 501.
[4] Ecclus. 9. 1–11; 19. 2, 3; 22. 3–5; 23. 22–26; 25. 14–28; 26. 6–12; 41. 17,
20, 22; 42. 6, 9–14.   [5] Another unrecorded proverb.

had befor. but and if shee chauns to bury her sekond huzband and loov also, þen þen[a] afterward if shee chauns to hav never so mani loverz, þe los of þem will greev her but A littl, for when shee hath A hol thorow her hart, shee kan never loov so whotly and konstantly az shee did befor. neiþer will þe los of her lover greev her inwardly very much.

Now sir, eevn az þe stat standeth with þe widow þat hath had ij husbandz, so hath it bin with mee in woing of dyverz women, az partly yee may perseiv bi þat which I hav befor written in woing matters. þe which women hav for A short tým geven me such kawz to think þat þei hav loved mee, þat I hav thouht þat þe Soon wold hav lost hiz liht befor þei wold hav chainȝed, and þeir inkonstansy hath greeved ⌈mee⌉ sumwhat Also. but yet, I am not only A lýv, but also þen I did both eat my meat, and drink my drink, and sleep well inowh. By þat which I do gaþer and hav lerned toching mi natiuite, if þer be ani kredit to be geven to *Astroloȝi*, I do think now þat at þe howr of my birth,[1] þe sýn *Virgo*, waz in þe *Horoskop*, and *assendant*, þe lord of whoz hows iz *Mercuri*. wherfor hee waz þe lord of my birth. Ðen do I read in owr aunsient poet sir Geffrey Chawcer, þat *Mercuri* and *Venus* be kontrary in þeir wurking and dispozision, and þerfor þe on of þem, falleth in þe oþerz exaltasion. yet do I imaȝin þat alþoh *Venus* was *retrograd at þe howr* of *my* birth, shee waz favorably aspekted with benevolent planets or sýns towardz mee, which mad mee to reseiv sum kommodite by sum women, alþouh þeir great goodwils toward mee did soon vanish away by þe means of her *retrogradasion*. It may bee þat *Mars*, þe *armipotent god*, waz also *retrograd* or very ny þe sam at þe tým of my birth, which added to my hindrans also of benefits þat I shiuld or waz lýk to hav had by warriarz or

---

[a] Dittography.

[1] Whythorne gives insufficient information to permit the exact calculating of his own birthday in 1528, according to Professors Curt Zimansky and Johnstone Parr who have kindly pondered this problem. But this passage and Whythorne's remarks on p. 95 show that he knew his own horoscope and occasionally turned his hand to casting others. His Chaucer reference is to lines 697-702 of *The Wife of Bath's Prologue*.

Marsians. Wheþer þat þe Soon, þe Moon and Starz, hąv any operasion or no, it iz to be rẹd in þe Salms,[1] and in þe .1. epistell to þe Corinthians & the .15. chapter.[2] And yet I do say þat God hath geven such powr vnto þọz hiz kreatiurz not þat þei shiuld rewll and do absoliutly withowt hiz will & permission, þat which by hiz gift hee hath appointed þem to do, but so far akkording to þeir limits az hee will suffer þem. and to prọv þat to be trew ye may fynd in þe skriptiur[3] how þat God did mąk þe Soon to stand still when þe childern of Israell wer fihting A battell against þeir enemiez. but if þat God wilnot let nor hinder þem, þen þei do wurk akkording to þeir operasions in all earthly things.

Dyverz filosoferz dispiuting togiþer of þat which an hiumąn kreatiur reseived from þe infliuens of þe planets, grew to þis opinion, þat Man, of Saturn had vnderstanding, of *Jupiter* 59ʳ strength, of *Mars* þe mýnd. of þe Soon vertiu. of ⟨Ve⟩nus moving. of Mercuri, sharpnes of wit. and of þe Moon þe nątiur of ʒenerasion. Ðe fizisions do sai, þat man in hiz kreasion reseiveth of þe Soon þe spreit. of þe Moon þe body. of Mars þe blood. of Mercury þe wit. of *Jupiter* dezýr. of *Venus* pleaziur, and of Sąturn moistiur. þez opinions of þe Filosoferz and Fizisions did I tąk owt of þe book named *The garden of pleaziur*[4] *&c.* If yee dezýr to know mọr of þe government of þe planets and sýns, þen read þerof in þe Sheppardz kąlender.[5] in þe book entiteled. *Breef introducsions both natiurall and pleazant,* and also *delectabull vnto þe art of Chiromancy or Manuell diuinasion.*[6] *&c.* And also in þe book of *Arcandam*[7] þe astroloʒian.

---

[1] Psa. 136. 8, 9: 'The sunne to rule in the day. . . . The moone & the starres to gouerne in the night . .' (Bishops' Bible, 1568) is an example.

[2] 1 Cor. 15. 40–41.   [3] Joshua 10. 12, 13.

[4] Whythorne has quoted directly from Ludovico Guicciardini's *Houres of Recreation* [or] *the Garden of Pleasure,* translated by James Sanforde, 1573, sig. H7ᵛ (*STC* 12464).

[5] *The Kalendayr of the Shyppars* (*STC* 22407–15) passed through many editions between 1503 and the time Whythorne wrote this passage.

[6] F. Withers' translation of Joannes ab Indagine's *Briefe Introductions unto the Art of Chiromancy* was first published in 1558 (*STC* 14075).

[7] The passage about Ptolemy occurs on sig. B1 of *The Most Excellent Booke to fynd the Fatal Desteny of Euery Man,* published under the pseudonym Arcandam [1562?] (*STC* 724).

in þe which book I ⟨did⟩ read þat *ptolomeus* saith, þat A wẏz man mai rewll þe starz, þe w⟨hich⟩ iz to sai, þat hee may lett and prohibit þe veri fiutiur effekts, wh⟨ich⟩ do proseed of þe starz, and þe infliuenses of þem, so þat þe starz do no⟨t⟩ enfors and konstrain vs overmuch to ani thing, exsept it be such az ar prọn and ready to be drawn bi þem, and such az will follow natiur rạþer þen reazon after þe maner of briut beasts. after þe which sor⟨t⟩ be þei who will embrạs venus darlings mọr þen reazon wold hạv þe⟨m.⟩

and if I hạv bin ọn of þem, now I will turn over A new leaf,[1] & will so estrainʒ mi self from all loving okkazions az far az I do know yet þat I wilbe shortly lẏk vnto A good fellow which being sumwhat step⟨ped⟩ in yeerz and had past þe snạrz of Venus darlings and bạbs. who kạ⟨m⟩ by chauns in to A sekret plạs, wher [hee] fownd A yoong man & A yoong w⟨o⟩man embrạsing and kissing togiþer, wherwithall hee stood still A littl, a⟨nd⟩ þen hee mạd A kros on hiz fọrhed with thomb, and þen with hand he mạ⟨d⟩ az it wẹr A penthows over hiz eies az ọn doth whọz siht iz trobled by þe brihtnes of þe Soon liht if he look toward it. þe which being doon hee said ʒezus, doth þis world last yet? az who wold [hạv] said doth þis embrạsing and kissing kontinew still? bekawz all such kẏnd of aksions wẹr past with him, hee thouht þat þei had bin doon with evri body els. and yet I wilnot swẹr þat I will do so, for when ọn doth swẹr þat hee will or wilnot do A thing, þen will þe Devl be ever tempting of him to break hiz ọth. but az I am ⌈þus advyzed⌉ I wilnot alter nor chainʒ my mynd in þat kas. I hạv staid yow to long in þis loving, howbeit if yow do mark well all þe aksions and speeches þerin it may bee for yowr good if yee chauns to hạv þe lẏk happen to yow, and now seing þat it iz lẏk to bee þe last þat I do entend to trobull yow withall after þis tẏm bear with mee and I will konkliud for þis matter az þus.

not long after my widow and I parted az iz affọrsaid, shee being whot in þe sear,[2] and of þe spur kowld tarry no lenger

---

[1] Proverbial; Tilley L 146.
[2] A metaphor meaning 'easily made to go off' (*OED* 1. b).

withowt A mąk, and þerfǫr in hast shee stumbled under an
hosteler, who now doth lubber leap her, for hee with rubbing
hors heels, and greazing þem in þe rowfs of þeir mowþs, gat so
much money az þerwith hee so bleard þe widowz eiz, þat shee
thinking all had bin gold þat shýned,[1] took him to bee her[a]
wedded spowz. so þat þe Dor[2] having flown all þe day abowt **59ᵛ**
emong herbz and flowerz, hath now shrowded her vnder A hors-
turd. and to say þe trewth hee iz sweet enowh for such A sweet
pees az shee iz, and þus I end of þis fǫrsaid matter.

After þis I went into þe kuntrei and waz with [A] ȝentilman to
teach hiz childern, (with whom I had bin A yeer or twoo befǫr
þis tým) who at my first kumming both hee and hiz wýf gąv
mee many fair promizes of good and grątfull konsideration for
my pains taking with þeir ⟨c⟩hildern, but þǫz promizes węr not
only slenderly performed, but ⟨al⟩so þei wold sumtýms offer to
abriȝ mee of þat which I had alredy in iws, and þen lo, I wold
sumtýms bestow A littl kolęr on þem, and þei seing þis, and
perseived þat I wold karri no kǫls,[3] wold talk of it behynd my
bak az who wold say þat I waz not well advýzed in þat I wold
not bear with such wurshipfull folks az þei bee, & þen wold
þei kunningly eiþer glauns at mee þem selvs, when I waz in þeir
kumpaniez, or els do it by attorney, þat iz to say by an oþer. but
konsidering þat þei both had bin my skollerz az well az þeir
childern, and þat I had never any thing of him for his own
teaching I wold shoot þeir bolts bak vnto þem again. and in þe
end I went from þem. imediately whervpon I wrǫt þus folloing—

Now þat þe trewth iz trýd[4]
of things þat bee ląt past
I see when all iz spýd
þat wordz ar but A blast[5]

---

[a] MS. reads 'hed'.

---

[1] See p. 28.
[2] A dung-beetle; this passage is based on Tilley B 221.
[3] Proverbial; Tilley C 464.
[4] An allusion to the proverbial phrase, 'Time tries the truth'; Tilley T 338.
[5] A variant to the proverb 'Words are but wind'; Tilley W 833.

And promẏz great
iz but A heat
If not performd at last

I kan bear it nomọr
it iz to great A pain
I hạv no strength in stọr
to toil for so small gain
I will forbear
mi wits to wear
And wạst nomọr in vain

To weak mi brains now bee
such wraingling waiht to weld
A bak not brọd yee see
big burdens karri seld
þen whi shiuld I
þus foolishli
Az thral be stil so held.

60ʳ

But to provyd in tẏm
þẹz trobuls to delay
and do no farder klẏm
but go an oþer waẏ
proving if I
kan elswhẹr spi
And fẏnd A better stay.

Heer nọt þat þe wurd weld. affọrsaid, alþouh it mai bee vnder-stoo⟨d to mean⟩ sustain, lift, or bear, in ọn plạs of þis fọrsaid song, so it mai be taken ⟨az þe⟩ nạm of þe parish whẹr my fọrsaid skollerz did dwell.[1] and whẹraz I ⟨do⟩ sa⟨y⟩ þat I will klẏm no farder, it iz bekawz þat when I waz to rẏd vnt⟨o⟩ þeir hows, I

---

[1] Because there are several places named Weld, Weild, or Weald, location of this parish and, by that means, identification of Whythorne's unpleasant employers, is not easy. He offers the single detail that it was situated on a hill. Weld in the hundred of Fawley, Hants, is one possibility, as is Weld, Herts., and North and South Weald, Essex. Perhaps the best case can be made for Weald Hall, South Weald, Essex, occupied after 1567 by Wistan Browne (d. 1580). Weald Hall, about 17 miles north-east of London, is very near Childerditch,

shiuld rẏd up A hy hill er I kạm at it, and þerfọr I d⟨id⟩ sai þat I will no farder klẏm þat hill.

when I had þus eazed my mẏn⟨d⟩ for þat matter, and kontinewing in London, what with þe variete of þe aksidents þat I had seen and felt befọr þis tẏm, and þat which I did now kontinewally see ọn way or oþer, and what with þe variete of matte⟨r⟩ þat I had red, with þat which by experiens I had learned. Az first þat which I had red in þe .3. cap. *Genesis*.[1] God said to owr first parent *Adam, in þe swęt of þi fạs shalt þow eat þi bred, till þow be turned again into þe ground, for owt of it wast þow taken. in asmuch az þ⟨ow⟩ art dust shalt þow be turned again.* þęs wordz węr not only spọk⟨en⟩ to Adam, but þei węr ment to all hiz posterite. þen I saw þat þe world ⟨iz⟩ so korrupt, þat whosoever knoweth not how to dissembull[2] kannot lẏv i⟨n⟩ quiet in þe world, nor who kannott flatter and glọz, seemeth to be eiþ⟨er⟩ e[n]viowz, or els iz taken to bee prow[d]. þe malisiowz do not reʒois somu⟨ch⟩ of þeir proper goodz, az [þei] do of þe hurts and hindranses of oþerz. of þe which sort of peopull *Aristippus* saith, *Si come la rugine consuma il ferro, cosi l'inuidia gli inuidi*.[3] which iz to say. eevn az þe rust doth konsium þe iron, so envi doth þe enviows. I see sum men so kovetows az þoh þei shiuld lẏv ever, and oþerz so prodigall az þei shiuld [die] presently. I do know sum þat do honour þe wikked rich men, and dispẏz þe learned and þe adorned[a] with vertewz. And to bee breef, towching þe kommen affairz of þe world. all vertew iz turned topsi turvy. whervpon kummeth þe dyverz kala[mi]tiez wherwith God doth vyzet both þe good [&] þe bad. Job. saith[4] in *cap* .14. Man þat iz born of A woman iz but of A few daiz. & þei be extinkt az

---

[a] MS. reads 'aþorned'.

where Whythorne's friend Adrian Schaell then served as vicar (see p. 218). Moreover, if this house, where Whythorne 'had bin A yeer or twoo befọr þis tẏm', is the same as the one in which he wrote the Testimonial for Sybil Slius, it would fulfil the requirement concerning the route to Hatfield Peverell (see p. 168).   [1] Gen. 3. 19.   [2] Proverbial; Tilley D 386.
[3] The source of this saying, evidently some Italian compendium, has not been found. Prof. F. P. Wilson points out that it is given by G. Torriano in *Piazza Universale di Proverbi Italiani* (1666), p. 121.
[4] Job 14. 1.

A flowr. þei flẏ az A shadow, and do not remain. þe preacher saith[1] in cap .1. vanite of vanite, althings ar vain. What profit hath man of all hiz labourz, in þe which hee doth trobull him self vnder þe Soon? I hạv saith hee, beheld all things þat bee doon vnder þe Soon, and behọld þei ar all but vanite, and affliksion of þe mynd.

so many waiz man iz wrapt in kalamitis, az ọn who throuh þe weaknes of hiz mowld is ready and prọn to be overthrown with þe blast of evry temptasion, az ọn þoh hiz abyding on þe earth be never so long, yet hee iz þe pray of Tẏm, and by him swalloed vp, and devowred. az ọn who iz subʒekt to evry chauns of fortewn on whom þei do trivmf daily, making him to play kontinewally 50ᵛ þeir dyverz komikall and traʒikall parts. az ọn who iz þe very imaʒ of inkonstansy, ever doing and vndoing, and never satis- fied nor quiet, and lastly az ọn who iz þe veri reseptakell of all worldli trobuls ⌜&⌝ perturbasions, whọz ofspring and childern, after þat þeir parents having plaid ⌜þeir⌝ parts and doth pai ⌜þeir⌝ detz to natiur, and get ⌜þem⌝ vnder ⌜þe⌝ skaffold, do okkiupi þeir faþerz plạs A small tẏm, and þen do follow þe sạm way þat þeir vaþerz[2] went befọr þem. vpon all þe which konsiderasions it seemeth ⟨þa⟩t owr old old[a] proverb waz first devyzed which saith. Ðis world ⟨iz⟩ but A skaffold for vs to plai owr kommediz and traʒediz vpon.[3] On ⟨þ⟩e which proverb with

---

[a] Dittography.

[1] Eccles. 1. 2, 3, 14.

[2] Note Whythorne's lapse into Somerset dialect.

[3] Because this comparison was a favourite of Shakespeare's, the search for early examples has been keen ever since the time of George Steevens. That none of Shakespeare's editors noticed Whythorne's madrigal for three voices on the subject, printed on f. 17 of his 1571 *Songes*, demonstrates how few copies survived. Equally significant is Whythorne's statement that when he wrote the poem early in the 1560's (about the time of Shakespeare's birth) the saying was regarded as 'owr old proverb'. Shakespeare's editors have found no English examples earlier than 1570. Tilley (W 882) adds the *Paraphrase of Erasmus upon the New Testament*, 1549 (*STC* 2854), in Matthew v, f. 39: 'Ye have a parte to playe in the stage of the whole worlde.' Steevens had ob- served the comparison in one of Petronius's fragments but, as Francis Douce later pointed out, Petronius was not available in translation until 1599. Pos- sibly it was the source of the slightly modified version which was reportedly chosen as the motto of the Globe Playhouse, 'Totus mundus agit histrionem'. Whythorne may have been familiar with the following passage in Erasmus's

Woodcut portrait of Whythorne

Made for his 1571 *Songes*, the same block was used again in his 1590
Duos with the bottom portion of the upper left quarter of his arms
slightly altered

þe rest þat goth befor it, when I had konsidered A littl, I devized
þis sonet folloing—

> *Ponder þe proof so far az þow*
> *in wo⌐r⌐ldly wurks be tried shall*
> *how vain þei ar in deed and show*
> *how dainȝerus to deal withall*
> *and nothing els þow shalt þen fýnd*
> *þe wurld þus wurking in hiz kýnd*
> *but wýd skaffold for vs ech on*
> *to plai owr traȝedies vpon.*

Now waz ⌐I⌐ kum very ny to þe end of þe wurk þat I purpozed
to put in print, and þerfor I konsidered with mi self what waz
needfull for me to do mor befor I did it. and þen kạm to mi
mýnd, þat seing þe books with þe miuzik in þem shiuld bee, az
my childern, bekawz þei konteined þat which my hed brouht
foorth (az it iz said þat þe greatest substans ⌐alþouh not þe
cheefest,⌐ wherof childern be prokreat kummeth from þe ⌐hed
&⌐ brains) Also bekawz þei shiuld bear my nạm, I kowld do no
les þen sett in evry ọn of þem, þeir faþerz piktiur or kounterfet,
to reprezent vnto þọz who shiuld ywz þe childern, þe form and
favor of þeir parent, þe which I offerd az it wẹr of good will to all
such who be þe loverz of Miuzik. and bekawz þat þe ywzerz of
þọs books shiuld see þat az in þe beginning of þem I do ad vnto
my nạm þe týtl of A ȝentilman, so I mean to shew my self to be
ọn azwell in þe owtward marks, az in þe inward man, of þe which
inward man þe miuzik with ⌐þe⌐ dittiez and songs & sonets þerwith ȝoined shall shew to þe suffisient ȝiuȝ in þat respekt. þerfor
I will set with my kownterfet such armes, az I hạv fownd to be
left vnto mee by my poor Aunseterz with þe which alþouh þei
hạv left mee no great revenewz to support and maintain þem[a]
withall, yet þarby þei hạv left mee A remembrans þat I am az

---

[a] MS. reads 'þen'.

Praise of Folie, translated by Sir Thomas Chaloner in 1549 (*STC* 10500),
sig. E3ᵛ: 'So lykewyse all this life of mortall men, what is it els, but a certaine
kynde of stage plaie: whereas men come forth . . . till at last the maker of the
play, or bokebearer causeth them to auoyde the skaffolde. . . .'

free A man born both by faþer and moþers sẏd, az hee þat mai
dispend thowzandz of powndz, of yeerly inheritans. þen bekawz
þe maner iz to set with arms sum word or sentens which lẏketh
þe ownerz of þe arms, I devyzed with my self what wurd or
sentens I miht best ywz.

whervpon þer kąm in my mẏnd to devẏz A sentens or word
vpon þe etimoloʒi of my nąm, and also vpon þe krest belonging
to my kot of arms. My nąm az I hąv spesialtiz to shew for witnes
61ʳ of þe sąm iz þus written. Whythorne. ʒoining þe .t. and þe .h.
togiþ⟨er⟩ az þus .th. and mẏn awnsetòrz węr kommenly kalled
þus. whyt horne, not ʒoining þe .t. and þe .h. togiþer. so þat þe
substans of my nam, i⟨z⟩ eiþer. thorn. or. horn, of þe which (eiþer
thorn, or horn) ⌜who so⌝ iz prikt or ⟨go⟩red, shall fẏnd þat þei
be raþer to sharp þen oþerwẏz or kontrary, also þe krest or
baʒ belonging to my kot of arms be fẏv lawnses, which weapons
at þe points be also sharp. what I am of mẏnd my self or in
kondision I will mąk yow my ʒiuʒ, and þoh I am sharp, yet not
to sharp. yee k⟨n⟩ow þat & if on do tread A worm on þe taill it
will turn again,[1] and yee ⌜kno⟨w⟩⌝ also þat evry thing þat moveth
iz subʒekt to a[n]ger eevn in it self.[2] þer iz A sertain disagreing
in natiur emong herbs and treez, az iz between þe Elm and þe
Ash. and also emong dead things, az þe li⟨ut⟩ strings þat be mąd
of sheeps guts, and of woulf guts, will never be⟨e⟩ browht to
stand in riht tewn togiþer.[3] I bring not þez ensampuls t⟨o⟩
kommend malisiowsnes, or anger to be in Mankẏnd, but I do
say þus much bekawz I wold shew yow how þat þer iz sertain
affeksions in þe hiuman natiur, az þer iz A sertain natiurall
disagreing in many worldly things, which hąv no moving of
þem selvz. wherfor bekawz I am not so pasient az pasient
Greezeld[4] waz I know þat I shalbee moved to anger sumtẏms,

---

[1] Once again Whythorne echoes Heywood (Tilley W 909).

[2] This proverb appears to be unrecorded.

[3] Neither the antipathy between elm and ash, nor that between sheep's and
wolves' guts is otherwise recorded in collections of proverbs.

[4] A play of this name, 'Compiled by Iohn Phillip', was printed *c.* 1569, and
may well have been performed earlier in the decade (Greg No. 52). But
Whythorne undoubtedly knew the story as told by Chaucer's Clerke.

and yet return to my former estąt again. þe proverb which saith
þat þe littl pot wilbe soon hott,[1] doth not exkiuz þe great hy
pot. and if þe littl pot be so az þe proverb sait⟨h⟩ þen it must
needz follow þat it wilbe soon kǫld again exsept þe he⟨at⟩ be kept
vnto it still. now sir, alþouh þe proverb iz kommenly applied
t⟨o⟩ littl folks, þe tall big folks az affǫrsaid be not exkiuzed
þerby, for ye⟨e⟩ shall fŷnd of þem þat wilbee assoon whot az
littl folks, and alþouh many of þem do not shew þeir anger so
soon az short folks, þat iz bu⟨t⟩ bekawz þer iz A longer distans
& passą3 between þe tall folks harts and þeir toongs, þen þer
iz of short folks, which maketh þat þe thowhts of þe short, doth
burst owt of þeir mowþs soner þen of þe tawll.

I hąv staid yow sumwhat long on kolerik, angri, and sharp
aksidents, which waz mǫr of purpǫz þen of oversiht bekawz þat
mi *bilis* & kolęr provoked mee to say sumwhat for short folks, in
azmuch az I am nǫn of þe tawlest. þez fǫrsaid sharp things (I sai)
mąd mee to mąk and set þis fǫrsaid sentens in Italien þat foloith
with my said kǫt of arms. þe which iz þus. *Aspra mà non troppo*.
which iz to say in english. Sharp but not to much. þis word
sharp. az I hąv set it and devyzed vpon it, and þe hǫl sentens,
may be taken eiþer for an *A3ektŷv*, or els for þe *imparatŷv mood*
of þe *verb* to sharp. wherfǫr I devyzed vpon þe devŷs þerof þis
þat folloeth—

Đe point of launs, þe end[a] *of horn, or prik of thorn to tuch
and mŷnd of him whǫz word þis iz, ar sharp, but not tomuch
bee þow þi self az hee iz sharp, mąk oþerz sharp also
but not tow sharp and þen þow dost Aspra mà non troppo.*[2]

---

[a] Written above 'sound'.

[1] Another Heywood proverb (Tilley P 497).

[2] These verses, and Barnam's poetical response to them, are written on the
inside cover of the manuscript under the woodcut of Whythorne, which because of an alteration in the arms, appears to be the 1590 *Duos* (see facsimile,
p. 211). It is significant to note that when writing them he dropped his 'new
orthografye' and reverted to ordinary spelling.

These versions read as follows:

Vpon the devyse afforesaide of. *Aspra mà non troppo*.

[*Note continued on next page.*

61ᵛ   At þis tȳm I waz in A ȝentilmans hows, who had to teach
hiz childern þe latten toong, A yoong man[1] which iz A very
proper skoller, and þerwithall kan mąk verses both in Lattin and
in English very well vnto whom I shewd my fǫrsaid english
verses which I had devȳzed vpon þe Italien sentens, whervpon
hee devyzed on þe sąm az þus—

Đe dint of spear, and prik of thorn, ar sharp vndowtedly,
but if þe points be over sharp þei break (yow know) quikly
eevn so for to be sharp iz good, az wȳz men hąv vs tawht
but over sharp iz not þe best, for over much iz nawht[2]

when my said frend had shewd mee þǫz hiz verses, I told him
þat I lyked þem well, and better I wold hąv doon if hee had
towched sumwhat of þe properti of A horn, az hee did of þe
lawns, and thorn. whervpon, hee devyzed þez verses þus foloing—

What ech thing iz in evri kȳnd, þe nąm doth well diskry
bi natiurz help þe first fȳnder, þe nąm did wel apply
whȳ thorn do prik, and horn do sound to almen it iz known
þe ǫn by natiur tąk hiz fors þe oþer being blown
þe thorn do moov with sum sharpnes, þe horn kal on ȝently
heer iz A ȝentil prikking thorn, þis whȳt horn sownd trimly

Note 2 continued from previous page.]

                        end
⟨T⟩h⟨e⟩ point of lawns, the sownd of horne, or prick of thorn to tuch,
              aboove named
And mynd of him whose wurd this is, ar sharp but not tow much.
Be thow, thy self, as hee is sharp, make others sharp also,
but not tow sharp, and then thow doost, *Aspra mà non troppo.*
              Thomas Whythorne
    Other wyse of the same by *Thomas Barnam.*

The dint of spear, and prick of Thorn, ar sharp vndowtedly,
but if the points be over sharp, they break (yow know) quickly,
Eevn so for to be sharp is good, as wyse men have vs tawght,
b⟨ut ov⟩er sharp is not the best, for over much is nawght.

    [1] This friend and fellow tutor, Thomas Barnam, wrote verses which were
prefixed to Whythorne's 1571 *Songes.* He was probably the Thomas Barnham
who matriculated at Clare College, Cambridge, in Lent 1563/4; he may have
been the son-in-law of William Feake, who left £200 'To my son in law
Thomas Barneham and Mary his wife' on his death, 7 May 1595 (H. F. Waters,
Genealogical Gleanings, Boston, 1901, p. 789).   [2] Cf. Tilley M. 1294.

þat which do moov þe flesh to God, iz lẏk A prikking thorn
þat which do moov to pleazant ȝoi rezembleth wel þe horn
so thorn and horn mai well agree, and help ech az with hand
and wheraz horn will not tạk plạs, let .t. befọr him stand
sumtẏm thorn mai in chamber bee, and horn in church mai sound
þei will (if þat yee ywz þem wel) to Godz glori redownd
þe horn in chamber may yow moov, þe thorn in church mai tuch
þen ywz þem bọth (my ȝentil freend) of ọn thing not to much.

wheras he saith befọr þat horn and thorn may bee ywzed both
in þe chiurch and also in þe chamber, hee saith þat bekawz hee
did know þat I had þen mạd miuzik to be sung in þe chiurch,
and also sertain meeterz and miuzik vnto þem to be sung for
pryvat rekreasion in howzes. when hee had þus mạd þis fọrsaid
sonet in kommendasion of my nam, I to gratifi him with þe lẏk
devyzed on hiz nạm (being kalled Barnam) þis þat folloith—

Not all for nowht þe fạþerz ọld gạv nạm to evri thing
bi privi tuch of sekrets hid, in folks from beginning
of which sum pạrt (alþouh not all) in Barnam I do spy
inkliuded in hiz nạm also, þe which lẏ privily
first of þe Bar, or[a] *Bear too sai, þerin I konseav*
þat whẹr þe Bar iz fixed fast, þe theef must ask it leav
þe Bear also hiz fors iz great, to keep him self from hurt
for whẏl hiz fọz seak hiz mizeaz hee laiz þem in þe durt
A Bar lẏkwẏz þe wẏz do set kondisions il to let   **62ʳ**
which mani tẏms þe wikked sọrt þeron þeir wyts do whet
þis Bar hiz piupulz pranks doth bar, and keeps þem in such aw
az þerbi þei mai pleaz God best and not to break hiz law.

At þis tẏm I did shew þe songs and sonets ȝoined with my
miuzik vnto dẏverz of my frendz, and also did let þem hear much
of my[n] sung. whervpon, sertain of þem who wẹr lea⌈r⌉ned,
did wrẏt verses in laten, in þe ko⟨m⟩mendasion of þe whọl wurk,
þe which verses þei did send to, and þen ⟨I⟩ did go to London
whẹr I plied my tẏm all þat I kowld to set foorth m⟨y⟩ miusik

---

[a] Written above 'and'.

in prýnt, þe which being browht to þe printerz very ny, d⟨id⟩ mąk mee very glad, and þervpon I wrǫt þis sonet folloing—

As restles hed doth alwaiz gýv
þe lýk sowr saws to mýnd and spreets
so do þei all at ons revýv
and irksum dulnes from þem fleets
when az þe hed to pas hath browht
þat which hee wold so fain hǫv wrowht

To þis fǫrsaid sonet I mąd A song of fýv parts and did set it at þe last end of all my songs. now konser[n]ing þe latten verses þe ⌈which⌉ my frendz had mąd in þe kommendation of þe whǫll wurk of my miuz⟨ik⟩ and sent þem to mee to print with my miuzik. alþowh þei bee nǫ⟨n⟩ of mýn own making, yet in azmuch az þei węr mąd and written only fo⟨r⟩ my sąk, and doth not konsern any mans wurks but mýn, I will s⟨et⟩ þem with mýn heer foloingly, and þeir nąms to þem who mąd þem—

In Musicen. Tho. whithorni[1]
Hexasticon ad Lectorem.
Candi⌈de⌉ sume tibi, lector, praeludia musae,
hocque lubens spectes, quod modo surgit opus
Authoris mentem metire. & consule recte,
Vt merita meritum laude fruatur opus
Nec multum curat, probat, improbat aemula turba
ipse bonis mauult, quam placuisse malis

Eiusdem carmen phaleucium
Siue Endecasyllabum.
Qui claro teneram nitore musam
Fecit, iam cupit is videre lucem
Rarum prodit opus whithornus ille
Et cuntis reserat suas camænas
plenas pegasei liquore fontis
Hic dat lautitias, iocos, lepores.

---

[1] These commendatory verses were printed in the Triplex part book of Whythorne's 1571 *Songes*.

Hic dat delitias, sonosque dulces
His iunxit numeros venustiores
Hauritque eloquium, phasinque nostram
Materno penitus sapore cultam:
Perpende has pretio, has ames, emasque,
Hæ curas minuunt, levant dolores
Tollunt tædia, si qua sunt molesta,
Aspires igitur pio Whithorno,
Præclaro ingenio faue, valeque.
   Tho. Couert.

  In Thomæ whithorni[1]
  Musicen Carmen
Terpsicore tacuit metuens maledicta Megæræ
  Nec valet, vt vellet, verba referre sua.
Iam verò vocem tollit (monitore Whithorno)
  Ac est in faciles auᵃ venire manus
Musarum varias formas perducit ad Anglos,
  Angelica vt possint voce sonare modos
Instruit, est facilis: delectat: grata peritis:
  Adiuuat, hac caminus dulciter ore deum.
Ergo concordi qui vult modulamina voce
  Concordes socios comparet, hæcque canat.

   Sapphicum in
   eandem.
Facta clarorum veteris solebant
Ad lyram nuda celebrasse voce
Hic sono possis homines, Deosque,
   tollere pleno.
Laus poetarum merito virescit
Qui suas tractant lepidè poeseis
Viuat idcirco celeber Whithornus
   tempus in omne.

ᵃ The printed version reads 'ausa'.

---

[1] Printed in the 1571 Medius part book.

Iunxit hic musis peramœna metra
In quibus motus videas iuuentœ
63[r]   *Atque maturœ grauiora vitœ,*
           inde senectœ.
Tho. Barnam.

In libros Thomœ Whithorni[1]
Octostichon.

Ludicra quœ iuuenum, quam sint prœuisa virorum
   Nec sat firma senum, consilia, acta, vices:
Versibus appositis, in idemque cadentibus apte
   Anglorum rythmis, ecce Whithornus habet
Vtque magis moueat: dulci modulamine vocum
   Musicus insignis, temperat omne metrum
Ergo cui numeri sunt cordi, & musica concors,
   Si lubet, vnanimes œre parato libros
        Adrianus Schœll.[2]

When I ⌐had⌐ printed mi miuzik, I *printed* þerwith in on of
þe books, serta⟨in⟩ latten verses, þe which hen⌐ri Thorn,⌐ had
mad long befor ⌐only⌐ in þe kommendasion of ⟨my⟩ miuzik, but
bekawz þei do not speak any thing of þis mi wur⟨k⟩ I do leav
þem owt in þis book. yet after þe printing of mi miuzik I
going into þe kuntrey wher þe sayd[a] henrye Thorn did dwell,
an⟨d⟩ showing him how I ⌐had⌐ put in print in my wurk of

---

[a] MS. reads 'siayd'.

---

[1] Printed in the 1571 Bassus part book.

[2] Adrian Schaell (1530–99) came from Germany to England about 1557,
and served as 'scholemaster' in the house of Lord John Grey (d. 1569). In
1561 Schaell was appointed Vicar of Childerditch in Essex, near Lord John's
seat at Pirgo. Probably Schaell addressed his verses to Whythorne about
1569–70, when Whythorne may have been living near by at Weald Hall,
South Weald, Essex (see p. 208).
  In July 1570, seven months after the death of Lord John, Schaell became
Rector of Higham, Somerset, a manor belonging to the Grey family. There
Schaell remained for nearly thirty years, leaving behind him a 'Memoir of
High Ham Church', written in 1598, from which these biographical details
have been gathered (*Proceedings of the Somersetshire Archaeological and
Natural History Society*, xl, 113–22). See also Rev. John Collinson, *Somerset*,
iii (1791), 446.

miuzik hiz verses þ⟨e⟩ which he had written in þe kommendasion of miuzik,[1] hee foorthwi⟨th⟩ devyzed þ̧ez verses in latten
folloing—

> *In Tho. whithorni*
> *musicen ad lectorem*
> Turpis in ignauo peritura est munera vita
>   Et celebri nomen funere fata prement
> Si nil præclari facias, nil nomine dignum
>   Si species tantum te probet esse virum
> Hinc homines summos meruerunt vocis honores
>   Quorum longæuo est laus celebranda die:
> Ingenuam, facili qui sic coluere Minerua
>   Artem aliquam, vt tandem floreat illa mâgis.
> Ex quorum numero Thomam memorare Whythornum
>   Qui pariter musas finxit, & apta metra.
> Ter binisque dedit mundo spectanda libellis
>   Et satis authorem comprobat illud opus
> Ergo legat placida quisquis sit mente benignus
>   Intereà taceat liuida turba. Vale.
>   .Hen. Thorne

63ᵛ

---

[1] Thorne's commendatory Latin verses were printed in the 1571 Contratenor part book. They read as follows:

    ❡ Musices Præconium.

Tædia depellit varij modulatio cantus,
  ingenium reficit, membraque fessa leuat.
Tristi mordaces expellit pectore curas,
  atque iuuat miris musica chorda modis.
    Aliud.
Post morbos, curas, cursus, aliosue labores
  dulcisonum recreat pectora lassa melos.
    Aliud.
Musica demissa est diuorum munus Olympo,
  quo mens lætari fracta labore queat.
    Aliud.
Musica grata Joui est, simul & mortalibus ægris,
  quemque iuuat dulcis nobile vocis opus.
    Aliud.
Musica captiuum solatur compede vinctum,
  hac minus indignum sentiet actor opus.
Quisquis cantandi contempserit inscius artem,
  ignarus, stupidus, bardus, asellus eat.

Ꝺe said henry Thorn wheraz hee saith befor. *Ter binisque dedit mondo*, it iz bekawz I told him þat I wold print in A book by þem selvz, all þe sonets þat I hav sett to my forsaid miuzik, so þat, þat book will mak six books þat I do sett foorth in þis wholl wurk.

At my return again to London, I went to my printer to know of him how my miuzik went awai owt of handz, and hee told mee þat it waz not bowht of him so fast az hee loked for. þen I told him þat I thouht þat it was ij kawzes þat hee sold þem not az yet very fast, þe first waz bekawz hee had printed miuzik heer tofor, þe which waz very fals printed, and þarfor it waz A diskredit to þat which shiuld follow in print heerafter, vntill such tým az mýn wer kommenly known þe trew printing wherof shiuld shadow þe falsnes of þe oþer. Ꝺe sekond kawz why my miuzik waz sold no faster, waz bekawz it is not az yet much known þat þer iz such A miuzik to be bowht, and þerfor I had devýzed A mean to mak it known and to furþer þe knowleȝ þerof az þus. I told him þat I had written into A book all þe songs and sonets which I had mad to be sung with my miuzik, and in þe sam book I had set þe rest of þe stavz and verses þat I mad to be sung with sum of þoz songs, þe which ar not set in þe books wher my miuzik iz, bekawz þei wold hav okkiupýd to great A room. Also I told him þat I had written into þat book not on[ly] my prefas to þe miuzik, but also all þe verses ⌈in latten⌉ which wer written by oþers konserning my miuzik, and if hee thowht good az I did to put þis book in print, I thouht þat it wold be an okkazion to manifest, and mak known þe sam þe mor and þe furder of. for alþouh þat þe book hath in it no great exsellensy of matter and maner, yet hedz þat do delýt to know evry mans devýs in wryting, will for noveltiez sak hav on of þe books when þe[i] bee printed, so þat when az it iz kommenly known abrod, (and þe raþer by þe means of þez said books) þat þer iz such A miuzik to bee bowht, þei who do dezier to hav veriete of miuzik will þe soner prokiur to hav it. Ꝺe which devýs of mýn my printer lýked well, and bekawz hee had þen somuch wurk to do of hiz own alredy, hee prokiured an oþer printer[1] to

---

[1] Of this projected volume nothing further is known.

do & print þe said book. and against þat þei shiuld go in hand I
devyzed A prefąs to be sett in þe beginning þerof az folloith—

> Sum rithms shall heer appeer, which strainȝ mai seem to skan
> wherin iz towcht sundri[a] affekts, þat hapneth vnto man,
> þat hapneth vnto man, and sundri waiz doth sound
> hath kawzd þez meeterz to bee mąd, in stąt az þei be found
> In stąt az þei bee fownd, so oþerz lýk ⟨b⟩egan
> To whǫz sonets I miuzik mąd to pleaz þem now and þan
> To pleaz þem now and þan, þat lýk my simpul trąd
> I meeterz of mýn own devýzd, in pląs of þǫz erst mąd
> In plas of þǫz erst mąd, axsept þǫz[b] mąd bi mee
> And all þe rest tąk in good part, þis do I krąv of þee
> Đis do I krąv of þee, also þat þow konsent
> To read þis book advyzedly, er þat þow gýv ȝiuȝmend.

64[r]

Now, yee shall vnderstand, þat alþouh I did sai in my prefąs[1]
befǫ⟨r⟩ my miuzik, þat I wold stay at þat tým what I kowld wrýt
in þe praiz of miuzik, yet bekaws it shiuld not be thouht þat
I staid to wryt it þan for þat I kowld not do it, I do now mean
to mąk yow A witnes what I kan say for miuzik in kommendasion þerof. First I will nǫt vnto yow such plases of þe skriptiur,
by þe which I do gaþer þat miuzik waz ywzed in heavn befǫr þe
world began. Đen will I shew yow ho⟨w⟩ þat it ⌐and instruments
belonging to it,⌐ waz invented on earth sins þe world began. þen
will I sh⟨ew⟩ yow how it waz ywzed of holy men and holy
women in such sort az þe sk⟨rip⟩tiur doth bear witnes of. And
þen will I rekownt vnto yow somuch ⟨az⟩ I hąv red in profąn
awtors, and az I hąv learned ⌐oþerwyz⌐ þat from tým to tym to
þis prezent tým how it waz and iz esteemed emong sum who
węr and ⌐be⌐ az well learned and az wýz or raþer wýzer þen
many of þ⟨ǫz⟩ who will kondempn it.

In þe xixth chapter of *Exodus*.[2] iz written þat when þe lord

---

[a] MS. reads 'sumdri'.   [b] 'ę' written above 'ǫ'.

[1] Line 94: 'What I cowld write in Musicks prays I will at this time stay.'
Note that Whythorne here quotes the 1571 printed version, and not the line
as given in the autobiography, p. 181 *supra*.
[2] Whythorne paraphrases Exod. 19. 16 and 19.

kam down to þe mount *Sinai*, and gav þe lawz to Moyzes, þer waz A trumpet sownded. In þe third chapter of St. *liuks* gospell[1] ye shall fýnd þat with þe Anȝell which appeerd to þe sheppardz (, in A feeld by Bethlem, named *Ader*,[a] whẹr Jacob kept hiz sheep) þe which Anȝell told þe sheppardz of þe birth of Chrýst, þer waz A great kumpany of heavnly ministerz which lawded God and did sing *Glori bee to God on hy &c.* Also yee shall fýnd in þe first, þe .8. þe .14. þe 15. þe 21. chapterz of þe *Apocalips*,[2] þat St *John* þe Evanȝelist hard both singing and also þe sownd of Miuzikall instruments in Heavn and þat yee may þe better beleev mee þerin, look in þe .22. chapter of þat book and ye shall fýnd þat hee saith. *I am Jhon which saw þez things, and hard þem.* Now konsydering þat it iz not to be dowted þat þer iz heavnly miuzik, or miuzik in heavn, it iz not oþerwýz to be thouht but þat it waz þạr ywzed befọr þe world began. or els yow must graunt þat it waz learned þạr sins þe world began, which iz ⌐not⌐ lýk to be trew. ⟨It⟩ ⌐iz⌐ mọr lýk þat God gav þe
64ᵛ sạm gift vnto hiz Angels and ministerz befọr þe world began. and az hee iz þe Awtor and wurker by means of all goodnes so hee geving þe sạm mạks it good, þowh sum do misywz it, and sum beasts do kondempn it for eevl and nawht.

Đus hạv I shewd yow mýn opinion for þe first invension of miuzik, and now will I shew yow of sum of þem who wẹr þe first þát invented it after þe world began. In þe fowrth chapter of *Genesis*,[3] yee shall fýnd how þat *Tubal*, *Lamechs* soon by *Ada* hiz wýf, invented þe harp and Organs, wherby it shiuld seem þat miuzik or at þe least singing waz ywzed heer er þe tým of þe invension of miuzikall instruments wẹr ywzed, oþerwyz how

---

[a] A superfluous opening parenthesis has been omitted.

[1] The passage is not in the third chapter of Luke, but 2. 8–14.

[2] Whythorne's references are to Rev. 1. 10; 8. 7, 8, 10, 12; 14. 2, 3; 15. 3; 21 is a mistake, probably for 18. 22; 22. 8.

[3] Genesis 4. 19–22. The confusion of Tubal for Jubal occurs in several sixteenth-century texts, and has been explained as being derived from the 1540 *Byble in Englishe*, sig. a2 verso. (See F. P. Wilson's note in his 'Supplement to McKerrow's Edition of Nashe', 1958, p. 22.) But the error has an ancestry more ancient, for it is found in Chaucer's *Book of the Duchess*, line 1162, and in some manuscripts of the *Origines* of Isidorus Hispalensis. Perhaps some early scribe (or more than one) mistook the first letter of the name when copying it.

kowld *Tubal* know þe distinksion of þe soundz and nots which
do mak þe agreement þat iz in miuzik (or Godz prezent gift
geevn to him az þe first mean wherby to mak it known in þe
world.)ª alþouh þat Cooper in hiz kronikell[1] saith þat *Tuball* invented þe siens of miuzik by þe stroks and noyz of þe hammerz
of hiz broþer *Tubalcan*, who waz A smith, for hee delyting in
þe sowndz of þe hammerz, by þe waiht of þem, hee perseived
þe proporsions and tewns þat þe hammerz gav, and þerby hee
devyzed þe prinsipuls of miuzik. Đen for þe kontinewans þerof
I did read in þe book intiteled *Đe treatis of moral philosophi*,
konteining þe saings of þe wÿz[2] *&c.* of *Mercurius*, and hiz pillerz
of ston, who is thouht to bee befor *.Noes.* flood. and if it wer
hee who iz said to invent miuzik, þen waz it prezervid, az
Astronomi waz prezerved, bekawz it waz graven in þe ston
pillerz of *Mercurius*. of þe which *Jamblicus*, and dyverz oþerz
do wrýt much, az þat book saith. and if þat miuzik wer klean
extinkt by þat flood, þen it may bee þat it waz invented by such
oþerz after wardz az wryting rekounts and rekordz vnto vs. In
þe dream of sir Geffrey Chawser[3] it iz said þat *Pithagoras* waz
þe first fýnder þerof. *Bullen* in hiz bulwark,[4] saith þat *Mercurius*,
florished abowt .164. yeerz befor Chrystes birth, hee waz kalled
A God, for hiz wunderfull wizdom, and invension of miuzik
and oþer arts. it iz said þat ⌐he⌐ did invent þe harp of þe bon or
shell & synewz of A *Tortes*. wheþer þis last *Mercurius*, and þe
oþer afforsaid wer both on, þat I will leav to yowr 3u3ment, for
in þe fortowched treatis it iz written þat þe first named *Mercurius*
waz of such fam and kredit emong þe *Egipcians*, þat þei did put
foorth all þeir wurks vnder hiz nam, & þe poets for hiz singiular
learning do mak him A God, and kall him þe messin3er of

ª MS. here has an opening parenthesis.

[1] Whythorne quotes with slight verbal changes from *Coopers Chronicle*
(1565), sig. A2 (*STC* 15220).

[2] For an earlier reference to William Baldwin's *Treatise of Moral Philo-
sophy*, see p. 165. Baldwin's account of Mercurius Trismegistus Hermes
occurs on sigg. B1–B3ᵛ (1550 edition, *STC* 1254).

[3] Chaucer, *Book of the Duchess*, lines 1167–70, probably derived his information from the *Origines* of Isidorus Hispalensis.

[4] William Bullein, *Bulwarke of Defēce* (1562), sig. diiᵛ (*STC* 4033).

Jupiter, whom þe ⌐poets⌐ do kall þe God of heavn & governour
of all. Ðe profet king David waz for hiz exsellent skill in miuzik
(and invension of þe Regals)[1] kalled þe exsellent singingman of
Israell, az rekordeth þe books of þe kings[2] in Diverz plases.

In þe book named þe *Pilgrima3 of Prinses*,[3] and in þe [a] ij parts
þerof, which iz of þe first inventors of arts & of miuzik, and
mirth, yee may read sumwhat of þe inventorz of miuzik, and of
þem þat ywzed it. In þe book named *Thesaurus Linguæ Romane
& Britanicæ*,[4] iz written how þat *Apollo* waz akkounted þe
poetikall god of miuzik (and also I hạv red þat hee invented þe
Shawlm.) þe poets fain þat *Amphion* did first invent þe pleazant
sownd of miuzik, and þe harp also, wherby he brouht þe stọns
65ʳ togiþer wherwith þe siti of *Thebe* waz builded. sum do apply
þis raþer to þe sweetnes of hiz eloquent Speches, wherwith hee
k⟨a⟩wz⟨ed⟩ þe peepull to býld it, þen to hiz sweet miuzik. In an
Italien book nạmed *F⟨a⟩brico del Mondo*,[5] iz written þat *Linus*
invented miuzik. *Apollo*, *Calliope*, *Alpheo*, and *Orpheus*, þe harp,
or violl, *Mercuri* þe pýp. And Marsia þ⟨e⟩ liut. Sum do say þat[b]
Dionisius invented miuzik. *Eusebius* saith þat *Zephus* did
invent it. *Solinus* saith, þat men of *Crete* did invent it by ⟨þe⟩
ring and sownd of bras. *Polibius* saith þat it waz first invented
by þe *Achadians*. *Pan.* þe poetikall God of þe Sheppardz, iz
said to bee þe first fýnder or inventer of þe Bagpýp. In þe
Thesawrus linguæ, afforsa⟨id⟩ do I read, þat *Cibele*, þe dawhter

---

[a] A space has been left here.   [b] MS. reads 'þe'.

[1] The regal is a primitive type of organ.

[2] Whythorne included the Books of Samuel among the Books of the Kings,
as in the Vulgate.

[3] In Lodowick Lloyd's *The Pilgrimage of Princes*, 1573 (*STC* 16624), two
chapters are entitled 'Of the first inuentours of artes, and of the vse of Sooth-
saying', and 'Of Musicke and mirth'.

[4] Some of this information is found under the entry for 'Apollo'; the information upon Amphion is drawn from *Fabrica del Mondo*, f. 13ᵛ, the compendium to which Whythorne refers specifically a few lines later.

[5] This refers to Francesco Alunno's *La Fabrica del Mondo* (Venice, 1526),
which was frequently reprinted. Whythorne quotes from the entry under the
sub-heading 'Musica' (ff. 13–14 of the 1548 Venice edition). His source for the
statements about Dionysius, Zephus, Solinus, &c., appears to have been Lloyd's
Pilgrimage of Princes (cited in note 3). Whythorne's many quotations from
Cooper's *Thesaurus Linguae* are usually found under the alphabetical entry.

of king *Minos*, and wẏf to *Saturn* fown[d] þe pẏp and *Tabor*, and also þe *Cimbals* emong þe Greeks. In þe sąm book do I read, þat þęr iz A great siti ni to þe mountain *Libanus*, kalle⟨d⟩ *Enos*, wherin dwelled 3iants, þat invented instriuments of miuzik. In þat book I do also read, þat in þe tẏm of *Darius*, waz A man nam⟨ed⟩ *Lasus*, who did wrẏt of miuzik. In þe sąm book, do I read also þat þe *M⟨u⟩ses*, węr ladiez and governorz of *Poetri*, miuzik and eloquens. In þe sai⟨d⟩ book do I read, þat *Ptolomeus* lẏved in þe tẏm of *Anthoni* þe Emprowr, who restored owt of darknes þe *Mathematicall* sienses (Ðe *Greeks* do kall þoz sienses mathematikall, which ar demonstrabull, or wherin on may mąk A plain demonstrasion bi number, az may bee of *Geometri*, *Arithmetik*, *Miuzik*, and *Astronomi*) In þe said book do I read also, þat *Pithagora⟨s⟩* fownd þe subtill konkliuzions and misteriez of *Arithmetik*, *Miuzik*, and *Geometri*. In þe fǫrsaid book do I read þat an ǫld Miuzisian nąmed *Terpandrus*, added vij strings to þe harp. Ðus hąv I shewd yow of þe first inventerz of Miuzik, and þe instriuments þerto belonging.

And now ⟨I⟩ will shew yow of þǫz who bǫth ywzed it and allowd it [in] þe Chiurch (az well as owt of it) to praiz þe Lord withall. In þe xvth chapter of *Exodus*,[1] y⟨ee⟩ shall fẏnd þe thanks and song which *Moizes*, and þe childern of *Israell*, did sing after þei had eskąped þe tiranny of *Pharo*, and hiz *Egipcians*. In þe first book of *Samuell*,[2] & þe xviijth chapter, iz written þat when king *Saul*, and þe prophet *Dauid* kąm from þe distruksion of þe *Philistians* þer kąm women owt of þe sittiez of *Israell* with instriuments of miuz⟨ik⟩ vnto þe which þei did sing praizes to God for þeir viktoriez. In þe ⟨.5.⟩ chapter of þe book of *Judges*,[3] shall yee fẏnd þe song and rendring of thank⟨s⟩ þe which *Debora*, and *Barac*, gąv vnto þe Lord for þeir viktory aga⟨inst⟩ *Sisera*. In þe first book of þe *Cronikels*,[4] and in þe .16. and .25. chapt⟨erz⟩ yee shall fẏnd þat þe singerz, and miuzisians of þe

---

[1] Exod. 15. 1–19.
[2] 1 Sam. 18. 6, 7. [3] Judges 5. 1–31.
[4] 1 Chron. 16. 5, 6; 25. 1, 6. Whythorne has varied somewhat the list of musical instruments.

Tempul, ywzed besýd þeir singing, instriuments of miuzik, az Organs, Vials, or Krowdz, Simbals, Salteriez, and Trumpets. In þe .16. chapter of *Judith*,[1] iz þe song and thanks geving of *Judith*, and her peepull for þe viktory, & distruksion of *Holophernes* & þe *Assirians*. *Heer* mýht bee rehersed þe yws of miuzik[a] mạd by þe profet king David befọr þe ark of God (and how þat hiz wýf skorning him þerfọr, waz mạd barrain) Also heer I miht rehers þe song of *Anna* (þe moþer of *Samuel*) Also of *Zachari*. 65ᵛ ⟨A⟩lso of St Mary, þe moþer of ȝezus krýst. And also of *Simeon*, And þe lýk of many oþerz þe which be spoken of in þe Bybull, but I will omit þem. In þe .44. chapter of þe book of *Jezus Sirach*,[2] Whẹr þe praiz of sertain holy men iz rehersed, az of *Henoch, Noe, Abraham, Izạc*, and *Jacob*, iz þez wordz foloing, *Let vs kommend þe nobul famowz men, and þe ȝenerasion of owr fọr elderz & faþerz. þei sowht owt þe sweetnes and melodi of Miuzik, and brouht foorth þe pleazant songs in Skriptiur.*

Saint pawll seemeth to allow of miuzik whẹr hee saith in þe third chapter to þe *Collossians*.[3] *Let þe word of God dwell plenteowzly emong yow in al wizdom, teaching and exhorting ọn an oþer in salms, himns, & spiritual songs, and Sing vnto þe lord in yowr harts.* Also hee saith in (*Timoth* .5.)[4] *praiz God in salms, and himms and spirituall songs, singing and making melodi to þe Lord.* St *Jạms*[5] (*cap* .5.) willeth þe mirth of *kristians* to be vttered by singing, and saith þus. *If ani man be meri let him sing salms.*

Now to pas from þe Sk[r]iptiurz towching þis matter. I will rehers sum of þe doktorz and oþerz of þe chiurch who ywzed miuzik, and who wrọt of it. I did read in *Thesaurus linguæ &c* of ọn named *Asaph*, who was A singing man in þe hows of God, to whom king David assigned sertain *týtls* of hiz Salms. I did

---

[a] MS. reads 'miuziz'.

---

[1] Judith 16. 1–21.   [2] Ecclus. 44. 1, 5.   [3] Col. 3. 16.
[4] Whythorne slipped here; he meant to refer to Eph. 5. 19.
[5] James 5. 13.

read in þe forsaid book þat *St Augustin* being konverted to þe kristian faith by St *Ambroz*, þat þei both being replenished with þe holy Gost did sing togyþer þe salm *Te Deum*,[1] awnswering mutiually þe on þe oþer. After which tym of þe konversion of St *Augustin*, hee wrýting of þe riht yws of miuzik, to be ywzed with þe salms of king David, hee saith þat þe verses of þe salms ar framed by meaziurz þat childern, or yoong peopull singing þem az songs[a] ⌈þat⌉ þey miht tåk deliht þerin. Also hee saith þat *Canticum*, and *Salmus* hav þis diffrens. *Canticum* iz when it iz sung only with þe mowth. and *Salmus* iz þat which iz also plaid or sownded with þe Saltery, Harp, or oþer instriument. And again speaking of Chiurch singing, hee saith þat wee shiuld not sing lýk birdz. for krowz, popinʒaiz, and piez, ar tawht to sound þat which þei vnderstand not. Hee saith also, þat God hath not graunted to birdz, but to men only to sing in knowleʒ. wherfor wee þat hav learned to sing Godz servis in þe Chiurch must mark well what wee do sing, and blessed iz hee þat vnderstand-eth þe song. I did read in an Italien Býbull, in þe argiument þat iz sett befor þe Salms of king David þis þat folloith.[2] Ðe seventy (or threeskor and ten) interpreterz hav kalled þis book, *Salterio*, of þe nam of A miuzikall instriument, vnto þe which wer sung þez salms. þe Hebriuz hav kalled it *Theilim*, A book of lawdz & songs devýn. þe Greeks hav kalled it. *Salmi*. þe which wurd doth

---

[a] This word crossed out, but 'stet' written above it.

[1] Whythorne is here quoting from the entry under 'Augustinus' in *Thesaurus Linguae*. The legend that Saints Ambrose and Augustine impro-vised the *Te Deum* by reciting alternate strophes at the baptism of the latter is found first in the *Chronicon* of Bishop Datius (now ascribed to Landulphus Senior).

Whythorne writes as if the conversion were at the same time as the impro-visation of the *Te Deum*, an indication that he lacked first-hand knowledge of the *Confessions*, which makes no mention of the *Te Deum* and, in any case, clearly distinguishes between the occasion of the conversion and that of the baptism (Book VIII, chap. 12; Book IX, chap. 6). Nor is all the information that Whythorne gives to be found in *Thesaurus Linguae*; it corresponds only vaguely to various passages in the *Confessions*, so presumably was taken from some intermediate source.

[2] This passage occurs in Antonio Brucioli's *La Biblia* (1562), where it is headed 'SALMI DI DAVID. / ARGOMENTO' (sig. 212ᵛ; f. 228ᵛ). Whythorne has translated loosely, with some omissions and a few interpolations.

66ʳ singnifi þe sownd of A harp, or of ani oþer instriument miuzika⟨ll
for⟩ ⟨a⟩z þ⟨e⟩ holy songs wẹr sung vpon or with sum miuzikall
instriumen⟨ts⟩ in þe kongregasion of þe peepull to lift vp þeir
harts, and to mạk þe⟨m⟩ attentif to þe wordz of þe sạm. (Ðen
after þat þer iz set foorth þe dyverz yowses þat þe salms wẹr
written for, it foloeth þus)

And it iz ⟨to⟩ bee noted, bekawz yee fẏnd dẏverz inskripsions
in þẹz salms, az s⟨um⟩tẏms *Salmo*, only. sumtẏms *Cantico*,
only. Also sumtẏmz *Salmo* of *Cantico*. and sumtẏmz *Cantico*
of *Salmo*, it iz to bee nọted, þat *Salmo* properli iz, when þe
instriument iz sounded only withowt þe hiumạ⟨n⟩ vois. And
Cantico kontrariwẏz iz þe vois withowt þe instri⟨ument⟩ (of þe
which opinion waz St *Augustin*, az iz A littl befọr rehersed⟨⟩).
þen *Salmo* of *Cantico*, iz when þe hiumạn vois beginneth, and
þe instriument doth follow. And *Cantico* of *Salmo*, iz when
þe instriume⟨nt⟩ beginneth, and þe vois doth follow. It iz to be
vnderstood or nọted ⟨al⟩so, þat when yee see in þe insk⌈r⌉ipsion
of sum of þe salms, *Al maestro de⟨l⟩ Canto &c.* which iz to sai,
to þe mạster of þe song, or harmoni, ye ow⟨ht⟩ to vnderstand
þat such songs partikiularly[a] be ordeined to be sung in þe holy
kongregasion of all þe kumpani of singerz and miuzisians, which
hạv aboov þem þe master singer (or chaunter of þe quier) to
govern þe miuzik. Ðe Hebriw wordz. *Alamoth*, *Neginoth*,
Giboth, and oþerz which bee in þe insk⌈r⌉ipsions of sum salms,
do singnifi A sort or kẏnd of miuzik ⟨&⟩ sertain meaziurz,
akkording to þe opinion of oþerz, sertain instriumen⟨ts⟩ and
after oþerz opinions, þe beginnings of verses, akkording to þe
meaziur⟨z⟩ of ⌈þe⌉ which ⌈þei⌉ be sung, az iz said in þeir plạs.
Bi þe which affọrsaid yee may gaþer þat emong þe kongregasions
of þe faithfull, in king Davidz ty⟨m⟩ and sins þat tẏm, þer waz
instriuments of miuzik ywzed, and ⌈also⌉ miuzik sung with
dyverz voises togiþer, azwell az with ọn tewn only.

I read in *Fabrico del mondo*,[1] affọrsaid, þat *Anastasio*, A

---

[a] MS reads 'parpikiularly'.

---

[1] Whythorne derives this information from the entry under 'Musica'.
See p. 224 and note 5.

byshop of Rǫm, did forbid þ⟨e⟩ yws of miuzik in þe chiurch, but þen I do read þạr also, þat *Ambrosio*, kommaunded, þat it shiuld be ywzed to provǫk owr mẏndz to devǫsion and r⟨e⟩liȝion, and *Agostino*, dispiuted *pro & contra*. Master John *Calvin* in A prẹfạs or epistell which iz set next befǫr sertain salms in Italien[1] mee⟨ter⟩ alloweth much of miuzik to be ywzed emong þe kongregasions of þe faithf⟨ull.⟩ hee saith þat þẹr iz ij maner of publik praierz. sum be mạd with þe wurd ⟨on⟩ly or simply, and þe oþer iz with singing, and þat iz not A thing fownd owt ⟨of⟩ lạt tỹm, for it waz ywzed sins þe first oriȝinall of þe chiurch. and (saith h⟨ee⟩) St pawll, also saith þat wee shiuld mạk praierz not only with þe mowth & word only, but with þe vois and song also. Heer to konkliud for miuzik in þe chiurch. Look in þe last of þe Queens maȝestiez Inȝiunksions,[2] and þạr shall yee fẏnd þat shee with þe konsent of all her klarȝy, do allow both of singing and also of sownding on miuzikall instriuments to be ywzed in þe Chiurch, (þe which shee hath daily ywzed in her own chappell[)].

when I waz in Itali, and in þe siti of *Venetia*, which waz in þe daiz of queen Marẏ, þe first, I was kredibli enformed þạr, þat þe stạt and m⟨a⟩ȝestrạts of þat siti, gạv vnto A notabull Miuzisian þạr, whǫz nạm waz ⟨*Adrian W*⟩*eillert*,[3] aboov iij hun- **66ᵛ** dreth krouns A year (evry krown being in valew of owr money

---

[1] This passage occurs in a volume entitled *Sessanta Salmi di David. Tradotti in rime volgari Italiane, etc.*, 1564, on f. 3ᵛ under the heading 'GIO[vanni] CAL[vino] a tutti cristiani e amatori de la Parola di Dio.' Paul Chaix, Bibliothécaire de l'Université de Genève, to whom I am indebted for this information, points out that in later editions of 1573 and 1585 Calvin's name is omitted.

[2] The Injunctions of 1559 (*STC* 10095), actually written by Archbishop Parker, contained specific provisions to encourage 'the lawdable scyence of musicke' by maintaining livings for musicians and choirs. It also permitted the use of hymns and anthems despite the desires of fanatic Protestants who wished to confine Church music to psalms. For a description of the Queen's own service, see Sir John Hawkins, *General History of Music* (1776), chap. cxiv.

[3] The Flemish composer Adrian Willaert (1480–1562) became *maestro di cappella* at St. Mark's in 1527, where he wrote a prolific series of masses, madrigals, and other music. Contemporary records show that at the period when Whythorne was in Venice (1555), Willaert's income was 140 ducats, approximately a quarter of the amount Whythorne reports it to have been. In 1556 it was increased to 200 ducats. See E. vander Straeten, *La Musiquє aux Pays-Bas* (Brussels, 1882), vi. 201, 203.

A nobull) þe which fee hee had for to kompǫz and to mạk þe
miuzik þat waz sung in þeir Chiurch. Ðạr waz not an organist
⌈in all Italẏ,⌉ of any akkownt for hiz skill in hiz profession, whẹr
iz daily servis in þeir chiurches, but hee had an hundreth Crowns
A yeer for hiz fee or wạჳes. Now to ⌈leav to⌉ speak of þe miuzik
ywzed ⌈openli and⌉ privatly to serv God withall and also to
sai sumwhat of þat which hath bin yvzed for privat rekreasion
⌈onli,⌉ yee shall fẏnd in þe sekond book of *kronikels*,[1] þat emong
oþer presiowz gifts, which þe queen of *Saba*, gạv vnto king
Salomon, þer wẹr instruments of Miuzik. In þe sekond
chapter of þe preacher, oþerwẏz nạmed *Ecclesiastes*,[2] yee
shall fẏnd þat emong þe pleaziurz, and kommoditiez þat king
Salomon provẏded for hiz hows, hee had men and women
þat kowld sing. To leav þe skriptiurz, and to kum to profạn
Awtorz who do wrẏt of þis matter. Yee shall vnderstand þat
plutarchus wrẏteth, how þe *Grecians*[3] did somuch delẏt in þis
siens, þat at þeir feasts and bankets, þei wold hạv sum ǫn or
oþer skilful in þis siens to sownd owt ჳẹsts, and akts of nobull
men on þe harp, or sum oþer sweet instri⌈u⌉ment miuzikall.
Erasmus in hiz ⌈.2.⌉ book, *Apothe*.[4] saith þat miuzik waz had in
great prẏs even of aunsient tẏm, az it apeareth bi þe *Lacedi-
monians*, who had no les kạr & respekt to miuzik both on instriuments and singing, þen þei had of þeir daily sustenans and oþer
þeir nesessariez, akkounting az well of þe ǫn az of þe oþer. for
az meat and drink with apparell iz nesessary to þe sustenans and
preservasion of þe body, so sweet miuzik iz þe revẏver and
norisher of þe spreits, bringing A fors with it lẏk vnto A heavnly
inspirasion. in somuch þat *Licurgus*, being þeir Law giver,

---

[1] 2 Chron. 9. 11. Actually, Solomon had lyres and harps made from algum
wood presented by the Queen of Sheba.

[2] Eccles. 2. 8.

[3] The basic source of this passage and also of the reference below to Licurgus is in Plutarch's *Moralia*, the 'Ancient Customs of the Spartans', 14–17;
Whythorne probably acquired his knowledge from some intermediate compendium.

[4] Whythorne gives a free translation of Erasmus's *Apophthegmata* (1550),
Book 2, p. 182. It is interesting to note that he used the Latin edition instead
of Nicholas Udall's translation, where this passage is omitted.

thouht it meet and konvenient to ʒoin with praktẏz of war, þe
study and pleazantnes of miuzik, wherby þe great ferventnes
of fiht, being temperạted bi þe sownd of instriuments, shiuld þe
mọr sooner put owt from þem, þe drẹd of death, and konfirm þe
mọr boldnes in þem. Đe sạm *Erasmus* in *hiz Adages*[1] saith, þat
it waz akkustomed in þe old tẏm, þat at þe end of evrẏ feast,
A harp waz karried abowt þe tabull, and if any man waz ingnorant
in miuzik so þat hee kowld not sing hiz song, hee had A Bay bow
browht and set befọr him to sing vnto. In *Tusculanarum ques-
tionum. liber*[2] .1. iz written þat þe Grecians did deem hy and
passing great knowleʒ or eriudision to bee in singing and plaing
on miuzikall instriuments. wherfọr *Epaminondas*, A prins of
Grees, waz in all kẏnds of miuzik perfektly instrukted. *Themis-
tocles*, A Diuk of *Athens*, for refiuzing to pley at þe tabull when
hee had banqueted, waz akkownted þe mọr ingnorant or les
learned. Such delẏt had *Sokrates* in miuzik (az saith *Xenophon.
lib .4. de dictis Socrates*) þat when hee waz kum to þe ạʒ of .lx.
yeerz, and upwardz hee gạv him self to study & learn how to
play on miuzikall instriuments, hee being notwithstanding ọn
of þe mọst wẏz and devẏn Filosoferz þat ever waz. In *Thesawrus
linguæ*[3] affọrsaid, I do read of *Adrianus*, A nobull and exsellent[4] **68ʳ**
wẏz Emprowr, who emong þe exsellent gifts which hee h⟨ad⟩
hee had knowleʒ in miuzik.[a]

---

[a] A deletion reads, 'In þis sam book do I read of *Hippias* who'. Whythorne
apparently made a false start; he preferred to introduce Hippias later, on
p. 235.

---

[1] In Erasmus's *Adagia* (Lugduni, 1550), p. 258, headed 'Canere ad Myr-
tum', derived from Plutarch.

[2] Cicero's *Quaestiones Tusculanae*. An edition by J. Dolman was published
in 1561 (*STC* 5317), but comparison of texts, especially the passage in a
later quotation (p. 235), indicates that Whythorne was himself translating
from the Latin. Since the earliest Latin edition published in England came
out in 1577, Whythorne may have used it promptly after publication, or he
could have used an earlier continental edition. The passage here quoted
occurs on p. 3 of the 1577 translation.

[3] From *Thesaurus Linguae*, subject 'Adrianus'.

[4] The foliation goes from 66 verso to 68 recto because the 'musical scrap'
(for which see Appendix III) was bound into the autobiography here when
the MS. was repaired.

I hąv red in Hawls Kronikl,[1] of king henrẏ þe ayht, ląt king of þis lan⟨d⟩ þat hee waz not only A great favorer of miuzik, but also waz so well s⟨killed⟩ þerin þat hee kompǫzed and mąd diverz songs very well. I hąv red in ⟨þe⟩ golden book of þe Emprowr *Marcus Aurelius*,[2] þat hee in hiz letter to *po⟨lion⟩* konfessed to learn miuzik him self, and also had it tawht to oþerz in h⟨iz⟩ hows, to þe entent to repres sertain vẏses þen raining in þe sąm. Also ⟨in⟩ þe sąm book[3] iz shewed how þat þe sam emprowrz soon and heir to hiz empier, learned miuzik. (how þe ⌐said⌐ emprowr *Marcus*, loved miuzik, lo⟨ok⟩ in þe .14. chapter of hiz book) heer peradventiur, sum ingnorant pers⟨on⟩ who knoeth not þe diffrens of degreez in ǫn funksion and vertew, wo⟨ld⟩ say þat in þe ᵃ chapter of þe sąm book, iz to be red how þat þe emp⟨rowr⟩ banished minstrels owt of Room. and how hangeth þis togiþer, þat ⟨hee⟩ banished þe proffessors of þat which hee learned him self? to þe which I do aunswer þat þis question of þeirz shall mąk for miuzisians, fo⟨r⟩ if it had not now kum ⌐so⌐ in question, az I had not bin drẏven to awnswer þe matter, þe diffrens of degreez, and nąms of professions of þǫz þat do after sum sorts profes miuzik, had az yet paradventiur bin vnknown vnto yow. Ever sins þat miuzik kąm to ani per-feksion and wa⟨z⟩ akkownted ǫn of þe seven liberall sienses, and also þat it waz yowz⟨ed⟩ of many, þęr hąv bin degreez þerof, az þęr bee of Devẏns, lawyerz, and fizisions. for az of devẏns, þęr be Doktorz, and bachelarz. so of lawyerz (I mean Sivell lawyerz) þerbee Doktorz and bachelarz. and also þerbe both Dok[t]orz and bachelarz of miuzik.

ᵃ Space never filled in.

---

[1] Edward Halle, *The Vnion of the Two Noble and Illustre Famelies of Lan-castre & Yorke*, 1550 (*STC* 12723). The Life of Henry VIII (f. 8) describes the king '. . . exercisyng hym selfe daily in shotyng, singing, daunsyng, wrastelyng, casting of the barre, plaiyng at the recorders, flute, virginals, and in settyng of songes, makyng of ballettes, & [he] did set .ii. goodly masses, euery of them fyue partes, whiche were song oftentimes in hys chapel, and afterwardes in diuerse other places.'

[2] Antonio de Guevera, *The Golden Boke of Marcus Aurelius*, 1535 and many other editions. In the 1566 edition (*STC* 12445a), the passage occurs on sig. C5ᵛ.   [3] Ibid., sig. G2ʳᵛ (chap. 14).

Now sir besẏd þe Dokterz and bachelarz, þer bee þat depend
and lẏv by devinite (of þe which sum be Dok[t]orz and also
bachelarz) ⌐az¬ þe Bishops, and so dissending, þer be Deans of
Chiu⌐r¬ches, Arch deakons, kanons, prebendariez, parsons,
vikkarz, kiurats, and such oþerz þe nạms of whọz plases ⌐and
offises¬ I do not remember. Now konser[n]ing lawyerz, þer be
also þat depend ⌐on þe sivell¬ law (of þe which sum be Dokterz
& Bachelar⟨z⟩) ⌐az¬ 3ud3es of þe sivell law, advokạts, prokterz,
and such oþerz, þ⟨e⟩ nạms of whọz plạses and offises I know
not all. Ðen of Miuzisions, þ⟨ẹr⟩ be also þat depend þerof (of þe
which sum hạv bin ⌐and be¬ doktorz and ⌐bachelarz¬ ⟨⟩) and sum
miuzisians vnkomenced ⌐also,¬ of þe which sort þer hạv byn and
be⟨e⟩ sum þat hạv setfoorth az great maestriez in miuzik az
ever did any doktor or bachelar of miuzik. þen iz þer Organ[i]sts,
in chiurches. þen be þer teacherz of miuzik, and also to sing
priksong. and to sownd on miuzikall instriuments, which be
named skoolmasters. þen þer be singerz in chiurches, of þe
which þẹr bee of childern or boyz, aswell az of men. þen owt of
þe chiurch þer bee þat do ⌐teach &¬ serv privatly, az sum in
nobulmens howzes & men of wurships howzes, and sum in
þeir own howzes.

lastly þẹr bee þ⟨ọz⟩ do ywz to go with þeir instriuments abowt
þe kuntreiz to sytiez, tow⟨nz⟩ and villa3es, whẹr also þei do go
to ⌐pryvat howzes to¬ such az will heạr þem eiþer publikly o⟨r⟩ **68ᵛ**
pryvatly, or els to markats, fairz, marria3es, assembliez, taverns,
Ạlhowzes, and such lẏk plases. and þạr to þọz þat will hear þem
þei will sell þe sowndz of þeir voises and instriuments. also to
banketterz, revellerz, mummerz, maskerz, daunserz, tumblerz,
plaierz and such lẏk, þei sell also þe sowndz of þeir voises and
instriuments. Ðẹz in awnsient tẏm wẹr named Minstrels. and
az þe fọrsaid *Marcus Aurelius*[1] did banish þis sort of peopull
for þeir misywzed lẏf, so hạv þei bin of lạt[2] in þis owr realm

---

[1] Ibid., sigg. G2ᵛ–G3ᵛ. The banishment followed trouble at the celebration of the feast of Berecynthia, Mother of the Gods, held on 4 May according
to Whythorne's sources.

[2] Tudor laws against vagabonds were very strict, calling for the pillory,
branding with a 'V', whipping until bloody, and loss of ears. Minstrels were

restrained sumwhat from þeir vakabond lýf, which sum of þem ywzed. Ðọz maȝestrạts and ȝiustizes be not well advýzed (⌐with reverens⌐ I do speak it) who do gýv lisenses vnto minstrels vnder þe nạm of miuzisians to go abowt þe kuntrey with þeir miuzik in such sort az iz befọr rehersed, and if þei do remember þem selvz, þe statiut nameth þem minstrels, and so owht þei to do in þeir lisenses geven to þem.

Having now az I do họp, satisfied yow in þe knowleȝ of þe dýverz degreez and sorts of þọz who do profes and lýv by miuzik, I will now tell yow mọr what I hạv red in *Thesaurus linguæ*[1] affọr said, of þem þat loved and ywzed miuzik, and first of *Nero* þe krewell emprowr of Room, who kawzed fier to be sett on þe siti of Room, and whýll it waz A burning hee plaid on hiz harp, and did sing þe distruksion of *Troy*. I do raþer wunder at hiz dývers and stranȝ appetýts and kondisions þen allow of hiz krewell deed, for it iz not þe property, or natiur and kondision of ọn þat loveth miuzik in deed to bee krewell. now again I do read in *Thesaurus &c. Olimpicum certamen* (saith hee) waz A gạm or prýz þat waz kept on þe hill *Olimpus*, and ọn of þe pryzes waz for miuzik. It speaketh also of ọn of þe nýn Miuzes, nạmed *Caliope*, which exselled all þe rest, in sweetnes of vois. It saith also þat þer waz A woman nạmed *Pandora* vnto whom þe poetýkall godz gạv sundry gifts, and emong þọz gifts *Apollo* gạv her miuzik. In þe sạm book iz also written þat *Pierides*, þe dawhterz of *Pierus*, kompared in singing with þe Miuzes, but being vanquished, and geving to þe miuzes reprochfull wordz, þei wẹr by þem turned into *Pies*. Also in þe said book iz written þat *Stesicorus*, A famowz poet, first fownd owt singing of songs in daunses. Again, þe said book saith þat *Thamyras*, waz hee who first plaid on A harp, withowt singing þerto. And þe sam book saith þat þer waz A kunning miuzisian named *Timotheus*,

specifically included among the classes so punishable in the statute of 1572 (14 Elizabeth, chap. 5) to which Whythorne probably refers. For discussion of the problem see Walter L. Woodfill, *Musicians in English Society from Elizabeth to Charles I* (Princeton, 1953), especially Part II.

[1] The following references may be found in *Thesaurus Linguae*, listed under each name.

who ywzed to tak of hiz skollerz which had learned with oþerz befor, dobull salary, þat hee took of which had never learned befor, saing, þat hee took with þem dobull laborz, þat iz to say, to mak þem to forget, þat which þei had learned korruptly befor, & þen to teach þem perfektly. Again þe forsaid book saith þat *Hippias*, who waz A *Rhetorisian*, he plaid exsellently on evry instriument, and did sing hiz own verses in all kÿndz which noman kowld amend. lastly, he speaketh of A miuzisian of *Chalcis*, named *Xenophilus*, which lyved .107. yeerz in great felicite and quietnes. I do read in þe forsaid book named *Fabrico del mondo*,[1] of *Chirone*, þe *Centaur*, who þe poets do fain to be 69ʳ half A man and half A hors. he waz ⟨skilled i⟩n m⟨iu⟩zik, in þe which hee waz master to *Achilles*, þe valient *Grecian*. In þe sam book do I read of *Arione*, who waz A perfet miuzisian. he wa⟨z⟩ of *Methinna*, A siti in *Lesbo*. and for hiz kunning waz much esteem⟨ed⟩ of *Periandro*, king of *Corintho*. Also in þe said book hav I red of *Orpheo*, who waz þe soon of *Caliope*, hee waz [of] þe kuntrei of *Thracio*. ⟨hee⟩ waz both A poet, A harper most exsellent, and A miuzisian. Ðÿs for þis purpoz shall suffÿz, and now will I not vnto yow such p⟨ro⟩fan and old awtorz az hav written in þe kommendasion of Miuzik. *Tulli*, in hiz *Tusculans que*[*s*]*tions*.[2] þe first book, saith þat þe sowll ⟨of⟩ man, iz A sertain intension or earnest konsyderasion of þe mÿnd, ⟨and⟩ iz disparsed thorow owt evri part of þe body, and evn az it iz in sing⟨ing⟩ or plaing on miuzikall instriuments which iz kalled harmoni, so dÿv⟨erz⟩ movings ar mad or kum of þe natiur and fygiur of þe hol body az sound⟨z⟩ ar mad in singing. Again in þe said book and þe first chapter,[3] iz said ⟨þat⟩ *Plato* by number mad A divizion of þe sowll into iij parts, and also þat *Xenocrates* said p[l]ainly þat þe sowll waz number. of þe which opinion wer þoz filosoferz, who said þat þe sowll iz devÿded into iij parts. þat iz to say, *Vegitatiue*, *Sensitiue*, and *Intellectiue*.

---

[1] These references are also found under 'Musica' in Alunno's *Fabrica del Mondo*. See p. 224 and note 5.

[2] Cicero's *Quaestiones Tusculanae*. For the text used by Whythorne, see note 2 on p. 231. In the 1577 edition the passages here paraphrased occur on p. 12.   [3] Ibid., p. 12.

which iz to say in english, inkreasing, sensibull, and vnder-standing.

of þe which opinion waz *Aristotell* also, who in hiz book *De Causis*, saith þat þe sowll of man hath iij operasions. þat iz to say, *Animalem, Intellectualem,* and *Diuinam.* which iz to say, lẏvly, vnderstandingly, and heavnly. so þat in þe respekt of number only þe sowll of man iz Miuzik, for þat part of Ret⟨ho⟩rik which iz kalled þe proporsions, iz taken owt of miuzik az þe Filosofer⟨z⟩ do bear witnes. for *Tulli* in his book *de oratore*, and many oþer learne⟨d⟩ men do say þat all learning both proz and Meeter or vers, towching number, quantite, and rithm, do depend on miuzik. *Plato*, in hiz first book of hi⟨z⟩ lawz, saith þat Miuzik doth kontein all kynd of learning, and þat miuzik kannot bee wurþely intreated ⟨o⟩f withowt all kẏndz of know-leȝ. *Henrici Cornelij Agrippæ*, saith þat emong mani of þe Gresians which wrọt of miuzik þẹr waz ọn named *Aristoxenus*, who said þat þe sowll of man waz miuzik, þe which dokiuments and lessons of *Aristoxenus*, konserning miuzik, *Boethius* trans-lated into Latten. hee speaketh of þạt miuzik which standeth in sownd and vois, and not of þat which konsisteth in meeterz, rithms, and verses. *Aristotell* in hiz book *de Mondo*,[1] saith þat miuzik doth render or yeeld A konsent or agreement of sharp and flat soundz, & of long and short soundz, mixed togiþer in dyverz voises and so bringeth þem all into ọn konkordans in þe end. Owr aunsient poet sir Geffrey Chawser, in þe beginning of hiz book named Ðe Assembly of fools,[2] saith þat þe Sphẹrs be þe wawls of miuzik. I fẏnd in þe xij chapter of þe book nạmed þe mirrowr of þe world, which book waz translạted owt of frenc⟨h⟩ into english by william Caxton, anno 1508.[3] þat of

---

[1] This supposititious work bore the title *De Mundo Aristotelis*, but no early English edition is known. The passage is found in the Basle edition of 1533, p.18, though Whythorne most probably found this quotation in a compendium.

[2] *Parliament of Fowls*, lines 59–63. Whythorne misquoted 'welle of musik' in line 62.

[3] No copy of the 1508 edition of Caxton's *The Myrrour of the Worlde* is known; the earliest edition is that of 1481 (*STC* 24762). Caxton reprinted the volume in 1490 and L. Andrewe reissued it about 1529. Whythorne derived this passage from the twelfth chapter.

þe siens of miuzik ku⟨meth all⟩ attemperans (I will wrẏt ⌐þe **69ᵛ**
matter of⌐ hiz wordz, az hee wrọt þem) and of þis ạrt, proseedeth
sum fyzik, for lẏk az miuzik akkordeth althings þat do diskord
in þem selvz, and remain þem to konkordans, riht so in lẏkwẏz
travelleth fyzik to bring nạtiur to point þat diznatiureth in mans
body, when any malady or siknes enkombreth it. but fyzik iz
nọn of þe number of þe .7. sienses of filosofy, but it iz A maestri
or A kraft, þat entendeth to þe helth of A mans body. and for to
preserv it from all maladiez, and siknesses az long az þe lẏf iz þe
body, and þerfọr it iz not liberall, for it serveth to heall mans
body. which els oftentẏms miht lihtly perish. and þer iz nothing
liberall ne free, þat groeth on þe earth. And forasmuch az siens
þat serveth to mans body leezeth hiz franchẏz, but siens þat
serveth to þe sowll, dezerveth in þe world to hạv nạm liberall. for
þe sowll owht to be liberall az thing þat iz of nobull being, az
shee þat kummeth of God, and to God will or owht to return.

and þarfọr be þe .vij sienses liberall, for þei mạk þe sowll ⌐all⌐
free, and on þat oþer pạrt, þei teach and ensign all þat in evry
thing owht properly to bee doen. And þis iz þe very reazon why
þez arts all vij, be named .7. sienses liberall, for þei mạk þe sowll
liberall, and deliver it from all evell. of þis art of miuzik þus
kum, þat shee akkordeth her to everich so well, þat by her þe
.7. sienses wẹr sett in konkord þat þei yet endiur. by þis siens of
miuzik be extrait and drawn all songs þat be songen in holy
chiurch, and all akkordans of all þe instriuments þat hạv diverz
akkordz and dyverz sowndz. and whẹr þẹr iz no reazon, and
entendement of soom things. Certes who kan well þe siens of
miuzik, hee knoweth þe akkordans of althings. and all þe kreatiurz
þat pain þem to do well, remain þem to konkordans. Ðe said
book saith þat miuzik iz þe sixt siens of þe liberall sienses. But
Master .*T. Wilson*. in hiz book of þe art of *Logique*,[1] doth set it
in ⌐þe middell,⌐ between þe seven liberall sienses, þe which he
setteth þus. *grammer, logique, Rethorique, Miuzik, Arithmetique,*

---

[1] Thomas Wilson, *The Rule of Reason, conteinynge the Arte of Logique*,
1553 (*STC* 25811). Whythorne refers to a poem on f. 2ᵛ, 'A brief declaration
in Metre, of the seuen liberal Artes'.

Geometri, and *Astronómi*. and miuzik so standing in þe midz
emong þe oþer six sienses may akkord her to evry of þem, þat
by her þe rest of þe sienses may be so sett in konkord þat þei will
e[n]diur, az iz said befor. *Aristotell*.[1] in hiz .8. book, *De Re pub*,
þe .4. chapter, saith þat miuzik after A sort belongeth to vertew.
it doth bring þe body in good lýking, by þe kustom of honest
pleziurz. it availeth to lýv by. it iz of fors, to attain wizdom. it iz
plased or set in such things az bring to vs þe greatest deliht. it
iz in assembliez. it iz þe kawzer of mirth. it availeth for þe
rekreasion of þe mýnd. it doth provók anger, klemensy, fortitiud, &c and it doth settl þe dispozision of þe mýnd to any thing
þat it iz enklyned vnto. Vpon þe opinion of *Aristotell* ⌈az⌉ afforsaid, þer iz on þat wryteth þus. Miuzik (saith hee) iz A siens
which kan riht well konstitiut and fram, þe habit and dispozision
of þe mýnd, which seing it iz so, yoong men no dowt ar to bee
70[r] brouht vp & instrukted in þe sam. yee mor over, it iz very fitt
and agreing to þeir na⟨tiurz and⟩ al⟨l⟩ things þat ar or bee
(exsepting þe very natiurz indeed) þer iz ⟨no⟩ mor si⟨ur⟩ and
trew, þen number, rithm, and miuzik. for þei do shew foorth,
and expr⟨es⟩ A similitiud and shap of wrath, klemensi, fortitiud, and temperans, & als⟨o⟩ of þeir kontrariez. yee, and of
mani oþer things towching mannerz. wee ⟨ak⟩kownt miuzik
(saith hee) in þoz things which bring with þem passing
pl⟨eziur⟩ and delýht, wheþer it bee bar of itself, or ȝ⟨oi⟩ned
with konsent.

Also he saith þat men do well ⌈to⌉ ad and ywz miuzik at feasts
in kumpaniez a⟨nd⟩ assembliez, for þat it iz þe worker and pro-
voker of pleaziur & deliht, ⟨þe⟩ yows wherof iz most akseptabull to evry aȝ, stat, and degree. I hav r⟨ed⟩ in þe forsaid *Fabrico
del mondo*, þat *Boetio*, in þe prohem of hiz miu⟨zik⟩ saith, þat
þe sam delyteth evry aȝ, and it iz of such fors, and powr, ⟨þat⟩ it

[1] This material occurs in *Thesauri Aristotelis Stagiritae Libri XIIII. Com-
mentariis Illustrati* (Paris, 1562), f. 105ᵛ. (The *STC* lists no English edition
before 1598.) Whythorne may have taken his other information from the
anonymous commentator quoted after his paraphrase; this is not, however,
the compiler of the 1562 *Thesaurus*.

chain3eth or altreth all men. Ðe sạm book[1] saith þat *Ari⟨sto⟩tell*, in hiz *Problemati* saith, þat whosoever iz sorowfull, or who þa⟨t iz⟩ mery, ywzeth miuzik, þe ọn to diminish þe sorow, and þe oþer to enkreas hiz mirth. I hạv red, in *Thesaurus*[2] affọrsaid, of *phrigium Melo⟨s⟩* which iz A melody or tewn of instriument wherin seemed to bee (az *Lucanus* saith) A maner of divẏn fiury (albeit *Porphirius* kalleth it *barbarows*). *Cassiodorus* saith, þat þe melody named *Dorium*, geveth wizdom, and chastite. *Ph⌐r⌐igium* stirreth to battell, and infl⟨ạ⟩meth þe dezẏr of fiury. *Aeolium* appeazeth þe tempests of þe mẏn⟨d⟩ and bringeth in sleep. *Lidium*, quikkeneth vnderstanding in þem þa⟨t⟩ be dull, and indiuseth appetẏt of selestiall things. *Gallenus*.[3] &. *Fucsius*, do say þat miuzik dooth appeaz þe dolowrz of þe mẏnd. lẏkwẏz sir Thomas Eeliot in hiz Castell of helth[4] doth allow of it ⟨for⟩ þat purpọz, alþowh in hiz Governowr hee doth invei against þem þa⟨t⟩ do not ywz it az þei owht to do.

Ðis for þis tẏm and purpọz shall suffẏz, and now will I rekownt vnto yow sertain historiez by þe which ye may vnderstand and perseiv of what powr and fors miuzik iz. In þe .vj. chapter of *Josue*,[5] ye shall fẏnd, þat throuh þe sownd of trumpets, kornets, and þe voises of þe peepull of *Israell*, þe wawls of *Jerico* wẹr thrown down to þe grownd. In þe .xvj. chapter of þ⟨e⟩ first book of *Samuel*, oþerwẏz named þe first book of þe kings[6] ye shall fẏnd þat when king Sawll waz feared and vexed with ⟨A⟩ malingnant spreit, it parted and fled away, when þe profet *Daui⟨d⟩* sounded with his harp befọr him. but now perchauns, yow wold sa⟨y⟩ þat alþowh it waz Godz will þat ⌐bi⌐

---

[1] Whythorne's source was again the article under 'Musica'. See p. 224 and note 5.

[2] *Op. cit.*, article 'Phrygium melos'.

[3] The opinions of Galen and Leonhard Fuchs are probably derived from some medical compendium.

[4] Sir Thomas Elyot's *Castel of Helth* (1539 and frequently republished; STC 7643–57). Whythorne apparently has in mind Book III, chap. 12, 'Of dolour or heuinesse of minde'. In Elyot's *The Boke named the Gouernour* (1531 and many later editions; STC 7635–42), chap. 7 describes 'In what wise musike may be to a noble man necessarie: and what modestie ought to be therin'.

[5] Joshua 6. 20.

[6] 1 Samuel 16. 14–23.

miuzik such great things shiuld bee browht to pas az iz afforsaid, yet þe aksion iz not kommen, neiþer iz þer left to posterite any kredibull remembrans þat ani mor such wunderfull things hav bin wrouht by miuzik sins þat tȳm, þe which I think to be trew. but þen I do say, þat if it pleazed God to wurk, or suffer to bee wrouht so good and great benefyts by miuzik, þen doth hee allow it wurþi of þe estimąsion of such A thing az it pleazed him to do good withall. I do read in *Fabrico*[1] &*c* afforsaid þat 70ᵛ *E*[*m*]*pedocle*, with h⟨iz miuzi⟩k did mitigąt, and put away þe ȳr and wrath of A yoong man, þe which wold hav killed[a] þe akkiuzar of hiz faþer. In þe sąm book[2] do I read þat *Arione* sailing into *Sicilia*, and from þens into *Itali*, hee had gotten by hiz miuzik in þoz kuntreiz A great deall of money, and after A sertain tȳm, hee being dezyrus to return to *Corintho* whęr hee dwelled, he gat into A ship belonging to þe sąm town, þe marinarz of þe which ship knowing þat hee had much money, and determining to hav it, þei did determin to kast him into þe Sea, bekawz hee shiuld not tell afterward, who robbed him, þe which hee perseiving began to pray þem þat þei wold spąr him hiz lȳf. but when hee perseivid þat hiz praierz węr in vain, hee requyred A tȳm befor hee shiuld be kast into þe Sea, þat hee miht sing with hiz harp, kloþed, and adorned[b] with most presiowz garments and ȝiuels þat hee had, þe which being grawnted vnto him, and hee on þe ships sȳd, after hiz song being sung, hee leapt into þe Sea, whęr he waz prezently reseived of A fish named A *Dolphin*, and on hiz bak sąfly brouht to þe Iland of *Tenaro*. and from þens hee went to *Corinth*.

I miht heer rehers þe storiez of *Amphion* who builded *Thebe* with þe sownd of Miuzik. And also of *Orpheo*, who by hiz miuzik fecht hiz loov, named *Euridice* owt of Hell, þe which storiez be written in þat book, but bekawz þei be poetikall I will bestow no lenger tȳm on þem. Lȳkwȳz do I read in *Thesaurus*[3]

---

[a] MS. reads 'lilled'.   [b] MS. reads 'aþorned'.

[1] *Op. cit.*, article 'Musica'. See p. 224 and note 5.
[2] *Ibid.*, article 'Musica'.
[3] *Op. cit.*, article 'Argus'; also 'Berecynthium cornu' and 'Halesina regio'.

&c afforsaid, þat *Argus*, for all he had so many eiez, waz by þe sweet harmony of *Mercurius*, brouht on sleep and so by him slain. In þe sam book did I read of *Berecynthium cornu*, which waz A horn wherwith þe preests of *Cibele*, wer stired and provoked to A raʒ and fiury. Also in þe sam book hav I red of *Halesina regio*, which iz A kuntrey wherin iz A well, þe water wherof being alwaiz quiet and plain, if on standing bi it do play on A Shawlm, or oþer lẏk pẏp, þe water of þe well will rẏz az [if] it daunsed, insomuch, þat at þe last it will mount and run over þe brim of þe well. and þe pẏp seasing, þe water will foorthwith fall and bekum quiet. In þe book named þe konkordans of historiez (oþerwyz kalled Fabians Kronikell[1]) I hav red þat A french king named Lews þe .xj. after þe akkount of þat book (and þe .x. after þe french akkownt) having A great diseaz in him (wherof hee died) kalled in Latten *Morbus Elephancie* hee kommaunded to be browht befor him, all þe kunning masterz of miuzik within hiz realm, þat by þe melodi⌐o⌐us sownd of þeir instriuments, hee miht be eazed of hiz pain, but when hee had assembled of þe best, an hundreth and twenty in number, A few sheppardz pẏps wer to him mor solas, þen all þe oþer, or any part of þem. þe which hee held still in hiz koort and kommaunded þat evry day þe sheppardz shiuld play and sownd þeir bagpẏps A sertain distans from þe plas wher hee waz. It waz told mee not long sins, þat þer iz A sertain serpent, of þe which if A man be stung,[2] hee shalbe foorthwith speechles, and also hee shall begin to dawns, and so kontinew in daunsing hee having in hiz mẏnd þerwith and whẏll hee iz A dawnsing þe tewn of sum dawns þe which hee dawnseth, and yet hee shalnot be habull to sownd owt þe sam by any means. wherfor to help and kiur him, þer iz brouht vnto him, such az kan play on miuzikall instriu- 71ʳ ments or els sing all þeᵃ daunses þat be⟨e⟩ ywzed in þat kuntrey,

---

ᵃ MS. reads 'de'.

[1] *The Chronicle of Fabian*, written by Robert Fabyan, was first published by Pynson in Latin in 1516. This passage is found in the English version of 1559 (*STC* 10664), ii. 479, 491.

[2] A variant on the tarantula myth.

and if any of þem kan chauns vpon þe tewn of þat dauns which soundeth in hiz hed and mýnd, hee iz foorthwith kiured of hiz diseaz. but if þei kannot hit vpon it, hee never leaveth daunsing, til⟨l⟩ hee doth fawll down dead.

It waz on A týmn told mee of A bagpýpe⟨r⟩ who went Abowt þe kuntrei to get hiz lyving, and on A týmn hee wa⟨z be⟩nihted befor hee kowld get from þem wher hee last waz, and his way ⟨hom⟩ward waz to go thorow A forrest, wher þer was many wýld beasts. when hee kạm to þe forrest, hee fearing ⟨þe⟩ wurst, gat him vp into A tree, and þạr sat all þe nyht. at þe break of þe day, þer kạm þat way wher hee waz A great woulf, who smelling þe man on þe tree bega⟨n⟩ to look vp to him, And when hee had spýd the man þe woulf began ⟨to⟩ howll, and so lowd, þat sum of hiz fellowz hard him, whervpon þer kạm vnto him A great many mọr of woulvz, who howld ⌈and⌉ mạd so grea⟨t⟩ A noyz þat þe man ⌈waz⌉ half Amazed at yt, for besýd þeir howling þe⟨i⟩ ⌈d⟨id⟩⌉ rýz vp against þe tree and also leap vp az hy az þei kowld to hạ⟨v⟩ reacht vnto him, and when þei did see þat þei kowld not kum by þe man þat way, þei with þeir feet digged or skraped þe earth from þe roots of þe tree, and with þeir teeth did být at þe roots, mýnding to pluk vp all þe roots, so þat þe tree myht fall, wherby þei miht kum to þeir pray. þe poor man seing how hard hee waz bested, and lookin⟨g⟩ for no ayd, þer kạm to hiz mýnd to proov an experiment, which ⌈waz⌉ to tạk hi⟨z⟩ bagpýp and to play þeron, and assoon az hee had mạd hiz pýps to go a⟨z⟩ lowd az hee kowld mạk þem, all þe woulvs ran away from þe tree i⟨nto⟩ þe forrest az fast az þei kowld. and when þe man perseived þat þe so⟨wnd⟩ of hiz bagpýps had dryven away þe woulvz, hee thanked God þat ⟨hee⟩ had put such A ⌈mosion &⌉ mean into hiz mýnd by ⌈þe⌉ which hee eskạped from such A perill and dainʒer, and þạrvpon hee kạm down from þe tree, and assoon az hee waz down, hee did sett hiz pýp to hiz mowth ⌈again, and⌉ so went ⌈plaing þeron⌉ thorow þe forrest (withowt any assawt of any beast) vntill hee kạm whẹ⟨r⟩ hee did know him self to be past all þat dainʒer.

Heer miht I rehers and bring to yowr mýnd, how miuzik

affekteth infants, who at þe singing of þeir nurses, or sownding
of sum miuzikall instriument or sh⟨uch⟩lẏk sownd, will many
tẏms stop & stay þeir kryeng. Heer mẏht I al⟨so⟩ shew yow how
miuzik doth affekt birdz, az yee mai perseiv by such w⟨hich⟩ be
kommenly kept in mens howzes, how þei will reʒois and sing in
þeir sort and kẏnd, when þat þei do hear ani miuzikall noyz.
Ðen for beasts I may shew how þat when þe fears hors doth hear
þe sownd of þe Trumpett, or þe Drum & fẏf, how hee bianby
advaunseth him self, and how ready he maketh him self to fiht,
by bẏting, and stryking with hiz feet & heels. Ðen for fishes, yee
may kall to mẏnd þe story of þe *Delphin*[1] afforsaid. Also I hạv
hard, and also I hạv seen it printed in A map,[2] þat at *Island*, and
Ilands þạrabowt, þer be þat do yowz to stand on þe Seashọr at
A sertain tẏm of þe yeer, and þạr sownd and play on bagpẏps,
þe which Melody doth kawz sertain sorts and kẏndz of fyshes
to kum ny vnto þeir shọr, & þen with nets, and such oþer **71ᵛ**
devẏses þei do tạk þe fẏshes.

Now will I towch þe ʒenerall estimasion of miuzik, with þe
appurtenanses belonging to þe sạm, and þen konkliud. Yee shall
vnderstand þat in þis owr realm, it waz ọn of þe trạdz and exersizes appointed and allowed for such ʒentilmen to lẏv by, az
wẹr yonger broþerz and neiþer lands nor feez, and goodz to
maintain þem. Yee shall fynd in þe book named. *Ðe Aksidens
of Armeri*,[3] þat A king of *Hẹralts* may gẏv arms to any þat iz
exsellently skilled in ani of þe seven liberall sienses (whẹᵣrᵌof
miuzik iz ọn) alþouh hee nor hiz aunsetorz miht never gẏv
any befọr.

In tẏm past miuzik waz cheefly maintained by *Cathedrall
chiur*ches *Abbeis. Colleges. parish chiur*ches, Chauntries, gẏls,
Fraternities &c. but when þe *Abbeiz*, and kolleʒes withowt þe

---

[1] See p. 240.

[2] Whythorne apparently had in mind the *Carta Marina* of Olaus Magnus
(woodcut, Venice, 1539; engraving, Rome, 1572).

[3] Gerard Legh, *The Accedens of Armory*, 1562, and frequently reprinted
(*STC* 15388–93). In the 1576 edition, f. 115, the passage reads: 'The fowerth,
what he is of condicion, whether clene of life, iust in promise, a keeper of
hospitalitie, cōning ī al, or anye one of the vii. artes liberal, or of Diuinitie,
Cosmographi, Historiographi, Phisike . . . etc.'

vniuersities, with gẏls, and fraternities &c wẹr suppres, þen
went miuz[ik] to dekay. To speak of miuzik in howzes, yee shall
vnderstand, þat dyverz nobullmen and women, in tẏm past,
imitating þe prins, wold hạv Organists, & andᵃ singingmen to
serv God after þe maner of þat tẏm with miuzik in þeir privat
chappels. but þat imitasion iz also left. þen for such az served
for prẏvat rekreasion in howzes, which wẹr for þe nobilite &
wurshipfull, þes wẹr no les esteemed þen þe oþerz, till tẏm þat
þe Raskall and of skumm of þat profession, who be, or owht to
bee kalled minstrels (alþoh now A daiz many do nạm þem
miuzisions) þẹz I say did and do mạk it kommen by offring of
it to evry ʒak, going abowt evry plas and kuntrey for þe sạm
purpọz, az partly it iz towcht affọr.

heer kummeth A prety ʒest to my remembrans between A
minstrell and A begger. when I did ly in A man of wurships hows
in þe kuntrey to teach hiz childern, þer kạm A minstrell to þat
hows to offer sum of hiz minstrelsy. and after þat hee shewd hiz
skill, þe ʒentilman of þe hows kalled þe minstrell to go owt of þe
dọrz to speak with of sum matterz, and when þe ʒentilman waz
withowt hiz dọrz, þạr waz A begger A stowt Rọg þat did beg
sum money of þe ʒentilman, þe which þe ʒentilman wold not
gẏv him, but did bid ọn of hiz servaunts to gẏv him sum meat
and drink, but þe Rọg wold not be so awnswered, but waz
importiunat vpon þe ʒentilman for sum money, wherwith þe
ʒentilman waz angry with þe begger, and ywzed sum hard
speeches to ⌐him.⌐ whervpon þe minstrell, said to þe begger,
good fellew yow ar to blam to trobull þe ʒentilman somuch, and
if hee wẹr dispozed to gẏv yow money yow shiuld hạv had it for
fewer wordz þen yow hạv geven to him. with þat þe knạv Rọg,
bent all hiz mallis and speech vnto þe minstrell, saing vnto him,
I kry yow mersy sir, I do know yow well inowh, for I ⌐hạv⌐ seen
yow walk þe kuntrey azwell az I, many tẏms er now, I wus man
yee need not to be so lusty, if yee do remember ⌐yow⌐ well, for
þer is nomor diffrens between yowr estạt and mẏn, but þat yow

---

ᵃ Dittography.

do go into þe hows, and I do stand withowt þe dọrz. at þẹz wordz
of þe disgrạs of þe minstrell þe ȝentilman did lawh very hertẹly,
and þen he kawld þe begger roging knạv, and so went hiz way.
by þis yow may see in what stạt þe minstrels ⌐be in⌐ when az
beggerz and rọgs do akkownt þem to bee þeir kompanions and
fellowz. yett for all þis kannot ⌐I⌐ but ⌐sai⌐ sumwhat mọr for **72ᵛ**
miuzik, for all þat it iz misywzed and diskredited by such az iz
b⟨efọr⟩ spoken of.

Now I will speak of ⟨þ⟩e yws of miuzik in þis tẏm prezent. First
for þe chiurch, yee do and shall see it so slenderly maintained in
þe kathedrall chiurches and kolleȝes ⌐& parish chiurches,⌐ þat
when þe old stọr of þe miuzis⟨i⟩ans be worn owt þe which wẹr
bred when þe miuzik of þe chiurch ⟨waz⟩ maintained (which iz
lẏk to bee in short tẏm) yee shall hạv few or n⟨ọn⟩ remaining
exsept it be A few singing men, and plaierz on miuzi⟨kall⟩ instriuments, of þe which ye shall fẏnd A very few or nọn þat
⟨kan⟩ mạk A good lesson of deskant, and yet þez wold be named
and akkou⟨nted⟩ miuzisians alþowh þer ⌐be⌐ nọn wurþi of þatt
nạm exsept þei kan mạk songs of ij, iij, iiij parts and so vpward
akkording to þe trew rewls þerof az iz befọr said. þer be An oþer
sort of miuzisians þat be named *speculators.*[1] þat iz to say, þei
þat do bekum miuzisians by studye withowt ⟨any⟩ praktis þerof.
þer hạv bin of such who hạv mạd songs and hạv prik⟨ked⟩ þem
owt, and yet kowld not ⌐sing⌐ A part of þem, þeim selvs. þer be
An oþer sort of loverz of miuzik, who do eiþer learn þe siens az
affor⟨said⟩ or to play and sownd on miuzikall instriuments, or
els to sing prikson⟨g⟩ for þat þei wold þerwith, eiþer setfoorth
Godz glory in þe chiurch, or els yowz it for þe sạm purpọz in
privat howzes, or els for þeir own rekreasion, and do not oþerwẏz
seek to lẏv or furþer þeir lẏvings þerby ani maner of way. þez
ar to be esteemed and preferred akkording t⟨o⟩ þeir estạts, and
also akkor[d]ing to þeir skill þerin aboov þọz who do learn þe
siens, or to play on miuzikall instriuments, or els to sing prik-

---

[1] This use of the word does not occur in *OED*, though 'speculation' and
'speculative', both terms of contrast with practical musicians, are quoted
from Morley's *Introduction to Music* (1597). See Appendix III.

song (az iz afforsaid) to lyv by or to furder þeir lyvings þerby. Ðoz þat do learn it az afforsaid, for þe loov þei hav to þe siens and not ⟨to⟩ ⌜l⟨yv⟩⌝ by az þe oþerz do, þez I say ar to be akkownted emong þe number of þ⟨oz⟩ who þe book named Ðe institusion of A ȝentilman¹ doth allow to learn miuzik. And also which þe book named Ðe Coortier,² doth will to learn miuzik, for þei wold hav þe great ȝentilmen, and þe koortier⟨z⟩ to learn miuzik in þat sort, and to þat end. Which kownsell of þoz books, þe nobilite, and þe wurshipfull do much follow in þez daiez for many of þoz estats hav skoolmasters in þeir howzes to teach þeir childern both to sing priksong, and also to play on miuzikall instriuments.

I kannot heer leav owt or let pas to speak of an oþer sort þ⟨at⟩ do lyv by miuzik and yet ar no miuzisians at all. And þoz be þei, w⟨ho⟩ after þei hav learned A littl to sing priksong, or els hav eiþer learn⟨ed⟩ by hand, or by ear, or els by tabulatiur, to play or sownd on miuzika⟨ll⟩ instriuments, such miuzik az hath bin and iz mad by oþerz ⌜and not by þem⌝ bianby þei will ywzurp on miuzik, and akkownt and kall þem selvz miuzisians. of þe which petifoggers of miuzik, þer be boþ skoolmasterz,ª singingmen, and minstrels. heer peradventiur yow wold say þat I hav given okkazion in þis last afforsaid to draw awai þe goodwils of sum who do favor miuzik, bekawz I do mak such distinksions of þe degreez & sorts of þe loverz and professorz of miuzik, and of þoz who be no miuzisans in deed. and wilnot allow þe meanest sort of þem, þe nam of miuzisians azwell az þe best sort. but þei þat loov þe furþerans of þe estimasion of miuzik in deed, wilnot mizlyk with þat which I hav now written þerin, but raþer allow myn opinion. bekawz þat it iz A Chaos, or A konfiuzed lum[p] of degreez and sorts heaped vp in A bundell, az most kommenly it iz ywzed now adaiz, and geveth kawz vnto þe ingnorant, ingnorantly, & þe malisiowz kontiumeliowzly

72ᵛ

ª MS. reads 'skoormasterz'.

¹ The Institucion of a Gentleman, 1555 and reprinted 1568 (STC 14104–5). The reference occurs on page Ciiii verso of the 1839 facsimile of the 1568 edition.

² Count Baldassare Castiglione, The Courtyer. Done into Englyshe by T. Hoby, 1561 (STC 4778). The reference is to sigg. Iii-iii.

or spỳtfully to impiut and ywz þe nąms of þe meanest and basest sort of þem, vnto þe best and hỳest sort, whęrby þe siens hath of ląt, bin þe les esteemed of many.

Đis, for þis purpọz shall heer suffỳz, and now to tell yow sumwhat of þe ȝenerall estimasion of miuzik in forrein realms, yee shall vnderstand, þat sumwhat I do know þerof in Italy, Frans, and þe Duchland. but cheefly in Italy whęr I perseived þat emong such az węr of any akkount, þei węr esteemed to bee but riudly and bąsly browht vp who had no knowleȝ in miuzik, or at þe least habull to play or sownd on sum miuzikall instriument or els to sing priksong, in such sort az þei węr habull to sing A part when þe[i] węr in kumpany of such who węr willing to sing songs of .ij. iij. iiij. pąrts &c. and for þat kawz, yee shall fỳnd in þat kuntrei, in mọst mens howzes þat bee of any repiutasion or akkount, not only instriuments of miuzik, but also all sorts of miuzik in print, having setts of books in þeir howzes for singing & for instruments, þat be of .ij. iij. iiij. v. vj. vij. and also of viij parts, and vpward. bekawz þat when þer be many in ọn kumpany togyþer who kan sing priksong parfektlye, ye shall in þọz books fỳnd songs of dỳverz trądz for þem to sing. and for þat þe printerz wold hąv evry day new songs to print, þei do fee þe best miuzisians þat þei kan retain, to þe end þat when þei do mąk ani new songs, þeir printerz may hąv þe only kopiez of þem to print, which enkoraȝeth þe miuzi[si]ans to emploi and gỳv hiz mynd and indevor þe mọr to hiz study þerin.

Đus hąv I shewd yow of þe awnsienti and antiquite of miuzik. Of þe inventorz þerof, and of þe inventorz of þe instriuments belonging to þe sąm. Of þọz who bọth ywzed it and allowd it in þe chiurch azwell az withowt, to praiz God withall. Of such profąn, and old awtors az hąv written in þe kommendasion þerof. Of sertain historiez by þe which yee may vnderstand and perseiv of what powr and wurking, þe sekret fors it iz of. How it affekteth infants, birdz, beasts, and fyshes. Of þe ȝenerall estimasion þerof azwell in þe tỳm past, az in þe tỳm prezent in þis realm. and of þe generall estimasion þerof in forrein realms. And if miuzik węr not A vertew to bee esteemed of, wold so many saints, and holy men and women, And also wẏz and learned men hạv learned, ywzed and esteemed of it az iz befọr spọken? Now ȝiuȝ yow, what franzy and madnes remaineth in þọz blokhedz, and dolts, who will so vtterly kondempn it. Ðer iz nọn þat do dispẏz it, but such az be eiþer delẏted to drudȝ and toill for þeir lyvings in servill, and filthy trạdz, or els be ingnorant in all sorts of learnings, and if þei be not so I warrant yow it iz but in ⌐such⌐ sorts, wherwith nesessite kompelleth þem to lẏv by. but and if þei bee learned, and lẏv not þerby, yet

73ʳ peradventiur þe old proverb may be fulled in þem, which saith þat Ðe greatest klarks be not wẏzest men.[1] And also it may be sa⟨id⟩ of þem þat þei bee so disdainfull, az þ⟨ei⟩ kannot lẏk to hạv any body for þọz vertewz þat þei hạv no skill in, to be⟨e⟩ esteemed any thing ny az þei bee, or els þei be so enviows, az þei kannot a⟨llow⟩ ọn who exselleth in A vertew of mọr estimasion þen þeirz iz of to bee esteem⟨ed⟩ mọr þen þei. And if þei be not towched with any of þọz fọrsaid vẏses, þ⟨en⟩ peradventiur þei be so malisiows þat bekawz sum of þat profession hạv ⟨of⟩fended þem, þei kan neiþer abẏd þe thing it self, neyþer þat þe prof⟨e⟩sso⟨rz⟩ þerof shiuld hạv þeir dew and dezerved estimasion. Now when I h⟨ad⟩ konsydered A whẏll vpon all þis kommendasion of miuzik, I devẏzed in meeter þervpon all þis þat doth follow—

Sith þat long tẏm I hạv profest A loover[a] *for to bee*
of þat sweet[b] *siens, which miuzik hiht, and sum tẏms to mee*
I took in hand to shew in þat how I had spent sum tẏm
(wherwith also I ȝoind sonets devẏzd in English rẏm)
in þe prefạs wherof I said, I wọld at þat tẏm stay
what I in praiz þerof kowld wrẏt,[c] *or els what I kowld say*
Now, lest yee shiuld think þat I towcht, mọr þen I kowld wel do
I wil breefly, heer to yow show, az kumz my mẏnd vnto
how it from tẏm to tẏm hath bin of hẏ, and low maintaind
az thing of valew too set bi, and not az fansy faind.

[a] Written above 'master'.   [b] MS. reads 'sweer'.   [c] Written above 'show'.

[1] Proverbial; Tilley C 409.

And first for þ'aunsi'entnes þerof mi mỹnd þerin to show
I think it [fit] er I in þis diskoors do farder grow
bekawz it mai þerby appeer, þat er þe world began
it waz in Heavn first fownd and ywzed, and after þat bi man.
I read in þ'old, and new Testments, þat soundz of melodi
both voises and ẹk instriuments, with sownd of trump on hy
hath oft bin hard in Heavn to bee, in sundri maner waiz
sumtỹm warning, or els thratning, and sumtỹm to Godz praiz
wherfọr sins miuzik hath so oft, bin hard in Heavn aboov
I mai þe sạfli'er bỹd þerbi, and do no farder proov
þat miuzik þạr waz ywzd befọr þe world did first begin
or els yow must graunt vnto mee, þat þeir skils þerin
þei learned sins þat in þis world it hath bin had in prỹs
and so God gạv þem þe knowleȝ, az t'wẹr of hiz devỹs
itᵃ mai not bee þat wee on earth, shiuld first inventorz bee
of such A thing az hee wil hạv somuch in Heavn to bee
for miuzik being A vertew rạr, from God at first it kam
(from whom proseedeth al vertewz) whọz þ'awtor of þe sam.
And after þat þe world began (I read in Genesis   **73ᵛ**
þatᵇ) Tubal first invented it, whò lỹkwỹz az said is,
þe Organs and þe Harp also, hee mạd by hiz devỹs
so þat sins him þ'invensions lỹk of oþerz did arỹs
I mean such az bee spoken of, in profạn awtorz ọld
of whọz devỹs in instriuments þeir fạmz þei hạv enrọld
to prosekiut mỹn enterprỹs I now begin again
of holy men and women bọth, sumwhat to towch þe train
who bi miuzik hạv ẹk deklạrd þe sạm to bee esteemd
and ywzd to dỹverz purpozes, az now and þen it seemd
az þat þe Isra'elỹts did sing, when þe Redsea þei past
in wh[i]ch Pharao, and hiz wẹr drownd, for all þei mạd such hạst
az þat waz mạd bi Delbora, Judit, and ẹk Mozes.
when az þe Viktori of þeir fọz, þei quietly did posses
az þat waz ywzd, when az þe wawls of Jerico down fell
az þat also which Dạuid mạd þe spreet in Sawl t'expell

ᵃ Written above 'þat'.   ᵇ MS. reads 'dat'.

az which which[a] *þe women did mąk, þat Dauid met họmward*
when hee þe hiuʒ Philistian slew with sling and stọn so hard
and þat which Dąuid mąd and sung befọr þe Ark of God
whọz wẏf for skorning him þẹrfọr from teeming was forbod
Egregius psaltes Israel, waz Dauid of sum nąmd
bekawz in miuzik hee exseld and þạrbi wunderz frąmd
þe verses of whọz salms iz said by Augustẏn þe great
to bee frąmed bi meaziurz good, þe eazier to repeat
so þat meaziurz being but meeterz, and meeterz rithms to bee
it argiuz þat þe họl salter with miuzik doth agree
if I wold stand vpon ech pląs, þat in sk[r]iptiur iz fownd
which for þe kredit of miuzik doth altogiþer sownd
if I of Doktors wọld alęʒ who miuzik did allow
azwell in chiurch az owt of chiurch Godz praiz þerwith to show
if I of þe philosoferz wold show who it loved
and which of þem kontempning it, węr þerfọr reproved,
if I of þaunsi'ent phizisions, shiuld shew how þei hạv said
what kiurz be wrouht bi miuziks fors, and what eev[l]s it hath staid
if I, (I sai) of all þe poets would show þeir devẏses
wherin fẏnly þei of miuzik, þe vertewz do expres

74[r]   *Ðis pamflet smawl A volium great shiuld þen be turned vntoo*
so þat I shiuld do mọr in þis, þen now węr meet to doo
þe skọp of miuzik is so larʒ, it towchet[h] evri thing
whear number iz, or meaziur iz, or ani agreing
al sorts of mirth, eevn hee (I sai) þat doktor meriman[1] *hiht*
A great number of diseazes doot[h] chąs and put to fliht
not only from þe ⌐sik bodẏ afflikted dyverz waiz,⌐
but also from þe pensif thouhts þat fowl dispair assaiz
and also þei being banished hee keeps þem from [hens] still
whęr þei harberd, whęr if þ'abọd, lẏk taints þei wọld þem sp⟨ill⟩
Lo heer, how mirth, which miuzik iz, how much it doth avail⟨l⟩
to man, hiz helth, and stai þerof þat it shal nowai quaill

---

[a] Dittography.

---

[1] i.e. Merryman or mirth, a proverbial expression. See Tilley D 427: 'The best DOCTORS (physicians) are Dr. Diet, Dr. Quiet, and Dr. Merryman.'

miuzik I sai it iz for why mirth of it self kan bee
in no plas if agreement bee not þar and ẙwnitee
al which togiþer by akkord, to konkord do enklẙn
and konkord of miuzik iz grownd, þus do I it defẙn
so þat whẹr mirth iz þar konkord doth bear þe cheefest sway
and whẹr konkord iz þar miuzik doth rewll þer iz no nay
wherfọr al stạts of all degreez bi miuzik do appear
to hạv þeir siur and agre'ing stạt devoid from strẙf and fear
lẙkwẙz free stạts, Kingdoms, Empẙrz, and Monarkiez mihty
do stand and florish no lenger þen miuzik þei stand by
but heer sum kiuriowz miuzisian perchauns wọld to mee say
þat diskord in miuzik mai bee tạken in so good way
az to þe hearerz t'will agree, and so þeir fansiez sitt
whẹr diskord too all þọz estạts wold pleaz þem nẹr A whitt
to which I sai it hath bin seen diskord so to bee ywzd
þat it hath brouht þem to akkord who konkord hạv refiuzd
Konsider now of þis heer said, and kawzes þow shalt see
for which miuzik shiuld still be had, and ẹk esteemd to bee
þouh sum arch doltz, nai rạþer beasts, do raill and rạv þerat
who bee much wurs þen hạrbrain fools, þat speak þei know not what
sum of which sots kontemptiowzly will flowt and also skorn
þe better by þe bạser nạm, which þei long tẙm hạv born
þẹrz nọn þat do kondempn miuzik, or do þe sạm envy
but such who do deliht to drudӡ, in trạdz þat be filthy
or els it mai be said of þem, þat eiþer þei so bee

Puft vp with dẙvlish enviowzne⟨s⟩, az mani be wee see,
þat þei kannot lẙk ani ọn, in whom such vertiwz rain
wherin þei hạv no skill at all, nor will for þem tạk pain
to bee esteemed for þe sạm az þei wold bee set vp
or els þei of dizdainfulnes, hạv swilled such A sup
az þei kannot abẙd ani who'exsell in perfektnes
in A vertew mọr to be'esteemd, þen þat which þei profes
to bee preferred mọr þen þei, and befọr þem tạk plạs
þẹz bee þe pangs of such frantiks, þat swelt in such A kạs
and if with nọn of þẹz vẙses affọrsaid þei bee towcht
yet mai þe spreet of mallis great within þem bee so kowcht

þat for þ'offens doon by sum on, which miuzik doth lyv[a] by
against þeir mỹndz, þei fret and fium, and kontiumeliusly
not only taunt against þe si'ens lỹk Bedlemz in mad mood[1]
but also' against her professorz þei rail az þei wẹr wood
all which, þei bee both ingnorant and void of such learning
þe which to evri ӡentil s⟨p⟩reet doth ӡoi and kumfort bring
and if not so, tiz but in sorts az warrant dạr mạk I
whẹrwith þeir need kompelleth þem to ywz and too lỹv bi
but if þei bee with learning fild, and do not lỹv þerby
peradventiur yet þe proverb I mai to þem apply
þe which oþerz, for oþer kawz, to oþerz now and þen
appli, which saith, þe greatest klarks bee not þe wỹzest men[2]
þe grạv and aunsi'ent learned men þei honowrd miuzik so
þat þei did graunt þeir free grạses, to such az sewd þem to
for to kommens and tạk degrees in þeir skools az grạdiuạts
þez not dizdaind þem to aksept and ywz þem az þeir mạts
of which sort of miuzisians wẹr of lạt yeerz and daiez sum
Both Doktorz and Bachelarz[b] ẹk þouh great wẹr not þe sum
sith þat I hạv heer towcht degreez of þọz who do profes
miuzik, I wil also rehers so ni az I kan gẹs
þe dỹverz sorts of þọz who do, it loov for þeir avail
az for delỹht or els for gain in which þei wold prevail
First of which sorts of miuzisi'ans, þẹr bee vnkommensed
mani, whọz fạms throhowt owr realm of sum be revrensed
I mean nọn els but such who hạv, set foorth sum works worþỹ
for which þe skilfull in þat ạrt, þat nạm to þem apply
Next þem skoolmạsterz also bee þe si'ens who do it teach
az singing, deskant, and kompọz such songs az hạv A reach

75[r]   Of pạrts for voises seuerall, konӡioned all in ọn
with such konsent, and har⟨m⟩onni az fạwt þerin iz nọn
skoolmasterz also þẹr be such, t'⟨i⟩nstrukt who vndertạk
to sownd on miuzik instriuments, such miuzik az þei mạk
in Chiurch þe Organist hath plạs, next hath þe singing man

---

[a] written above 'set'.   [b] Written above 'bachelarz and doktorz'.

---

[1] Proverbial; Tilley B 199.   [2] Proverbial; Tilley C 409.

þe qui'erister az piune hee must kreep vp az hee kan
Owt of þe Chiurch dẏverz estạts, hạv for privạt pleziur
such of þeir own, az kan both sownd and also sing full siur
þẹs differ not from þọz fọr towcht, and ar to bee termed
az þ'oþer bee in þ'exersẏz þat þei hạv professed.
Heer kumth to mynd þọz kounterfets, who lẏk to Esops krow
do dek þem with oþerz feþerz, and þerwith mạk great show
az þouh þei sung, or plaid, or tawht, nọn but þeir own miuzik
whẹr az in deed þei kan mạk nọn, þouh þei at þis wil kik
twẹr good þat nọn shiuld bee sufferd in publik or pryvạt
to teach to pley on instriuments, on which mai bee þ⟨e⟩ rạt
of mọr þen ọn part of miuzik at ọn instant sounded
eksept þat first[a] þei hạv kompọzd twoo songs þat bee grounded
on miuziks lọr, in such good fowrm and in suc⟨h⟩ desent wẏz
az good allowans of þe sạm miht wurþely arẏz
from þe masterz þat of þat siens awtorized shiuld bee
t'alow of such who seek bi þat, to kum to such degree
and ech of which twoo songs shiuld bee[b] of semibreefs þe sum
of ọn hundreth and not vnder, what overplus did kum
þe ọn of three parts on plainsong, þ'oþer az þei fansy
but of fẏv parts, þis last shiuld bee þeir kunnings for to try
þe which kunning till þei had shewd nọn shiuld admitted bee
but for vsherz, and by lẏsens, of masterz in degree.
Also owt of þe chiurch þer bee þat miuzik do lẏv by[c]
who with þeir instruments þerof all kuntreiz far and ny
sitti, and town, villạʒ, and hows þei vizit evri plạs
to Fairz, markats, and konvensions of peopull hy and bạs
to see who þạr will hear þem plai, or sownd, and sing þerto
þẹz of lạt daiz wẹr minstrels ⌐kald,¬ þouh now þei would sai no
þọz maʒestrạts and ʒiustizes who grawnts þeim lẏsenses
by þe nạm of miuzisians now kuntriez both mọr and les
to go abowt þei do not well by þat nạm þem to kall
az þouh of miuzik þei wẹr cheef whẹr þei be meanst of all

---

[a] Written above 'befọr'.　　[b] Written above 'hav'.　　[c] This line
deleted, after a false start, eighteen lines above.

þei shiuld þem nạm az þe statiut doth term þem evrichọn
which iz by þe nạm of minstrels, and let þ'oþer alọn

75ᵛ *I sai not þus in þe kont⟨e⟩mpt, of a⟨n⟩i sort heer said*
but for order which shiuld be had az reazon hath thing⟨s⟩ waid
for miuzik iz ọn of þe sẹvn, nạmd s⟨i⟩'enses liberall
and þerfọr shiuld hạv no misyws, az thing þat wẹr ⌐in⌐ thrall
I wold not hạv yow now to think þat ani maner way
in ⟨þ⟩is fọrsaid I mean to towch, þọz who do learn to play
on instriuments, or els to sing, or songs for to kompọz
for miuziks loov þat it in þem, shiuld wurk and so dizpọz
þe good effekts þat it wurketh,ᵃ and not for oþer gain
az þạrby to gaþer riches, and for þat tạk such pain
þez do I honour in mi hart, mọr þen I do þe rest
az þoz who with good natiur bee enricht aboov þe best
for who miuzik doo loov in deed, to vertiuz beᵇ enklӳnd
plẹzant of mood, grasi'owz also, and not of kriwell mӳnd
what ma⟨y⟩ be mọr of miuzik said, let oþerz it kommend
for I, with þis þat foloith will, konkliud and mạk an end

Đe konkliuzion.

Đe miuzik tiuns of vois or sownd
doth help þe earz and doth expell
all sorows þat þe hart doth wownd
also þe wits it cherishth well
it sowpleth sinewz of ech wiht
and ẹk þe faint it filz with miht.

To þis fọrsaid konkliuzion and sonet I mạd A nọt or song of fӳv parts þe which I did print with þe oþer songs of fӳv parts befọr spoken of.

when all þez fọrsaid sirkumstanses wẹr þus finished abowt þe printing of my miuzik, þẹr waz A mosion mạd vnto mee to serv Doktor parker of lạt Archbyshop of *Cantorbery*,[1] and þat

---

ᵃ Alternative reading 'doth wurk'.   ᵇ Written above 'ar'.

---

[1] The date of Whythorne's appointment as Master of the Archbishop's Chapel is unrecorded, but it was probably shortly after the publication of his 1571 *Songes*. John Day, who had printed Parker's *Whole Psalter* in 1567, may

I shiuld be þe master of þe miuzik of hiz chappell. þe ⌐which¬
servis I refiuzed not bekawz I did know þat by hiz pląs hee waz
þe most honorabl man in þis realm next vnto þe Queen. and
when I waz with him, hee willed mee to mąk A nǫt and song
of fowr pąrts to A pees or staff of þe .107. salm (þe which hee
had transląted and turned into English vers) for to ⌐be¬ sung in
hiz chappell, þe which I did perform. And when þat waz doon,
þen kąm to my mŷnd, of þe ⌐meditasion mąd vpon þe¬ *Lordz
praier* (*or, pater noster*) þe which az ⌐I¬ told yow befǫr¹ in A plas
when az I did ly in A ʒentilmans hows to teach hiz childern ⌐I
did mąk.¬ wheraz þe sąm praier waz mąd but in prǫz, I did mean
⌐now¬ to turn þe sąm into English vers, but er I ⌐do¬ wrŷt þat
which iz in vers I ⌐will¬ wrŷt þat which iz in prǫz, and þen þe
oþer folloingly. þat which iz in prǫz beginneth þus—

O owr eternall, and everlyving Go⟨d al⟩þouh ow⟨r⟩ wikkednes 76ʳ
and sin befǫr owr ei⟨es d⟩oth so akkiuz vs ⟨þ⟩at wee must needz
say. Faþer wee hą⟨v⟩ offended þee, and ar not wurþy to [bee]
kalled þi childern, yet wee do b⟨eleev⟩ þow art þat most mersy-
full Lord, whǫz property iz alwayz to h⟨ąv⟩ mersy, and woldest
not þe death of A sinner, but þat hee s⟨hiu⟩ld ⟨repent⟩ and bee
konverted. and also woldest þat wee shiuld not b⟨e slow⟩ to run
vnto þe trǫn of þi heavnly grąs for mersy. þow hast ⟨told⟩ vs by
þi dear soon owr saviowr Jezus Chrŷst to kall þee faþ⟨er and⟩
kall on þee az A Faþer, and to hǫp and assiur owr selvz in þ⟨ee
az⟩ þe chŷld doth in hiz faþer. and alþouh *Đowᵃ art in Heavn*
yet ⟨þow⟩ seest and regardest þe simplest kr⟨e⟩atiur vpon þe
earth ⟨so⟩ þat ǫn hear of þe hed of him who feareth and loveth
þee sha⟨lnot⟩ perish. þi devŷn powr stretcheth throuhowt þe
heavns. by ⟨þee all⟩ things ar mąd, and withowt þee nothing
waz, nor iz m⟨ą⟩d. fo⟨r all⟩ þe world by þee waz mąd and iz

ᵃ MS. reads 'Dow'.

---

well have been the intermediary. The only record of Whythorne's connexion
with Parker is the name of 'Mr. Whithorne' among the Archbishop's pall-
bearers at his funeral, 6 June 1575 (John Strype, *Life and Acts of Matthew
Parker*, 1821, ii. 432–4). The psalms and other music that Whythorne set for
Parker are not known to be extant. ¹ See p. 104.

governed by þee, yee, þow ⟨best⟩ knowest þe thouhts of all
lyving kreatiurz, and it iz not possib⟨ull⟩ for any thing to stand
nor remain withowt þee. Daiz, moneths yeerz, liht, and darknes,
be not only ⟨m⟩ạd by þee, but þei be⟨e⟩ also konservid by þee.
and for asmuch az þow art þat omnipotent *Jehova*, and God
almihtye. *Halloed be þi n⟨ạm,⟩* þi nạm be mangnifi⟨ed,⟩ praized,
and extolled for ever. vnto þi nạm be all honour & glo⟨ry.⟩ all þe
kreạtiurz vpon þe earth owht to glorify þi nạm, not o⟨nly⟩
bekawz þow art þeir kreator, but also bekawz þow art alway
⟨be⟩nefisiall vnto þeim, yee, eevn þọz who do know no God
at all. graunt þerfor þat þi gloriouz, and holy nạm may bee
known throuhowt all þe họl world, to all þọz ⟨p⟩eopull who
know þee not. and þat it bee of all infydels, or vnbeleeving mis-
kreants, love⟨d⟩ and mangnified alwaiz, aswell az ⌈it⌉ iz emong
þi kristian flok. graunt also þat *Ðiᵃ kingdom mai kum*, þat þi
kingdom of grạs m⟨ay⟩ kum vnto vs in þis world, and þat wee
may finally kum to þi e⟨ter⟩nall kingdom in Heavn, evermọr
to bee with þee, and partisip⟨ator⟩ orᵇ partaker of þi everlasting
glory, and heavnly inheritans w⟨ith⟩ þi only begotten soon Ʒezus
krÿst, and to bee in þe number of þ⟨ọz⟩ to whom hee shall or will
say at *Dọmz* day, and þe last day of Ʒiuʒment, *kum yee þe blessed
of my Faþer, do yee posses þe kingdom prepared for yow befọr þe
beginning of þe world.* & wee dezÿr also þat þis kingdom ons in
vs begun, may bee dayly enkreased, and go forward mọr and
mọr, so þat all subtill and sekret hạt or slewth, which wee hạv
vnto goodnes bee not suffred to rewll ⌈so⌉ in vs þat it shall kawz
vs to look bak again and fall into sin but þat w⟨ee⟩ may hạv
A stabull purpọz and strength, not only to begin þe lÿf ⟨of⟩
inosensy, but also ⟨to⟩ proseed ⟨stedfa⟩stly foorth in it, and þat
wee may walk wurþely, pleazing þee in all þe frewts of A lÿvly,
wu⟨r⟩king and frewtfull faith, growing and inkreasing dayly in
þe trew knowleʒ of þee, and ⌈of⌉ þi blessed will.

76ᵛ

And for azmuch az owr, redeemer and media⟨tor,⟩ Ʒezus
krÿst, referred hiz will vnto þi will what tÿm he praid ⟨vnto⟩ þee

---

ᵃ MS. reads 'Ði'.   ᵇ Written above 'and'.

þat þe kup of hiz passion miht pas away from him, much ⟨m⟩or owht wee mizerabull sinnerz to say to þee at altymz, azwell in adversite az in prosperite. *Ðy will* (and not owrz) *bee doon in earth az it iz in Heavn*. for þow how soever it seem vnto owr weak & kor⟨r⟩upt ʒiuʒments dost know what iz most meet for vs þen wee owr selvs do. þerfor, lyk az þi holy Angels, and Saints in *Heavn*, do ⟨n⟩ever seas, ne shall seas, to fulfill þi holy will and pleaziur in ⟨al⟩things, and þat most redily, gladly, and withowt any maner of grudʒ⟨i⟩ng, or rezisting þervnto, knowing sertainly and siurly þat þi will iz alwaiz þe best, graunt evn so þat wee þi childern (by adopsion[a] and gras) heer on earth, may kontinewally by owr good lyf, honour, praiz, and glorify þee, and so mortify owr own natiurall, korrupt, and sinfull appetyts and wils from tym to tym, þat wee mai be ever ready lyk loving and obedient childern, humbly, lowly, and obediently, [to] approov, allow, and akkomplish þi will in all things, and to submitt owr selvs w⟨ith⟩ all owr harts vnto þe sam akknowleʒing þat whatsoever iz þi will, þe sam iz þe best and most expedient and needfull. And az althings lyving do wait and look for at þi hand, þat þow shiuldest[b] gyv þem not only meat in dew tym, but also all oþer nesessariez for þe sustentasion of þem in þis owr transitory lyf.

and when þow dost gyv vnto þem, þei shall gaþer, and when þow dost open þi hand þei shalbe filled with all goodnes, so wee dezier þee to *Gyv vs þis dai owr daily bread*. not only of materiall bread, not only of þe bread with þe which wee do sustain owr korporall lyf. not only of worldly needfull things suffisient so long az wee shall lyv heer vpon þe earth, but first and prinsipally heavnly bread, with þe which wee may sustain owr eternall lyf. þat lyvly bread which kam from Heavn to bee broken for owr redempsion. to eat þat delykat bread with þe which owr saviowr and redeemer did at hiz tabull feed hiz Apostels. gyv vs þis bread loving faþer, þat wee may hav it heer in þis lyf for þy gras, and in þe lyf to kum for glory. let vs hav it withowt tarrieng or withowt any delay, bekawz þat kontinewally

---

[a] MS. reads 'aþopsion'.   [b] In the margin opposite this line Whythorne wrote a Bible reference, apparently ⟨S⟩al. ⟨10⟩4.

wee hav need of þis bread, withowt þe which owr sins be deadly, owr sowlz famish and dy for hunger, þer is no hop at all to bee looked for, and faith loozeth hiz hold and handfastnes. so þat þe sekond death stryketh vs, damnasion thrusteth vs down hedlong, and Hell with hiz botomles pitt gapeth to devowr vs. from whens to return and kum again, þer iz no ransom nor **77ʳ** redempsion, but þar to abŷd still, and for evermor, wher wee shalbe ever ⟨dyin⟩g and never dead. graunt vs also þat az wee lŷv not only bi korporall food and oþer ⟨ne⟩sessariez, but cheefly by Heavnly food, and also with evri word ⟨þat⟩ pro- seedeth from þi mowth, so wee may be tawht þe vndowted & tr⟨ew⟩ woord owt of þe Testaments of þi holy will. and þat wee may hav p⟨rea⟩cherz and teacherz of þi word. in whoz harts and mowþs may be þe ⟨words⟩ of trewth, and not such az babbull foorth þe fond fansiez of þ⟨eir⟩ dreaming and heedles hedz. not such whoz talk iz for þeir own ⟨de⟩monish gain, and ambisiows aspyring. not such who be world⟨ly⟩ men plezerz, and serverz of þe tŷm, not having respekt to þe akkount þat þei must mak of þeir Bailywiks, and feeding of þeir hung⟨ry⟩ and thirsty flok. but such who in teaching and preaching of þi wo⟨rd⟩ may shew þat þei hav þee alwaiz in memory and fear, and such ⟨who⟩ in þe deklaring of þe trewth may not bash to speak þe sam befo⟨r þe⟩ peopull, even azwell to þe hiest, and greatest of þem, az to þe l⟨owest⟩ᵃ and basest¹ of þem. Ðow faþer doost rezist þe prowd, and vnto þe hu⟨m⟩bull þow gevest gras, for hiumilite iz A Sakrifŷz vnto þee. who kan say my hart iz klear and I am piur from sin? þer iz no body so goo⟨d⟩ vpon þe earth but þat hee sinneth. yee, þe rihteowz man offendeth seven tŷms A day to þee, and if þe rihteowz man so sinneth, kan wee wreches ȝiustify owr selvz in þi siht? no no, it iz wee þat owht to say, O most mersifull Faþer *Forgŷv vs owr tres- passes.* owr ⟨ma⟩nifold sins and wikkednesses, which wee from tŷm to tŷm most gr⟨e⟩vowzly hav kommitted against þy devŷn

---

ᵃ An illegible interlineation appears here.

¹ A marginal note at this point reads '*Sal./138./.Sal./.51.*', alluding to Psalms so numbered.

maȝesty. siurly, if wee wold say þat wee hav no sin wee shiuld
begẏll owr selvz, and þer iz no trewth in vs.

Alas poor mẏzerabull, and wreched kaytẏvz, exsept þow gẏv
vs þi gras wherby wee may stay owr selvz, wee ⟨do⟩ run ⌐hed
long⌐ dayly and howrly into Sathans kingdom. And seing
wee shal be forgeven owr trespasses no oþerwyz þen *As wee do
forgẏv þem þat do trespas against vs*, grawnt vs such pasiens
wee do beseech þe, þat. when any body doth to vs, or speaketh
any thing again⟨st⟩ vs, þat wee ⌐be⌐ not angry þerwith, neiþer to
offer ani violens wit⟨h⟩ owr hands, nor to revẏl, or kurs, nor
murmer, or seek revenȝ ⟨in⟩ any oþer way against owr adver-
sariez and enemiez þerfor, but þa⟨t⟩ wee may kommit þe revenȝ-
ment vnto þee, to whom it belongeth, and wee to say well of
þem, do well to þem, and to pray to þee for þem, þat þow wilt
forgẏv þem, and not impiut þeir offenses to þem, and wish þem
þe sam good, gras, and glory, þat wee wold dezier to owr selvz,
and also when need iz, to help þem az wee be bownd by kristian
charite. Ðow loving faþer, art trew and faithfull, and wilt not
suffer vs to be tempted mor þen wee may bear & overk⟨um⟩ but
þow wilt mod⟨er⟩at þe temptasion so, þat wee weak wretches **77ᵛ**
may sustain and overkum it. wee pray þe O lord *Lead vs ⌐not⌐
in to temtasion*, nor ⌐yet⌐ suffer vs to be led into temtasion,
but gẏv vs gr⟨a⟩s to withstand it, let vs not be overkum with þe
assawts of þe ⟨del⟩ites of þe wikked world. þe mosions ⌐of⌐ þe frail
flesh, and þe kon⟨k⟩iupisenses þerof. and also þe malisiowz serpent þe Dyvell. þe Dy⟨v⟩ell (I say) who, lẏk A wood, and mad
Lion raȝeth and runneth abowt, and with hiz subtill sly sleihts
ever seeketh how hee may de⟨v⟩owr vs. And if by owr fraill
natiur, wee, throuh hiz temtasion do fall into ⌐þe⌐ thraldom of þe
Divell by sin, yet wee dezier þe þat þow wilt soon deliver vs
from it, mak vs so free from it þat it mai not tak ro⟨ot⟩ in vs, and
þat it may not rein in vs ani thing at all. Also wee pray þee to
Deliuer vs from all evell, from all worldly and gostly affliksions,
trobuls, and adversitiez. also wee prai þe to deliver vs from all
such sin az shall kawz þi heavy displeaziur to grow on vs, þat
wee may bee defended not only from it, but also from all þe

kawzerz, wurkerz, and provokerz þerof, who, be Sathan and hiz Angels. þat suttl serpent þat begýled owr first parents *Adam and Eve*. þat old enemy of mankýnd. þat governour þat rewleth in þe eyr. þe spreit þat now wurketh in þe childern of vnb⟨e⟩leef, þat prins of þe world, who raineth over all þe sam (exsept þi littl poor flok) þat God of þis world which hath blýnded þe mýndz of þem which beleev not, least þe liht of þe Gospell of þe glory of Chrýst (which iz þi ima3) shiuld shýn vnto þem. Deliver vs O owr protektor from þat owr kankard enemy, & from all hiz powr and tiranny, for hee iz þe spring and prodiuser of all iniquite, and iz not only him self an homisyd or manqueller and also A lier, and A hater of þe trewth from þe beginning, but also iz þe very root, and okkazion of all mischef and sin, and also A hinderer of all vertew and goodnes. it iz hee who by hiz mallis and subteltiez, seeketh kontinewall to entýs and draw vs to sin. wherby wee miht finalli be browht vnto perpetiuall damnasion. þe which he wold siurly bring to pas if þow wilt not set to þi helping hand, to let him of purpoz and intent, for þer iz no hiuman and worldly powr vpon þe earth, þat iz to bee kompared to hiz. And how much iz owr own wizdoms to prevaill against hiz wit? in az much az hee iz þe full of vnderstanding emong earthly vnderstanding[1] kreatiurs, and so bee hiz Angels and ministerz (þe childern of darknes) wýzer in þeir 3enerasion, þen þe childern of liht, and lastly how much iz þeir mallis, and hat against vs who (I say again) do seek nothing somuch to be **78ʳ** browht to pas az þei do owr dampnasion. þat for, wee having well kon⟨side⟩red and ima3ined ⟨all⟩ þez afforsaid eevls and temp- tasions, and of þis terribull beast a⟨nd⟩ hiz adherents, þat wold so violently rap and pull vs with þem in⟨to⟩ eternall fier. and also knowing þe debilite and weaknes of ⟨owr⟩ selvs, þe which (withowt þi assistans and ayd) by no means kan ⟨re-⟩zist neiþer him nor hiz. eevn az childern fearing þe menases ⟨an⟩d thr⟨eat-⟩ nings of any body, for þat þei do not trust in þeir own strength & pow⟨r⟩ to defend þem selvs, do run for help and aid vnto þeir

---

[1] A marginal note at this point reads '*16*. ⟨*L*⟩*uk*.'

parents, ⟨lẏk⟩wẏz do wee by þis owr praier run vnto þee O
Heavnly fa⟨þer,⟩ krieng, O lord *Delyuer vs from all eevl*, from
⟨all⟩ owr enemiez, from all þoz forsaid eevls, and from all oþer
eevls what soever þei bee, O þow, owr defens, owr refiuӡ owr
to⟨wer⟩ of strength,[1] and owr kastell, owr Horn of helth and
salvasion. ⟨To⟩ þe end þat wee from þem being delyvered
and eskaped (w⟨it⟩h þ⟨e⟩ assistans of þẏ good gras) mai serv þee
in holines and rihteow⟨znes⟩ in þi siht all þe daiz of owr lyfe.
Ðis wee do know ⌜assiuredli⌝ þat þow kan⟨st⟩ doo, for þow art
þe lord over all, and heavn and earth ar full of þe maӡesty of þy
glory. þow art þe faþer of an infinit maӡesty. þow art omnipotent, almihty and all in all, so þat *Ðẏn iz þe kyngdom þe powr
and glory for ever and ever*. And az þow art so, and althing iz
þẏn, so wee do know sertainly, þat þow w⟨ilt⟩ grawnt þe petisions
and praierz of þe faithfull, espesially when þei be dezẏred and
mad in þi Soons nam. wherfor mersifull Faþer, wee beseech
þe to grawnt v⟨s⟩ þez owr[a] petisions and praierz þat wee hav
now mad vnto þee for þe loo⟨v⟩ of þi only soon owr only saviowr
Ӡezus krẏst, to whom, with þee, and þe holy Gost, be all honowr
And glory world withowt end. Sobeit ⟨.⟩

After þat I had mad and written owt þe meditasion afforsaid,
I ma⟨d⟩ and turned þe sam into English meeter in such sort az
folloith—

*Ðow þat entendst to God to pray, þis lesson learn of mee[2]
þat þow be not A gaz in Chiurch, nor street for folks to see
but sekretly with humbled hart, if if[b] with knee down bowd
put foorth þi Vois, and babbul not, with wordz þat bee to lowd*

*And if þow hav not ready pend, þat which þow doost dezi'er
but willingly þow woldst say þat wherin þow mihtst requi'er
althings needfull, þen kryst hath tawht, vs all how wee shiuld pray
on which þis folo'ing iz devẏzd þe which þow maist þus say.*

---

[a] MS. reads 'owt'.   [b] Dittography.

[1] A marginal note at this point reads '*2. Sam .22.*'
[2] Opposite the first line is a marginal note: '*Math. cap.6.*' Below, in a box
in the margin, Whythorne wrote: '*Ðe first staf of þis meditasion, hath a not
of .5. parts*'.

O þow'eternall, everlyving, þe God onli'almihty
alþouh owr sin, and wikkednes, iz still befọr owr ey,

78ᵛ And doth enfo⟨rs v⟩s evermọr vnto þee for to say
Faþer wee hạv offended þee, alwaiz both niht and day.

And not wurþi, for þi childern, to bee ons so nạmed
⟨n⟩or to reseiv any good grạs, þat may stand vs in sted
yet wee do know þat þow alwaiz, art þe lord mersifull
and woldest not þe death of þọz, whọz sins be rÿp and full

Neiþer woldst þow þat wee shiuld fear þe Trọn to run vnto
of þi free grạs for mersy which altÿms we'hạv need to do
for wee be tawht bi þi deer soon owr savi'or krÿst ʒezus
alwaiz to kall þee owr Faþer for all þat needeth vs.

And þouh in He'avn þow art alwaiz, þow hast to vs regard
þi powr devÿn throuh He'avns do pears althings on earth t'award
by þee [þis] world iz gouerned of all þow knowst þe thowht
Daiz, weeks, months, yeerz, lyht and darknes, and althings els
þow'ast wrouht

And se'ing þat þow art only hee þe'almihti ʒe'hovah hy
vnto þÿ nạm be all honour, praiz, lawd, and all glory
all þe kre'atiurz þa⟨t⟩ be on e'arth shiuld glorifi þi nạm
bekawz þow'art þeir only kre'ator, and keepst þem all in frạm,

Graunt þerfọr lọrd þi holi nạm throuhowt þe world may bee
of all miskr⌐e⌐ants, and infidelz, known, az belongth to þee
in all such sort, az þat þe sạm, to trew kristi'ans iz known
emong all such, az þÿ piur word, hath bin preached & sown.

Graunt also lọrd, þat þi kingdom of grạs may kum vs to
and fÿnalli to þi'eternall kingdom wee mai kum to
to bee with þee, and partaker, of þe'everlasting blis
with þÿ soon krÿst, and to be'of þọz, when þe ʒiudʒment day is

To whom hee will sai kum all yee, of my Faþer blessed,
do yee posses, and ẹk enʒoy, þe kingdom prepared
er beginning of world waz mạd, þe sạm do yee posses
to yowr great ʒoi, and kumfort lÿk, with all trew happ[i]nes

And wee dezier þat þis kingdom, ons in vs þat's begun
may daily bee enkreased so. az wee þe sạm had wun
so þat all sekrẹt hạt or slewth, which wee hạv to goodnes
be not sufferd in vs to rewll, but þow þe sạm repres.

And þat A stabull purpọzd strength, þat wee m⟨a⟩y hạv wherby **79ʳ**
not only to begin þe lỹf, of trew innosensy
but þat also wee may proseed foorth in þat ernestly
þee pleazing in A faith þat iz frewtfull & ẹk lỹvly

And for asmuch az owr Saviowr to þi will referd his
what tỹm hee praid þe bitter kup of hiz passi'on to mis
much mọr owht wee to sai and prai in owr adversity
what so befall vnto vs all, be'it far of or be'it ny

Ði will bee doon (and not owrz lord) in all þe world below
az þe sạm iz, in Heavn aboov, which all þỹn þạr do show
for all þe'Anʒels and Saints in Heavn do nẹver seas ne shall
þe Heavnly will for to fulfill az þọz who bee þi thrall

And az þei do mọst willingly withowt anỹ grudʒing
fulfill þi will in evri thing withowt ons rezisting
graunt vs þi grạs to do þe lỹk O Heavnly fạþer deer
az owr dewtiez in evri thing to þee þei may appeer

Althings do wait and trust in þee to gỹv þem what þei need
and if þow do restrain þi gifts great want shalbee þeir meed
for when þow gỹvst, þei shall gaþer, and when þow op'st þi hand
þei shalbee fild with all goodnes eevn throwhowt all þe land

So wee dezi'er þee to gỹv vs þis day owr dayly bred
not only þat materi'all bred wherwith owr bodiez be fed
nor only'of goods þat bee wor[l]dly solong az wee lỹv heer
wherby wee fill and dek owr selvz þat stowt wee mai appeer

But first and cheefly Heavnly bred with which wee do sustain
eternall lỹf þe which with vs wee mai still hạv remain
þat lỹvly bred þat kạm from Heavn for vs to bee broken
and for to pay owr ransom þat keeps vs from Sạthans den

To eat þat bred which owr savior did at hiz tabull break
to'hiz apostels when hee to þem hiz passi'on did forspeak
gýv vs þis bred loving faþer in þis frail lýf[a] for grąs
and in þe lýf to kum for glory' in þi hy Heavnly pląs

If wee want þis owr sowls famish for no hǫp do wee look
Faith loozeth hold, sekond death strýkth damnasion with hiz hook

79ᵛ puls into Hell, and Hell with hiz botomles pitt tąkth vs
from whens to kum þer iz no hǫp but lýv in plas grevovs

No ransom þen will vs prevail but þar to'abýd wee must
tým withowt end, þis siur it iz for þǫz þat bee vnʒiust
whęr wee shalbee for euer ⌐mǫr,⌐ kontinew'ally A di'ing
and yet alþowh wee fayn wold dy yet shal wee bee living

Again of bred graunt vs also, þat az wee do not lýv
bý korp'ral food, & oþer things needful which þow dost gýv
but cheefly by þý Heavnly food, and with þe word also
þat doth proseed from þýn own mowth wherby þi will to kno[b]

So wee may bi þe Testaments of þi most holly will
effek⟨t⟩iu'ally, & trewly tawht þi will for to fulfill
and þat wee mai hąv preachers trew[c] þi Gospell for to preach
in all whǫz harts & mowpz þi sprýt may be þi trewth to teach

Not bablerz foorth of fond fansiez, nor hedz þat bee dreaming
not such whǫz talk iz for þeir gain, and ambisi'owz ryzing
nor such worldlings & men pleazerz, and serverz of þe tým
þat hąv respekt to nothing mǫr þen how þat þei may klým

Not kąring for þat great akkownt which þei to þee must mąk
for feeding of þeir hungry flok which þei did vndertąk
but such preacherz az do þee fear only and oþerz nǫn
teaching þi trewth withowt all fear of worldlings everichǫn

Thow Fąþer doth rezist þe prowd, to þe'humbul þow gývst grąs
hiumilite for sakrýfýz with þee hath alwai pląs
who' iz hee kan sai my hart iz klear? and I from sin am piur
þer iz not ǫn so good on earth from þat kan him assiur

---

[a] MS. reads 'lyk'.   [b] MS. reads 'kro'.   [c] Written above 'piur'.

Đe ʒiust man sinth sęvn tẏms A day, wheron þi wrath dependth
and if rihte'owz do so sin, and þee so oft offendth
kan wee poor wreches ʒiustify owr ⌐own⌐ selvs in þi siht
no, no, wee all to þee must say, not ǫn, but evri wiht

O þow owr God, full of mersẏ forgẏv'vs owr trespasses
owr manifold sins and mizdeedz, and all owr wikkednes
which wee at tẏms mǫst greevowzly by mani waiz sundry   80ʳ
kontrary to þi holy will, and devẏn maʒesty

If ⟨w⟩ee wold say wee hạv no sin owr selvz wee shiuld dẹseiv
and az for trewth, þat, from owr selvz, wee shiuld siurly bereiv
alas poor kaytẏvz,ᵃ wreches all, exsept þow gẏv vs grạs
dayly' and howrly Sathan wold pul vs to hiz grạsles plạs

And se'ing þat all wee must forgẏv, þǫz þat do' vs much offend
befǫr þẏn anger for owr fawts, to vs shal hạv an end
gẏv vs pasi'ens wee þee beseech when ani'il wordz do saẏ
or deedz do doo, þat wee be not with anger ani waẏ

So overkum þat wee to kurs, or murmor at þeir deedz
or seek revenʒ against owr fǫz to pay þem for þeir meedz
but to kommitt þe revenʒment to whom it doth belong
þat onli'iz still to þẏn own self for to remoov owr wrong

And wee to say, and do þem good, þat hạv doon vs trespas
and pray to þee þat þow þeir fawts will spạr and over pas
wisshing to þem, þe sạm þi grạs, and also þi glory
wee wish to'owr selvz, az wee be bownd, bi kristi'an charity

Đow art faþer, faithfull and trew, and loov'st þi childern dear
and wilt not lead in temptasion, such who in loov þee fear
nor suffer þem to bee tempted mǫr þen þat þei bear may
but moderạt þe temptasi'on þat it mai pas away

Wherfǫr wee prai þee lead vs not into temptasion mǫr
þen wee mai bear, nor suffer not, þẏn to bee so forlǫr
but gẏv vs powr to withstand it, and not be overkum
with all þ'assawts of all owr fǫz, þowh great be not þe sum

ᵃ MS. reads 'kayvẏvz'.

Az þe vain world, and all hiz showz, az plęzant az A flowr
þe weak and frailtiez of þe flesh þat tempth vs evri howr
and þe malisiowz drągon fell, þe Dẏvll (I sai) eevn hee
who with hiz sleihts and ʒingling triks, entẏs vs hiz to bee

But if þat wee by frail natiur, throuh þęs temptasi'ons fall,
yet wee dezier þat þow wilt soon defend vs from þem all
þat þei mai not tąk root in vs but mąk vs free and kleer
and þat þei may not rain in vs whẏl þat wee do lẏv heer

80ᵛ

Also wee prai & þee dezier to be delẏvered
from all such eevls and from such kąrz wherby wee bee kumbred
from all affliksions boþ gǫstly, and worldly þat do breed
A desprat mẏnd þat lǫþz to lẏv how so þat wee do speed

Also wee prai þee to keep vs, from all such deadly sin
az shall kawz vs for to enkur, & þi displeaziur win
defend vs lǫrd, from þe kawzerz, and all þe provǫkerz
who az iz said bend þeir studiez, owr riu'in to bee workerz

Who iz Sąthan (and hiz Anʒels) þat subtil serpent vẏl
þat did entẏs owr first pąrents, and þem did both begẏl
he'iz þat prowd spreit þat rewls ⌐al⌐ þe'eir, and prins ⌐on earthlẏ
* mold⌐ᵃ*
exsept over þi littl flok, by whom he'iz oft kontrold

He'iz God on earth which hath blẏnded þeir myndz þat do rezist
lest þat þe lẏht of þe Gospell of þe glory of krẏst
(which iz þi'imaʒ) shiuld shẏn to þem, and so þei saved bee
and it A greef iz stil to him, þat [þei] shiuld kum to þee

Đęrf⟨ǫ⟩r wee kno'ing owr own weaknes (withowt þi helping
* hands[)]*
by no means kan hiz rąʒ rezist, nor keep vs from hiz bands
eevn az childern fe'aring þeir fǫz, not trusting þer own miht
run to þeir faþerzᵇ for þeir aid, þeir kawzes for to riht

ᵃ Written above 'in all þe world'.   ᵇ Written above 'parents'.

Lýkwyz do wee by þis owr pra'ier, O faþer run to þee
kri'eng O delyver vs from all owr enemiez þat bee
and from all eevls, whatso'ever þei [bee], O owr refiuʒ and towr
owr strength, owr Horn, and owr kastell, þat sąvth vs evry howr

Ðat wee be'ing þus delyvered, and with þe'aid of þi grąs
mai serv þe'in rihte'owznes of lýf till wee kum to þi pląs
þe ʒoiz wherin, kannot be told, þei do surmount owr wits
þowh sum þe sąm hąv roved at, and dre'amd þeron bi fits

Al þis wee know assiuredly, þat þow þe sąm kanst do
for þow'art þe great lord over all, and no God els iz so
for Hea'vn and earth ar full of þe maʒesti'of þý glory
Omnipotent, yee all in all, and lord God almihty

Ðýn iz þe kýngdom and þe powr, glory for ever and ay   81ʳ
þe which all þýn will never seas both for to think and say
and az þow'art so az wee hąv said, and þat althing iz þýn
so wee know sertainly þat þow wilt graunt þoz þat bee þýn

Espesially when þei bee krąv'd in þe nąm of þi Son,
wherfor mersifull faþer now graunt þis owr petisi'on
for þe loov of þi only soon krýst ʒezus owr savi'owr
to whom, with þee, and þ'hǫly Gǫst, be'al glori ever mǫr.

When I had ended and finished þis *Meditasion* affǫrsaid, I
vnderstan⟨ding⟩ that my fǫrsaid lord and master had A good
lyking to þe miuzik þat I m⟨ąd⟩ vnto hiz salm affǫrsaid, I mąd
⌈þen⌉ an oþer salm of fowr parts. at þe f⟨irst⟩ I mąd it ⌈to⌉ A
salm of ⌈hiz⌉, but afterward I turned þat salm after my⟨n own⟩
devýs in Such sort az folloeth—

Psalm. lxxxvj.

Bow down þýn ear, O lord hear mee[1]
for I am poor and in mizery
prezerv hiz sowll þat trusth in þee
for I will kall on þee dayly
komfort þe sowll of þi servaunt
O lord mi God þis hest mee graunt

---

[1] In a marginal box Whythorne wrote: '*Ðis hath A nǫt of 4. parts.*'

Heer kumz to my mẏnd, A sentens, in Italien þe which I
devẏzed when I waz in Italy, þe okkazion wherof being, þat
whẏl I waz þạr, and tasting sumtẏms þe overthwarts of inkonstant fortewn, I wold wish for better hap. and having red at þat
tẏm in an Italien book[1] þis sentens of *Aristotels þus foloing.
Felicita è fine di tutte le cose da esser desiate. Alcuni hanno detto
la feli[ci]ta esser prosperi di fortuna, alcuni virtu. &c.* Ðe which iz
to *say* in English. Feli⟨site⟩ iz þe end of althings þat be desyred.
sum hạv said felisite to bee þe prosperite of fortiun, sum
oþerz of vertew &c. now at þis tẏm I akkownted good fortewn
to be ⌐Godz gift, and⌐ A great felisite and happines. wee wẹr
wount to say þat hee þat waz A happy man waz A fortiunạt man,
and þat happynes to be felisite, vpon þe which I devẏzed þis
sentens folloing in Italien az þus—

> *Spero per il fortunato giorno*
> *Cosi dice Thomazo Whythorno.*

81ᵛ   Ðe English wherof iz. I họp for þe fortiunạt day. Seing þat
I hạv said enowh of forti[u]n in dyverz plạses befọr in þis book, I
will now say sumwhat of họp bekawz I hạv sum kawz þerto in
þis sentens affọrsaid. St *peter*[2] in þe .1. ⌐epistell & .i.⌐ chapter of
his epistell. and St matthew.[3] *cap* .12. saith þat þe họp in God,
⟨iz⟩ krẏst. St pawll saith.[4] Rom. *cap* .5. Ðe họp iz not konfounded.
St pawll saith[5] ⟨.1. Th⟩ess .5. họp iz owr helmett. St pawll saith[6]
Effe .4. owr họp iz eternall lẏf. St pawll saith.[7] Rom .8. wee ar
saved in họp. St pawll saith.[8] Rom .12. yee owht to reȝois in họp.
St pawll saith[9] Rom. cap .8. þe họp þat man seeth iz not họp.
St ȝon, in hiz first epistell, and þe .3. chapter, wryteth[10] þus of
họp. Dearly beloved, now ar wee þe soons of God, and yet it
doth not ap⟨p⟩ear what wee shalbe, but wee know þat when
it shall appeer, wee shalbe lẏk vnto him, for wee shall see him,

---

[1] Whythorne's immediate source for this quotation has eluded the editor.
[2] 1 Pet. 1. 21.
[3] A mistaken reference. Perhaps Whythorne had in mind Rom. 12. 12.
[4] Rom. 5. 5.   [5] 1 Thess. 5. 8.   [6] Eph. 4. 5.
[7] Rom. 8. 24.   [8] Rom. 12. 12.
[9] Rom. 8. 24.   [10] 1 John 3. 2–3.

eevn az hee iz. and whosoever hath þis hǫp in him, doth piurify him self, lẏk az God iz piur. so þat whosoever hath faith, hee doth lay vp hiz hǫp to God in *Heavn* of þe per⟨form⟩ans of such things az hee iz promyzed in þe word of God. After þat I had gaþered þęz fǫrsaid sentenses and had written þem I mạd þer vpon az folloith—

> *Not only Hǫp, but Faith also*
> *withowt all dowt assiureth mee*
> *þe lasting ʒoiz to kum vnto*
> *whęr I mẏ God shall alwai see.*

Ðis fǫrsaid Italien sentens I ywzed A long tẏm to wrẏt wher I lẏked after my return into England. And when I kạm to kạmbriʒ, I shewd þe sạm vn⟨t⟩o A freend of mẏ⟨n⟩, who had good knowleʒ in þe Italien toong and lan⟨g⟩waʒ. and hee not lẏking my devẏs þerin very well, bekawz I nạmed fortewn þerin, and also being willing to amend it, hee devyzed þis folloing—

> *Vuoi tu vedere il felice giorno?*
> *Aspetta dice, Thomaz Whythorno.*

Ðe English wherof iz þus. Woldst þow see þe happy day, abẏd or tarry A whẏll saith. T. W. þis last sentens did I ever ywz afte⌈r⌉ þe devẏs þerof, az I did þe oþer befǫr, and at lenkth I mạd þeron þez sentenses in meeter az do follow—

> *Woldst þow þe happy day now see*
> *Abẏd and bear þi kros with mee*

I do mean þe happy day to bee þat, wherin it shall pleaz God to ⌈kall⌉ vs owt of þis vạl of mizery into his everlasting kingdom of heavn. And þe bearing of my kros be all þǫz krosses myzeriez, vexasions, trobulls, and kalamitiez bǫth of þe body & mẏnd, which I do suffer and shall suffer whẏll I do lẏv heer vpon þe earth. þe which be inflikted, and do happen vnto vs kontynewally—

> *Ðe happi day woldst þow see ⟨now⟩*
> *þen of trew faith sum frewts shew þow*

82ʳ

Ðe difinision of Faith iz set down by St pawll in þe .xj.th chapter of hiz episte⟨ll to⟩ þe *Hebrews*. wher hee saith.[1] Now faith iz þe grownd of things w⟨hich ar⟩ hoped for, and þe evydens of things which ar not seen. For bẏ it owr eld⟨ers wer⟩ well reported of. Throuh faith wee vnderstand þat þe world waz ⟨ordeynd⟩ by þe word of God, so þat þe things which wee see, ar not mad of t⟨hings which⟩ did appear. If ye will read mor of faith þen read in þez chapterz folloing. evry on owht to prov hiz faith. 2.*cor*.13.5. Continewans of faith. *col.* ⟨1.23.⟩ þe shield of faith. *Ephes*.6.16. *Christ praieth* for Peterz faith. *Luk*.22.3⟨2.⟩ *Faith* kummeth by hearing. *Rom*.10.17. þe ⌐a⌐postels pray to hav þeir faith i⟨ncreased⟩ *Luk*.17.5. *Faith* in *God* by krẏst .1.*peter*.⟨1.21.⟩ *Mat.* 12.21. Faith ჳoined with charite .2.*Tim*.1.5. Faith iz A gift of God. ⟨*Phil.*⟩.1.29—2. *peter*.1.3. The end of Faith iz þe salvasion of owr sowls. 1.peter.⟨1.9.⟩ þe faith of *Abraham*. Gene.15.6. and .21.7. þe faith of þe faþerz. *Heb* .11. by ⟨faith⟩ þe spreit iz reseived. Gal.3 2. By faith þe harts ar piurified. A⟨ct.15⟩.9. John.15.3. by faith wee rezist þe Devell .1.*pet*.59. Faith wi⟨thow⟩t wor⟨k⟩s iz ⟨dead.⟩ *Jam* .2.17. þe faithfull ar þe childern of *Abraham*. *Rom*.9.8. þe faithfull shall n⟨ot⟩ com into kondemnasion. John .5 24.—

woldst þow now see þe happy day
abẏd and seek þe direkt way

To seek þe direkt way vnto þe happy day, and perfekt filisite, iz þat after wee bee baptyzed or reჳenerated, and ჳiustified by krẏst, to hav þe riht, & trew kristian faith. which iz not only to beleev þat þe holy sk[r]iptiur, and a⟨ll⟩ þe artikels of owr faith ar

---

[1] Heb. 11. 1–2. This quotation was taken verbatim from the Geneva version of the Bible, the first English edition of which appeared in 1560. No previous English translation had used verse numbers, which Whythorne cites for the first time in the quotations on 'Faith' which follow. It is amusing to observe that Whythorne merely copied his brief quotations and references from the heading 'Faith' in the Seconde Table, an index at the end of the Geneva Bible: 2 Cor. 13. 5; Col. 1. 23; Eph. 6. 16; Luke 22. 32; Rom. 10. 17; Luke 17. 5; 1 Pet. 1. 21; Matt. 12. 21; 2 Tim. 1. 5; Phil. 1. 29; 2 Pet. 1. 3; 1 Pet. 1. 9; Gen. 15. 6 and 24. 7; Heb. 11; Gal. 3. 2; Acts 15. 9; John 15. 3; 1 Pet. 5. 9; James 2. 17; Rom. 9. 8; John 5. 24. Whythorne's 2 Tim. 1. 5 is an error; the 'seconde table' refers to 1 Tim. 1. 5. He also errs in giving Gen. 21. 7, which should be Gen. 24. 7.

trew, but also to hạv A siur trust and konfidens ⟨in⟩ Godz mercy-
full promyzes, promyzed in ⟨þe⟩ holy sk[r]iptiurz affọrsaid to be
save⟨d⟩ from everlasting damnasion by krẏst. herof doth follow
A l⟨oving⟩ hart to o⟨bey⟩ hiz kommaundements, and not to pa⟨s⟩
þe tẏm of þis owr prezen⟨t l⟩ẏf vnfrew⟨t⟩fully and idelly, not
kạring how few ⟨goo⟩d works wee do, to þe glory of Go⟨d⟩ and
þe profet of owr neyburz. St John,[1] in hiz first epistell, and þe
.2. chapter, saith also, þat hee, who doth keep Godz word and
kommawndement, in him iz trewly þe perfett loov of God, which
iz charite, for charite bringeth foorth good works. þe works of
mersy ⌈be,⌉ az St *Mathæw*[2] saith .25. To ⌈gyv meat to⌉ þe
hungry & ⌈to gẏv drink to þe⌉ thirstye, to harber þe strainӡer,
to cloþ þe naked, to vyzit þe sik and þe prẏzone⟨r⟩ ⌈þe works do
witnes of faith. *philem* .5. *Hebru* .6.10. *pet* .1.5.⌉[3] þe which
works of ⌈mersy⌉ do proseed of charyte oþerwẏz named loov.
loov exsell⟨eth⟩ faith and họp.[4] 1. *cor*.13.13. loov envyeth not.
1. *cor*.13.4. þey loov God þat ke⟨ep⟩ hiz kommawndements.
loov iz not provoked to anger. 1. *cor*.13.5. loov iz þe fulfilling
of þe law. *Rom* .13.8. þe loov of God in owr harts. *Rom* .5.5.
in whom þe loov of God iz perfett. 1. John .2.5. loov ọn an oþer.
John .13.34. to loov þe strainӡer az þi self. *Leuit* .19.34. to loov
þẏn enemiez *Mat*. 5. 44. hee þat loveth an oþer hath fulfilled þe
law. *Rom*.13.8. hee þat lov⟨e⟩th krẏst keepeth hiz kommaundements. John .14.15.21. God so loveth þe world þat hee hath
gevn hiz soon &c. John .3.16.—

> *Ðe happi day now see woldst þow*
> *þen ywz þat which þow first did vow.*

---

[1] 1 John 2. 3, 5.
[2] Matt. 25. 35, 36. This reference is found under 'Workes of mercie' in
the 1560 Geneva Bible.
[3] Philem. 5; Heb. 6. 10; Pet. 1. 5. These references are found under
'Workes . . . of faith' in the Seconde Table of the 1560 Geneva Bible. Whythorne's Pet.1.5 is another error; the Geneva index gives 2 Pet. 1. 5.
[4] The following references are found under 'Love' in the Seconde Table
of the 1560 Geneva Bible: 1 Cor. 13. 13; 13. 4; 1 John 2. 5 (this reference was
accidentally omitted by Whythorne); 1 Cor. 13. 5; Rom. 13. 8; Rom. 5. 5;
1 John 2. 5; John 13. 34; Lev. 19. 34; Matt. 5. 44; Rom. 13. 8; John 14. 15, 21;
John 3. 16.

Ðe which iz þat which owr godfaþerz and godmoþerz did
promyz on owr behalf when wee weʳ baptyzed. þat iz to say, þat
82ᵛ wee shiuld forsąk þe Devll, and all hiz works. þe vain pomp,
and glory of þe world, with all ⟨þ⟩e kovetowz dezierz of þe sąm,
þe karnall dezierz of þe flesh, and also ⟨to⟩ beleev all þe artikels
of Apostels Cręd.—After I had þus az afforsaid ⟨en⟩ded to wrẏt
my fansy of þǫz sentences, yet I ment to hąv ǫn mǫr on ⟨þe⟩
sąm. for wheraz I waz willed by my forsaid lord and master to
mąk ⟨a nǫt⟩ or miuzik to þe .107. salm þe which hee had mąd
into English ⟨me⟩eter az afforsaid. Now I purpozing to mąk
dittiez of mẏn own vnto ⟨a⟩ll þe mi⟨u⟩zik þat I do mean to mąk
(exsept it ⌐be⌐ Latten) I devyzed again vpon ⟨þ⟩e forsaid Italien
sentens of .*Vuoi tu vedere &c.* and of þe sąm meeter ⟨o⟩f þe salm
afforsaid, þis þat folloeth—

> *Woldst þow prezently see þe happi day?*[1]
> *abẏd þow A whẏll, and heer what I say*
> *Ðe happy dai to see, iz to bekum happẏ,*
> *An⟨d⟩ happines I do defẏn, az heer iz said breeflẏ*
> *from si'ens þe vertew great, doth kum az I do read*[2]
> *And of vertiu þe only good, lẏkwẏz it doth prosead*
> *þe only good þat iz, þe Heavnly pląs on hy,*
> *from whens þe sowll iz ȝenerąt, by powr of þ'almihty.*
>
> *which sowll after hee doth forsąk, þe pląs hee had in man*
> *from whens hee kąm, to Heavn again, hee will if þat hee kan*
> *⟨fo⟩r to behold þe Heavnly lǫrd, iz hiz felisitee*
> *for þat az cheef of ani thing, hee mǫst dezierth to see*
>
> > *woldst þow prezently, see þat happy day*
> > *abẏd A tẏm, and tąk þe riht way*
> > *which if þow woldst do, & not saill on shelf*
> > *Loov God aboov all, and man az þi self.*

Now, being entred again into A konseit and vain of making of
miuzik, I entred into A determinasion (if it shiuld pleaz God to

---

[1] In the margin within a box Whythorne wrote: '⟨Ð⟩is hath ⟨A⟩ nǫt of [ ]
⟨p⟩ąr⟨t⟩s' followed by what appears to be another word, now illegible.
[2] Opposite in the margin is the word ⟨L⟩actan⟨t⟩ius.

furder mẏn intent) not to leav of þe sạm till I had mạd forty[1]
Diuos, or songs of ij pạrts. And also, wheraz I had printed, with
my forsaid ⌐miuzik⌐ but fowrteen songs of iij parts, I now determined to mạk so many mọr to þem az shiuld mạk vp forty songs
of three parts, to awnswer to þe forty Duos affọrsaid. Also I
determyned to enkreas þe number of þe printed songs of iiij
parts, being ny abowt forty, vnto A xxvj. mọr bekawz most of
þem bee but short, and þerfọr wold not okkiupy any great room,
and I ⌐entend to⌐ mạk þem þe mọr willingly bekawz þat songs
of fowr parts be most in request. þen wheraz I mạd & printed,
but twenty songs of fẏv parts, I now entended to mạk twenty
mọr vnto þem. besẏd all þe which I entended to mạk sum songs
of six, and seven parts, whatsoever I did els. Now sir to kum to
þe end of my purpọz in þez aksions, þe dittiez þat shalbe set 83ʳ
vnt⟨o þọz f⟩ọrsaid songs shalbe ⟨all⟩ of mẏn own devẏs and
making (exsept þọz þat shalbe of Latten)⟨. And⟩ now, I began
A new to read and rẏm ⌐and to konsyder again of worldly
a⟨ffairz⟩⌐ and to mạk ever az m⟨ẏ lei⟩ziur served mee. and þe
dittiez hạv I written heer foloingly az I ⟨mạd⟩ þem. and bekawz
þat tẏm must be had to bring to pas such ⟨aksions⟩ and great
wurk, I began to wryt first of Tẏm az folloeth—

Of Tẏm[2]

Đouh many ʒiuʒ and gẏv sentens
Vpon whọz sẏd þei think wel ⟨on⟩
þat for wizdom þe pre'hemi⟨nens⟩
owht not ọn ʒọt from þem be gon
and who gain saieth mạks great offens
yet Tẏm sai I who attainth all
for wizdom wear þe garland shall.

---

[1] Of the songs Whythorne planned to write, only the duets are known to
have been completed, fifty-two instead of the projected forty being published
in the 1590 *Duos*. Twenty of these songs appear among the poems at the end
of the autobiography.

[2] In the margin opposite each of the following songs Whythorne placed
a box containing the words (slightly varied on occasion) 'Đis hath a nọt
of [   ]'. His intention was to record the number of parts, once the music
for each song was written. In only two instances did he complete the information of the number of parts. See pp. 277 and 282.

.Oþerwÿz of Tÿm.

Althings þat hạv A beginni[n]g. Tÿm bringz þem ⟨to⟩ bee seen
and Tym þe sạm konsiumz again az þei had nẹver been
no new things bee, but Tÿm iz hee, þat doth invent þem all
and of ọld things, þe reʒister, þat þem to mÿnd do kall
it iz þe sạm, þat hath in siht, of all þe beginning
þe midz, and also of all things, þe end and finishing
in summ it hat⟨h⟩ aboov althings ⟨lordsh⟩ip and domin⟨ion⟩
exsept it bee over Vertew, ⟨who⟩ forseth not þeron

Tÿm trieth þe trewth.[1]

Tÿm tri'eth þe trewth in all
in what so'ever it bee
whẹr it be great or small
in tÿm yee shall it see.

Of needfull things oft harmfull

Of needfull things þat oft disgrạs
be þẹz follo'ing az I hạv plạst
þe witt iz first, wordz next tạk plạs
þen kompani, and drink iz last.

Of kounsell geving

To gÿv kounsell, to'oþerz iz rÿf
for of althings, þe'eazi'est it iz
83v   *but good kounsell, to wurk good lÿf*
þe sạm oftÿms, mani do mis
whẹr good kounsel, and deedz lÿk bee
of all oþerz, happy iz hee.

Of things, of most men dezyred
and to many most dainʒerows

Auktorite, mọst do dezi'er
⟨And⟩ mọst do dezier þeir eaz to hạv

---

[1] For an earlier use of this proverb, see p. 207.

also mani ar set on fi'er
when þei behold đạm bewty brạv
þęz with delihts, do bring dainȝerz
when to reazon þei bee strainȝerz

Of things þat do sumtẏms
mạk þe wẏz to *seem* fools

Đe great dezier, to get riches
and vainglory þat mani hạv
þe loov þat som seek to posses
A fiury great þat mạks sum rạv
do mạk wẏz folks for to seem dolts
and to ⟨sh⟩oot foorth mani fools bolts.[1]

Of ⟨th⟩ings þat wee do karry
a⟨bow⟩t with us, and yet mọst
tẏ⟨m⟩s þey do karry us.

Affeksions strong, þat do moov vs
to passi'ons great, for want of skil
owr toongs þat vain things will diskus
when owr fansiez do follow wil
þowh wee do bear þęz evry dạy
yet þei with vs do bear great sway

Of things þat wee do most
set by, & ar least siur of

Who doth not much esteem of helth?
and oþerz loov do much set by
who kovetth not, to hạv much welth?
and wold rạþer to lẏv þen dy
þęz forsaid things wee much do krạv
and smal se'wrty of þem wee hạv.

---

[1] An allusion to 'A fool's bolt is soon shot' (Tilley F 515).

Such experiens iz gotten ın
tỷm az mąketh wỹz.

what mąks yoong folks simpul in shew
liht of beleef, and drawn ech way
but wizdomz want, exsept in few
til experi'ens in þ⟨e⟩m bear ⟨sway⟩
for til þat tỷm experi'en⟨s bring⟩
þei want wizdom aboov a⟨lth⟩ing

A mans mỷnd is wavering
and full of passions.

Ðe mỷnd of man doth chainȝ hourly
sumtỷmz in họp, sumtỷmz ɩn fear
sumtymz in mirth, and sodenly
all chainȝed iz, hiz mery chear
his mortall lỷf doth littl see
and at þe end hiz thouhts vain bee.

Of þe prow⟨d⟩ man, and
of such a⟨z⟩ do fear God.[1]

Ðe lord abhorth al such az bee o⟨f p⟩rowd and h⟨awty ha⟩rt
and þowh þei ȝoin þeir handz ⟨in h⟩andz, yet ⟨will he mąk⟩ þem
    smart
with mersy and with faithfu⟨lnes⟩ great sinz b⟨ekum bu⟩t mean
and by þe fear of God þe lọrd eevl shalbe'esche⟨wed clea⟩n
when þat A man wil walk such waiez az hee may pleaz þe lọrd
hiz enemiez to be hiz freendz hee wil soon bring to'akkord.

Of riches well or ill gotten[2]

Better it iz with rihteowsnes, A littl to posses
þen wrongfully by any means to get vs great riches
A man devỷzeth in hiz hart, hiz own do'ings good or il
but yet þe lọrd doth order þem akkording to hiz wil

---

[1] In the margin Whythorne wrote: 'Proverb. Cap.16.'
[2] In the margin opposite the title there is a fragmentary reference,
'Prover.6.'

Ðe lord mạd vs þat wee shiuld serv him,
and þat wee shiuld do good vnto oþerz

Wee shiuld not lẏv, for owr own sẹlvz, alọn and for no mo
but wee shiuld study and họv kạr, for al oþerz also
þe mạker of þe Heavns and earth, and al þat in þem bee
did mạk þem þat þei shiuld him serv az þei bee in degree.

How wee shiuld ⌜win⌝ vs honowr   **84ᵛ**

Hee þat to him honor wọld win, let him þe sạm þen tạk
bi hiz own deedz, not bi reports, þat oþerz for him mạk

Ðe labor of þe good
and frewts of þe wikked

⟨Ðe⟩ labow⟨r of þe ri⟩hte'ow⟨z⟩ man it tendeth all to lẏf
but þe frewts ⟨of þe⟩ wikked ons, of sinfulnes iz rẏf

Saluator mundi domine[1]

O savior of þe world so wẏd
which saved hast all vs þis day
vs to protekt for vs provyd
þis nyht and ay

Draw neer to vs, and spar vs all
remoov from vs owr hainowz fawts
lihten owr sowls let vs not fall
in dark assawts

Let no⟨t þ⟩e ⟨s⟩leep owr mẏndz oppres
nor en⟨emiez⟩ away vs tạk
let vs ⟨be k⟩ept from filthines
for þẏn own sạk

Ðow reformer of owr senses
wee þee dezier with mẏnd and hart
þat with chạst mẏndz from owr kowches
wee may depạrt

---

[1] The marginal box contains the information: '⟨Ðis ha⟩th ⟨A nọt of.⟩3.
parts.'

To God þe Faþer and þe Soon
and also to þe holy spreit
be al glory and domini'on
Amen sobeit

Of worldly pleaziurz

Ðe pleaziurz of þis world ar al but vain[1]

85^r

Of things þat do
abat prẏd.

Ðe long anoy þat pẏns þe flesh away
þe skarsity þat brings great poverty
and bondaჳ great, who þẹz must needz assay
þeir prẏd wil bat look þei never so hy

Of hiumility

Hee doth well know hiz own weaknes
þat iz of lowly' and humbul mẏnd
hee kovets not to know or ges
mọr þen þe lord hath him assẏnd
hee feareth God and doth konfes
þat from him kummeth al goodnes

Hee lookth not hy but down below
and doth not lawh withowt great kawz
many vain wordz hee doth not show
but soft and sweet be al hiz sawz
hee nothing doth but with good grạs
and prẏd in him kan tạk no plạs

God dwelleth with þe humbul m⟨an⟩
hee honord iz of mọr and les
hiz nạm þei never kurs nor ban
but raþer þei þe sạm do bles
and he alọn þe frewt shal gain
þowh humbulnes prokiur him pain

---

[1] This verso page ends with the correct catchword 'Of things'.

.Of pasiens.

A stefast mynd þat willingly
doth suffer wrongs by word or deed
doth heap hot kọls on þ'enemy[1]
þowh pasi'ent folks do hardly speed
and þowh A martirdom it bee
yet pasient folks prevail wee see.

pasi'ens wee need when eevls do hap
whẹr wee A salv kannot provỹd
if aksydental eevls vs hap
az wordz and deedz mai vs betỹd
if owr dezart prọkiur such il
þen may wee thank owr wilfull wil.

Đe reward of þọz, who do fear, or not fear God.

Yee þat do serv þe God of loov
þe God of peas, and glori al
yee shal reseiv from him aboov
such help az yee no wai shal fal
for hee regardeth so al his
az þei hiz aid shall never mis

But if þat yee from him deklỹn
az dizobedi'ent childern ywz
þen will hee suffer yow to pỹn
and will yow vtterly refiwz
þus may yee chiuz of pain or rest
þe whi⟨c⟩h of both þat yee lỹk best

Of knowleʒ and ingnorans.

Knowleʒ hath nọn so great A fo
az ingnorans him self doth sho

---

[1] Proverbial; Tilley C 468 (Rom. 12. 20).

no kontrari'ez be gretter þen þei bee
briut beasts be'inferior to mankynd
and somuch kum þei þem behynd
az þeir ingnorans from þem iz in degree
þouh natiurz gifts in sum beasts gro
az lẏk in man yee kannot fynd
if man did want þ'immortal gǫst
þe which in mankynd God doth plǫs
  þen of beasts þe mǫst
wẹr mankẏnd and void of al grǫs

Of þǫz þat do tạk
many things in hand
at ǫns

86^r

If dyverz wurks þow tạk to do
of kontrary effekts þat bee
hard shal it bee to bring þem so
az þat þei may best kontent þee

Who manẏ irons hạv in fier[1]
shall not þem al mạk in ǫn heat
ne shal þei hạv al þeir dezier
þat to know al þeir wits þei beat

Đe meats þat liht bee to diȝest
requi'er no stomaks þat be strong
and stomaks weak kan tạk no rest
when gros meats into þem be throng

Đẹz ensampuls good lessons ar
for vs þat wee owr wits not bend
to deal in things þat do pas far
owr reach, to bring þem to good end

Of trusting

Hee þat wil trust þis lesson learn of mee
and tạke good heed of þis þat I tell þee

_____
[1] Proverbial; Tilley I 100.

alþowh sum say, in trust I treazon fўnd[1]
yet trust will I az reazon doth mee bўnd

If ọn I trust, and hee doth mee deseiv
I beshrew him þat kraft so well kan weiv
if hee deseiv mee twỹs þen shrew vs twain
him for deseit, I þat did[a] *trust again*

But if þe third tỹm, him I put in trust
and doth deal with mee again vnȝust
mỹn own self þan beshrew I and no mo
bekawz I did þe third tỹm trust him so

Of þọz þat kan
keep no kownsell.

Đe belly Godz þat swill[b] *in drink, till þat þeir wits bee owt*[2]
þe noddy foolz þat ween þem wỹz, in all þei go abowt
þe sely chỹld þat means no gỹl, and perils non doth kast
what in þeir mỹndz do kum to speak, frankly þei foorth do blast

86^v

Of three things which be
seldom or nẹver kiured

Three things þer bee which seldom kan
hạv remedy in any man
frenzў iz first, nex[t] herezў
and last of all iz ȝelozў.[3]

Of being over lyht.

Not over liht þouh pleazant þow dost sho
but of þat lihtnes dyverz hiumors ȝudȝ
sum sai shee[c] *iz lỹht, sum to þat sai no*
þus sum be pleazed, whyl[d] *oþerz do gruȝ*

---

[a] This phrase written above 'mee þat wold'.   [b] Written above 'powr'.
[c] Written above 'þat'.   [d] Written above 'and'.

---

[1] Proverbial; Tilley T 549.   [2] An echo of Tilley B 293.
[3] Proverbial; Tilley F 672.

Nothing iz sertain

Nothing iz sertain in þeȝ daiz
but subȝekt still to chainȝes all
þerfor tis best wee chainȝ owr waiz
þat no mishap to vs do fall.

Of trobuls well sent,
by þe attempt of þe
.S.

Þe trobuls past on vs[a] *did grow*
for owr[b] *trespas, and tȳm il spent*
yet þei mad vs our[c] *God to know*
and for þat kawz þei wẹr well sent

hiz hart revȳved
when þe .S. fled.

87ʳ

Revȳved waz mi hart and mȳnd
when þat my fọz wẹr forst to fly
tȳl þen my wọz kowld no eaz[d] *fȳnd*
but stil enkrẹst my mizery

Of Fạm[1]

When rạr[e] *attempts, being good o⟨r i⟩l*
be browht to pas, and mạk great show
þen Fạm doth fly with vois az shril
az Trumpets sownd þe sạm to'owt blow

Of prȳd and hiumanite.

Az hawhty prȳd oppresseth loov
and breedeth hạt withowt remọrs
hiumanite doth it re[p]roov
expelling quȳt al hạtful fọrs

---

[a] Written above 'mee'.   [b] Written above 'my'.   [c] These two
words written above 'mee my'.   [d] Written above 'rest'.   [e] Written
above 'great'.

---

[1] The marginal box reads: 'Þis hath A nọt of .5. parts.'

and wher dispẏt wold work dizgrạs
þạr ʒentilnes wil her displạs

Of þe swiftest thing
in þe world.

If þow woldst know þe swifte⟨st thing⟩
þat passeth throwh þe world ech ⟨day⟩[a]
and nothing kan restrain or bri⟨n⟩g
þe sạm ọn ʒọt to any stay
þe thowht of man þe sạm iz hee
þat nọn kan let from passing free

Of *Vertiw*

No exersẏz kan hạv good end
neyþer of body nor of mẏnd
exsept on vertiu it attend
whọz waiz þei must bọth seek & fẏnd
withowt vertew wee do no good
by whom al il must bee withstood

Of *K[l]emensy.*   87ᵛ

To'ywz good for il much better is
þen il for il az mallis wold
for klemensy siur wilnot mis
t'o enkrẹs grẹt fạm, and honor họld
mani good frewts shal al such get
who klemensy do not neglet

Of overkumming appetẏts,
wyth oþer lusts hurtfull.

In overkumming appetẏt
and lisensi'owz konkiupissens
also from plesiurz þee to'akquẏt
þat mai þee wurk sum grẹt offens
A viktori þow þen dost gain
þe lẏk wherof few kan obtain

---

[a] Perhaps 'way'.

Of overmuch offensif
speech.

When speeches to much, and owt of good frạm,
do kawz much offens, to honest wўz earz
þe toong þen iz blạmd þat plaid hath such gạm
and þerto iz ʒoind þis foloing vers
þe wizdom of Fools, in þeir toongs remain
but þat of þe wўz, in þeir harts mọst rain[1]

How to ywz A dissembling
Frend

Who spẹks þee fair vnto þi fạs
and ywzeth þee in owtward sho
az þowh þow stoodst in hiz good grạs
wheraz inward hee meanth not so
do þow him spẹk and ywz lỳkwỳz
but trust him not in any wўz

　　　　　họp þe most kumfortablest
　　　　　thing in þis world.

Of all þe things þat wee fўnd best
which in þis world mọst rẹdi is
họp iz þe sạm on whom wee rest
and hold fast by to help owr mis
for when althings be gọn and lost
yet wee on họp do depend most

Of Diliʒens

Diliʒens iz ọn of þe dawhterz cheef
of vertew, from [whom] springeth all goodnes
þe mọst tediows things shee maketh but breef
and also eazỳ, for shee kan repres
mọst kawzes þat bring ani grevows greef

---

[1] A conflation of two proverbs, Tilley H 312 and M 602. Utilized again
on p. 287.

Of *maintaining*
þe trewth.

Maintain þe trewth for best
þowh sum li'arz wil sai no
for þerof kummth gret[a] *rest*
whẹr ever þat þei go
þe trewth iz sumtẏm blạmd
emong þe vnwẏz sort
but trewth shalnot be shạmd
for al þeir il report

Of vntạmed will

Vntạmed wil þat wilnot yeeld
to reazons lọr when hee doth teach
brings good attempts to pas but seeld
so far þei bee beyond hiz reach

Oþerwẏz of will

Long framed waz my mynd to do
þat which my wil did draw mee to
and had not reazon drawn mee bak
wil wold hạv wrowht my vtter wrak
but Grạs did help my reazon so
þat wil from reazon needs must go
til þat my wil did yeeld az thral
alway to'obei to reazons kal.

88ᵛ

Of winning[b]

If þat I kowld ons win
þe thing þat I dezier
þen shiuld ⌐*þat*⌐ *stạt begin*
þat I did ay requier

---

[a] Written above 'siur'.   [b] Written above a deleted earlier title,
'Oþerwẏz of will'.

A good mosion
of fansy.

Not al forgot my fansy said
good kownsel now do þow follow
trust þow vpon dąm vertewz aid
wherby to þee sum good may grow

Of had I wist

Fly had I wist[1] az thing not good
repentans it doth bring to ląt
if in diu tỹm it be withstood
þow shalt posses A better stąt

Of þe mean estąt

Đe meri mean þat[a] pąrt wold I[2]
of al pąrts sing with mǫst goodwil
bekawz in þat þe melodi
iz best lẏked of men of skil

Try er þow trust[3]

Tri er þow trust for so maist þow
þe trew and faithles frend owt fỹnd
when faithful frend to þee doth show
þen trust and bee þow not vnkỹnd

89ʳ

Of A kontented mỹnd

Đe quiet mynd iz not offended
with evry thing þat krosseth it
but hǫps when al il haps be'ended
sum better chauns on him shal hit

ᵃ MS. reads 'þar'.

---

[1] Proverbial; Tilley H 8.
[2] Based on one of Heywood's proverbs, 'Measure is a merry mean';
Tilley M 804.
[3] Proverbial; Tilley T 595.

Ðe toong of A wẏz man iz in[1]
hiz hart, but þe hart of A fooll[2]
   iz in hiz toong.

Ðe wẏz mans toong iz in hiz hart
who wẏzly waith what hee wold say
but þe fools hart iz in hiz toong
who lets fools bolts to hạv þeir way.

Of þe kovetowz man.

Who pondreth wel þe trobuls mani' A wai
and dainȝers great þat niggardz do assai
wilnot kovet of world[ly] welth nomọr
þen reazon wold hạv þem to keep in stọr

Ðe gredy mẏzer moils alway for muk
þe which to him hee seaseth not to pl⟨uk⟩
hiz gredi mẏnd A vertew seemz to him
so doth þat vẏs hiz vnderstanding dim

Ðe poor do fẏnd of mani things A want[3]
þe kovetowz of al things hạv A skant
for þe niggard nọn shal þe better bee
and to him self þe very wurst iz hee

Ðe gaping Hel þat sowls do gulch and gull
þe perdision þat never wilbe full
iz lẏk þe eiez of þem þat kovett all
for satisfied þei never bee ne shall.

Of things þat do good
and harm.

As ⌈þe⌉ qui'et rest, and ȝoiful hart, with þe di'et moderạt   **89ᵛ**
az needful bee, az fiziks skil, for man in evri rạt
so sorow saws akkompni'ed, with ⌈fowl⌉ desparasi'on
and also solitarines, bring hạsty death vs on

---

[1] Marginal note reads '.Proverbs.'   [2] See p. 284.
[3] In the margin Whythorne wrote '.Seneca.'

Ðe beginning of þe
.71. Salm.

In þee O lord hav I trusted, my hop iz al in þee
let not konfiuzi'on mee oppres, nor ons tak hold on mee
but rid þow mee from al trobuls in þi great rihte'owsnes
enklÿn þÿn ear vnto my wordz and sav mee from distres

Of bewty.

Of gret bewty t'is often seen, it fadeth in short spas
and mani vÿl vÿsis of mÿnd, ar harbard in þat plas
of ⌈þe⌉ kommodite it brings, but few hav liht þeron
yet many hav bin browht þerbi, to'vtter distruksion

Ðe good estat of A
happy lÿf[1]

Ðe reȝiment of happi lÿf, iz fownd owt þus by skil
þe mÿnd on God, with lÿvli faith, and þen to'obei hiz wil
þe ȝoiz of Heavn and glory þar, to seek and for to gain
þe memory to bee on death and fear to feel Hel pain

Ðe prai'erz devowt, short and often, to keep þe mÿnd on hy
þe works verteowz, charitabul, and ywzed moderatly[a]
þe wil not wavring, but stedfast, both reasnabul & rÿp
þe speech littl honest, and trew þe kontrari t'owtwÿp.

Ðe konversasi'on grav, humbul, and þarwithal pleazaunt
þe body klean it must be kept, þat nastines not haunt
þe garment kumly, konveni'ent, and meet for ech degree
þe sports honest, short, and seldom, þus must þei ywzed ⌈bee.⌉

Ðe yws of sleep, waching, women, siuperfliously doth hurt
þe diet temprat, þe mealz sertain, A strong body doth wurk
Ðe meats not moist, nor korruptibul, but lyht and klenly drest
þe kawz of raw and il hiumourz, to bee refraind iz best

90ʳ

---

[a] Written above 'profitably'.

---

[1] The marginal box reads: 'Ðe first staf of þis hath A not'.

Ðe natiural akkustomd purȝing, ⌜ywz⌝ and maintain
þ'exersyzes of þe body with sum klean trąd tąk pain
þe travel of þe body not exsessẏv nor violent
þe'eyr helthsom þe hows lihtsom, with living kompitent

Of frewtles frendz or fǫs

Of frend or fo to chiuz þe ǫn
if þow of bǫth ǫn chois must mąk
þe frewtles frend to tąk alǫn
or hurtles fo, which woldst þow tąk?

If I of bǫth shiuld shew my mẏnd
how I of bǫth my fansy leeks
az il I kownt þe helples frẏnd
az fo, who harmz to mee nǫn seeks.

Of vnfayned faith

Vnfained faith, þe prẏs þerof iz much
for faith vnfaind, no toong kan iel þe meed
so great þerof, þe sk[r]iptiurz do pr⟨ẏz⟩
wherfǫr let faith, þi ankor hold be suc⟨h⟩
az may not slip, and so tąk þow siur heed
þat þow hold fast, az now I þee advẏz

Ðe thouht iz free

Ðe thouht iz free,[1] non knowz but God þe sąm
no saint nor man, nor devl[a] kan it bewrai
wherfǫr tąk heed, in ernest or in gąm
what þow entendst or what þow meanst to sai

---

[a] Written above 'feend'.

---

[1] Proverbial; Tilley T 244.

Of *sekret* things

In things sekret þat be not to bee known
let sekresy, be ywzed in such sort
az desentnes, in þat ƙạs doth requier
but if þat blab hạv ons sekrets owt blown
and þerof mạd, her tatling and report
þen sekresy, iz wasted az with fier.

90ᵛ

Of vowz making

Perform þi vow, if þow dost anẏ mạk
but er þow vow, advẏz þee wel þerof
lest þẏn advẏs, in error do þee tạk
and so þi foz of þee do mạk A skof.

A perswazion to pasiens

Hạv pasi'ens stil, þowh God þee towch
    with krosses mani' A way
when kros iz past þen grạs wil kum
    wheron þow shalt hạv stay

Oþerwẏz of þe sạm

Hạv pasi'ens still þowh God þee try
with krosses strainȝ and mani' A way
which tạk for sins þat þow hast doon
when kros iz past þen grạs bi'anby
wil kum wheron þow maist hạv stay
and so bee helpt and eazed soon

Of Họp

Assewred họp much lẏk iz vnto faith
az tree from root dost kum and grow wee see
so faith from họp doth spring and spred lẏkwẏz
By faith wee lay owr họp in Heavn on haith
kryst iz owr họp by him wee sạved bee
and so eternal lẏf to vs doth rẏz

Of Felisite

Felisite þe prosprowz end
iz of al things þat wee dezi'er
but trew felisite iz þ'end
wherto by vertew wee aspi'er

How to asswaȝ anger

If þow wilt mittigǫt anger
ywz speech ȝentil, pleazing & trew
Or with pasient sylens suffer   **91ʳ**
or els bi'absens þe sǫm eschew.

Salm .96.

O sing vnto þe lord A song, þat plęzant iz and new
sing to þe lord al þe hǫl earth, hiz praizes þat be dew
sing to þe lord and praiz hiz nǫm of hiz salvasion tell
to þe heaþen and al peepul hiz wonderz þat exsell
þe lord iz great and wurþely hee kannot bee praized
hee much mǫr iz þen oþer Godz to bee loovd and feared
az for þe Godz of þe heaþen þei bee but idolz dum
*it iz þe lǫrd þat mǫd þe Heavns from him*ᵃ *althings do ku⟨m⟩*
glory and powr, worship, honour, ar in hiz sanktiuary
askrÿb þerfǫr yee kynredz al hiz praiz diutifully
wurship þe lord in þe beawty of desent holines
let þe hǫl earth be'i⟨n fear o⟩f him, and foorth þe sǫm expres
tel þe heaþen þe lor⟨d raineth a⟩nd world hee mǫd firmly
and þat hee þe peepul ⟨shal ȝiudȝ⟩ eevn rihteowsly
O let þe Heavns and ear⟨th be glad⟩, let seas & floudz mak nois
let feeldz and woodz, an⟨d al in⟩ þem befǫr þe lǫrd ⟨reȝois⟩
for hee kummeth to ȝiudȝ ⟨þe⟩ ęrth & world with rihteowsnes
and þe peepul hee with hiz trewth wil ȝiudȝ both mǫr & les.

ᵃ Written above 'whom'.

Audi vide tace

I see how sum kontrol ech on
whom þei do see or hear to'offend
az þowh it wer þeir charȝ alon
bẏ wai of chek such things to'amend
but if þat þow wilt lẏv in peas
þen hear and see and hold þi peas[1]

Sum sai to hold þeir peas at þoȝ
who talk and do mor þen þei owht
þei flatter þouh þei nowht disklóz
but I þis lesson siur hav bowht
þat hear and see and sai þe best
iz mean riht good to purchaz rest

91ᵛ

Let Momus mok and mow hiz full
let Zoilus frown and karp lẏkwẏz
yet when þei both so pluk and pull
nowht els shal get for þeir devẏs
but to bee tawht to'obtain þeir pace
ever to'*Audi vide* and to *tace*

Ðe giltles thowht
sets fam at noht

Ðouh flikring fam who mani'A plas hath sowht
and flown on hy, and spred abród below
al such konseits az kreep into þe thowht
of mani'A on, yet þus much wil I show
Ðe giltles thouht sets Fam at nowht

It iz m⟨or mize⟩rabull to be born
⟨in⟩to ⟨þe wor⟩ld þen to dy and
⟨be⟩ buried—

For ⟨to be born⟩ az infants bee
þe st⟨   ⟩ so to set bẏ

---

[1] Proverbial; Tilley N 275.

az iz þeir stạt whọz end wee see
bekawz þei'ar rid of mizerẏ
lament wee shiuld at childerns birth
and at þeir death to shew sum mirth

No man iz happy vntill þat
hee happely dieth—[1]

Đe worldlings ʒiudʒ þat man happy
þat worldly welth hath at hiz wil
and þat honour doth set on hy
wherby hee mai hiz wil fulfil
but Solon said, nọn waz happy
til happily þat hee did dy

In adversity trew frendz
be disserned from þe fained[2]

---

[1] Proverbial; Tilley M 333.

[2] The presence of a catchword, '*Lẏk*', shows that the manuscript continued with more songs. This is the end of a gathering, so possibly there were many more songs and perhaps other matter at the end of the manuscript.

APPENDIX I

LOCATION OF COPIES OF WHYTHORNE'S PRINTED SONGS

OF the five part-books of Whythorne's 1571 *Songes for three, fouer and five Voyces*, three copies of each book are known, but no perfect set exists. The Henry E. Huntington Library at San Marino, California, has the only set with all five; they came from the Britwell Court Library, selling as lot 160 on 15 December 1919. Unhappily, each volume is mutilated to some degree; all lack title-pages and some other leaves, front and back, are missing but supplied in facsimile.

Christ Church, Oxford, has four of the books, a handsome well-preserved set consisting of the Tenor, the Triplex, the Medius, and the Bassus, but lacking the Contratenor volume. For many years it was suspected that the Contratenor had been stolen in the nineteenth century, but examination of a manuscript catalogue made by Dr. Charles Burney in November 1778, still preserved at Christ Church, shows that among the music kept on the '4th Shelf' was Whythorne's *Songes*, and Burney added the note, 'N.B. but 4 Books'.

The British Museum also has but four of the part-books, lacking the Tenor volume.[1] Several of them have missing or mutilated pages, supplied in facsimile. The Triplex and the Contratenor have the name 'J(?) Johnsone' and 'Thomas Johnsone' scribbled on the end-papers of each respectively. The Bodleian has only the Tenor volume, but it has the signature 'Thomas Johnson' several times on the final leaf. This argues that the Bodleian volume was once part of the set at the British Museum, a set once preserved in a Johnson family. Oddly enough, the Bassus book in the Huntington set also has the name 'Johnson Thomas' on its second leaf.

The only other volume known is a copy of the Contratenor book in the New York Public Library. It may be the copy formerly owned by E. F. Rimbault and described in the *Bibliographical Miscellany* (part 4, 1854) which is otherwise untraced. The book came to the New York Public Library with the Drexel Collection; a note inside the cover shows that it was purchased for £3. 2s. 6d. A possible relationship between this and other extant part-books may be found by some later investigator through examining the vellum leaf of a Latin manuscript with rubricated initials in which it is bound.

[1] Purchased as lot 527 in the Oliphant sale, 24 Apr. 1873.

The Huntington copies of the Tenor, the Medius, and the Bassus books also retain the portions of vellum leaves in which they were anciently bound, the latter two containing music and Latin text.

The collation of the five part-books is as follows:

Contratenor	AAa–JJi⁴
Tenor	AAA–DDD⁴
Triplex	Aa–Ii⁴, Kk²
Medius	AA–KK⁴
Bassus	A–I⁴K²

In the Christ Church copy of the Medius book, sheet DD has been printed or folded in the wrong order, namely 1, 4, 3, 2, the leaves being numbered 13, 16, 15, 14.

A distinctive feature of the music is the printing of Whythorne's name within the staves of music to fill out blank spaces at the end of the songs (see illustration). Sometimes his whole name is given and at other times it is variously abbreviated, tailored to the amount of space available.

The 1590 *Duos* are even more scarce than the 1571 *Songes*. Both volumes are found in the British Museum[1] and in the Cashell Library in Dublin. Bodley has only the Bassus volume. Both volumes collate: A–F⁴, G². Signature Diii of the Bassus volume is mis-signed Ciii.

The woodcut of Whythorne appears on the back page of the *Duos*; the same block used in the 1571 *Songes* was utilized and shows some deterioration. The scallop in his coat of arms has been altered by being given a dark background. A proof copy of the altered woodcut was sewn (now pasted) on the verso of the title-page of the manuscript of the autobiography; that it is a proof copy instead of a leaf from the 1590 *Duos* is shown by the lack of printed matter on the reverse side.

The reprinting of Whythorne's songs began in 1903, when Rudolf Imelmann inserted the words from the 1571 Triplex book into the *Jahrbuch der deutschen Shakespeare-Gesellschaft*, pp. 140–78, with selected musical settings. Next, Peter Warlock in 1927 published twelve of the songs with new settings (Oxford). Then in 1947 Manfred F. Bukofzer edited three additional songs ('Such as in Love', 'Thou shalt soon see', and 'When Cupid had compelled me') with slight alterations in the dynamics and tempo markings (Music Press, New York). At least two of Whythorne's songs have been broadcast by the B.B.C., 'Grace before Meat' and 'Buy New Broom'.

---

[1] Purchased from J. Lilly, 23 Jan. 1856.

APPENDIX II

WHYTHORNE AND THE DUDLEY FAMILY

BECAUSE of Whythorne's usual reluctance to reveal the names of his employers, patrons, and friends, it has been difficult to identify most of the persons with whom he was associated. Enough hints are given, however, to suggest that he benefited intermittently over forty years from the patronage of the Dudleys, a family second to none in the power complex of sixteenth-century England.

The first hint occurs about 1551, when Whythorne received the offer of a position in the household of a duchess to be tutor to her daughter (p. 55). This offer was a blow to the pride of his current employer, the Suds-of-Soap widow, who by combining tears with a steep increase in wages kept Whythorne from transferring his services to the duchess. Soon after this, Whythorne's employer suffered a fall in fortune (p. 60), which preceded a 'worse fall' by the duchess and her husband a short time later. Whythorne used this break in employment to travel on the Continent.

After Whythorne's return from approximately two years abroad (c. 1555), he was engaged as 'chief waiting man' and music tutor in the household of a nobleman who, as Whythorne informs us, was heir to the 'noble woman . . . aforesaid' (p. 85). This duke's son, we learn, 'did fall also, yet being afterward set at liberty again, he lived very honourably by the living which he had by his lady and wife'. During the period of Whythorne's employment, the nobleman was 'called to serve . . . [at St. Quentin], where to recover his honour before lost, he consumed much of his lady's land and substance' (p. 85). These financial reverses forced the nobleman to revoke an annuity he had promised to Whythorne. Prudence born of disappointment now caused the 'chief waiting man' to decide to seek greener pastures, so Whythorne left the duke's son, and took a position in the household of a Privy Councillor (p. 86).

The details of the story fit neatly with the history of the Dudley family. By 1551 John Dudley, recently created Duke of Northumberland, had become the most powerful man in England. Promptly, he humbled his chief opponent, Edward Seymour, Duke of Somerset, who was executed in January 1552.[1] Despite Northumberland's

---

[1] Possibly the fall of the Suds-of-Soap gentlewoman was connected with the broken fortunes of the Somerset party.

driving ambition for political dominance, he emphasized cultural values in the upbringing of his children. His wife Jane, daughter of Sir Edward Guilford, had presented him with thirteen children, eight sons and five daughters, several of whom had died in infancy. By marrying his son Guilford to Lady Jane Grey, Northumberland attempted to capture the crown of England for the Dudleys. His failure temporarily ruined the family fortunes, and a 'worse fall' can scarcely be imagined, for the duke, his wife, and five sons were confined in the Tower, whence the duke, his son Guilford, and his daughter-in-law Lady Jane went to the executioner's block.

By 1554 the surviving sons began to emerge from political disgrace and return to the political sunlight. After the death of John, the eldest son, in October 1554 (at Penshurst, the home of his brother-in-law Sir Henry Sidney), Lord Ambrose Dudley (1528–90) became the head of the family. Upon his mother's death a year later, Lord Ambrose inherited most of her property, a relatively small holding compared to the lands of his wife Elizabeth, Baroness Tailboys, whom he had married when the Dudleys were riding high in 1553. In 1556 Lord Ambrose sold two manors belonging to his wife,[1] and in the following year took a leading part in the expedition to St. Quentin. The glory he earned in the victory was the prelude to an eminent career during the reign of Elizabeth and his elevation to the earldom of Warwick.

In support of the case that Whythorne served Lord Ambrose Dudley in 1556, before his departure with the expedition to St. Quentin, it should be remembered that in 1551 the dukes in England could be counted on the fingers of one hand. Indeed, after the execution of the Duke of Somerset in 1552, of Northumberland in 1553, and of Suffolk in February 1554, Norfolk remained the only duke alive. Moreover, Northumberland was the only duke who had a son that fought at St. Quentin, according to available information.[2] This evidence by elimination combines with the details given by Whythorne to identify the Dudley family as his patrons in the decade before the accession of Elizabeth. The proffer in 1551 of an appointment to tutor the daughter of the Duke of Northumberland, and the attempt of Lord Ambrose Dudley in 1556 to tie Whythorne to his household by dangling an annuity before him are manifestations

---

[1] He sold these manors on 18 June 1556, the day after he had been confirmed in possession of lands held through his wife. *Lincs. N. & Q.* xi (1911), p. 253; *Cal. of Patent Rolls 1555–7*, pp. 533–5.

[2] A list of those involved will be found in *Hist. MSS. Comm. (Foljambe)*, *Fifteenth Report*, Appendix, Part V, pp. 5–6.

that Whythorne's abilities were highly regarded well before his thirtieth birthday.[1]

Because the Duke and Duchess of Northumberland had five daughters, several of whom died in infancy without their birth-dates being recorded, and because the duke arranged child marriages to bind the wealthiest noble families of England to the Dudley line, it cannot be determined with certainty which of the daughters Whythorne was invited to teach. Lady Mary became the wife of Sir Henry Sidney in 1551, her first child, Sir Philip Sidney, being born three years later. The only other surviving daughter was Lady Catherine (1548–1620), who would have been too young in 1551 to benefit from lessons on the virginals or in singing pricksong.[2] When Lady Catherine was only 6 years old, in May 1553, her father married her to Henry Hastings, later third Earl of Huntington. It is interesting to note that years later, in 1590, Whythorne dedicated his second publication, the *Duos*, to Francis Hastings, brother to the Earl of Huntington.

[1] John Heywood may have been involved in recommending Whythorne to Northumberland. The duke was one of Heywood's patrons, and a manuscript containing several of Heywood's plays was listed in the inventory of Northumberland's estate. (*Hist. MSS. Comm., Second Report*, Appendix, pp. 101-2). John Harley, Master of Magdalen College School from 1542 to 1548, when he became chaplain to Northumberland, provides another link.

[2] The other three sisters were Lady Margaret, who died in her tenth year; Lady Catherine, who died in her seventh year; and Lady Temperance, who lived for only one year. The fact that another daughter was named Catherine argues that the first one was an early child. See A. Collins, *Letters and Memorials of State* (1746), i. 32, and R. Davies, *Chelsea Old Church* (1904), pp. 49–53.

APPENDIX III

THE 'MUSICAL SCRAP'

THE loose slip of paper, now bound between folios 66 and 68 of the manuscript, has been called the 'musical scrap' for reference purposes. The contents reveal Whythorne in his old age writing down the names of 'Doktorz and Bachelarz of Miuzik in England', first those 'of aunsient tẏm', and on the reverse side, those 'of lạt tẏm'. Two simple pen ornaments suggest that the 'aunsient tẏm' side is intended to be read first.

The subject of Degrees of Musicians was a favourite with Whythorne, as the passage on pp. 232–3 reveals. Perhaps he jotted down these notes to serve as illustrations to this thesis. His action can be dated some time after July 1592, because of the events that he mentions in connexion with John Bull, Thomas Morley, and Giles Farnaby, to be discussed later. But now for Whythorne's 'musical scrap'.

Of Doktorz and Bachelarz of Miuzik In England

Đọz of aunsient *tẏm*, wẹr, *doktor* ⌐*Newton*, who waz also A bachelar of Diuinite & master of Arte.⌐ *Farfax. doktor Cooper.* and *dokter. Tye. Doktor Farfax* waz

of þe Abbey at St Albọns. dokter Cooper waz of þe Abbey at St Edmondz bury. And dokter *Tye*, waz

of þe kathedrall chiurch at Elye. Đen of bachelarz, þạr waz mr parrat and mr Whẏt. mr parrat

waz of Mawdlin kolleʒ in Oxford, and mr Whẏt waz of *Trinite* Colleʒ in Cambridʒ when hee Commensed

Đe mọst famowz master of miuzik (vnkommensed) of aunsient tẏm waz mr John Taverner who dwelt at Boston.

more the blynd harpar. pygott, mr Sheppard waz of þe Queens chappell.

⌐*Đạr* waz in king henry þe eihts daiez A Doktor of miuzik nạmed doktor newton. it iz reported þat hee waz bọth A

master of Art, A bachelar of diuinite, and also A Doktor of miuzik. but þe miuzik which hee mạd, waz by spe-

culation, and not by praktẏz, for when hee had mạd A song, hee kowld not sing A part of it when hee had mạd it.

⌐ The beginnings of this line and those following have been cancelled by a large cross.

The 'Musical Scrap'

Dr. Newton is the mystery figure of this list, since no candidate of this name occurs in histories of music. Nor does any likely Newton appear among the graduates of Oxford or Cambridge in the pages of Foster or Venn. C. F. Abdy Williams, who made a special study of *Degrees in Music at Oxford and Cambridge* (1893), lists no Newton, or any similar name.[1] Yet Whythorne is so specific that he must have had evidence for his statement. Possibly he recalled information heard in the household of John Heywood.

Most of the others are well known or easily identified. Robert Fayrfax (1464–1521), director of the choir at St. Albans, received the Doctor of Music degree from Cambridge in 1504, and from Oxford in 1511. Of Robert Cooper little is known beyond the facts that Cambridge awarded him a Doctorate in Music in 1502, and that his songs exist in various collections. That Cooper was of the Abbey at Bury St. Edmunds was previously unrecorded. Christopher Tye, a well-known musician, received his Mus.D. at Cambridge in 1545, and was incorporated at Oxford in 1548.

Robert Perrot, or Porrot (d. 1550), had been master of the choristers at Magdalen, Oxford, and undoubtedly was remembered there during Whythorne's residence (1538–46), though by that time Perrot had apparently gone on to an administrative career. Unknown to Whythorne, Perrot had been granted the D.Mus. degree at Oxford in 1516. Robert White (d. 1574) received the degree of Mus.Bac. from Cambridge in December 1560, but there is no other record of his having been at Trinity. Whythorne probably had personal knowledge of the matter, since his own residence at Trinity began in the following year.

John Taverner (1495?–1545), the Boston organist and composer, was well known in his century. William More (1492?–1565) served as chief harper to four sovereigns, apparently the last to occupy the official position.[2] His blindness enabled him to carry messages from Roman Catholic prelates without arousing suspicion (M. C. Boyd, *Elizabethan Music*, p. 188). Richard Pygott (1485?–1552) associated himself with Cardinal Wolsey and enjoyed a royal pension. John Shepherd (*c.* 1520–63) was instructor of choristers at Magdalen

---

[1] The best candidate is John Newton, sometime Fellow of the Queen's College, Oxford, who acquired his B.A. in 1508/9, and later proceeded M.A. and B.D. But there is no record of his having written any music, 'by speculation' or otherwise; he seems to have become a clergyman. Francis Newton (d. 1572), Vice-Chancellor of Cambridge in 1563, seems too late to fit Whythorne's list.

[2] Whythorne had copied out some of his 'songs and sonets' (p. 14), none of which seem to have survived.

College during the latter part of Whythorne's residence there (1542), and became a Gentleman of the Chapel Royal in 1552.

On the other side of the 'musical scrap' Whythorne jotted down the names of many contemporary musicians:

Ðe doktorz and Bachelarz of Miuzik of lat tým, wer þez foloing.

Doktor Bull. & dokter Dally. Doktor Bull, iz of þe Queens maȝestiez chappell. and Doker Dally,

waz of *Trinite* kolleȝ in Cambriȝ. Ðe bachelarz of Miuzik wer ⌈master⌉ morley, who iz also of þe

Queens chappell, mr Dowland, and mr Farnabye.

Ðe most famowz miuzisians in þis tým ⌈unkommensid bee⌉ mr Thomas Tallis, ⌈mr Sheppard,⌉ mr willam Birde, who

be also of queens maȝesties chappell—Also mr Parsons. mr Farant. mr Strgers.

mr Munday the elder, and the yoong—mr Farmer—mr Bath— John Cosen—

Johnson the preest—And Johnson A player of wynd Instruments. Cobbold—Damon—

More the blynd harper—Sheppard—Applebe. preston—

John Bull (1562?–1628), the famous organist and composer, received his Bachelor of Music degree at Oxford in 1586, and his doctorate from Cambridge by 1592, in which year (7 July) he was incorporated at Oxford. Doctor Dally of Trinity College, Cambridge, seems to mean Thomas Dallis who taught at Cambridge, evidently the Dr. Dallis mentioned by Meres (*Palladis Tamia*, 1598, ed. D. C. Allen, 1938, f. 288ᵛ). Thomas Morley (1557–1603), who had received his B.Mus. at Oxford in 1588, became a Gentleman of the Chapel Royal on 24 July 1592. John Dowland (1563–1626), the renowned lutenist and composer, had taken his B.Mus. at Oxford in 1588. Giles Farnaby (1565?–1640) had received his Oxford degree on 7 July 1592.

Thomas Tallis (1505?–85) and his pupil William Byrd (1543–1623) are two of the best-known musicians in Elizabethan England. They held a near-monopoly of music publishing beginning in 1575. Three musicians named Parsons are possible: Robert (d. 1570) of the Chapel Royal; John (d. 1623), probably son of Robert; and William (1515?–64?) of Wells Cathedral. Similarly, several musicians named Farrant are available, the most likely being John Farrant, composer and organist of Hereford Cathedral about the time Whythorne wrote these notes. Of Nicholas Strogers little is known except his music.

William Mundy (1529?–91?), Gentleman of the Chapel Royal from 1564, was father of John Mundy (d. 1630), organist to Queen Elizabeth; the son received the degree of B.Mus. from Oxford in 1585, and in 1624 that of D.Mus. John Farmer published psalm-tunes in 1591, and the following year contributed to Thomas East's *Whole Booke of Psalmes*. William Bathe (1564–1614) attended Oxford without taking a degree before publishing in 1584 *A Briefe Introduction to the True Art of Musicke*; by the time Whythorne wrote these notes Bathe had gone to Spain, where he ended his days. Little is known about John Cosyn, who published in 1585 *Musicke of Six or Five Partes Made upon . . . the Psalmes*. Johnson 'the Preest' was Robert Johnson, a Scot who fled to England, and whose music is found copied into several manuscripts. Concerning Johnson 'a player of wynd Instruments', there is insufficient evidence to identify him with any of the musical Johnsons listed in Grove's *Dictionary*.

William Cobbold (1560–1639), organist of Norwich Cathedral, was one of the ten contributors to East's *Whole Booke of Psalmes*, 1592. William Damon (1540–91), a court musician, published a book of psalm-tunes in 1579, which was republished in a revised version in 1591. More and Shepherd are named here; the earlier reference is written between the lines, indicating that Whythorne transferred them to the 'aunsient tỹm' list. For some reason he did not transfer the last two names on this list, Thomas Appleby (c. 1488–1562) and Thomas Preston, both of whom also flourished early in the century.

APPENDIX IV

TWO DELETIONS (see page 5)

The first deletion seems to be a simple cancellation:

> As he doth vse the .k. in stead of .c. in this word .consonant. as thus .konsonant. As he doth vse the .s. for .t. in this word .derivation. as thus .derivasion.

Whythorne's purpose in cancelling this passage is not clear, for he followed Hart in these points.

The second deletion is substantial, running to six and a half lines. The material deleted is identical with a passage that occurs lower on the page, where Whythorne makes the transition from orthography to begin the account of his childhood. (Printed as the middle paragraph on page 6: 'I hav sumwhat degressed . . . þe songs and sonets foloing.')

This mistake argues strongly that Whythorne was copying the account of his 'new orthografye' from an earlier draft.

APPENDIX V

THE ICONOGRAPHY OF WHYTHORNE

SOME of the most interesting pages of Whythorne's autobiography are those in which he tells of the portraits of him that were painted. Somewhat surprisingly, he sat for his portrait four times, the first occasion being when he was 20 or 21 years old (p. 20). He tells that he had a picture of himself playing the lute painted as a decoration on his virginals, to match a picture of Terpsichore, also playing the lute. This occurred about 1549, after he had left the service of John Heywood, and when he was living independently in London.

The second portrait was painted about a year later, after Whythorne had recovered from a long attack of the ague (p. 49). His declared purpose was to see how much this illness had changed his appearance. The painter had recently made for Whythorne a copy of his portrait of the 'Suds-of-Soap' widow, and the musician decided to have one done of himself. This was before Whythorne left for his continental travels in 1551.

The third portrait dates from about 1562, when Whythorne was 34 and had returned from Cambridge to London. Whythorne visited the studio of the same painter who had done his portrait 'ny a Dozen yeers' earlier (pp. 133–5). The new painting showed Whythorne's long, full beard, wrinkled face, hollow eyes, and other signs of maturity. The details of the studio that Whythorne gives make us wish for more, but he does not name the artist. Neither this painting nor the two earlier ones are known to have survived.

Paradoxically, the fine portrait that serves as frontispiece to this book, dated 1569, is not mentioned in the autobiography. It is now the property of Miss Winifred Hill of Worthing, Sussex, who has kindly permitted its use in this volume. It formerly belonged to her father, the late Arthur F. Hill, F.S.A., a partner in the well-known London firm of violin-makers. Earlier it had belonged to Dr. W. H. Cummings and was sold with his collection at Christie's, 17 December 1915, as lot 136: nothing is known of its provenance before that. The painting is on a panel, 12 × 10 inches; it was exhibited at the Queen Elizabeth Exhibition in London in 1933, where it was no. 177.

Although Whythorne does not mention the painting of this portrait, he describes the making of the woodcut from it to adorn the 1571

X

songbooks. His purpose was to show the 'outward marks as in the inward man', namely, the arms and dress of a gentleman. The woodcut was again used in the 1590 *Duos*, but for some reason the upper left quartering of the arms was slightly altered (see illustration opposite p. 211). The copy of the woodcut sewn inside the cover-leaf of the autobiography has this alteration and so provides further evidence that Whythorne kept the manuscript by him until the last years of his life.[1]

The artist of this fourth portrait is not known, but may have been George Gower. Mr. David Piper of the National Portrait Gallery suggests that the style of the painting is very similar to those that can be definitely ascribed to Gower, especially in the moulding round the eyes. Though no portraits by Gower have been dated before 1573, his self-portrait, painted in 1579, shows a man aged about 40; hence, Gower would have been about 30 when Whythorne's portrait was executed.

What is known of these portraits of Whythorne raises a larger question: the fact that a man in his relatively modest station had his portrait painted four times invites speculation about the habits of greater and more affluent Elizabethans.

[1] On the woodcut stitched to the verso of the title-leaf Whythorne twice wrote the couplet:

> *Though now chainged yet thus was I*
> *When I of age was twice twenti.*

For other verses on this page, see p. 213, n. 2.

APPENDIX VI

INDEX OF FIRST LINES

THIS index lists all Whythorne's known poems, together with a few other verses found in his *Autobiography*. The spelling is taken from the manuscript, except for the verses found only in his printed volumes of 1571 and 1590. The number of known lines of each poem is given in parenthesis: where the number in a printed source differs it is noted in parentheses after the appropriate reference.

The first column gives the page-number where the poem appears in this edition of the *Autobiography*.

The second column gives the location of verses printed in Whythorne's 1571 *Songes*, using the foliation of the Triplex part-book.

The third column gives the location of verses printed in the 1590 *Duos*, but here the figure shows the number of the piece in the Cantus part-book.

The fourth column contains brief notes, such as psalm-numbers given by Whythorne and identification of verses not by him. The symbol PW indicates songs included in Peter Warlock's edition, Oxford, 1927.

First Line	Page	1571	1590	Notes
A stefast mynd þat willingly (12)	279			
A tyranny not lasting long (1)			49	12th Canon
Acceptable is nothing more (1)			50	13th Canon
Accompany the good (1)			19	
Affeksions strong, þat do moov vs (6)	275		36 (1)	
All þat which fansy heer brouht foorth, þi fansẏ to revẏv (2)	120			
All ye þat serv þe blynd god loov (12)	59	11		
All yow þat list þe trewth to know, who shee iz þat iz heer (44)	168			
Almihty God, þi loving kạr (12)	163	21ᵛ		PW 538
Althings that hạv A beginning, Tẏm bringz þem to bee seen (8)	274			
And I will walk at liberty			12	
As restles hed doth alwaiz gẏv (6)	216	38		
As þe qui'et rest, and ȝoiful hart, with þe di'et moderạt (4)	287			
As t'iz A sẏn of persons grạv (6)	117	30		PW 362
As tẏm doth alter evry wiht (2)	135			

First Line	Page	1571	1590	Notes
Assewred hǫp much lẙk iz vnto faith (6)	290			
Auktorite, mǫst do dezi'er (6)	274		34 (1)	
Az, for her aunsientnez, shee standz aboov all in degree (12)	84			
Az hawhty prẙd oppresseth loov (6)	282		24 (1)	
Az mani hedz hǫv mani witts, so diuerz men of verteuz hǫv (4)	177	2ᵛ		
Az þi shadow it self applieth (8)	29	33		PW 362
Be faithful to thy friend (1)			17	
Behold, now praise the Lord (4 vv.)		26		Ps. 134
Better it iz with rihteowsnes, A littl to posses (4)	276			
Bewǫr how sorowz thee oppres (4)	142	6ᵛ		
Blessed are those that are unde-filed in the way			1	Ps. 119
Bow down þẙn ear, O lord hear mee (6)	267			Ps. 86
But Solon said (1)			44	7th Canon
By new broom, by new broom, yee may be siur (12)	90	35ᵛ		
Diliȝens iz ǫn of þe dawhterz cheef (5)	284			
Er Vulcǫn with hiz Fiery bank, konsiumed Bucerz chest (30)	122			
Felisite þe prosprowz end (4)	291			
Fly had I wist az thing not good (4)	286			
For reazon now (4)	199			
For to be born az infants bee (6)	292		41 (1)	4th Canon
For to reklaim to frend A froward fo (6)	81	7ᵛ		
For your goodwill look for no meed (2)	44			Not by Whythorne
Gẙv ear lady vnto my plaint (40)	49			
Gẙv not þi mẙnd to heavines (10)	156	36		PW 364
Hǫv pasi'ens stil, þowh God þee towch (4)	290			
Hǫv pasi'ens still þowh God þee try (6)	290			
Hee doth well know hiz own weaknes (18)	278			
Hee þat contemneth injuriez, hiz stǫt will better appeer soon (4)	118			
Hee þat to him honor wǫld win, let him þe sǫm þen tǫk (2)	277			
Hee þat wil trust þis lesson learn of mee (12)	280			
His mortal life (1)			40	3rd Canon

First Line	Page	1571	1590	Notes
I am þe tabull of þe point (2)	63			
I hard of lat how on did prat, and search althings to know (18)	47			
I hav er þis tým hard mani on sai (14)	189	13	14 (5)	PW 356
I hav not only read, but ek by proof hav trýd (4)	172	31ᵛ		
I kannot deem þem happi siur (6)	139	11		
I seek all notions, plain or shrewd (8)	39			
I see how sum kontrol ech on (18)	292			
I will yeeld thanks to þee (56)	161	(8)		Ps. 138
If dyverz wurks þow tak to do (16)	280			
If evri on þat goth abowt (8)	176	2ᵛ		
If flattered be þe wicked (4)	171	34		
If I had not forseen, þe chainȝes newly hapt (4)	114	15ᵛ		
If þat I kowld ons win (4)	285			
If þow þat hast A faithfull frend (20)	166	34ᵛ		
If þow wilt mittigat anger (4)	291			
If þow woldst know þe swiftest thing (6)	283			
In counsel be thou close (1)			18	
In frendz of ech estat look for equalite to bee alway (2)	82	4ᵛ		
In overkumming appetýt (6)	283		25 (1)	
In publik plas nothing wryt þow (2)	63			Also p. 120
In þee O lord hav I trusted, my hop iz al in þee (4)	288			Ps. 71
In things sekret þat be not to bee known (6)	290			
In weall and wo be pasient (6)	81	32ᵛ		
It doth belong mor of good riht (8)	65	33ᵛ		PW 363
It doth mee good in Zeph'rus rain (10)	21	12		PW 360
It hath bin proved both eevn and morrow (14)	51	13 (6)		
It iz A world sum sotz to see (6)	140	10ᵛ		
Iz þer no chois for mee, but still to tast þis strýf (4)	85	18		
Knowleȝ hath non so great A fo (12)	279			
Lament we should at children's birth (1)			42	5th Canon
Let thy loving mercy come also unto me			11	
Like as the birds that swallows hight (1)			45	8th Canon
Long framed waz my mynd to do (8)	285			

First Line	Page	1571	1590	Notes
Of greet bewty ti's often seen, it fadeth in short spąs (4)	288			
Of miuzik þouh þe cheef knowlęȝ hath long tým hindred been (148)	178			
Of nątiurz gifts witt iz þe cheef (6)	73	15ᵛ		
Of needfull things þat oft dis-grąs (4)	274		32 (1)	
Of Vertewz all endeuowr þow to know (12)	18			
Out of the deep have I called unto thee, O Lord		27ᵛ		Ps. 130
Perform þi vow, if þow dost anẏ mąk (4)	290			
Ponder þe proof so far az þow (8)	211	17		
Prefer not greet bewty befǫr vertew (20)	27	12ᵛ (6)		
Press not to hear other's secrets (1)			21	
Remember him þat hath not yow forgot (12)	101			
Revẏved waz mi hart and mẏnd (4)	282			
Shall I this wo sustain (8)	79	36ᵛ		
Sins I embrąs mi ladies grąs in sort az I dezier (8)	42			
Sins I embrąs þe heavnly gras In sort az I wold hąv (8)	157	20		PW 357
Sith þat long tým I hąv profest A loover for to bee (196)	248			
So feigned friends (1)			46	9th Canon
Such as in loov wold hąv long ȝoy (4)	55	3ᵛ		Edited by Bukofzer
Sum rithms shall heer appeer, which strainȝ mai seem to skan (12)	221			
Tąk heed of wordz þow maist not vowch (6)	62	10		
Take from me the way of lying			8	
Teach me, O Lord, the way of thy statutes			9	
That my ways were made so direct			2	
Ðe ardant loov of women all, and pleazant wẏn of þe flaggon (2)	76			
Ðe belly Godz þat swill in drink, till þat þeir wits bee owt (4)	281			
The conditions of man (1)			48	11th Canon
Ðe dint of spear, and prik of thorn, ar sharp vndowtedly (4)	214			Not by W.
Ðe diverz chauns þat God doth send (8)	147	18		
Ðe dowtfull stąt þat I posses (24)	141	17ᵛ (6)		PW 361

INDEX